New Directions in German Studies

Vol. 33

Series Editor:

IMKE MEYER

Professor of Germanic Studies, University of Illinois at Chicago

Editorial Board:

KATHERINE ARENS
Professor of Germanic Studies, University of Texas at Austin

ROSWITHA BURWICK
Distinguished Chair of Modern Foreign Languages Emerita,
Scripps College

RICHARD ELDRIDGE
Charles and Harriett Cox McDowell Professor of Philosophy,
Swarthmore College

ERIKA FISCHER-LICHTE
Professor Emerita of Theater Studies, Freie Universität Berlin

CATRIONA MACLEOD
Frank Curtis Springer and Gertrude Melcher Springer Professor in
the College and the Department of Germanic Studies, University
of Chicago

STEPHAN SCHINDLER
Professor of German and Chair, University of South Florida

HEIDI SCHLIPPHACKE
Associate Professor of Germanic Studies, University of Illinois
at Chicago

ANDREW J. WEBBER
Professor of Modern German and Comparative Culture,
Cambridge University

SILKE-MARIA WEINECK
Professor of German and Comparative Literature,
University of Michigan

DAVID WELLBERY
LeRoy T. and Margaret Deffenbaugh Carlson University Professor,
University of Chicago

SABINE WILKE
Joff Hanauer Distinguished Professor for Western Civilization and
Professor of German, University of Washington

JOHN ZILCOSKY
Professor of German and Comparative Literature,
University of Toronto

Volumes in the Series:

1. *Improvisation as Art: Conceptual Challenges, Historical Perspectives*
by Edgar Landgraf

2. *The German Pícaro and Modernity: Between Underdog and Shape-Shifter*
by Bernhard Malkmus

3. *Citation and Precedent: Conjunctions and Disjunctions of German Law and Literature*
by Thomas O. Beebee

4. *Beyond Discontent: "Sublimation" from Goethe to Lacan*
by Eckart Goebel

5. *From Kafka to Sebald: Modernism and Narrative Form*
edited by Sabine Wilke

6. *Image in Outline: Reading Lou Andreas-Salomé*
by Gisela Brinker-Gabler

7. *Out of Place: German Realism, Displacement, and Modernity*
by John B. Lyon

8. *Thomas Mann in English: A Study in Literary Translation*
by David Horton

9. *The Tragedy of Fatherhood: King Laius and the Politics of Paternity in the West*
by Silke-Maria Weineck

10. *The Poet as Phenomenologist: Rilke and the New Poems*
by Luke Fischer

11. *The Laughter of the Thracian Woman: A Protohistory of Theory*
by Hans Blumenberg, translated by Spencer Hawkins

12. *Roma Voices in the German-Speaking World*
by Lorely French

13. *Vienna's Dreams of Europe: Culture and Identity beyond the Nation-State*
by Katherine Arens

14. *Thomas Mann and Shakespeare: Something Rich and Strange*
edited by Tobias Döring and Ewan Fernie

15. *Goethe's Families of the Heart*
by Susan E. Gustafson

16. *German Aesthetics: Fundamental Concepts from Baumgarten to Adorno*
edited by J. D. Mininger and Jason Michael Peck

17. *Figures of Natality: Reading the Political in the Age of Goethe*
by Joseph D. O'Neil

18. *Readings in the Anthropocene: The Environmental Humanities, German Studies, and Beyond*
edited by Sabine Wilke and Japhet Johnstone

19. *Building Socialism: Architecture and Urbanism in East German Literature, 1955–1973*
by Curtis Swope

20. *Ghostwriting: W. G. Sebald's Poetics of History*
by Richard T. Gray

21. *Stereotype and Destiny in Arthur Schnitzler's Prose: Five Psycho-Sociological Readings*
by Marie Kolkenbrock

22. *Sissi's World: The Empress Elisabeth in Memory and Myth*
edited by Maura E. Hametz and Heidi Schlipphacke

23. *Posthumanism in the Age of Humanism: Mind, Matter, and the Life Sciences after Kant*
edited by Edgar Landgraf, Gabriel Trop, and Leif Weatherby

24. *Staging West German Democracy: Governmental PR Films and the Democratic Imaginary, 1953–1963*
by Jan Uelzmann

25. *The Lever as Instrument of Reason: Technological Constructions of Knowledge around 1800*
by Jocelyn Holland

26. *The Fontane Workshop: Manufacturing Realism in the Industrial Age of Print*
by Petra McGillen

27. *Gender, Collaboration, and Authorship in German Culture: Literary Joint Ventures, 1750–1850*
edited by Laura Deiulio and John B. Lyon

28. *Kafka's Stereoscopes: The Political Function of a Literary Style*
by Isak Winkel Holm

29. *Ambiguous Aggression in German Realism and Beyond: Flirtation, Passive Aggression, Domestic Violence*
by Barbara N. Nagel

30. *Thomas Bernhard's Afterlives*
edited by Stephen Dowden, Gregor Thuswaldner, and Olaf Berwald

31. *Modernism in Trieste: The Habsburg Mediterranean and the Literary Invention of Europe, 1870–1945*
by Salvatore Pappalardo

32. *Grotesque Visions: The Science of Berlin Dada*
by Thomas O. Haakenson

33. *Theodor Fontane: Irony and Avowal in a Post-Truth Age*
by Brian Tucker

Theodor Fontane

Irony and Avowal in a Post-Truth Age

Brian Tucker

BLOOMSBURY ACADEMIC
NEW YORK · LONDON · OXFORD · NEW DELHI · SYDNEY

BLOOMSBURY ACADEMIC
Bloomsbury Publishing Inc
1385 Broadway, New York, NY 10018, USA
50 Bedford Square, London, WC1B 3DP, UK
29 Earlsfort Terrace, Dublin 2, Ireland

BLOOMSBURY, BLOOMSBURY ACADEMIC and the Diana logo are
trademarks of Bloomsbury Publishing Plc

First published in the United States of America 2021
This paperback edition published 2023

Copyright © Brian Tucker, 2021

For legal purposes the Acknowledgments on p. viii constitute
an extension of this copyright page.

Cover design by Andrea Federle-Bucsi
Cover image: William Frith, *Pope Makes Love to Lady Mary Wortley Montagu*,
1852, oil on canvas. Auckland Art Gallery Toi o Tamaki,
gift of Sir Frank Mappin, 1974

All rights reserved. No part of this publication may be reproduced
or transmitted in any form or by any means, electronic or mechanical,
including photocopying, recording, or any information storage or retrieval
system, without prior permission in writing from the publishers.

Bloomsbury Publishing Inc does not have any control over, or
responsibility for, any third-party websites referred to or in this book.
All internet addresses given in this book were correct at the time of
going to press. The author and publisher regret any inconvenience
caused if addresses have changed or sites have ceased to exist,
but can accept no responsibility for any such changes.

Library of Congress Control Number: 2021935682

ISBN: HB: 978-1-5013-6835-6
      PB: 978-1-5013-6839-4
      ePDF: 978-1-5013-6837-0
      eBook: 978-1-5013-6836-3

Series: New Directions in German Studies

Typeset by Integra Software Solutions Pvt. Ltd.

To find out more about our authors and books visit www.bloomsbury.com
and sign up for our newsletters.

Contents

Acknowledgments	viii
Note on Editions and Translations	ix
Introduction	1
1 The Dilemma of Choice in *Irrungen, Wirrungen*	33
2 The Broken Word: On the Rhetoric of Trust and Honor in *Schach von Wuthenow*	61
3 *Graf Petöfy* and the Empty Vow	89
4 *L'Adultera*, Adulteration, and Avowal	113
5 *Unwiederbringlich*, or the Impotence of Being Earnest	147
6 Haunting Ambivalence: The Rhetorical Education of *Effi Briest*	185
7 All Talk: In Lieu of a Conclusion, *Stechlin*	219
Bibliography	237
Index	245

Acknowledgments

Let me set aside irony for a moment and begin with a sincere expression of gratitude. I'm grateful first to Imke Meyer, a model of editorial efficiency, for her guidance and encouragement throughout the publishing process. Thanks are due to the two outside readers, whose thoughtful suggestions improved the manuscript in many places, as well as to the numerous colleagues who commented on parts of the project while it was still a work in progress. They include, among others, Fritz Breithaupt, Todd Kontje, May Mergenthaler, Peter Pfeiffer, Lynne Tatlock, and Holly Yanacek. John Lyon has become an indispensable conversation partner on all things Fontane, and I've profited from our collaborative endeavors. John's challenging questions helped me sharpen my argument, especially in the introduction.

Most of this book was written during a sabbatical in the island nation of Palau. I owe a heartfelt *mesulang* to everyone who made it such a warm and welcoming place to work on the project. I couldn't have asked for a better writing retreat. And without a lot of behind-the-scenes support back home, it wouldn't have been possible to make steady progress on the manuscript while away. I'm grateful to Greg Redding and Jane Hardy for temporarily shielding me from the day-to-day duties of running an undergraduate language program. Rachel Barclay provided much-needed research assistance, making multiple trips to retrieve books from the stacks and scan pages. Karen Longerbone and Allen and Christy Tucker ran an international book import/export service for me, via both parcel post and personal luggage. To my family, to Paul and Nina: I'm especially grateful for having the space to work in the morning and more than enough reason to get up from my desk in the afternoon. Thanks, finally, to Danielle, for reading everything, as always, for being earnest and reliable when it counts and wonderfully ironic when it doesn't.

Note on Editions and Translations

For citations of Fontane's works, this study relies primarily on the *Große Brandenburger Ausgabe* and secondarily on the *Nymphenburger Ausgabe*. I have cited whenever possible from the *GBA*. References to Fontane's narrative fiction, which constitutes the first *Abteilung* of the *GBA*, appear parenthetically with volume and page number. Parenthetical references to other *GBA Abteilungen* give the *Abteilung* as a Roman numeral, followed by the volume and page number. At the time of this writing, some materials were not yet available in the *GBA*, and in those instances, I have referred to the *Nymphenburger Ausgabe*, cited parenthetically with the abbreviation *NA*, volume, and page number. Reference information for both editions is provided in the bibliography. Citations from Fontane's novels also refer to a published English translation whenever one is readily available. Where no English source is cited, the translation is my own.

Introduction

Theodor Fontane spent the summer of 1852 in London. During his five months in the English capital, he served as a correspondent for the Prussian press, submitting cultural reports about his impressions and experiences. One of the things he did in London was attending the National Gallery's annual Summer Exhibition, a juried show to which artists of any caliber may submit their work.[1] Fontane, whose journalistic career involved both theater and art criticism, including regular reviews of the Berlin Exhibition, describes feeling overwhelmed by the quantity of paintings on display.[2] He objects primarily to the exhibition's excess: there are too many rooms, with too many paintings of uneven merit. Nonetheless, within this welter of mediocrity, his discerning eye picks out several works of genuine quality.

One painting that struck him was William Frith's 1852 "Pope Makes Love to Lady Mary Wortley Montagu," where "makes love" is an antiquated formulation for "declares his love" (see this book's cover image). We know that Fontane was taken with the painting, first because he compares it favorably to works by the revered Adolph Menzel, and second, because he recreates the visual scene in intricate detail. As its title suggests, the painting depicts the moment when the poet Alexander Pope bares his heart and declares his love to Lady Montagu. More precisely, it depicts the emotional aftermath of Pope's declaration, as it delivers a superb image of unrequited love. Fontane's description homes in on the two figures' appearances, on their clothing, pose, and posture, but mostly on their sharply contrasting expressions. While

---

[1] On Fontane's journalistic work in England, see Sonja Hillerich, *Deutsche Auslandskorrespondenten im neunzehnten Jahrhundert* (Berlin: de Gruyter, 2018), 159–61.
[2] On Fontane's art criticism, see Carmen Aus der Au, *Theodor Fontane als Kunstkritiker* (Berlin: de Gruyter, 2017). On the theater reviews, some aspects of which I address in Chapter 1, see further Clarissa Blomqvist, "Realism on Stage: Reflections on Language in Theodor Fontane's Theatre Reviews," *Monatshefte* 104, no. 3 (2012): 337–45.

Pope sits, turned away from Lady Montagu, "mit einem unvergleichlichen Ausdruck von Scham, Wuth und Rache" (*NA* 17:67, with an incomparable expression of shame, fury, and vengeance), the Lady herself, standing at a table, tilts her head back in laughter.[3] What grabs Fontane's attention in the painting is its juxtaposition of two diametrically opposed moods and expressions. The poet has just exposed himself in the most intimate, sincere, and vulnerable way possible, yet Lady Montagu's reaction is lighthearted and flippant. In this fraught moment, she cannot take him seriously. What is to him most serious is to her merely amusing.

Fontane's report provides context by citing from the exhibition catalog, where Frith recounts the depicted event: "Zu der schlechtestgewählten Zeit von der Welt, wo die Lady alles andere eher als eine 'Erklärung' erwartete, gestand ihr der Dichter seine Liebe, und zwar in so leidenschaftlichen Ausdrücken, daß trotz aller Anstrengung, ernst und ehrbar zu bleiben, ein lautes Lachen der Lady doch endlich ihre einzige Antwort war" (*NA* 17:66, At the most inopportune time in the world, when the Lady least expected a "declaration," the poet avowed his love to her in such passionate terms that, despite her best efforts to remain serious and respectable, a loud laugh was ultimately her only reply). It is not hard to see why this painting in particular would strike a chord with Fontane. This is just the sort of anecdote that he would collect from newspapers, letters, or society gossip and then transform into the plot of a novel. His literary works often include—at least as an underlying force—similar dynamics of desire, courtship, and rejection. In *Frau Jenny Treibel*, Jenny rejects Wilibald Schmidt, a bit of background that foreshadows the broken engagement between Leopold and Corinna, just as Effi's mother, Luise, rejects Geert von Innstetten before matching him with her daughter in *Effi Briest*. But the most obvious overlap between the Frith painting and Fontane's novels occurs with Holk's humiliating rejection at the hands of Ebba in *Unwiederbringlich*. Holk goes to Ebba to bare his heart and soul. Like the anguished poet Pope, he confesses his love and tells her the truth about how he feels. Ebba's reaction, however, is incredulous. Like Lady Montagu, she can hardly take his declaration seriously—she shrugs it off—and she cannot understand why he would take her insincere flirtations as seriously as he did. His misplaced sincerity makes him laughable.

The correspondence between Frith's image and Fontane's novel thus goes well beyond the thematic level of courtship, declaration, and rejection. More striking is how both scenes play out a conflict between

---

[3] Aus der Au cites the description of Frith's painting as an example of Fontane's art criticism. Aus der Au, *Theodor Fontane als Kunstkritiker*, 253–4.

two juxtaposed modes of expression. On the one hand is a form of communication that is earnest, sincere, authentic, and credible. When Pope or Holk declares his love, one knows that he means what he says. Love and desire are *no laughing matter*, and this form of expression is careful to treat serious topics with the seriousness and solemnity they deserve. On the other hand, the women in these scenes, Lady Montagu and Ebba, react in counterpoint to their suitor's earnest, sincere speech. They embody an opposed mode of expression, one that is flippant, ironic, unserious, and hence unreliable.[4] Their ironic indifference allows them to chuckle at those who, in David Foster Wallace's words, expose themselves "to others' ridicule by betraying passé expressions of value, emotion, or vulnerability."[5]

I believe that Fontane is enamored of Frith's painting because it reflects in a single image a conflict and concern that would occupy the writer throughout his career. For Fontane, the figures of Lady Montagu and Pope represent two opposed attitudes toward language, meaning, and truth—one frivolous and insincere, the other earnest and open. Fontane's shorthand designation for these two fundamental attitudes is *Scherz* and *Ernst*—an opposition that contrasts what is playful or facetious (*Scherz*) with what is meant in all seriousness (*Ernst*). And in the mouths of speaking subjects, these two attitudes lead to two different modes of language, which one might call, in Fontane's German, *scherzhaft* and *ernsthaft*, and which the present inquiry will label in English as irony and avowal.

Language that is *scherzhaft* is not merely in jest; it is facetious and tongue-in-cheek. It treats serious matters with deliberate flippancy. Such language functions as verbal irony insofar as it undermines the very ability to distinguish between the serious and the unserious. As Friedrich Schlegel writes in a fragment on Socratic irony, "everything in it should be jest [Scherz] and everything should be earnest [Ernst]."[6] It is not so much that Fontane draws on a specifically Romantic discourse of irony, but rather that Schlegel's statement delineates fundamental components of irony that would have persisted well into the nineteenth

---

[4] In these two instances, the conflict divides along gender lines, such that the women are ironic and flippant, whereas the men are earnest. But that duality does not hold as a general rule in the society novels. Works such as *L'Adultera*, *Schach von Wuthenow*, *Effi Briest*, and *Der Stechlin* show that, for Fontane, gender does not predetermine one's manner of speaking. The men in these novels are just as likely to engage in irony, empty talk, and dissimulation.

[5] David Foster Wallace, "E Unibus Pluram: Television and U.S. Fiction," *Review of Contemporary Fiction* 13, no. 2 (1993): 181.

[6] Friedrich Schlegel, *Kritische Friedrich-Schlegel-Ausgabe*, ed. Ernst Behler, Jean Jacques Anstett, and Hans Eichner (Munich: Schöningh, 1958–), 2:160.

century. Karl Heinz Bohrer argues, for instance, that the polarization of "Ernst" and "Scherz" is a product of the early nineteenth century and that the semantic sphere of "Scherz" more closely resembles contemporary notions of irony.[7] Language that is, in nineteenth-century parlance, *scherzhaft* or, in contemporary terms, ironic thus stands in contrast to everything that is earnest, sincere, and reliable. My aim in this book is to demonstrate that the tension between unserious and serious speech, between irony and avowal, constitutes, in ways that have not been fully appreciated or explored, a central conflict in Fontane's works. More specifically, I will argue that Fontane's most well-known society novels play out a struggle between the incompatible demands of these two modes of speaking.

Before defining irony and avowal as oppositional terms, I want to draw attention to two further points in Fontane's reception of the Frith painting. First, what is at issue between the two depicted parties? It is not merely the question of whether they should be lovers, nor the anguish of unrequited love. At issue, rather, is a prior or more fundamental question—namely, whether Pope's declaration should be taken earnestly, whether it even merits serious consideration. His expression of shame and rage, as Fontane reads it, reacts not only to Lady Montagu's rejection, but also to the fact that she flips something exceedingly weighty and sincere into its opposite, into something trivial and laughable. Pope's consternation derives, at least in part, from an instability or rapid oscillation between sincerity and insincerity. Some of that instability is reflected in the sculpture of two figures kissing in the background: what might initially have read as a portent of romantic fulfillment now stands in sardonic counterpoint to Pope's rejection. It will take some time, but over the course of the next several chapters, I will try to show that similar disagreements and misunderstandings—struggles over whether to take language earnestly or ironically—feature prominently in Fontane's novels. Moreover, the uncertainty that irony generates in the reception of language proves to be a motor of conflict and discord.

Second, observe, as Fontane does, that Lady Montagu's laughter is involuntary. Although she tries to remain solemn and react earnestly, she cannot. There is something infectious and uncontainable in her reaction, and this constitutes a key point in Fontane's critique of irony in particular and unreliable speech in general. Even though Fontane is widely regarded as a writer of ironic prose, his novels often dramatize a

---

[7] Karl Heinz Bohrer, "Sprachen der Ironie—Sprachen des Ernstes. Das Problem," in *Sprachen der Ironie—Sprachen des Ernstes*, ed. Karl Heinz Bohrer (Frankfurt am Main: Suhrkamp, 2000), 11.

profound concern with regard to irony.[8] For Fontane, irony provides an exemplary instance of a discrepancy between language and meaning, a loosening of the ethical bond between words and the things to which they ostensibly refer. His novels investigate the extent to which human relationships—personal, social, political—can continue to function in the face of pervasive irony and the erosion of language's credibility.

I do not mean to keep Fontane at a distance from early modernists such as Thomas Mann and Alfred Döblin by making him out to be an irony scold. The notion of uncontrollability depicted in Lady Montagu proves important here. The disconnect between what one says and what one means—the hallmark of verbal irony—might work perfectly well in the service of witty dinner party banter, but Fontane's novels repeatedly ask what happens when the unreliable element of language escapes its boundaries, when it leeches out of unserious contexts and into serious ones—into marital intimacy, contractual obligations, and even political calculations. What happens when certain fashionable forms of unserious speech prove to be contagious, when they begin to adulterate and weaken communicative spheres that rely on honesty, trust, and sincerity? Fontane suggests an answer to this question on two distinct but related levels, the personal and the historico-political. The novels identify an irreconcilable discrepancy between word and deed as both the root of emotional discord and the proximate cause of historical and political upheaval. What is more, Fontane is masterful when it comes to capturing this dynamic in snippets of dialogue, which is another reason why Frith's painting of a dialogic conflict between avowal and irony appears retrospectively as a seed. The scene it portrays contains *in potentia* many of the issues and concerns that Fontane's society novels will develop.

---

[8] It is difficult to provide any single definitive citation for what appears to be a widespread consensus in the secondary literature. Here are three references, chosen more or less at random, to Fontane's ironic tone. Goetschel describes Fontane's irony as an authorial attitude of "non-binding ambivalence." Willi Goetschel, "Causerie: On the Function of Dialogue in *Der Stechlin*," in *New Approaches to Theodor Fontane: Cultural Codes in Flux*, ed. Marion Doebeling (Columbia, SC: Camden House, 2000), 121. Johnson locates a "cynical irony" in *Frau Jenny Treibel*. David Johnson, "Ironies of Degeneration: The Dilemmas of Bourgeois Masculinity in Theodor Fontane's *Frau Jenny Treibel* and *Mathilde Möhring*," *Monatshefte* 102, no. 2 (2010): 150. White casts Fontane's irony as a complement and counterpoint to his tendency "to allow things to speak for themselves." Michael White, *Space in Theodor Fontane's Works: Theme and Poetic Function* (London: MHRA, 2012), 41. Scholars often discuss Fontane in terms of a lightly ironic tone, and my task will be to complicate that narrative by pointing out how the novels depict the pernicious effects of ubiquitous irony.

Irony and Avowal

It is important, at the outset, to define the cardinal terms and establish how the present inquiry sees them functioning in Fontane's writings. Irony, in particular, is a thorny topic in philosophy and critical theory, and using it as shorthand for an unserious, unreliable mode of speaking does not make matters any easier. Nonetheless, the term provides a fitting designation for the forms of language use that Fontane observes, and to see why, we can begin with a canonical nineteenth-century definition of irony. Søren Kierkegaard, in his 1841 Magister dissertation, *The Concept of Irony*, writes, "The most common form of irony is when one says something seriously which is not seriously intended. The other form of irony is when one says something facetiously, as a jest, which is intended seriously."[9] Kierkegaard's delineation of irony turns on the disconnect between what is earnest and what is facetious, between the serious and the unserious. It has to do with the speaking subject's intention, its attitude or relationship to its own language, and it occurs through a discrepancy. The attitude that the subject presents deliberately runs counter to and conceals its actual relationship to what it says. To put the point in Fontanean terms, verbal irony exists through the opposition of *Ernst* and *Scherz*, through the performance of faux solemnity and earnest facetiousness. One finds both forms of irony in Fontane's works, as well as many hybrid, in-between forms. Indeed, one of Fontane's favored labels for language that is coy, potentially ironic, and difficult to pin down is "halb ernst-, halb scherzhaft" (15:144, half in earnest, half joking),[10] that is to say, language that dwells in a gap between the purely earnest and the completely facetious.

Kierkegaard identifies irony's most salient feature as the rhetorical deployment of a gap or discrepancy. It is a divergence between phenomenon and essence, form and content, rhetoric and grammar, and he writes that it is "a determination present in all forms of irony, namely, the phenomenon is not the essence but the opposite of the essence."[11] The most basic and familiar form of irony is to say the opposite of what you mean—to assert sincerely what is not meant sincerely, or to say ostensibly in jest what is actually a sincerely held belief. How, then, can Lady Montagu be said to personify an ironic rhetorical bearing? Her laughing, dismissive reaction does not align perfectly with Kierkegaard's descriptions, as there appears to be nothing put on or self-contradictory about her laughter. The irony in this instance comes

---

[9] Søren Kierkegaard, *The Concept of Irony*, trans. Lee M. Capel (Bloomington, IN: Indiana University Press, 1965), 265.
[10] English from Theodor Fontane, *Effi Briest*, trans. Hugh Rorrison and Helen Chambers (New York: Penguin, 2000), 90.
[11] Kierkegaard, *Concept of Irony*, 264.

about dialogically. The incongruence and indirection cannot be located solely in Lady Montagu's reaction. It must be located, rather, in the discrepancy between the seriousness of the rhetorical context and the insincerity of her response. By avowing his love, Pope has made himself vulnerable and dependent on her response. Her reaction is to him a matter of the utmost weight and importance, and yet she delivers it as if it were all merely in jest. Herein lies the Kierkegaardian discrepancy that marks this as an example of irony: she delivers a rejection that is, in essence, sincerely devastating (*Ernst*) through the phenomenon of lighthearted amusement (*Scherz*).

Fontane, as we shall see, is interested in capturing similar moments of ironic discrepancy. The society novels devote a significant amount of attention to depicting how people talk to one another and how they interact. To the extent that these novels reflect the social norms and conventions of the late nineteenth century, they portray modes of speaking as anything but straightforward. Social communication appears in these works as both strictly regulated and increasingly frivolous and problematic. If we read Fontane's novels as relatively realistic and reliable portraits of the society from which they emerged, we get the impression that, in the modern social order of Wilhelmine Germany, it had become fashionable and indeed expected to speak ironically. One finds ample instances of this dynamic in Fontane's works. They depict an urbane society in the thrall of irony, one whose constituents are bound by the negative freedom of not needing to mean what they say.

But Fontane will also subsume the strict form of irony under a broader concern with unreliable language. Irony's characteristic discrepancy between phenomenon and essence delivers a particularly vivid example of the erosion of meaning and certainty. Language becomes less reliable and meaning becomes less certain as speaking subjects loosen the indexical bond between words and the things to which they refer. In the present inquiry, irony will refer to specific instances of ironic verbal expression (saying the opposite of what is meant) but will also point to an entire relationship to language and truth, one characterized by discrepancy, tension, unreliability, and uncertainty. A parallel broadening of scope also exists in the critical treatments of irony. Beda Allemann, writing on literary irony, suggests, for example, that reflections on irony should move away from the insistence on stark opposition and toward the notion of "an ironic field of tension."[12] Irony, in this view, does not require what is meant to be the direct opposite of what is said. Rather,

---

[12] Beda Allemann, "Ironie als literarisches Prinzip," in *Ironie und Dichtung*, ed. Albert Schaefer (Munich: C.H. Beck, 1970), 30.

irony names a more general tension between meaning and its expression in language.

This broader sense of an unspecified tension is already evident in the classical sources on irony. Cicero, for example, in *De Oratore*, classifies as ironic instances "when your words differ from your thoughts, not in the way of which I spoke earlier, when you assert exactly the contradictory [...], but when the whole tenor of your speech shows you to be solemnly jesting, what you think differing continuously from what you say."[13] Taking Socrates as his model, Cicero speaks here of irony as "urbane dissimulation" (*urbana dissimulatio*), and the term "dissimulation" recurs in Quintilian's discussion of irony as the difference between a statement and its underlying intent.[14] Dissimulation implies pretense, concealment, and false appearances.[15] It is a form of rhetorical posturing and misrepresentation, which makes it particularly apt for connecting the specific sense of irony to Fontane's broader concern with unreliable language.

The society novels repeatedly present situations in which people do not mean what they say and do not say what they mean. Or, to sharpen the stakes of the dilemma: they present situations in which it is impossible to determine whether people mean what they say and say what they mean. This unreliability will manifest itself in a variety of forms, from the recitation of hollow phrases (with their pretense of intellectual depth) to broken promises, empty vows, and statements that can read as earnest and ironic at the same time. But these various symptoms all trace back to an underlying affliction. Borrowing from the language of adultery novels, one could call this scourge "Wortbruch," or "infidelity to the word one has given," not only in the strict sense of breaking one's word, as in breaking a promise, but in the more general sense of allowing for an open relationship between words and what they signify.[16]

---

[13] Cicero, *De Oratore*, trans. E. W. Sutton and H. Rackham (Cambridge, MA: Harvard University Press, 1948), 2.67.269.

[14] Quintilian, *The Orator's Education*, ed. and trans. Donald Russell (Cambridge, MA: Harvard University Press, 2001), 9.2.44. Quintilian remarks, though, that dissimulation is not a perfect synonym because it does not cover all aspects of irony.

[15] The phrase "urbane dissimulation," Dane writes, "would become standard in descriptions of irony." Joseph Dane, *The Critical Mythology of Irony* (Athens, GA: University of Georgia Press, 2011), 49. See further Ernst Behler, *Irony and the Discourse of Modernity* (Seattle: University of Washington Press, 1990), 77–9.

[16] "Wortbruch" occurs via the phrase "Wort- und Treubruch" in *Schach von Wuthenow* (6:121), the novel that constitutes the focus of Chapter 2. Giorgio Agamben coins the phrase "infidelity to the word" in *The Sacrament of Language: An Archaeology of the Oath*, trans. Adam Kotsko (Stanford: Stanford University Press, 2011), 6.

Irony thus points to a mode of speaking that always puts its own sincerity and credibility into question. In *Der Stechlin*, the narrator casts irony as the tendency to place "hinter alles ein Fragezeichen" (17:8, a question mark behind everything). And Dubslav's habit of continual ironization and self-negation has a particular effect—namely, to leave "seine Hörer jedesmal in Zweifel darüber [...], ob er's ernsthaft oder scherzhaft gemeint habe" (17:9, his listeners each time in doubt as to whether he meant it seriously or ironically). Fontane's novels explore how this profound uncertainty, to the point of indeterminacy, infects social discourse, attenuates credibility, and makes communication all the more problematic and precarious.

There is a second point to make regarding the understanding of irony as urbane dissimulation, and that is its implication of agency and intention. Dissimulating requires one to dissemble, to conceal something behind a pretense or false appearance—all of which is carried out consciously, deliberately. To put it plainly, ironic dissimulation is something that one aims to do; it does not happen by accident. Now, there is a poststructuralist view that takes irony as a condition of possibility for language in general and literary language in particular. Kevin Newmark, for example, reads the discrepancy that Kierkegaard identifies in irony as an "originary discrepancy," such that "the possibility of language is therefore always already dependent on the possibility of irony."[17] I want to make clear that I will not be trying to impose this line of argument on Fontane's novels. Fontane is after something different. He is not out to portray a general *Sprachskepsis* or crisis of language, as if his characters were just waking up to the fact that language is always already constituted over a fundamental discrepancy between arbitrary signifiers and things in the world. In other words, Fontane is not the kind of writer, I think, to marvel at how communication ever takes place, or how one is ever able to convey meaning in a stable, reliable way. His writings are concerned, rather, with what happens when a lax relationship to language and meaning comes to dominate social discourse. This is not to claim that representation is, for Fontane, entirely straightforward and unproblematic. I want to claim instead that, when Fontane pursues a concern with unreliable communication, the issue is not inherently broken language but rather disingenuous rhetoric. People no longer *try* to bridge the gap between words and referents; indeed, they deliberately exploit this gap in pursuit of duplicity and dissimulation.

---

[17] Kevin Newmark, *Irony on Occasion* (New York: Fordham University Press, 2012), 42.

In this regard, the object of Fontane's anxiety resonates with Harry Frankfurt's notion of "bullshit," whose essence Frankfurt characterizes as a "lack of connection to a concern with truth" and an "indifference to how things really are."[18] This sort of indifference is certainly evident in *Irrungen, Wirrungen* when Botho epitomizes upper-class social interactions. He tells Lene and the Dörrs, for instance, "Es ist alles ganz gleich. Über jedes kann man ja was sagen […]. Und 'ja' ist gerade so viel wie 'nein'" (10:28, It makes no difference at all. You can say something about anything, and whether you like it or not. And a "yes" is as good as a "no").[19] For the people in Botho's social circle, "yes" is just as good as "no" because their speech is neither motivated nor guided by a concern with truth. It does not matter whether they sincerely mean what they say because the verbal exchange has become an end in itself rather than an instrument to convey meaning about the world.[20]

At this point, one could be justified in encouraging Frankfurt and Fontane (and me) to lighten up already. What, after all, is the harm in playful, insincere banter? People go to parties, drink, and speak haphazardly, saying things they don't really mean. This does not exactly constitute a vexing cultural crisis. But Frankfurt, like Fontane, sees a corrosive cumulative effect to indifferent speech, especially when it gets taken too far. He writes, "Through excessive indulgence in [bullshitting], which involves making assertions without paying attention to anything except what it suits one to say, a person's normal habit of attending to the way things are may become attenuated or lost."[21] His point is, first, that a disregard for truth and accuracy can infiltrate one's speech, occupying ever-larger swaths of territory, and, second, that an excessive indifference in language can degrade the very ability to discern and evaluate how things really are. To return to the example of *Irrungen, Wirrungen*, one finds in the character of Käthe a similar exacerbation of the disregard for truth and credibility. Käthe's incessantly unserious chatter is governed by one criterion—that what she says be witty and amusing. Indifferent to how things actually are, it is not guided by a concern for truth and accuracy. As I will try to work out in Chapter 1, she is so committed to an idiom of unserious banter that she has lost the ability to speak in more serious, efficacious ways. More

---

[18] Harry Frankfurt, *On Bullshit* (Princeton: Princeton University Press, 2005), 33–4.
[19] English from Theodor Fontane, *On Tangled Paths*, trans. Peter James Bowman (New York: Penguin Books, 2010), 28.
[20] This state of affairs accords with Georg Simmel's notion of "Geselligkeit" or sociability, in which "discourse becomes an end in itself" as an "art of entertaining oneself, with its own artistic laws." Georg Simmel, *Grundfragen der Soziologie* (Berlin: de Gruyter, 1970), 61.
[21] Frankfurt, *On Bullshit*, 60.

ominously, she seems unable to distinguish between the serious and the unserious, the important and the trivial. She models Frankfurt's point that an inordinate indulgence in an indifferent manner of speaking can corrupt one's capacity for discernment and judgment.

The example shows that the society novels are not occupied with irony merely as a mode of speaking. The anxiety centers, rather, on the possibility that an unserious, ironic mode of speaking could metastasize—as it does in the above instance—into a mode of being. The canonical sources also frequently establish "hierarchies of irony" by differentiating, for example, between an "irony of words" and an "irony of manner" or of being.[22] Socrates provides the model of a person who does not make stray ironic remarks but rather embodies an existence of thoroughgoing irony. The critical reception is divided on the value of ironic existence, perhaps reflecting the ambivalent, double-edged nature of irony itself. On the one hand, some thinkers take an ironic bearing as the condition of possibility for self-reflection, critical distance, and humane life.[23] On the other, there is the concern that irony as a purely negative force leads to a nihilistic dead-end. Richard Bernstein reads in Kierkegaard, for example, a paradoxical experience of "pure irony," which is to say, a rigorously consistent irony. He observes that, although irony can provide a necessary liberating moment, "the more one pushes this ironic stance to its extreme," the more it becomes "enslaving and disastrous," and "self-destructive."[24] Bernstein pursues through the rigor of philosophical reflection the same concern that Fontane plays out in narrative fiction.

To put the dilemma in terms that resonate with Kierkegaard's dissertation, how can one master the moment of irony so that it is redemptive rather than destructive? How can one avoid becoming mired in pure negativity and nihilism? Kierkegaard emphasizes the necessity of mastering irony—limiting and controlling it, isolating it in a dialectical moment—but he has much less to say about how one accomplishes that task.[25] In the conclusion to his dissertation, he says that irony can be a "bath of rejuvenation and regeneration," but it is crucial that one notice how he casts irony as a temporary respite, like a pose or mask that one

---

[22] Dane, *Critical Mythology*, 48.
[23] See, for example, Jonathan Lear, *A Case for Irony* (Cambridge, MA: Harvard University Press, 2011), 9, where he connects the capacity for irony to human excellence.
[24] Richard Bernstein, *Ironic Life* (Cambridge: Polity Press, 2016), 89–90.
[25] Kierkegaard briefly addresses irony "as a mastered moment" in the last few pages of his dissertation. Kierkegaard, *Concept of Irony*, 336–42. See further Bernstein, who calls the answers to these questions "extremely sketchy and elusive." *Ironic Life*, 91.

must discard as soon as its work is done. Of the person who cannot understand irony, he writes, "He does not know the invigoration and fortification which [...] comes from lifting oneself up and plunging into the ocean of irony, *not in order to remain there, of course,* but healthily, gladly, lightly to clad oneself again" (my emphasis).[26] The rejuvenating potential of irony can be actualized only through its limitation and restraint; this is what Kierkegaard means by having mastery over irony.

Fontane's society novels take up this issue and essentially make the point that the Kierkegaardian task—to partake of irony and then set it aside—is easier said than done. They repeatedly stage situations in which irony and other forms of unreliable speech cannot be so easily contained. They suggest that irony is unstable and uncontrollable, that what Kierkegaard calls "the wild infinity wherein it storms consumingly forth" will not be restrained by whatever limitations one tries to impose on it.[27] Returning to the metaphor of bathing in an ocean of irony, one could say that Fontane expresses the insight that this ocean is subject to the movement of powerful cultural tides. When one steps into this ocean, one could easily be carried away by the current, such that it becomes impossible to get back to solid ground. This is the big idea that one observes over and over again in Fontane—a concern with the possibility that individual speakers and indeed entire societies can become trapped by irony, can become ensnared in a nihilistic mode of speaking in which nothing matters and no one can determine whether what is said overlaps with what is sincerely meant. And the danger is that this relationship to language and truth cannot be donned and doffed like the jacket one wears at a private club. If it proves impossible to extricate oneself from ironic expression, the risk is that this way of speaking could develop into a way of being in the world. When the speaking subject finds it impossible to master irony, it is possible that irony has mastered the speaking subject.

The possibility of irony's excess is also evident in the German Romantic tradition that provides a foil for Hegel's and Kierkegaard's reflections. Even Friedrich Schlegel, the great critical proponent and practitioner of irony, identifies an ironic ambivalence in our relationship to irony. In his trenchantly ironic essay on incomprehensibility, he acknowledges that we grow weary of irony "when it is offered to us everywhere, all the time," and he recognizes the danger "that one cannot reemerge from irony," a danger that the essay realizes through its own rhetorical performance.[28] Where Kierkegaard imagines a

---

[26] Kierkegaard, *Concept of Irony*, 339.
[27] Kierkegaard, *Concept of Irony*, 338.
[28] Schlegel, *Kritische Ausgabe*, 2:369.

refreshing dip in the waters of irony, Schlegel envisions a potentially fatal undertow. At one point, he even claims, "Irony is nothing to joke about [scherzen]. Its effects can continue for an incredibly long time."[29] Schlegel once again relates irony to a fundamental dynamic of *Scherz* and *Ernst* and highlights its long-lasting effects. These are useful quotations because they show even Friedrich Schlegel being aware of irony's potential excess and enthralling power. Whether he means these warnings earnestly or ironically is anyone's guess, and more critical ink has been spilled over Schlegel's ironization of irony than I have the space to address here.[30] But to identify that concern in one of the central critical treatments of irony is important because it puts Fontane and Schlegel closer to each other than one might expect. It will sometimes sound as if the present book wants to cast Fontane in opposition to a philosophical and critical tradition inhabited by Socrates, Schlegel, Kierkegaard, and Benjamin. In fact, the realization that one can get sick of irony's instabilities, that irony is nothing to take lightly, these insights belong to the core of influential reflections on irony. When Fontane explores the possibility that irony could become too prevalent, and that its very prevalence could have unanticipated, pernicious side effects, this critical bearing does not set his novels in opposition to the European tradition of irony. It locates them within it. In *The Magic Mountain*, Thomas Mann has the character Settembrini voice the rational humanist resistance to irony: "Ah yes, irony!" he says to Hans Castorp, "beware of it in general as an intellectual stance. When it is not employed as an honest device of classical rhetoric, […] it becomes a source of depravity, a barrier to civilization, a squalid flirtation with inertia, nihilism, and vice."[31] Fontane's novels repeatedly dramatize how ironic, unreliable speech can become both a vice and a drawback to civilization.

The concern in Fontane with empty language has ethical, aesthetic, and political dimensions. The discrepancy between words and things, especially when exploited in the realm of promissory language—contracts, oaths, vows, promises, and so on—severs the all-important bond between words and future deeds. In short, the speaking subject has an ethical obligation to be faithful to her word, to actualize the promise of language through future action. In novels such as *Schach von Wuthenow* and *Graf Petöfy*, the focus of Chapters 2 and 3, Fontane probes the consequences of an indifference to that obligation. It raises ethical issues insofar as infidelity to one's word degrades not only language's

---

[29] Schlegel, *Kritische Ausgabe*, 2:370.
[30] Ernst Behler is an indispensable reference on Schlegel's irony. See, for example, Behler, *Irony and the Discourse of Modernity*, 82–9.
[31] Thomas Mann, *The Magic Mountain*, trans. John E. Woods (New York: Knopf, 1995), 262.

comprehensibility but also its credibility. It is a question not just of whether one can know what other people mean but also whether one can trust people to act in accordance with their given word. In *Die Poggenpuhls*, for example, Leo is quick to sound generous, so long as those around him don't misunderstand his offers of generosity as sincerely meant. His sister, who knows him all too well, says, "du willst dich nett machen, wo du nicht beim Worte genommen wirst" (16:26, you want to make nice—as long as no one takes you at your word).[32] Irony and insincerity function like trapdoors within the ethical bonds of trust, fidelity, and credibility. "Yes, I promised to do *x*," the cynical ironist might say, "but wasn't it obvious that I didn't mean what I said?" J. L. Austin classifies vows and promises as explicitly performative utterances, as speech acts that *do* something via their very utterance, and he describes such insincerity as an abuse of the procedures of performative language. If one promises in bad faith or without the requisite intention, then the speech act is "professed but hollow."[33] The destabilizing force of irony ensures, however, that questions of earnestness and intent are never so transparent and easy to adjudicate.

From an aesthetic perspective, the inadequation of words and things is a problem of representation, not just for the speaking subject, but for art and literature as well. Already in his programmatic 1853 essay "Unsere lyrische und epische Poesie seit 1848," Fontane characterizes realism as a poetic program devoted to maintaining a reliable connection between words and the world they signify. Hugo Aust writes: "The concept of realism stands for a tight relationship between art and reality," and he refers to its way of perceiving the world as a "gaze that registers how something actually is."[34] To the extent that realism indicates a literary movement, it names in language and via language a relationship to truth and a concern for how things actually are. Fontane writes of realism, for instance, "er will das *Wahre*. Er schließt nichts aus als die Lüge, das Forcierte, das Nebelhafte, das Abgestorbene" (*NA* 21.1:13, it wants what is *true*. It excludes nothing but what is false, forced, nebulous, dead). This fundamental conflict between truth and falsehood reveals an aesthetic aspect to the issue of language's reliability. His concept of realism is guided by a concern for true and accurate

---

[32] English from Theodor Fontane, *The Woman Taken in Adultery and The Poggenpuhl Family*, trans. Gabriele Annan (Chicago: University of Chicago Press, 1979), 151.

[33] J. L. Austin, *How to Do Things with Words* (Cambridge, MA: Harvard University Press, 1962), 18. See further Lecture IV, where Austin cites as an example of lacking proper intention, "'I promise,' said when I do not intend to do what I promise" (40).

[34] Hugo Aust, "Fontanes Poetik: Realismus," in *Fontane-Handbuch*, ed. Christian Grawe and Helmuth Nürnberger (Stuttgart: Kröner, 2000), 413, 416.

representations, and the "lie" that he identifies in other literary epochs could be reframed as a disregard for truth, for how things are in actuality.

In this sense, Fontane's realism acts as the functional opposite of or the antidote to Frankfurt's notion of bullshit. Fontane's realism has no patience for an "indifference to how things really are."[35] Instead, as he writes elsewhere, the realist novel must deliver "ein unverzerrtes Wiederspiel *des* Lebens [...], das wir führen" (*NA* 21.2:653, an undistorted counterpart of the life that we lead), the key criterion in this passage being one of accuracy and recognizability. It might sound a bit stilted and heroic, but Fontane casts realism as an antidote, in the aesthetic realm, to the decadence of idle talk, to the erosion of reliability and credibility. This is why one should be cautious in describing Fontane's style as ironic. The sort of verbal irony that Fontane criticizes exploits a discrepancy between words and meaning and introduces the possibility of destabilizing referential aberration. It thus runs counter to the realist program that Fontane espouses, with its reliable, efficacious, and mimetically accurate representations.

Finally, the historical settings of Fontane's novels also reveal the social and political consequences of a culture in the thrall of unreliable language. What happens, they ask, when the dominant mode of discourse in a society is based on empty banter, hollow phrases, irony, insincerity, and indifference to the truth? One answer is that it becomes increasingly difficult to go against the grain, to speak in ways that are forthright, transparent, and reliable. In the *Wanderungen*, for example, Fontane refers to the sculptor Johann Gottfried Schadow as a representative of Berlin irony, "der trostlosesten aller Blüten, die der Geist dieser Landesteile je getrieben hat" (V.4:339–40, the most dismal blossom that the spirit of these regions ever produced). He notes that this local variant of irony was in full bloom during Schadow's time in the mid-nineteenth century, "und da es für den einzelnen mehr oder weniger unmöglich sein wird, sich gegen einen die Gesellschaft beherrschenden Ton abzuschließen, so adoptierte denn auch Schadow auch diese Sprechweise" (V.4:340, and since it will be for the individual more or less impossible to wall oneself off from the tone that dominates society, thus Schadow too adopted this manner of speaking). According to Fontane, there is a tipping point beyond which the ironic manner of speaking takes on a life of its own and acquires the power to co-opt the language of individual speakers. They assimilate to the dominant tone and adapt their speech to meet its expectations.

---

[35] Frankfurt, *On Bullshit*, 34.

The society novels demonstrate that there are costs associated with a cultural commitment to empty, ironic speech. When it comes time to speak seriously about serious matters—when transparency, honesty, and credibility are of paramount importance—one might find oneself unable to drop the pose of ironic indifference and insincerity. When Fontane depicts society's obsession with empty, unreliable speech, the historico-political settings are not a coincidence. He often chooses to set his novels in societies on the verge of calamity: Prussia in 1806, just before defeat at Napoleon's hands (*Schach von Wuthenow*, Chapter 2), Hungary in the era and aftermath of its failed revolution (*Graf Petöfy*, Chapter 3), or Copenhagen in the years leading up to the Second Schleswig War of 1864 (*Unwiederbringlich*, Chapter 5). These carefully crafted historical settings suggest that an ironic indifference to truth and accuracy can act as a catalyst, hastening political and military downfall. When the dominant mode of speaking makes communication less reliable and less efficacious, when it becomes a mode of being that erodes the ability to perceive the world as it actually is, societies find it increasingly difficult to respond effectively to the challenges they face.

The corrosive side effects of a socially dominant tone simultaneously suggest a line of political resistance. Precisely because it is so easy to be swallowed up by a ubiquitous, fashionable mode of discourse, to speak otherwise—to differentiate oneself via a voice that is sincere, straightforward, and reliable—becomes a political act in its own right, an act of resistance. *L'Adultera* depicts this resistance most vividly through the figure of Melanie van der Straaten, who transgresses Berlin social norms not only by leaving her husband and children but also by dropping the tone of perpetual self-ironization and speaking frankly (see Chapter 4). The idea of speaking against the grain of ironic, unserious speech brings me to avowal, the second key term for understanding Fontane's representation of conflicting relationships to language and truth. Against the backdrop of irony's erosion of reliable communication, the society novels present an alternative to irony in the form of avowal, veridiction, *Wahrsagen*, or truth-telling.

I draw the term "avowal" from a series of lectures that Michel Foucault delivered in 1981 on wrongdoing and truth-telling. Here he develops a definition of avowal as "a verbal act through which the subject affirms who he is, binds himself to this truth, places himself in a relationship of dependence with regard to another, and modifies at the same time his relationship to himself."[36] He calls this act "avowal"

---

[36] Michel Foucault, *Wrong-Doing, Truth-Telling. The Function of Avowal in Justice*, ed. Fabienne Brion and Bernard Harcourt, trans. Stephen Sawyer (Chicago: University of Chicago Press, 2014), 17.

(*l'aveu*), and the corresponding term in Fontane's German is *Bekenntnis*, along with the verb form *bekennen*, which can mean both to avow and to confess. Across languages, these terms are united through their concern with conveying personal truth earnestly and accurately. Foucault's definition refers to several elements that specify the nature of avowal and distinguish it from a basic declaration. For instance, he first differentiates avowal by noting that it occurs only when the stakes and potential costliness are high. His primary example is a patient's avowal of madness, but he also describes the costs of speaking truth in a context more relevant to Fontane's novels, writing, "when someone declares his love, it is an avowal if this declaration runs the risk of being costly."[37]

Second, the person who avows freely chooses to bind or obligate herself to what has been declared. Returning to the example of love, Foucault says that a statement such as "I love you" can often be just a simple declaration. He then adds: "But when the sentence 'I love you' functions as an avowal, it is because one passes from the realm of the unspoken to the realm of the spoken by voluntarily constituting oneself as a lover through the affirmation that one loves."[38] Part of the passage's point is that avowal must be voluntary, that it cannot be extracted by force. It seems that, without the element of volition, the subject could not create for itself a new mode of being or commit to the obligations it entails. Foucault envisions how the subject, in the moment of avowal, becomes a lover or, in the confessional mode, takes on the identity of the criminal.

He goes on to argue that avowal differs from other forms of declaration because it involves submitting oneself to the exercise of power and authority. For Foucault, this power structure holds not only in institutional contexts such as the church or the court of law where avowal occurs in a confessional mode; it also pertains in more personal relationships. The patient who admits to being mad accepts the doctor's authority over him, and in similar fashion, the person who avows his love bestows authority on the other person's response. (See above Pope, Alexander.) The Foucauldian sense of avowal provides a template for viewing the novels' acts of veridiction (truth-telling) as a counterpoint to ironic expression, as certain characters attempt to step outside the game of irony and engage in a different kind of speaking. In subsequent lectures, Foucault connects avowal and veridiction to the ancient virtue of *parrhesia*, which "consists in telling the truth without concealment, reserve, empty manner of speech or rhetorical ornament which might

---

[37] Foucault, *Wrong-Doing, Truth-Telling*, 16.
[38] Foucault, *Wrong-Doing, Truth-Telling*, 16.

encode or hide it."[39] He goes on to elaborate an opposition between reliable and unreliable speech when he contrasts *parrhesia* with rhetoric, defined as "a set of processes which enable the person speaking to say something which may not be what he thinks at all."[40] This opposition reflects in brief the conflict between avowal and irony, between speaking frankly and deliberately saying something other than what one thinks, feels, or believes. Avowal, as used in this book, thus names the capacity to speak against the grain of society's dominant ironic tone, to step out of the ocean of irony, and to access a mode of communication that remains candid and sincere.

Though I do not treat Fontane's novels in chronological order, one can still perceive in his work a kind of trajectory to avowal's promise as an antidote to irony. *L'Adultera*, the inaugural society novel, first published serially in 1880, presents the strongest case for avowal's power to cut through irony and unserious talk. Painting in broad strokes, one can trace a gradual attenuation of avowal's promise through the course of Fontane's oeuvre. In mid-career novels, such as *Unwiederbringlich* of 1890, there is no decisive moment in which avowal triumphs over irony. Indeed, candid sincerity appears misplaced, powerless, even ridiculous in the face of ironic indifference, so much so that the Frith painting of Pope and Lady Montagu comes to look like a portrait of avowal's impotence. In the late novels such as *Effi Briest* and *Der Stechlin*, the decline of serious communication has advanced even further. *Effi Briest* (1895), the focus of Chapter 6, studiously avoids moments of face-to-face conflict (the ritualized conflict of the duel notwithstanding), preferring instead to let letters stand in for human speech. Avowal as a conscious, volitional act does not occur in that text. And *Der Stechlin*, Fontane's last finished novel, the book edition of which was not published until after Fontane's death, in late 1898, consists of little more than superficial social chatter, suggesting that the tide of empty, unserious talk will not be turning anytime soon.[41] In this regard, the conflict between irony and avowal that runs through Fontane's works reflects at a macro-level a trajectory that is familiar from the fates of individual characters: they begin with defiance and resistance, move through complication and failure, and end up in a state of quiet resignation.

---

[39] Michel Foucault, *The Courage of the Truth (The Government of Self and Others II)*, ed. Frédéric Gros, trans. Graham Burchell (New York: Palgrave Macmillan, 2011), 10.
[40] Foucault, *Courage of the Truth*, 13.
[41] Hans Blumenberg, *Gerade noch Klassiker. Glossen zu Fontane* (Munich: Carl Hanser, 1998), 7.

Relationship to the Scholarly Literature

By attending to irony and avowal in the society novels, I aim not only to produce new readings of these works but also to revisit and complicate the critical understanding of Theodor Fontane in two main respects. The first of these has to do with the relationship of historical change to language change. It goes almost without saying that Fontane is regarded as a master at portraying dialogue and interpersonal communication. His work demonstrates a deep sensitivity to patterns of speech, contemporary mannerisms, and the way people talk to each other. The critical view reflects Fontane's own assessment of his authorial strengths. He writes in a letter to his daughter, for instance, "Meine ganze Aufmerksamkeit ist darauf gerichtet, die Menschen *so* sprechen zu lassen, wie sie *wirklich* sprechen."[42] (My complete attention is focused on letting people speak the way they *actually* speak.) At the same time, and perhaps paradoxically, he is also seen as presenting communication as empty, fragile, or even meaningless. Moreover, Fontane's novels seismographically trace the disruptions and instabilities of a society in turmoil. His writing reflects the destabilization of social order that results from rapid modernization and industrialization, from the fall of the aristocracy, and presents the ensuing cultural confusion and disorder. Randall Holt, for instance, sees Fontane's characters struggling to negotiate the "breakdown of the meaningful order of social structures."[43]

These two threads come together in the explanatory narrative that says that the communicative breakdown depicted in Fontane's novels mirrors an extra-literary societal breakdown. Rapid technological development, urbanization, and modernization created a rupture, a sense of uncertainty, and a loss of meaning in the world, all of which gets reflected in language, in the way people speak, write, and interact.[44] David Gross summarizes the cultural climate of the late nineteenth century, writing that in the wake of the Industrial Revolution, "it seemed that culture was becoming inherently meaningless and despiritualized and consequently

---

[42] Theodor Fontane, August 24, 1882, *Der Dichter über sein Werk*, ed. Richard Brinkman (München: Deutscher Taschenbuch Verlag, 1973), 2:302.

[43] Randall Holt, "History as Trauma: The Absent Ground of Meaning in *Irrungen, Wirrungen*," in *New Approaches to Theodor Fontane: Cultural Codes in Flux*, ed. Marion Doebeling (Columbia, SC: Camden House, 2000), 103.

[44] For a recent example of the strengths of a contextualizing approach, see Iwan-Michelangelo D'Aprile's extensive portrait of the era, *Fontane. Ein Jahrhundert in Bewegung* (Hamburg: Rowohlt, 2018), which documents the influence on Fontane's writing of globalization, political movements, and revolutions in media, transportation, and technology.

was losing touch with people's inner lives."[45] Given this cultural milieu, the "meaninglessness of speech" depicted in Fontane's novels thus appears as "the implicit corollary to the confusion of the social order."[46] On this view, the fragility of human communication must necessarily be seen as symptomatic of much broader historical forces.

In what follows, I'll be pointing out how Fontane's novels draw attention to the corrosive social effects of empty, unreliable speech as a dominant manner of speaking. Doing so allows me, if not to reverse the direction of fit in the above narrative, then at least to complicate the vectors of influence. Fontane's writings on the emergence of a distinctive Berlin idiom and its penchant for irony evince a more nuanced and idiosyncratic view of the relationship between language and history. From his perspective, it is not so much that historical change shapes or even breaks language, but rather that changes in the way people choose to speak—linguistic changes—have the power to shape history. Empty talk, far from being an inevitability imposed on these characters by historical circumstances, is actually a cultivated attitude, a sophisticated affectation, and a relationship to language adopted willingly and admired widely among Berlin's upper classes. At stake in this distinction is the potential for political agency within language. If language has been broken by the ruptures of rapid historical development, then there's nothing one can do to resist the erosion of meaning and reliability. Individual speakers will just get tossed about by the waves of historical change. Even though Fontane is clear-eyed about the difficulty of contradicting society's dominant tone, he also sees a potential path of resistance. The earlier novels in particular hold out hope that it is still possible to speak forthrightly, to insist on truth and meaning, to align words and deeds. Language use presents as an aesthetic issue, but also as an ethical and political issue.

One finds a parallel argument in George Orwell's essay "Politics and the English Language." He begins with the assumption that language mirrors societal conditions and therefore cannot be improved: "Our civilization is decadent, and our language—so the argument runs—must inevitably share in the general collapse."[47] Orwell disagrees with this

---

[45] David Gross, "*Kultur* and Its Discontents: The Origins of a 'Critique of Everyday Life' in Germany, 1880–1925," in *Essays on Culture and Society in Modern Germany*, ed. Gary Stark and Bede Karl Lackner (College Station, TX: Texas A&M University Press, 1982), 71.
[46] Russell Berman, *The Rise of the Modern German Novel: Crisis and Charisma* (Cambridge, MA: Harvard University Press, 1986), 149.
[47] George Orwell, *In Front of Your Nose, 1945–1950*, vol. 4 of *The Collected Essays, Journalism, and Letters of George Orwell*, ed. Sonia Orwell and Ian Angos (New York: Harcourt, Brace, Javanovich, 1968), 127.

view. He sees language instead as an instrument that people decide how to use. Habits—both good and bad—can be acquired and discarded. He furthermore discusses the collapse of meaning and clarity in terms that resemble key characteristics of irony. "The great enemy of clear language," he writes, "is insincerity. When there is a gap between one's real and one's declared aims, one turns as it were to long words and exhausted idioms, like a cuttlefish squirting out ink."[48] The Fontanean equivalent of "exhausted idioms" is the *Redewendung*, the trite expression or hackneyed turn of phrase. For Orwell too, the impediments to effective communication are insincerity and dissimulation—the willful exploitation of a discrepancy between phenomenon and essence. Orwell's essay is helpful because it captures in a succinct source the stakes of the disagreement over Fontane's notion of language and history. Orwell opposes the argument "that language merely reflects existing social conditions, and that we cannot influence its development" because he wants to hold onto individual agency and a capacity for speaking subjects to shape the state of language use. In 1946, he remains optimistic that "the decadence of our language is probably curable."[49]

Fontane could have written a similar sort of essay on politics and the German language, or politics and the Berlin idiom. He, too, sees language as an instrument whose use is dictated by the designs of individual speaking subjects. Yes, the dominant discourse is a top-down phenomenon that threatens to consume the individual speaker. At the same time, though, that dominant discourse is nothing but the aggregation of language choices made by individual speakers. In the discussion of Schadow, for instance, Fontane casts irony's ascension to Berlin's dominant discourse not as the side effect of historical upheaval, but rather as an instrument of resistance and self-defense. He claims in this instance—though he will present a different genealogy in the later "Berlinertum" essay—that Berlin's distinctive irony arose as a natural consequence from the fact, "daß einer Ansammlung bedeutender geistiger Kräfte die großen Schauplätze des öffentlichen Lebens über Gebühr verschlossen blieben" (V.4:340, that a group of significant intellectual forces was unduly denied access to the primary venues of public life). If the public sphere affords certain intellectuals no space in which to say what they think, then irony acts as an instrument of disguise and detour, allowing them to express their thoughts by saying something other than what they mean. In such cases, the discrepancy between what is said and what is

---

[48] Orwell, *In Front of Your Nose*, 137.
[49] Orwell, *In Front of Your Nose*, 137.

meant should be a "transparent opposition," such that the intended audience readily perceives the underlying message.[50]

The problem that Fontane explores is how that sort of irony transitions from being an instrument of intellectual resistance to a fashionable, ubiquitous way of speaking. At that point, one would require a new form of resistance and self-defense, something to defend against the negative, corrosive power of irony. Fontane identifies the antidote here as "the free word." He writes in a somewhat puzzling passage, "Das freie Wort ist endlich der Tod der Ironie geworden und wird es täglich mehr" (V.4:340, The free word was finally the death of irony and becomes it more so every day). It is puzzling, first, because "being the death of something" is a quality that should not admit degrees of variation. One cannot kill something off, and then do so more and more over time. It's puzzling, moreover, because Fontane locates irony's death in the mid-nineteenth century and then persists through the subsequent decades to explore ongoing issues of irony and unreliable speech. What could Fontane mean by this apparently self-contradictory statement? It is best understood, it seems to me, along the lines of "the king is dead, long live the king." That is, freedom of expression made one particular form of irony obsolete. Once people had a public forum to express their ideas freely, without distortion, irony as an intellectual defense mechanism was no longer necessary. And yet irony had not been truly killed off, since it lives on through the speech mannerisms and rhetorical choices of individual speaking subjects—hence the assertion of an ongoing conflict between the free word and ironic dissimulation. The "free word," for Fontane, now means being able to say what one means sincerely, forthrightly, and unambiguously. This authentic, reliable mode of speech, described here as avowal, is required more and more to counteract the negative force of irony.

The present study also reassesses Fontane's relationship to irony as a narrative quality. It is basically taken for granted that Fontane is an ironic writer, which establishes his work as a touchstone for Thomas Mann's intellectual irony and locates him closer to the works of fin-de-siècle modernism. But it is surprising that more scholarly work has not been devoted to the relationship between Fontane's narrative irony and the treatment of irony within his works. The two most focused studies of Fontane's irony of which I am aware both appeared in the 1970s; these include Fritz Martini's chapter on "ironic realism" and Pierre Bange's monograph *Ironie et Dialogisme*, which has received less attention than it deserves, probably because it was never translated from the French.

---

[50] Allemann, "Ironie als literarisches Prinzip," 28.

Both writers interpret irony in the direction of multiperspectival representation, and both find in Fontane's works a positive, productive form of irony. I will of course want to complicate this line of interpretation by showing that Fontane is not nearly so sanguine about the prospect of irony as a common and representative form of unreliable language.

In the 1970 volume *Ironie und Dichtung*, Martini connects realist irony to the potential for critical distance and self-conscious reflection within narrative. He characterizes it as "a capacity for distancing" and "an act of keen critical consciousness." One should note that this is a far more positive and constructive notion of irony. Rather than dwell on its potential for nihilism and infinite negation, Martini sees irony as making possible the critical portrait of contemporary society that has become synonymous with European realism. Irony names the ability to maintain a critical distance from narrative's object, to be unaligned with any particular perspective, and thus to stand above the fray. In fact, it would not be going too far to say that Martini casts irony as the condition of possibility of Fontane's realism: "It is a means to secure the perspectival distance that allows one to mold a realist narrative into an autonomous work of art."[51] Without ironic detachment, one could not produce realist narrative as autonomous art. Martini fails to observe, however, that Fontane's critique of Prussian society also involves a critique of its empty, ironic language. Irony is not simply the instrument that provides critical distance and allows Fontane to critique the society in which he lives. As a symptom of unreliable language, irony is also an object of that critique. When Martini concludes, writing, "Already with Fontane, irony thus became the language of the epic artistic spirit," that conclusion overlooks Fontane's misgivings with irony and his attempts to portray its negative, destructive force.[52]

Bange's book on irony and dialogism attends similarly to the multiperspectival nature of Fontane's works. As the title suggests, Bange connects Fontane's irony to a Bakhtinian notion of dialogic narrative. Equating the ironic and the dialogic, he writes, for example, that novels such as *Cécile* and *Irrungen, Wirrungen* "aim to establish an ironic (dialogic) view of the world."[53] And from the outset, he uses Bakhtin's

---

[51] Fritz Martini, "Ironischer Realismus," in *Ironie und Dichtung*, ed. Albert Schaefer (Munich: C.H. Beck, 1970), 115.

[52] Martini, "Ironischer Realismus," 141. While Martini does note a resistance in Fontane to certain forms of irony, the characterization remains overwhelmingly positive.

[53] Pierre Bange, *Ironie et Dialogisme dans les Romans de Theodor Fontane* (Grenoble: Presses Universitaires de Grenoble, 1974), 139.

terminology to define what that view of the world would look like. He writes that the dialogic (or ironic) novel is "the novel of interminable questioning, of ambivalence, the novel of the divided man, stripped of his illusory completeness [plénitude]."[54] Bange quite correctly identifies an ironic aspect that occurs repeatedly in the society novels. His definition of a dialogic-ironic view accords with Fontane's notion of self-irony as a cultivated stance of ambivalence and uncertainty, of placing a question mark after every statement, as he puts it in *Der Stechlin*. Again, however, I think these readings go wrong when they view irony as enabling critical distance but fail to see the daylight of critical distance between irony and the narrative voice of Fontane's novels. In other words, they take irony as an instrument of critical reflection without acknowledging how the novels reflect critically on this selfsame ironic tone. Treatments of Fontanean irony must countenance the fact that the novels are, at a minimum, ambivalent about the widespread adoption of an ironic stance. More often, they will show how irony strips away not only illusions but also sincerity, authenticity, and communicative reliability.

None of this need imply that Martini and Bange are wrong about what they observe in Fontane's works. Evidence of detachment, dialogism, critical distance, and societal self-reflection is in abundant supply in the society novels. Those authors might well respond that the disagreement here could actually be resolved through a finer typology of ironies—the deliberately disingenuous forms of verbal irony that Fontane depicts held apart from intellectual irony at the level of narrative. But "irony" is still not the most felicitous term for the narrative stance in these novels because it is not the term that Fontane, in his capacity as literary critic and author, would have used. This usage of irony is rather a retrospective imposition, as Fontane understood narrative irony in a different, more pejorative sense. For Fontane, "irony" denotes an inferior narrative disposition, one that strives for above-the-fray detachment but cannot achieve it. On the topic of humor, for example, he makes an unfavorable comparison between Willibald Alexis and the great Walter Scott. The comparison begins with the following principle: "Der Humor hat das Darüberstehn, das heiter-souveräne Spiel mit den Erscheinungen dieses Lebens, auf die er *herab*blickt, zur Voraussetzung" (*NA* 21.1:211–12, Humor has as its precondition the stance of standing above the cheerful-sovereign play with the phenomena of life that it looks *down* upon). The passage indicates the components that go into true humor: detachment, critical distance, and an Olympian gaze

---

[54] Bange, *Ironie et Dialogisme*, 7.

unaffiliated with any particular diegetic perspective—all things that Martini and Bange would subsume under the rubric of irony. And yet Fontane differentiates these characteristics from what he calls irony.

In his view, Scott achieves a sovereign stance, whereas Alexis does not. "Wo W. Alexis eine ähnliche Position einzunehmen versucht, bleibt er, als Kind seiner Zeit und seines Landes, in der *Ironie* stecken. Er spöttelt, er persifliert; aber seine Seele bringt es zu keinem olympischen Lachen" (*NA* 21.1:212, Where W. Alexis tries to occupy a similar position, he remains, as a child of his time and his country, mired in *irony*. He mocks, he satirizes; but his soul never achieves Olympian laughter). Irony appears here not as the condition of possibility of realist art but rather as a shortcoming and a dead end. It marks the inferiority and narrowness of Alexis's perspective relative to Scott's. The passage echoes Schlegel's concern that one could become trapped in an irony from which it is impossible to escape. Sure, the ironist can mock and humiliate—one thinks here of van der Straaten's mortifying tone—but that is all. It is not the royal road to sovereign detachment or narrative humor on a grand scale. One should note furthermore that Fontane attributes Alexis's dead-end irony to his being a product of a particular time and culture—namely, Berlin in the mid-nineteenth century. Another symptom of his era, Alexis cannot get beyond the negative freedom of irony, cannot achieve the positive freedom of artistic and intellectual autonomy. If irony points out what is lacking in Alexis's prose, then one can easily see why Fontane would resist applying that label to what he admires in Scott's works, and why it is problematic to apply that same label to what many critics admire in Fontane's works.

This question—of whether Fontane's narratives critique, endorse, or even adopt a stance of thoroughgoing irony—might not seem like an essential critical crux, but it in fact goes to the heart of Fontane's literary practice and his status as a realist writer. Erich Auerbach, for instance, in his immensely influential book *Mimesis*, gives a backhanded compliment when he states, "Only in the case of Fontane [...] is it possible to discern the rudiments of a genuine contemporary realism." His point is that, with the exception of Fontane, one finds in German-language literature little in the way of a modern realist style. Even in the case of Fontane, that realism remains rudimentary, and one encounters it only in his final works from the 1890s. On the one hand, Fontane stands out as a more accomplished realist than any of his German-speaking contemporaries; on the other, he lags behind—behind his French counterparts—because his realism is just beginning to develop at the end of his career and life. Why does Fontane remain mired in a rudimentary realism? Auerbach attributes the shortcoming to a deficiency in tone. He writes that the rudiments of contemporary realism in Fontane "do not develop fully because his tone after all never goes beyond the half-seriousness [*halben Ernst*] of pleasant, partly optimistic, partly resigned conversation."[55] Recall that Fontane repeatedly refers to his characters' ironically ambivalent tone as one that is "half joking" (13:220), partly facetious and partly earnest at the same time.[56] Auerbach lays this half-serious tone at Fontane's feet and blames it for his underdeveloped style of realism.

This misattribution, however, is precisely why it is so important to see how Fontane examines that half-earnest, do-I-mean-it-or-not ironic tone from a vantage point of critical distance.[57] The fatal flaw that Auerbach identifies in Fontane's prose is actually the fatal flaw that Fontane's prose means to identify in Prussian society. In fact, one could adapt Auerbach's judgment to paraphrase Fontane's diagnosis: Prussian society cannot "develop fully" as long as its tone "never goes beyond the half-seriousness of pleasant, partly optimistic, partly resigned conversation." It is the achievement of Fontane's realism to depict that ironic tone so realistically, with such a high degree of mimetic accuracy, that it gets mistaken for the author's own. Disentangling Fontane's relationship to irony helps to set his achievement in more obvious relief. In the most emphatic instances, his novels present that ironic tone as cynical, pernicious, and potentially uncontainable. Even in the subtler instances, one can at least say that Fontane is deeply ambivalent about contemporary culture's penchant for irony and other forms of unreliable language. For those who would insist that Fontane remains at heart an ironist, here is the path forward: one could claim that Fontane is such a rigorous and systematic ironist that he is ironically ambivalent even about the prospect of ironic ambivalence. As Bernstein writes, "If the ironist is to be thoroughly consistent, he must turn his irony against his own ironic stance."[58] To do otherwise would be to undermine irony with earnestness. I see Fontane differently, though, more along the lines of Kierkegaard at the conclusion of his dissertation, as he steps back

---

[55] Erich Auerbach, *Mimesis: The Representation of Reality in Western Literature*, trans. Willard Trask (Princeton: Princeton University Press, 2013), 519.

[56] See further Zuberbühler, who identifies the interplay of *Ernst* and *Scherz* and the reader's suspension between them as constitutive elements of the well-known "Fontane-Ton." Rolf Zuberbühler, "'Excelsior!' Idealismus und Materialismus in Kellers und Fontanes Altersromanen *Martin Salander* und *Der Stechlin*," in *Gottfried Keller und Theodor Fontane: Vom Realismus zur Moderne*, ed. Ursula Amrein and Regina Dieterle (Berlin: de Gruyter, 2008), 104.

[57] Mecklenburg prudently cautions against taking character speech as a mouthpiece for authorial intent when it could just as easily be an object of critical scrutiny. Norbert Mecklenburg, *Theodor Fontane. Romankunst der Vielstimmigkeit* (Frankfurt am Main: Suhrkamp, 1998), 152.

[58] Bernstein, *Ironic Life*, 89.

from the nihilism of pure irony. Like Kierkegaard, Fontane holds out hope for the possibility of irony as a "mastered moment," as a rhetorical tool that could be used judiciously, sparingly, and held in check by the forthrightness of avowal. And yet the novels repeatedly express the concern that this hope is naïve, that irony cannot be quarantined or contained, and that it will eventually contaminate every last aspect of human interaction.

Fontane's relationship to irony is an issue that has been taken for granted in the secondary literature without ever being run to ground in a satisfactory fashion. The promise of revealing a skepticism in Fontane vis-à-vis irony's negative, destabilizing force and thereby reorienting our understanding of some of his best-known works makes it worthwhile to revisit questions that seem settled but are in fact not.

In a Post-Truth Age

The subtitle "Irony and Avowal in a Post-Truth Age" refers, first of all, to the condition of reading Fontane in the light of our contemporary age, which, at the time of this writing, includes the *Fontanejahr* of 2019, the 200th anniversary of the author's birth. Revisiting Fontane's novels in a post-truth age brings the conflict between irony and avowal into sharper relief and makes legible the stakes and contours of our own post-truth condition. The year 2016 inaugurated what we tend to think of as the contemporary post-truth era. It witnessed a "voluminous stream of lies, scandals, and shocks" during the US elections that year, including a disinformation campaign waged by Russian intelligence,[59] as well as an avalanche of bad-faith claims in the lead-up to the Brexit vote in the UK.[60] No wonder, then, that *Oxford Dictionaries* selected "post-truth" as 2016's word of the year.[61] Nor is the sense of a post-truth era confined to the English-speaking world. The Society for German Language, observing similar cultural trends, named "postfaktisch" ("post-factual") its word of the year in 2016.[62] As I write this in 2020, we still live in a world where the victims of mass shootings are likely to be dismissed as so-called crisis actors and whatever statistics the administration cites are likely to be "alternative facts" made from whole cloth. Everywhere one looks, people worry about not being able to tell fact from fiction, not being able to believe their own eyes

---

[59] Michiko Kakutani, *The Death of Truth* (New York: Tim Duggan Books, 2018), 142.
[60] Matthew D'Ancona, *Post-Truth: The New War on Truth and How to Fight Back* (London: Ebury Press, 2017), 18.
[61] D'Ancona, *Post-Truth*, 8–9.
[62] Gesellschaft für deutsche Sprache, "GfdS wählt 'postfaktisch' zum Wort des Jahres 2016." https://gfds.de/wort-des-jahres-2016/

and ears. Politicians and pundits seem indifferent to the truth, and it is increasingly unclear whether people actually believe or mean what they say, even in official, public forums.

From 2015 on, the media struggled with how to report on Donald Trump's campaign and subsequent administration, with its unprecedented disregard for the truth. Take, as a telling example, a minor campaign skirmish that has long been forgotten, having been buried under many more dangerous crises and egregious falsehoods. In spring of 2016, Carrier Corporation announced plans to move manufacturing jobs from Indiana to Mexico, which prompted then-candidate Trump to claim, "we're not going to let Carrier leave." A few months later, it was your fault if you had taken him at his word: "I said 'Carrier will never leave,'" he recalled, "but that was a euphemism."[63] The statement does not really constitute a euphemism—or the term "euphemism" functions here as a euphemism—because the import is simply that he did not mean what he clearly said. This sort of back and forth gave rise to Salena Zito's widely quoted lines, "When he makes claims like this, the press takes him literally, but not seriously; his supporters take him seriously, but not literally."[64] Though Zito's judgment struck a chord, it remains a bewildering task to take someone seriously but not literally. He means something, and he apparently means it seriously, but it would be naïve to proceed as if what he means necessarily overlaps with the straightforward meaning conveyed by his words. It is a conundrum that reactivates the bewilderment experienced by numerous characters in the society novels. As Woldemar puts it in *Der Stechlin*, "zugespitzte Sätze darf man nie wörtlich nehmen" (17:279, one can never take pointed sentences literally). In a post-truth age, one must be attuned to a general discrepancy between the phenomenon of language and the essence of meaning. In other words, one must be ever alert to the possibility of irony. Reading Fontane in this cultural context makes certain aspects of his work more perspicuous. Given the contemporary alarm over unreliability, falsehood, and indifference to the truth, it is perhaps easier post-2016 to perceive in Fontane's works a profound concern with language that is not reliable and not meant to be taken literally.

At the same time, though, there is an intentional ambiguity in the subtitle's phrase, "in a post-truth age." It is not only that we are reading Fontane from the perspective of a post-truth age, but also that Fontane

---

[63] Jonah Goldberg, "Take Trump Seriously but Not Literally? How Exactly?" *L.A. Times*, December 6, 2016.
[64] Salena Zito, "Taking Trump Seriously, Not Literally," *The Atlantic*, September 23, 2016.

portrays a conflict between opposed modes of language because he believes the age in which he is writing to be a post-truth age. He would not have used that term, of course, and there are certainly many differences separating the current moment from the late nineteenth century.[65] To name but one example, the rise of the internet and social media has played an enormous part in creating the current post-truth condition. As D'Ancona puts it, "The web is the definitive vector of Post-Truth precisely because it is indifferent to falsehood, honesty, and the difference between the two."[66] The contemporary digital media landscape would be unrecognizable to Fontane, but the concern with not being able to differentiate between honesty and falsehood would not. It is thus not an anachronistic imposition to think of the last decades of the nineteenth century as a post-truth age in its own right. Despite all that separates the contemporary world from the late nineteenth century, Fontane presents a necessary corrective to the post-truth condition—namely, to counteract irony with avowal and to replace indifference with a keen eye for distinguishing between the serious and the unserious.

Current attempts to come to grips with the post-truth condition often sketch out an intellectual history in which postmodernism appears as the philosophical precursor to the widespread popularization of post-truth thinking. According to these accounts, by "substituting the notions of perspective and positioning for the idea of truth" and viewing language as always "unreliable and unstable (part of the unbridgeable gap between what is said and what is meant),"[67] postmodernist theory unwittingly laid the groundwork for a world in which fact and fiction are functionally indistinguishable, climate science can be dismissed as a matter of personal belief, and political operatives sneer at the benighted simpletons who still reside in "the reality-based community."[68] There are of course vast differences between postmodernism's efforts to fracture grand narratives, to decenter and democratize society, and bad-faith appeals to epistemological nihilism in the service of a nativist, exclusionary agenda. But Albrecht Koschorke, considering the transition "From Postmodernism to the Postfactual Age," notes that,

---

[65] McGillen cleverly refers to the late nineteenth century as a "pre-truth age." Petra McGillen, "Fontane Goes to J School. Theodor Fontanes Englandjahre und die Entstehung journalistischer Autorität im *Pre-truth*-Zeitalter," forthcoming in *Colloquia Germanica* 52.1–2 (2019).
[66] D'Ancona, *Post-Truth*, 53.
[67] Kakutani, *Death of Truth*, 48. On postmodernism as contributing to post-truth, see further D'Ancona, *Post-Truth*, 89–109, and Lee McIntyre, *Post-Truth* (Cambridge, MA: MIT Press, 2018), 123–50.
[68] Ron Susskind, "Faith, Certainty, and the Presidency of George W. Bush," *New York Times*, October 17, 2004.

"what started as part of a liberatory, leftist project seems to have turned into an instrument for advancing the power claims of right-wing, sometimes extremist, movements."[69] Maurizio Ferraris locates the Nietzschean dictum "there are no facts, only interpretations" at the base of the postmodern project and traces how its emancipatory hopes were dashed on the shoals of populist media.[70]

Setting aside the question of whether popular accounts do justice to the intricacies of postmodern thought, as well as whether the current cultural climate can really be laid at the doorstep of abstruse critical theories, I want to focus instead on the idea of contagion.[71] For this is something that recent explanations of post-truth's genesis share in common: they are not so much narratives of cause and effect (postmodernism *caused* post-truth politics) but rather narratives of contagion from one cultural sphere to another. Koschorke writes, for example, that many aspects of postmodern thought "are becoming virulent" in a political landscape radically different from that of the 1960s.[72]

The idea in popular accounts is that radical critiques of objectivity and epistemology might have their place in the graduate seminar or the academic conference, but even abstract theories can have pernicious real-world consequences when they are popularized, politicized, and weaponized, which is to say, deployed to further an ideology diametrically opposed to that of the postmodern thinkers who allegedly engendered this very line of thinking. McIntyre writes in this vein, "It's all fun and games to attack truth in the academy, but what happens when one's tactics leak out into the hands of science deniers and conspiracy theorists, or thin-skinned politicians who insist that their instincts are better than any evidence?"[73] This notion of "leaking out" is especially important, as it suggests vectors of influence that run from rarefied, intellectual circles to the public at large. Such an account lands much closer to Fontane's explanations of how a particular brand of irony and wit came to be the dominant tone in nineteenth-century Berlin society. In the Schadow discussion, for example, he traces the roots of Berlin irony back to a cluster of intellectuals who adopted an ironic tone that

---

[69] Albrecht Koschorke, "Facts Shifting to the Left: From Postmodernism to the Postfactual Age," trans. Michael Thomas Taylor and Sasha Rossman, *PMLA* 134, no. 5 (2019): 1155.
[70] Maurizio Ferraris, "Was ist der Neue Realismus?" trans. Malte Osterloh, in *Der Neue Realismus*, ed. Markus Gabriel (Frankfurt am Main: Suhrkamp, 2014), 54–5.
[71] For a lucid introduction to postmodernism and its intellectual inheritance, see Behler's chapter "Modernism and Postmodernism in Contemporary Thought." Behler, *Irony and the Discourse of Modernity*, 3–36.
[72] Koschorke, "Facts Shifting to the Left," 1150.
[73] McIntyre, *Post-Truth*, 145.

subsequently spread throughout society. Or in the "Berlinertum" essay, which I treat in more detail in Chapter 1, he refers to the development of a Sanssouci tone in the circle of Frederick the Great, a way of speaking that then migrated through the various social classes. Without endorsing simplified characterizations of postmodern thought, I want to make the point that irony functions in Fontane the way postmodernism often does in current genealogies of the post-truth condition: it develops in restricted, elite discourse communities, but then gets popularized and spreads throughout society until it contaminates politics, commerce, and intimate relationships. The word "metastasize" will occur more than once in this book, as irony begins as one thing, in one particular setting, but then mutates into something else entirely and spreads throughout society.

One could also make the point that there need be no special connection between Fontane's time and today, because every era tends to perceive itself as a decadent, post-truth age. And it is certainly not as if strategies of misinformation were invented in the twenty-first century. One need look no further than the propaganda machine of Nazi Germany churning out the big lies in the 1930s and 1940s. Hannah Arendt writes that totalitarian propaganda in the twentieth century exploited a blend of gullibility and cynicism among the masses: "In an ever-changing, incomprehensible world, [...] they would, at the same time, believe everything and nothing, think that everything was possible and nothing was true."[74] Orwell, writing in 1946—that is, closer to Fontane's time than to our own—argues similarly that the political philosophy of totalitarianism "demands a disbelief in the very existence of objective truth."[75] The conviction that one lives in a post-truth world does not mean that truth no longer exists. It is, rather, a diagnosis that the contemporary culture (or, a significant segment of contemporary culture) has adopted the posture that truth no longer exists.[76] It occurs when people behave as if there are no fixed, stable truths on which to base one's convictions and decisions. Everything is malleable, negotiable, perspectival, and in flux.

Fontane's characters express post-truth sentiments on various occasions. In two of the novels analyzed in this book, they refer, for example, to Pontius Pilate's famously mocking, skeptical question. When Jesus says that he came into the world to "bear witness unto the truth," Pilate

---

[74] Hannah Arendt, *The Origins of Totalitarianism* (New York: Meridian Books, 1958), 382.
[75] Orwell, *In Front of Your Nose*, 64.
[76] See again McIntyre, who writes that the prefix "post" points to "the sense that truth has been eclipsed—that it is irrelevant." McIntyre, *Post-Truth*, 5.

retorts, "What is truth?"[77] The consensus view is that Pilate is speaking in jest, not in earnest. This kind of question, which could be classified as a rhetorical question, delivers a prime example of irony's ability to disrupt the referential work of language. Pilate's question ostensibly asks for a definition or explanation of truth, and yet the ironic, jesting trope suggests that there's nothing to explain because truth does not exist. Had Pilate not immediately walked away, one could be forgiven for mistaking his question as earnestly intended. As it stands, his rhetorical, ironic question implies that there is no truth to which one could bear witness. In Pilate, we have an early example of a post-truth posture. Christ's sentencing and crucifixion thus occur not just under the banner of a denial of truth, but a denial of truth that is expressed via irony.

When Fontane's characters refer to Pilate's "What is truth?" retort, they reference both the perspectival questioning of truth and its expression in an ironic mode. To take the analysis just a step further, observe that Jesus is being questioned in a juridical proceeding. His statement—his confession, if you will—is an act of avowal. He says who he is and obligates himself to that role. It is actually a meta-avowal: he avows that he has come to avow; he tells the truth about his identity as a truth-teller. The questioning that precedes the crucifixion plays out as a conflict between Christ's avowal and Pilate's irony. It is a biblical crucible for every conflict in Fontane in which one party wants to speak the truth in earnest and the other turns to irony. And what is more, Fontane's characters refer to this conflict between irony and avowal during their own conflicts over irony and avowal. Graf Petöfy, for instance, attacks his sister's earnest piety, saying, "Ach, die Wahrheit? Glaube mir, Judith, die Welt bleibt ewig in der alten Pilatusfrage stecken" (7:200, Oh, the truth? Believe me, Judith, the world is forever mired in Pilate's old question). For Petöfy, it would make no sense to talk about an isolated post-truth era, because he sees the despair of truth as an eternal condition. Every age is a post-truth age, or better yet, there never was an age in which truth was apparent in its unconcealment. In *Unwiederbringlich*, Pilate's question has become a trite expression of cynicism, serving as an unofficial motto for the entire Danish court (13:79). It reflects the post-truth bearing that reigns in Copenhagen and to which Holk gradually acclimates himself. The exchange between Pilate and Christ, like the Frith image of Pope and Lady Montagu, represents a conflict between irony and avowal. This conflict—its contours, stakes, and consequences—is what many of Fontane's novels work through, and it constitutes the central object of inquiry in this book.

---

[77] John 18:37-38, King James Version.

One The Dilemma of Choice in *Irrungen, Wirrungen*

Irrungen, Wirrungen provides fertile ground for exploring the themes of language and communication because here, perhaps more clearly than anywhere else, Fontane presents a stark contrast between two opposed relationships to language in the form of serious and unserious speech. The novel attentively depicts the penchant for empty, ironic banter among Berlin's higher social classes and contrasts it with a form of speech that is more earnest, authentic, and reliable. The novel begins in 1870s Berlin with a summer love affair between Botho von Rienäcker, a baron and military officer, and Lene Nimptsch, a young seamstress from a working-class background. Because of the vast differences in their social standing, class, and education, the relationship seems doomed to fail from the start. Indeed, despite their deep affection for one another, the affair comes to an abrupt end when Botho's family insists that he marry his cousin Käthe, who is both an appropriate match for someone of Botho's aristocratic standing and wealthy enough to stabilize the family's precarious financial situation.

The novel is structured around Botho's difficult choice between Lene and Käthe, and the differences between the two women crystallize into two radically divergent relationships to language. Lene, on the one hand, represents for Botho an ideal of straightforward, honest communication, "mit ihrer Einfachheit, Wahrheit und Unredensartlichkeit" (10:124, with her simplicity, truthfulness and lack of empty talk).[1] The last of these characteristics might well be the most telling, as "Unredensartlichkeit" indicates that she has no need for formulaic expressions or empty turns of phrase. Käthe, on the other hand, is diametrically opposed to this description of Lene. The narrative juxtaposes their different demeanors by noting on the same page that although Käthe is

---

[1] Fontane, *On Tangled Paths*, 114. Further references to this translation in this chapter are given parenthetically.

charming in social situations, "auch das Beste, was sie sagte, war oberflächlich und 'spielrig,' als ob sie der Fähigkeit entbehrt hätte, zwischen wichtigen und unwichtigen Dingen zu unterscheiden" (10:124, even the best of what she said was superficial and frisky, as if she lacked the ability to distinguish between important and unimportant things, 114). Even at its best, her language remains *scherzhaft* rather than *ernsthaft*. It plays at the level of surface and phenomenon, detached from any essence of underlying sincerity.[2] Käthe, it seems, can never go beyond the superficial phrases that have no place in Lene's speech, and much of the novel's second half is devoted to portraying how Käthe's insincere banter amuses everyone around her except Botho.

Prominent readings of Fontane have seized on this novel as a prime example of how rapid changes in nineteenth-century society impinged upon the ability to communicate clearly. From an historicizing perspective, these interpretations take Käthe's unserious chatter and Botho's decisions as the inescapable side effects of broad historical forces beyond the characters' control. The gist of the arguments is that the destabilizing or indeed traumatizing movement of history has led to a dearth of discernible meaning in the world. Modernity's chaotic uncertainty has eroded the reliability of meaning and the efficacy of interpersonal communication. Take, as an initial example of this line of argument, a passage from Russell Berman regarding "small talk," which is a short-hand formulation for the kind of insincere banter at which Käthe excels. He writes, "'Small talk' is not laudable, but it is the sole sort of speech—or narration—with which bourgeois culture can hope to master the semiotic chaos engendered by capitalist modernization. It is only through such speech that meaning or the illusion of meaning in an otherwise meaningless world is possible."[3] The quotation sketches in brief the main argument—namely, that Germany in the late nineteenth century finds itself in the midst of rapid modernization, which has created semiotic chaos and the sense of a world devoid of meaning. Under such circumstances, the ineffectual chatter of the upper classes becomes the only possible response, and it is a weak response indeed. Small talk is so unreliable, so small, that one cannot even be sure whether it presents actual meaning or merely the illusion of meaning without genuine substance.

---

[2] Stefan Willer, attending to play in the novel, cites this passage to extend forms of play to language. Stefan Willer, "Gesellschaftsspiele. Fontanes *Irrungen, Wirrungen*," in *Herausforderungen des Realismus: Theodor Fontanes Gesellschaftsromane*, ed. Peter Uwe Hohendahl and Ulrike Vedder (Freiburg: Rombach, 2018), 134.

[3] Berman, *Rise of the Modern German Novel*, 151.

In contrast to these readings, I maintain that Fontane depicts no crisis of meaning in *Irrungen, Wirrungen*, at least not in terms of an outright inability to communicate, and that meaningless small talk is not the only mode of speech available to the characters. To arrive at such a conclusion requires one to disqualify Lene as an alternative model of language use. *Irrungen, Wirrungen* presents unreliable, insincere talk not as the inevitable side effect of historical change but rather as a fashionable and cultivated rhetorical pose, something that upper-class Berlin society perceives as a mark of sophistication. Through the opposition elaborated between Lene and Käthe, the novel foregrounds an antagonism that runs, in various guises, through much of Fontane's novelistic output. One finds in this book a clear staging of the conflict between the two tendencies that I have labeled irony and avowal. Irony designates a mode of speech that is intentionally frivolous and unserious, one that blurs the distinction between sincerity and insincerity, whereas avowal describes the promise of speech that is more efficacious and reliable. If the protagonist chooses Käthe's meaningless charms over Lene's simple authenticity, this should not be taken as a sweeping generalization about linguistic breakdown but rather as a narrowly tailored statement on how the choices of individual speaking subjects aggregate to form a dominant idiom of empty, ironic detachment. It is ultimately not social upheaval but rather the "ossified life-style of the Prussian nobility, trapped by social convention and outmoded class arrogance"[4] that stands between Botho and more serious forms of communication.

Lene and Käthe: Two Opposed Embodiments of Language Use

My analysis of *Irrungen, Wirrungen* begins from a fairly obvious point—namely, the opposition that Fontane establishes between Lene and Käthe and their opposed ways of speaking. This aspect of the novel has been widely commented upon in the secondary literature. Holt writes, for instance, that "Fontane clearly sets up a dichotomy between Lene and Käthe, contrasting the two largely through their differing modes of communication."[5] The opposition constitutes a well-established point in the scholarship, but the problem, as I see it, is twofold. First, scholars who comment on this dichotomy tend not to recognize it as the novel's center of gravity, preferring instead to focus on other issues such as class

---

[4] Wolfgang Mommsen, *Imperial Germany 1867–1918: Politics, Culture, and Society in an Authoritarian State*, trans. Richard Deveson (London: Arnold, 1995), 120.
[5] Holt, "History as Trauma," 110.

obligations or the decline of the Prussian nobility.⁶ It is important, however, to hold onto the distinction between how Lene and Käthe speak, for this is the most emphatic way in which the novel differentiates and opposes the two women. Botho repeatedly couches his nostalgic yearning for the happiness he experienced with Lene in terms of an admiration for her straightforward, candid style of speech. In contrast, his dissatisfaction with Käthe is presented almost entirely in terms of her flippant, unserious talk. In both cases, Fontane uses differing manners of speech as synecdochic figures to sketch whole characters. The primary confrontation in the novel is as much as about choosing between unadorned, authentic communication (Lene) and meaningless banter (Käthe) as it is about social hierarchy and the pursuit of happiness.

Second, even when scholars do attend closely to this dichotomy, they are often inclined to see it as an illusory opposition, one in which Lene represents only a chimerical or nostalgic ideal, not an actual alternative to the ironic banter of the upper classes. There is thus the tendency to oppose "the reality of [...] Käthe's verbose irrelevance" to "the promise of authentic but inaccessible interchange with Lene."⁷ On this view, Lene and Käthe no longer embody two simultaneous possibilities of speech. Instead, they are separated temporally: Lene stands in for an idealized past possibility that has been precluded by the contemporary reality of disorder and uncertainty. They present a trajectory of communicative and cultural entropy, in which Lene is relegated to an earlier stage of communicative innocence, prior to the gradual decline into semiotic disorder. Of course, a large part of my aim here is to demonstrate that the confrontation between reliable and unreliable forms of speech constitutes an important yet underacknowledged conflict in Fontane's work. And presenting *Irrungen, Wirrungen* as exhibit A in making that case tips my hand, I want to see Lene and Käthe as coequal alternatives in part because the tension between their competing relationships to language is operative not only in this novel but throughout Fontane's work. Botho's difficult choice in the novel—the source of all his confusions and delusions—reflects broader cultural choices that, for Fontane, carry aesthetic, political, and ethical implications.

There is no question that the stark contrast between Lene and Käthe centers on their respective uses of language. In addition to admiring Lene's simplicity, truthfulness, and lack of phrases, Botho also praises her to her future husband Gideon Franke for the honesty of her

---

6   Holt illustrates this tendency. Though he addresses the contrast of divergent communication styles, in his view it is not the novel's primary concern. Holt, "History as Trauma," 110.
7   Berman, *Rise of the Modern German Novel*, 150.

speech. He describes their first encounter, saying, "an der Art, wie sie dankte, sah ich gleich, daß sie anders war als andere. Von Redensarten keine Spur" (10:151, from the way she thanked me I could immediately tell there was something different about her. There were no empty phrases at all, 139–40). What distinguishes Lene is something as simple as how she expresses gratitude. That brief exchange suffices to reveal her exceptionality, and here, too, one learns that Lene has no use for empty phrases or trite expressions. Botho's praise for Lene does not suggest a world in which meaning is indiscernible or communication impossible. Instead, it casts her straightforward manner of speech as a laudable quality. Lene's earnest speech may not conform to contemporary expectations of what is fashionable or sophisticated, but it is there, it is possible, and presumably it is a desirable trait in a prospective spouse.

Lene's manner of speaking matters to the characters, furthermore, because it evinces a tight, reliable bond between phenomenon and essence: "Denn so heiter und mitunter beinahe ausgelassen sie sein kann, von Natur ist sie nachdenklich, ernst und einfach" (10:151, although she can be cheerful and at times exuberant, by nature she's thoughtful, serious and straightforward, 140). Her earnest mode of speech cannot help but derive from a thoughtful, earnest nature. As Botho puts it later, while revisiting one of Lene's letters, "Alles was sie sagte, hatte Charakter und Tiefe des Gemüths" (10:167, Everything she said showed character and depth of feeling, 153). This connection between language and character, between speech and depth of feeling, is one of Lene's most attractive qualities, and it is precisely what is missing in irony, small talk, and empty chatter.

Botho goes on to tell Francke that Lene prides herself, "alles grad heraus zu sagen und keine Flausen zu machen und nichts zu vergrößern und nichts zu verkleinern" (10:152, [on] always talking straight without any evasions or making things out to be more or less than they really are, 141). Because Lene is a straight talker or, as Foucault might say, a parrhesiast, her language does not distort its object. Whatever it portrays, it does so without enlarging or diminishing it. Lene's language is, in this sense, realistic: it communicates reliably and effectively. Moreover, Botho's reference to "Flausen" in the above statement subtly serves to reinforce the contrast between Lene and Käthe, for "Flause" carries two different meanings. As Botho uses it above, it refers to excuses or evasions, such that Lene's speech is never evasive. However, the primary meaning of "Flause" remains "nonsense" or "gibberish." When Botho uses this phrase to describe Lene, it is not hard to hear the term's other meaning alluding to Käthe and her knack for idle chatter. The two senses of "Flause" are actually bound together in Käthe's speech, as it is her tendency to produce nonsense or rubbish that makes her seem evasive to Botho. No matter how much she says, her language never leads below the surface to a more serious form of communication.

The meeting with Franke gives Botho the chance to reflect on his relationship with Lene and to articulate what he found so attractive about her. Another such opportunity comes through his conversation with Rexin, who seeks out Botho's advice regarding a love affair remarkably similar to Botho's own relationship with Lene. Rexin announces his place in this novel's central dichotomy, saying that he has no need for "alles, was wie Feierlichkeit und schöne Redensarten aussieht" (10:173, anything that looks like solemnity or flowery language [empty phrases], 159). Rexin stands with Botho and Lene on the side of simplicity, sincerity, and forthrightness. He eschews both faux solemnity and trite expressions because both are empty, false, and constituted over a discrepancy. It is worth noting, too, that Rexin is a fellow officer, so that the novel's contrast in styles of speaking does not map perfectly onto class differences. To be sure, there are classist connotations to the two men's shared taste for the true, the simple, and the unadorned.[8] In both cases, the desire for authentic communication leads them to consider going against the social obligations of class.[9] But one sees here at least that Botho is not a complete outlier among the nobility, as he assumes a wide straddle with a foot in two separate social realms. Rexin's predicament, and especially its presentation in terms of a recognizable rhetorical stance, suggests that there exists a more broadly felt internal tension among the upper class regarding not only its strictures but also its accepted forms of communication. In other words, just as Pitt, Serge, and Balafré will demonstrate that Käthe is not anomalous in her taste for idle chatter, so Rexin's presence shows that Botho is not alone in his discomfort with the speech mannerisms of the upper classes.

---

[8] For a different take on how class perceptions structure the dichotomy between the novel's central women, see Brian Tucker, "To Have an Eye: Visual Culture and the Misapprehension of Class in *Irrungen, Wirrungen*," in *Fontane in the Twenty-First Century*, ed. John B. Lyon and Brian Tucker (Rochester, NY: Camden House, 2019).

[9] The novel associates transgressing class boundaries with crossing an enemy line and taking friendly fire. When Botho admits to himself that he is delaying the inevitable engagement with Käthe because he loves Lene, artillery fire interrupts his train of thought (10:106). This occurrence seems more meaningful when considered alongside the ride with Rexin. As they set out, Rexin verifies the route, saying, "In die Tegeler Schusslinie werden wir ja wohl nicht einreiten" (10:172, I assume we won't be crossing the line of fire at Tegel, 158). The allegorical import is clear: by counseling Rexin against marrying outside his social class, Botho will help him avoid taking fire from his own allies. See John B. Lyon's insightful *Out of Place* (New York: Bloomsbury, 2013), 153. According to Lyon, even natural spaces reinforce hierarchical social structures.

The Dilemma of Choice in *Irrungen, Wirrungen* 39

Rexin bears his heart to Botho and describes his love for Jette, saying, "ich kann ohne sie nicht leben, sie hat es mir angetan" (I can't live without her; she's captivated me, 160) and admiring "ihre Natürlichkeit, Schlichtheit und wirkliche Liebe" (10:174, her naturalness, simplicity and true love, 160). The three qualities Rexin chooses to highlight echo both formally and semantically Botho's descriptions of Lene from earlier in the novel. In another instance, Botho formulates the same thought slightly differently, praising her "Einfachheit, Wahrheit, Natürlichkeit. Das alles hat Lene, damit hat sie mir's angetan" (10:106, simplicity, truth and naturalness. Lene has them all, that's been her fascination for me, 98). These passages, with their repetitions and synonymous attributes, suggest that Lene and Jette are synonymous characters. And to drive the point home, Fontane even has both men use the same participle, "angetan." In a different age, one would suspect that Fontane has produced Rexin's dialogue by cutting and pasting from Botho's feelings for Lene.

The qualities that Lene and Jette represent come into clearer focus when contrasted with the general milieu of empty, unreliable talk that surrounds Botho. There are two key scenes in which Botho describes that milieu, and I treat them here in reverse chronological order. First, in the moment when his mother's letter convinces him that he must marry Käthe, he offers a clear-eyed appraisal of the happiness he must forgo and the future he will face. "Ich hab' [...] einen Widerwillen gegen alles Unwahre, Geschraubte, Zurechtgemachte. Chic, Tournüre, savoir-faire,—mir alles ebenso hässliche wie fremde Wörter" (10:106–7, I have an aversion to everything that's inauthentic and artificially concocted, *chic, tournure, savoir-faire*—words as ugly to my ears as they are foreign, 99). He is at best indifferent and at worst entirely put off by the salon rhetoric of the educated upper class. Perhaps most notable is how he ends this thought with two three-word series, which recall the triple lists of features that Botho and Rexin ascribe to their working-class lovers. Indeed, this parallel is not accidental, for the excerpt comes from the same scene in which Botho attributes to Lene the best in life—simplicity, truth, and naturalness. Peter James Bowman also notes Lene's fundamental candor and describes her relationship with Botho as "a situation of communicative authenticity," one that is threatened by "normative discursive practices" of platitude and banality.[10]

In this crucial moment of decision, the opposition between Lene and the world of the salon could not be clearer, since Botho formulates the conflict through two roughly antonymic lists. The untrue or inauthentic stands against Lene's simple truth, while contrived affectations represent

---

[10] Peter James Bowman, "The Lover's Discourse in Theodor Fontane's *Irrungen, Wirrungen*," *Orbis Litterarum* 62, no. 2 (2007): 154, 148.

everything that Lene in her straightforward manner is not. It is not just that Botho contrasts Lene's noble simplicity, to borrow a classicizing phrase, with the mannerisms of fashionable conversation. He puts it in much starker terms than that: the choice between Lene and Käthe is, at its most fundamental level, a choice between truth and falsehood, *Wahrheit* and *alles Unwahre*. Whereas Lene says what is true in clear and credible ways, Käthe is indifferent to whether her statements are accurate.

As if to give voice to the affectations he disdains, Botho follows his first list with another of modish loan-words from the French: *chic, tournure, savoir-faire*. The middle term merits further scrutiny because the French *tournure* has multiple related meanings, all deriving from the Latin root for "turn" or "turned." Thus, in its orthographically German form, "Tournüre" refers to a curved French bustle that was fashionable in the late nineteenth century. But in French, *tournure*, with its basis in "turning," also denotes a turn of phrase, as in the German equivalent *Redewendung*, or *Redensart*. And if *Redensart* is an acceptable German translation for *tournure* (as in *tournure de phrase*), we have arrived at the very phrases—empty turns of phrase—that contaminate much of contemporary speech but from which Lene remains immune. Reading this subtle reference to figures of speech in Botho's statement is, I believe, not just a bit of hermeneutic exuberance. The point is that these fashionable trends—whether sartorial or rhetorical—are related. Both the bustle and the turn of phrase are empty forms that give shape and contour, but without any actual substance. Both exploit a discrepancy between the outward phenomenon and the inward essence by creating the illusion of depth. And it is precisely this illusion that Botho means to deride with his list of French words: these are the sort of expressions that world-wise people employ to make their speech seem more intelligent and substantial than it actually is. They are, like the bustle, contrived and artificial, and ultimately hollow.[11]

One gets a sense of just how hollow the prevailing forms of speech are in an earlier scene when Botho characterizes high-society socializing for Lene, Frau Nimptsch, and the Dörrs. He gives an impromptu lesson on how to make polite conversation, assuring them, "eigentlich ist es ganz gleich, wovon man spricht. […] Über jedes kann man ja was sagen und ob's einem gefällt oder nicht. Und 'ja' ist gerade so viel wie 'nein'" (10:28, it makes no difference what you talk about. […] You can

---

[11] See, for example, the 1923 edition of the *Handwörterbuch der Sexualwissenschaft*, which describes the bustle or *Tournüre* as a "pillow or air bag in the form of an artificial 'cul.'" The bustle's salient features are that it is hollow and artificial. *Handwörterbuch der Sexualwissenschaft*, ed. Max Marcuse (Berlin: de Gruyter, 2001), 54.

say something about anything, and whether you like it or not. And a "yes" is as good as a "no," 28). Botho's point is that such conversation is utterly inconsequential: it does not matter what topic one discusses, nor does it matter what one says about any given topic. And contrary to the biblical exhortation to let one's "yes" mean "yes" and one's "no" mean "no" without the guarantee of any oath, here the distinction between incompatible opposites no longer carries any meaning.[12] One is free to speak haphazardly when there is no expectation that one's language be consistent, credible, or accurate.

This scene has become an important piece of evidence for the erosion—or even absence—of meaning in Fontane's portrayal of language and dialogue. Berman puts it in stark terms when he argues that "Fontane's conversations display the futility of speech," and he goes on to observe of this scene in particular that "conversation is ultimately about nothing and serves only to obscure the meaninglessness of perfunctory social encounters."[13] Botho's characterization of small talk makes such an assessment difficult to dispute. If it does not matter what one says, if "yes" is just as good as "no," then speech has become, in a sense, futile and meaningless. But it is important to ask whether this futility applies to Fontane's conversations in general, that is, whether Fontane's novels suggest that conversation *as such* is futile and meaningless.

Scholars fall on the totalizing side of this question when they see Botho's enactment as symptomatic of a widespread "breakdown of meaning and communication" and a "meaninglessness in which opposites collapse into one another."[14] To put it another way: on this view, the emptiness of Botho's language in this moment does not mark it as significantly different from normal speech. Rather, it marks speech in general as meaningless and futile and reveals "the fallibility of the established network of signifiers."[15] Such a conclusion stands to reason when it derives from a broader argument about language without meaning reflecting a modern world without discernible meaning. If rapid social change and modernization are the hammer that broke communication, then every superficial conversation comes to look like evidence of that destruction.

---

[12] See Matthew 5:37. Although this group of verses speaks primarily against swearing an oath, one also hears an insistence on fidelity to one's word and a clear demarcation between "yes" and "no," a distinction that no longer exists in Botho's circle.
[13] Berman, *Rise of the Modern German Novel*, 148–9.
[14] Holt, "History as Trauma," 105.
[15] Marion Doebeling, "Breaking the Mimetic Chain—Pattern of Cultural Unground," in *New Approaches to Theodor Fontane: Cultural Codes in Flux*, ed. Marion Doebeling (Columbia, SC: Camden House, 2000), xii.

In this same scene, however, the way Lene and her neighbors react to Botho's performance indicates that they view his model conversation as anything but typical. Frau Dörr leads the way with a series of incredulous interjections: "Und so sprecht ihr!" (So that's how you talk!), "Herr Baron, das geht doch nicht" (But you can't, Herr Baron), and then twice in a row, "Ist es möglich?" (10:27–8, Well I never, 27–8). To Frau Dörr, Botho's demonstration of sophisticated but inconsequential small talk is unfathomable. She doubts that it would even be possible to speak in the way Botho suggests is perfectly normal. Of course, a large part of this scene serves to reinforce the portrait of class differences between Botho and Lene. Her working-class world is so far removed from his that her neighbors have no sense of, and indeed can hardly believe, how the nobility interact with each other. So some of this interaction, to be sure, is intended to establish the disparities that would need to be overcome, in the manner of Eliza Doolittle's training in Shaw's *Pygmalion*, if Lene were ever to become a suitable partner for Botho.

What I find interesting about these reactions, however, is how they flip the critical reception of the novel's empty talk on its head. Often enough, Käthe's idle chatter is seen as demonstrating the reality of communicative futility, whereas Lene functions like a mirage of genuine speech within a desert of meaninglessness. But for the characters in Frau Nimptsch's home, it is exactly the opposite; it is Botho and the chatter of the upper classes that seem impossible and unbelievable. The people around Lene doubt the viability of Botho's small talk as a means of social communication. Within the fictional world of Fontane's novel, empty small talk strikes them as completely foreign and fanciful.

One should thus be careful not to arrive at overly broad conclusions about Fontane's portrayal of language based on Botho's demonstration. What one sees here is not the breakdown or futility of language as such; the others' disbelief shows clearly that empty, ironic banter is not a given, nor is it prevalent throughout the various layers of German society. One finds instead the emptiness of a particular kind of speech, one that is most prized and employed among a particular class of people. Gabriele Brandstetter and Gerhard Neumann write, for instance, that the speech depicted in Fontane's novels appears "no longer as a pure phonographic duplication of speech acts [Redeakten] in a naturalistic sense, but rather as the simulation and critical observation of those 'differentiating' speech-events [Sprech-Ereignisse] of a specific social class and social age."[16] This distinction (all speech versus the sophisticated

---

[16] Gabrielle Brandstetter and Gerhard Neumann, "'Le laid c'est le beau': Liebesdiskurs und Geschlechterrolle in Fontanes Roman *Schach von Wuthenow*," *Deutsche Vierteljahrsschrift* 72, no. 2 (1998): 247.

and fashionable speech of the upper class) matters because where one falls on this question influences how one understands the relationship between history and language use in Fontane's work. The "all speech is futile" view accords with an interpretation of cause and effect, in which the cause is the erosion of meaning in the modern world, and the effect is a breakdown of meaning within interpersonal communication. Lene, then, represents a prior, prelapsarian stage of communication, one whose possibility is nullified by the disorienting effects of modernization.

But if one understands Fontane here not to be evoking a general language crisis but rather to be caricaturing the interactions of a narrow class, that understanding upends the overarching view of historical change and the degradation of language. It is important to keep in mind that the kind of speech Botho presents is one that is cultivated and affected. It is not the "natural" state of language in nineteenth-century Berlin; it is both artificial and culturally contingent. In short, the people with whom Botho socializes choose to talk this way. Lene addresses the element of volition in this mode of speech, saying, "wenn es alles so redensartlich ist, da wundert es mich, dass ihr solche Gesellschaften mitmacht" (10:28, I'm surprised you go to entertainments like that if it's all just empty talk, 28). With the word "redensartlich," Lene draws the central contrast with her own nature and lack of empty phrases. In doing so, she implies a difficult question: why play along? The import is that one could just as easily choose not to attend social events at which one is expected to perform in this way and erode the indexical bond between language and meaning. There can be no real crisis of communication if the solution is as simple as choosing not to participate in it.

Moreover, the characters in Botho's social circle do not simply choose to talk this way; they strive to affect an ironic and frivolous tone. Käthe exemplifies this sort of speaking in the novel precisely because she is so good at it. Everyone finds her charming, "weil sie die Kunst des gefälligen Nichtssagens mit einer wahren Meisterschaft übte" (10:134, as she was a truly consummate practitioner of the art of aimless but winsome chatter, 123). And when the narrative reports Botho's embarrassment, it describes "das enorme Sprechtalent seiner Frau" (10:136, his wife's tremendous facility of speech, 125). Lest one think that meaningless speech represents some kind of failure or breakdown, the narrative repeatedly presents it as an art, a skill, and a talent—something that one must cultivate and refine. It is harder than it looks to talk a lot and still say nothing, but it is a skill that Käthe has mastered. Rather than depict Käthe as a particularly dire case of communicative crisis, the narrative casts her as the most sophisticated and talented practitioner of a certain kind of empty socializing. And it is only when the narrative departs from the perspective of Käthe's social circle and juxtaposes her speech with an alternative model that it all comes to seem more pernicious than amusing.

Käthe's role in the novel is to reflect the upper-class penchant for engaging in ironic, frivolous banter. She functions as a synecdoche for the communicative decadence of a particular stratum of Berlin society. Botho makes this observation when he reads Käthe's letters and then comments (again) on her gift of gab: "Welch' Talent für die Plauderei! [...] Aber es fehlt etwas. Es ist alles so angeflogen, so bloßes Gesellschaftsecho" (10:147, What a flair she has for gossip! [...] But there's something missing. It's all so glib, just an echo of society talk, 136). Käthe's glib way of talking merely echoes that of high society, so that whatever is missing from Käthe's speech is missing in general from the prevalent forms of unreliable, unserious communication in the upper class. It is precisely this lack or absence in Käthe's speech and in society talk that marks the difference between communication and chatter, and it is this same lack that Frau Dörr finds so astonishing.

Fontane on Language and History

It is important for my reading to see empty talk as a choice, a preference, and a desirable skill. It would be unsettling to see in Fontane's work the diagnosis that people try to say what they mean, but that the disorienting shifts of a changing world have broken communication and made meaning difficult to ascertain. But it is even more unsettling that people *choose* to speak unreliably and ineffectually, that they would deliberately turn away from the act of meaningful communication. Such a diagnosis means, in effect, that the erosion of meaning comes about not through some exogenous, historical factor but rather through an endogenous force. It suggests that the root cause is internal to society itself. In other words, it was not the hammer of historical change that destroyed communication. Instead, *Irrungen, Wirrungen* presents social communication as having been hollowed out from within.

The various readings of *Irrungen, Wirrungen* agree, then, that the novel attends to themes of speech and communication, and that it frequently presents that communication as troubled and problematic. Departing from that basis of consensus, the crux of the disagreement lies in ascertaining what exactly the novel means to say about the issue of empty talk in nineteenth-century Berlin. Why do people speak the way they do? Why do differences in speech patterns exist among various social classes, and how does one account for regional variations? How do such discourse communities come about?[17] What factors shape

---

[17] Foucault discusses closed, regulated communities of discourse in "The Discourse on Language," included as an appendix in *The Archaeology of Knowledge and the Discourse on Language*, trans. A. M. Sheridan Smith (New York: Pantheon, 1972).

the way people interact with each other? The novel pushes its readers to weigh broad questions such as these regarding language change, identity, and communication. But they are also questions to which Fontane gives considerable thought, not only in his fictional works but also in a popular press piece on cultural history.

Irrungen, Wirrungen situates its characters in 1870s Berlin, and it does so emphatically, with numerous details meant to specify the novel's particular time and place. John Lyon, who writes that "Fontane repeatedly asserts the significance of places," notes of this novel in particular that "Fontane gives the reader a definite location, landmarks that would have been current in the 1880s."[18] Indeed, when the novel appeared in print in 1888, its setting was obviously Berlin, and its era was clearly the 1870s. Moreover, many of its characters are unmistakably marked as upper-class Berliner. For Fontane, the Berliner, or collectively, *das Berlinertum*, represent a distinctive cultural group with its own attitude, mentality, tone, and speech patterns. And in 1889, just one year after the publication of *Irrungen, Wirrungen*, he wrote for the *Deutsches Wochenblatt* a semi-speculative piece of cultural history on "Die Märker und die Berliner und wie sich das Berlinertum entwickelte."

Fontane's essay begins with the point that Berlin was populated by people from throughout the wider region of the Mark of Brandenburg, and yet today (in 1889) one perceives a Berliner spirit and tone that it is quite different from the general regional culture. What is it, Fontane asks, that produced the spirit and tone specific to Berlin (*NA* 19:744)? He establishes a large historical frame within which to pursue that question, from the late seventeenth century into the nineteenth century. It is interesting to note that when Fontane goes searching for the proximate causes of contemporary Berliner culture, he rules out some of the most obvious historical factors. Addressing a topic with which he was by background personally well acquainted, Fontane asserts, for example, that the influx of French Huguenots to Brandenburg-Prussia in the late seventeenth century did not exert a decisive influence on the development of what belongs distinctively to Berlin. These Puritans, he writes, were just too "steif" (rigid) and "ernsthaft" (earnest) to contribute to the urbane and quick-witted spirit that took root in Berlin and culminated in a trenchantly ironic tone (*NA* 19:744). Eighteenth-century upheavals in France get similar treatment: "Noch geringer war der Einfluß der Französischen Revolution" (*NA* 19:751, The influence of the French Revolution was even smaller).

---

[18] Lyon, *Out of Place*, 151 and 149. See further Bade, who similarly notes the novel's "topographical precision" in its depiction of Berlin. James Bade, *Fontane's Landscapes* (Würzburg: Königshausen & Neumann, 2009), 60.

Now, Fontane in this piece never addresses his contemporary era of the 1870s and 1880s; he sees the primary components of Berliner culture already in place by the 1830s. So he is silent here on topics such as the Industrial Revolution or ongoing capitalist modernization. But my point is that, if one is trying to discern how historical events may or may not shape language use in *Irrungen, Wirrungen*, one would do well to consider this essay as a template for Fontane's notion of language use as an historically and culturally contingent phenomenon. When Fontane constructs his version of how *das Berlinertum* developed as a distinctive speech community, he tells a story not of sudden historical upheaval and communicative crisis but rather one of gradual and internal cultural influence.

Perhaps idiosyncratically, he locates the first stirrings of a Berliner spirit and tone in King Friedrich Wilhelm I's *Tabakskollegium*, a regular social gathering in which a group of men close to the king would gather to smoke, drink, and talk. Fontane lists a number of prominent and influential participants in these gatherings, and then writes, "Der Ton, in dem alle diese sprachen, drang auch nach außen und übte da seine Macht" (*NA* 19:746, The tone in which they all spoke pressed outward and exerted its power there). There are at least two points to make here. First, in Fontane's history of the citizens and culture of Berlin, language use plays an outsized role. It would be difficult to overstate the importance of speech particularities to Fontane's understanding of cultural and historical development. Second, Fontane espouses here a top-down version of how language use develops. The impetus for a distinctive Berlin tone comes from the king and his private circle, and this group then exerts its influence gradually over the rest of society. In fact, Fontane asserts that in the first half of the eighteenth century, the king himself was more influential in this regard than the men assembled around him. On Fontane's view, new mannerisms and patterns of speech radiate outward from the monarchy and its privileged discourse community—a fact that helps explain the class differences Fontane observes in language use and perhaps also the classist speech differences between Käthe and Lene that he emphasizes in *Irrungen, Wirrungen*.

Although Fontane locates the origins of the Berlin tone in the eighteenth-century *Tabakskollegium*, that is not the end of the story. The true shift does not occur until the second half of the eighteenth century, late in the reign of Frederick the Great. At this point in Fontane's historical narrative, the nobility and the royal court, which had long represented common sense and practical jokes, acquire a more literary sensibility, so that "diese Kreise wurden jetzt Repräsentanten des Witzes, der Pointe, der Antithese" (*NA* 19:748, these circles now became representatives of wit, pointe, and antithesis). As the tone of an earlier regime gets refined through exposure to literature and philosophy (Voltaire's time in Sanssouci is mentioned), polite society shifts gradually from an era of good humor and common sense to one that prizes cleverness and witticism. And Fontane argues that by 1786, "mit Hilfe dieser auf das Pointierte gestellten Sanssouci-Sprache" (with the help of this trenchant Sanssouci-language), the *Berlinertum* was much closer to having the attributes that make it distinctive in the nineteenth century (*NA* 19:748).

Note the character of the particular tone that develops around Sanssouci in the late eighteenth century. It displays a penchant for quips, witticisms, *bons mots*, irony, clever replies, antitheses, and punch lines. Fontane writes of this age of refined wit, "alles durfte gewagt werden, wenn das 'Reparti' witzig war" (*NA* 19:748, anything could be dared, as long as the repartee was witty). With the prioritization of the clever, amusing retort, it is not hard to see a familial resemblance between the language of Sanssouci and the language of Käthe and her social circle. Käthe is entertaining, charming, and amusing, but the polished surface of her speech comes to seem thin and brittle. It is a language that delights in the play of conversation and in formal dexterity, but without depth or earnestness. Its playful or indeed ironic insincerity cannot be taken seriously. The first and most prominent parallel between Fontane's essay on the development of the *Berlinertum* and *Irrungen, Wirrungen*, then, is that Käthe's speech comes to resemble an exacerbated form of the distinctive Berliner tone that developed and disseminated around the turn of the nineteenth century. The essay helps to situate Käthe's speech patterns historically, not as the unfortunate side effect of rapid modernization, but rather as the latest refinement in a long series of cultural developments that owe their genesis to the confluence of the nobility, the military, and the world of letters.

The second parallel between the essay and the novel is the attention both pay to how different social classes use language differently. Fontane's notion of how language use changes over time believes that new developments occur first within an elite and privileged circle and then slowly make their way through the rest of society. Of the pointed, witty language employed at Sanssouci, for example, Fontane notes that it was "nur die Sprache bestimmter Gesellschaftsschichten, deren Verbindung mit dem eigentlichen Volk gering war" (*NA* 19:749, only the language of certain social classes whose connection to the actual populace was slight). Thus, the second question that Fontane explores in the essay is how new speech patterns spread throughout a society stratified by class. His answer, primarily, is that the military drives the dissemination of language innovations. It brings people together from disparate areas and walks of life and then disperses them back into the civilian population, where they introduce to the middle and working classes the speech mannerisms they acquired while serving in the military. He sees this happen, for instance, as a result of the general mobilization for the German Campaign against Napoleon in 1813, after which one could identify "Schlag- und Witzworte [...], die vom Thron bis zur Hütte gingen" (*NA* 19:752, catchphrases and humorous expressions that ran all the way from the throne to the cottage).

Fontane makes his case with reference to specific historical events, but I want to emphasize that he does not cast events such as the campaign against Napoleon as the cause of linguistic change—he does not, that is, characterize the conflict as a violent impediment to effective communication. Instead, he casts the military campaign as a catalyst for disseminating innovations that appear to have arisen from a process of cultural evolution among the nobility. Fontane's cultural archeology of the Berliner idiom stands out as more distinctive when contrasted with other contemporaneous accounts. Hans Meyer's *Der richtige Berliner in Wörtern und Redensarten*, which first appeared in 1878, exemplifies a different understanding of how language change comes about. In the foreword, for example, he writes:

> Die rasche Entwicklung des großstädtischen Lebens vom Omnibus bis zur elektrischen Bahn, vom Rad bis zum Automobil, von der Postkarte bis zum Telefon, von der Hökerin bis zur Markthalle, vom Weihnachtsmarkt bis zum Warenhause und was sonst als Fortschritt belobt oder beklagt wird, alles hat der Volkssprache neue Blüten entlockt.[19]

> (The rapid development of metropolitan life, from the omnibus to the electric tram, from the wheel to the automobile, from the postcard to the telephone, from the Christmas market to the department store, and whatever else is lamented or extolled as progress, all that has elicited new blossoms in popular speech.)

While Fontane emphasizes long-term cultural evolution, Meyer attends to rapid changes in technology and transportation. To readers today, Meyer's account probably looks more modern; he tells a familiar story about how industrial and technological developments exert influence on how people live and speak. Fontane, in contrast, focuses on the gradual movement of cultural influence from the nobility to the lower classes.

Here we arrive at a difference between Fontane's essay and the fictional world of *Irrungen, Wirrungen*. In the historical account, the ironic

---

[19] Hans Meyer, *Der richtige Berliner in Wörtern und Redensarten* (Berlin: Hermann, 1904), iii.

tone particular to Berlin has made its way through all levels of society by the mid-nineteenth century. By that point, there are phrases and expressions that one would hear at court just as easily as at the market. But *Irrungen, Wirrungen* paints a different picture of Berlin society. In the novel, people in the lower classes are astonished by the frivolity and flippancy of upper-class social interactions. And it is not simply a matter of different social strata using different vocabularies. Although Botho expresses his exasperation with fashionable loan words from the French, the salient difference pertains to tone and sincerity. It is clear that, in terms of language use, the different classes live in different worlds. The turn away from sincerity and genuine communication that Käthe and others in her circle exhibit has not made its way to the modest homes of Frau Nimptsch and the Dörrs. Indeed, they find it hard to believe that one would actually speak the way Botho performs for them.

How should one understand this discrepancy between the novel and the essay, especially when the essay appeared right on the novel's heels? One possible answer is that, while the journalistic piece traces linguistic and cultural developments that shaped Berlin up to around 1850—up to the point, that is, of a dominant ironic tone—it does not deal with contemporary Berliner culture. As an historical narrative, it stops short of the current era and does not speculate on what has been evolving over the last few decades. And this point, the 1870s at least, is where *Irrungen, Wirrungen* picks up the thread. It imagines more recent developments in Berliner language and culture and shows how these new speech patterns are still clustered among the upper classes of the nobility and the officer corps. By drawing contrasts between the utterly unserious tone of the upper classes and the unadorned directness of the lower classes, the novel demonstrates that the latest developments in ironic, empty tone have not yet migrated from the salon and the soirée to the outlying areas and the lower classes.

Moreover, when one reads the novel alongside Fontane's account of the Berliner idiom, it casts Käthe's speech mannerisms in a new light. Her way of speaking appears, from this angle, to be a further heightening or exacerbation of the developments that took root at Sanssouci in the late eighteenth century. In Käthe's speech, the literary refinement of that earlier era, with its taste for the clever quip and the witty reply, gets taken to an extreme. The atmosphere around Sanssouci may have prized witty repartee, but Käthe presents an aggravated form of this tone. For her, wit and amusement are not merely what make the taboo permissible. They are the sole criteria for social interaction and the only way she engages with the world. Botho comes to this realization toward the end of their honeymoon, and after a few years he concludes that Käthe is incapable of carrying on an earnest conversation.

The problem with Käthe's speech is that she never goes beyond the level of quips and banter. Her extreme version of the Sanssouci tone that Fontane identifies is no longer a way of speaking that one could put on and take off, like a ball gown for special occasions. For her, it has become the only way of speaking and in fact a way of being. To Botho, it is "als ob sie der Fähigkeit entbehrt hätte, zwischen witchtigen und unwichtigen Dingen zu unterscheiden" (10:124, as if she lacked the ability to distinguish between important and unimportant things, 113). Since Käthe never takes anything seriously, she has lost the capacity to discern what would constitute an object of serious conversation. Confirming Frankfurt's warning about the attenuation of discernment, her refusal to differentiate in language between the *scherzhaft* and the *ernsthaft* has mutated into an inability to apprehend that difference in life. "Und was das Schlimmste war, sie betrachtete das alles als einen Vorzug [...] und dachte nicht daran, es abzulegen" (10:124, And the worst of it was that she regarded all this as a virtue [...] and had no notion of giving it up, 114). What Botho sees as a character flaw, and what some readers have diagnosed as a symptom of communicative crisis, Käthe treats as a virtue. Because she views her tone as a talent or asset, it is impossible to persuade her to change. There is a sense of decadence in this unstinting proclivity for unserious talk—the feeling that the evolution of Berliner speech has tipped toward its own excess and degradation. It is a refinement that results in the ability to rid one's speech of meaningful content, to talk at length while saying nothing of consequence.

Fontane's essay on the evolution of *das Berlinertum* thus provides a crucial piece of evidence for his understanding of the relationship between language use and historical change. When Fontane takes an historicizing view of language development, he does not reiterate the familiar narrative of rapid change and cultural disorientation, all of which is then mirrored in the breakdown of social communication. Instead, he produces a long-term account of how cultural institutions—the royal court, for example, or the military—generate and disseminate new speech patterns that eventually shape the character of an entire society. This view of how language use evolves provides important context for understanding the particularities of Käthe's speech. On Fontane's view, there are indeed historical factors that contribute to the ironic, insincere speech Käthe represents, but these factors stretch back much further than the technological and industrial innovations of the mid-nineteenth century. Furthermore, the factors that Fontane foregrounds are cultural developments within society itself. He identifies key institutions and junctures at which attitudes toward thinking, speaking, and self-presentation changed. Fontane's view of Berlin's dominant idiom, then, could be more accurately described as a gradual process of evolution, often in response to environmental factors, but not one in which historical shifts suddenly undermine the foundations of meaning and communication.

Avowal in an Ironic Mode

In *Irrungen, Wirrungen*, the tension between serious and unserious speech comes to a head when Käthe returns home from her curative trip to Schlangenbad. The days leading up to Käthe's arrival constitute an important turning point in the novel. Over the course of these few days, Botho pays his final respects at Frau Nimptsch's grave, tries to free himself from Lene's emotional grip by burning her letters, and braces himself for Käthe's return. As Botho thus takes his final leave from Lene and turns his attention to making his peace with Käthe, the novel symbolically reiterates the painful choice that Botho made earlier in the novel, for Käthe and against Lene. In fact, the narrative insists on this latent repetition after the fact. Botho, passing the time and avoiding company before Käthe returns, goes out riding and just happens to take the same route he did before when he resigned himself to ending his relationship with Lene. Even though three years have passed since he left Lene and proposed to Käthe, his wife's return is nonetheless fraught with feelings of ambivalence shading into regret.

This is the frame of mind in which Botho receives his wife, and the narrative of her return repeatedly stages a tension between the two modes of speaking—serious and unserious, authentic and ironic—embodied by Lene and Käthe. When Käthe first arrives back at the apartment, for instance, the household greets her with a welcome sign on which one "l" of "Willkommen" is unfortunately missing. The misspelling is important for two reasons. First, it reinforces the same class differences in education and language use that were evident between Lene and Botho, as well as between Lene and Käthe. Neither the maid nor the cook notices the error; it's up to Käthe to point it out. Second, the misspelling resonates all the more strongly with Lene's style of speech because Botho has, just a few days before, gone back through Lene's letters, noticed her numerous spelling errors, and been charmed once again—before consigning it all to the fire. Botho feels that her imperfect writing is "besser als alle Orthographie der Welt" (10:166, better than the most perfect spelling in the world, 153), and this sentiment—this pining for a language that is unpolished but all the more attractive for its imperfections—casts its shadow over the misspelled welcome sign.

Käthe's reaction to this greeting is furthermore telling, as she laughs it off in her typical lighthearted, ironic way, saying, "Willkommen! Aber blos mit einem 'l,' will sagen nur halb. Ei, ei. Und 'L' ist noch dazu der Liebesbuchstabe. Nun, du sollst auch Alles nur halb haben" (10:179, "Welcome"! But with only one *l*, so only half meant. Oh dear! And *l* is for "love" too. Oh, well. I suppose I'm only to have half of everything, 165). Her response in this instance exemplifies the kind of quipping, witty reply that became fashionable among the Sanssouci salon crowd in the late eighteenth century. The cleverness of her response lies in her decision to interpret the missing "l" not as a simple oversight but rather as a meaningful slip of the pen, almost as a Freudian slip *avant la lettre*.[20] In her half-joking repartee, the missing "l" unintentionally reveals something about the sentiment that gave rise to the greeting. *Willkommen* with only one "l" indicates to her that the welcome she receives is only half-meant and half-felt. What is worse, the letter "l" stands for love, which is perhaps lacking in the reception she receives from her husband.

The scene elicits a certain awkwardness. Although Käthe does not mean in earnest what she says—she never says anything in earnest—she nevertheless expresses in jest an ambivalence that her husband has struggled to conceal. He has been trying to suppress his dread and alienation while anticipating her arrival, so that the welcome she receives really is only half-meant and half-felt. That ambivalence runs deeper, though, because the spelling error echoes the language of Lene's letters, the very language that Botho had to destroy in an effort to disenthrall himself from her bond. In fact, it is not lost on the reader that Käthe's playful reading of the misspelled word might itself be a misreading, or at least an incomplete reading. The missing "l," which Käthe interprets as a signifier for "love," could just as easily stand for "Lene." In this sense, what is missing from Käthe's welcome is the love that Botho still feels for Lene. Much of the narrative leading up to this scene has dealt with Botho's internal conflict, with the juxtaposition in his heart of Lene and Käthe. It is thus telling that the crucial error in his welcoming of his wife occurs at the meeting point in *Willkommen* of "l" and "k."

It is also worth noting that this section of the novel revives the issue of Botho's will, his *Wille* in German, as he struggles to master his own desires and impulses. For instance, when he burns the last traces of Lene's language, he asks himself, "Ob ich nun frei bin? ... Will ich's denn? Ich will es *nicht*. Alles Asche. Und *doch* gebunden" (10:167, Am I free now? ... Do I even want to be? No, I do *not*. Nothing but ashes. And yet still I am bound, 154). Much of Botho's confusion stems from this internal conflict over what he wants, *was er will*, and that question of desire resurfaces in the word *Willkommen*. To say that someone is

---

[20] On the notion of parapraxis, see Freud's "1901 *The Psychopathology of Everyday Life*," in *The Standard Edition of the Complete Psychological Works of Sigmund Freud*, ed. and trans. James Strachey (London: Hogarth Press, 1953), vol. 6.

welcome, in its most concrete sense, means that one person's arrival accords with another person's will or desire. But this accordance is precisely what is lacking in Käthe's reception. Botho does not really want her to come home, at least not right way. By destroying Lene's letters and resigning himself to life with Käthe, he goes against his own will, and this distortion of will, this truncation of desire, can be felt in the truncated formulation of welcome that greets Käthe upon her return.

The tension between Lene's and Käthe's modes of communication verges on open conflict the next day, and at this point, their opposed manners of speaking become more closely aligned with the conflict between irony and avowal. The impetus for conflict occurs when Käthe goes to the fireplace and notices, incongruously because it is mid-summer, a pile of ashes in the hearth. Botho happens to come in at this moment and is caught off guard by his wife's discovery, "als Käthe mit dem Zeigefinger auf die Asche wies und in ihrem scherzhaftesten Tone sagte: 'Was bedeutet das, Botho? Sieh, da hab ich Dich mal wieder ertappt. Nun bekenne. Liebesbriefe? Ja oder nein?'" (10:187, when Käthe pointed to the ashes and asked in her most jocular tone, "What's all this, Botho? See, I've caught you out again. Now confess! Love letters, yes or no?," 172). Rather than being split over two characters, the tension between opposed ways of speaking belongs in this instance entirely to Käthe.

When Käthe points to the ashes and demands an explanation, she speaks in the register of what Foucault would call an "inquisitorial procedure." Foucault seeks to show in his lectures how avowal took on a fundamental role within judicial practices. He says, for example, of Europe in the late eighteenth century that "the establishment of the truth through the avowal of the culprit became once again an important piece of the procedure."[21] In Fontane's scene, Botho occupies the position of the culprit, a position underscored by Käthe's inquisitorial rhetoric. He has been caught, and confronting him with the evidence of his crime, Käthe now demands his "avowal" or *Bekenntnis*. The relationship to recognition (to *erkennen*) that one hears in the German verb *bekennen* is an important component of avowal, for avowal demands of the culprit not only that he recognize his own crime and his own guilt. In avowing, the culprit must also recognize the authority of the law to which he is subject. Foucault notes, "In the modern system, avowal consists not simply of recognizing one's crime, [but] at the same time recognizing, through the recognition of one's crime, the validity of the punishment that one will suffer."[22] All of these demands are implied in

---

[21] Foucault, *Wrong-Doing, Truth-Telling*, 203–4.
[22] Foucault, *Wrong-Doing, Truth-Telling*, 207.

Käthe's order to confess. Botho must recognize not only his transgression but also the validity of the law of marital monogamy, and he must furthermore subject himself to the authority of that code.

This entire exchange could be a moment of high stakes and high drama—an anagnorisis, in which Botho's concealed conflict finally comes to light—except that Käthe presents it in the most playful, ironic way. This is the point of the novel at which the poles of irony and avowal collide, the point at which avowal is demanded in the form of irony. Käthe has already been accused of not being able to differentiate between what is important and what is not. She reinforces that impression here by taking a deeply serious personal conversation and conducting it in the least serious way. Although Botho at first fears that his secret has been discovered, it is the ironic overlay in her questioning that allays his concern.

Botho at first tries to evade the interrogation, but she insists on his avowal. After she asks whether these are the ashes of love letters, the dialogue continues:

> Du wirst doch glauben, was du willst.
> Ja oder nein?
> Gut denn; ja.
> *Das* war Recht. Nun kann ich mich beruhigen. Liebesbriefe, zu komisch. (10:187)

> You must think what you please.
> Yes or no?
> Very well, yes.
> *That* was right of you. Now I can be easy. Love letters, how comical! (172)

The ironic tone that initiates the inquisition is matched by its unserious conclusion. In response to Käthe's accusation, Botho has just provided the powerful proof of avowal, the "veridiction of the crime by its perpetrator."[23] He has confessed, in essence, that yes, what she sees in the fireplace are indeed the ashes of love letters that he was burning, presumably because he did not want her to know of their existence.

This revelation could constitute a crucial turn of events in the novel. Should there be any objection that the discovery of old love letters is not that serious, one need recall only the devastation that ensues from Innstetten's discovery of old love letters in *Effi Briest*. In that novel, his discovery sets in motion a series of events that lead to divorce, death,

---

[23] Foucault, *Wrong-Doing, Truth-Telling*, 210.

and despair. It is entirely conceivable that the outcome in *Irrungen, Wirrungen* could be the same. And while the letters in *Effi Briest* provide incontrovertible evidence of an extramarital affair, it is surprising that Käthe never bothers to pursue the inquiry further, never asks whether the letters are old or new, never seems to worry about the prospect of infidelity, even though the letters surface approximately three years into their marriage. Botho's avowal, which one thinks would unleash a barrage of further questions and recriminations, suffices to end the conversation.

The most plausible explanation for Käthe's reaction is that she takes Botho's confession as ironically and playfully as her questioning.[24] Käthe struggles to differentiate between what is serious and what is not. To present important matters as if they were trivial, or to present something serious in a flippant way—these are canonical forms of ironic expression. From the other side, the consequences of irony include ambivalence and uncertainty. Irony makes it hard to tell whether someone is speaking in earnest or in jest. Käthe, in this moment, exemplifies both the expression and consequence of irony. First, she delivers a serious accusation in a lighthearted, ironic way. Second, the breakdown in communication stems from her misreading of Botho's speech, from her inability to discern whether he is speaking earnestly or ironically. When Botho eventually gives in and answers her question, he responds as Lene might. His single-word avowal is direct and honest, without any more evasions. But Käthe is unaware of Lene's existence and unaware of her way of speaking. Her error is to assume that Botho speaks along with her in the same tone, and that the jocular, teasing play of her questioning also characterizes his response. In short, her ironic demeanor blinds her to the fundamental truth of his response.

One sees through this exchange that Botho and Käthe really cannot have an earnest conversation. Everything that is serious and meaningful to him is, for her, just another occasion for merriment and amusement. The single most important conversation of their married life to date—the moment in which Botho stands prepared to confess his deepest internal conflict—is immediately dismissed as a joke. It recalls the Frith painting that Fontane saw in London in 1852: here Botho sits, like Pope, in anguish over the prospect of a lost love, while his interlocutor

---

[24] There are other ways to understand Käthe's reaction. While this reading focuses on rhetorical artifice, another approach could highlight how gender roles and expectations constrain women's choices. At a time when divorce was not socially acceptable, it is in Käthe's interest not to pursue the conversation, to treat it all as a joke. This perspective foregrounds how gender and social context might reinforce the tendency to react flippantly.

cannot help but find it comical. The incongruity between Botho's avowal and Käthe's reaction only grows as she flits to the next topic without a moment's reflection. No sooner has Botho confessed to burning love letters than Käthe is already on to her next amusing anecdote about a Russian woman who wasn't actually Russian at all. The anecdote's content only reinforces the ironic discrepancies of the preceding exchange: the Russian who was not really a Russian reflects the conversation that was not really a conversation and the avowal that was not really taken as an avowal. Käthe dismisses Botho's serious story about an absent woman in favor of her own superficial society talk about an absent woman.

At the end of this scene comes a moment in which Käthe pauses and notices Botho's reticence. "Aber Botho, Du sprichst ja nicht, Du hörst ja gar nicht" (But Botho, why don't you say something? You're not even listening), to which he replies, "Doch, doch, Käthe" (10:188, I am, Käthe, I am, 173). Botho insists that he does indeed hear, and what he hears is incessant idle chatter. He hears all too clearly the discrepancy between the sort of language for which he pines and the superficial speech that surrounds him in his marriage. The final twist is the misattribution of not hearing one's spouse. While Käthe accuses Botho of not hearing what she says, it is actually Käthe who fails to hear Botho's avowal and confession. Enthralled by her own ironic banter, she is oblivious to what is earnest, honest, and serious.

Speech Mannerisms and Side-Taking

Irrungen, Wirrungen contrasts two different modes of speech through Lene and Käthe, and I believe it is clear, through scenes such as those discussed above, that the novel presents Käthe's speech as inferior and insidious. Though her tone can be charming and seductive, it is ultimately harmful in its cumulative effect. Nonetheless, there remains in the secondary literature disagreement about the extent to which the novel favors one form of speech over another. Despite the praise that Botho heaps upon Lene's speech and the criticism he aims at Käthe's, the novel's events, some would argue, muddle the attempt to identify a clear hierarchy between these opposed ways of speaking. After all, Botho ultimately chooses Käthe over Lene, even if his choice is also an act of resignation, and by the novel's conclusion, Käthe is chastising Botho for not speaking more like she and her friends do.

Furthermore, as mentioned above, scholars have sometimes interpreted the opposition between Lene and Käthe as a false dichotomy, such that Lene represents a bygone, foreclosed alternative to Käthe's unserious speech. Berman goes so far as to suggest that the novel favors Käthe's lighthearted tone because it more closely resembles the "feuilleton style with its priority of entertainment" that Fontane adopted from the English press and then introduced in Germany.²⁵ Berman writes, "Despite the novel's apparent sympathy for Lene and its denigration of Käthe, Käthe is the one who in the end defends the communicative mode associated particularly with Fontane."²⁶ On this view, the novel appears to side with Lene and her straightforward speech, but the ostensible sympathy is misleading, because in the end, the novel champions the rise of an unserious, amusing tone that reflects aspects of Fontane's journalistic writing.

But focusing on the English feuilleton style associates Fontane and Käthe via a relatively narrow slice of Fontane's published work. And Franziska asserts in *Graf Petöfy* that even "das beste Feuilleton für eine Zeitung nicht ausreicht; es muß noch etwas Ernsthaftes hinzukommen" (7:133, the best feuilleton isn't enough for a newspaper; there also has to be something earnest too). What the feuilleton lacks is the earnestness and sincerity that Lene's speech exemplifies; by itself, language that is merely *scherzhaft* quickly becomes tiresome. Further arguing against the favoring of Käthe's speech are numerous documents in which Fontane contrasts two forms of language use and then speaks in favor of something that looks much more like Lene's simple, unadorned language or criticizes precisely the forced, artificial style of speech at which Käthe excels. Clarissa Blomqvist, for instance, has examined Fontane's theater reviews and his frequent reflections on theatrical language. She finds that he consistently praises authors who employ a simple, straightforward style of speech on the stage and disparages those who overburden their works with flowery language. Blomqvist writes that when Fontane considers the form of speech most effective in the theater, he "despises artificial, empty language" and "condemns 'the turn of phrase.'"²⁷ The contrived language and the empty phrases that Fontane criticizes in the theater are already familiar—these are the same empty phrases that characterize Käthe and her friends' speech and that Lene avoids.²⁸

In another theater review, this one of a play by Ernst von Wildenbruch, Fontane praises the work for employing a language without frills or affectations. He admires in particular the play's characters, "die [...] eine lapidare Simplizitätssprache sprechen, eine Sprache, die [...] in einem merkwürdigen Widerspruche zu dem schön und mitunter sogar konfus Redensartliche steht"²⁹ (who speak a lapidary language

---

[25] Berman, *Rise of the Modern German Novel*, 150.
[26] Berman, *Rise of the Modern German Novel*, 151.
[27] Blomqvist, "Realism on Stage," 339, quoting Fontane in the second passage.
[28] Mecklenburg outlines "the many forms of distorted knowing and speaking that Fontane includes under terms such as 'phrase' and 'lie.'" Mecklenburg, *Theodor Fontane*, 146.
[29] Blomqvist, "Realism on Stage," 338, again quoting Fontane.

of simplicity, a language that stands in a curious opposition to pretty and occasionally even muddled expressions). The passage outlines a central aesthetic opposition in Fontane's notion of theater and theatrical language, and it shows him clearly taking a side. On the one hand, the best character portraits allow figures to express themselves through an unadorned language, one that is concise, elegant, and meaningful at once. On the other hand, there is the muddled language of trite expressions and empty turns of phrase.

Readers will by now have recognized the key pejorative term "das Redensartliche" in the quoted passage, since the notion of *Redensarten*—and whether one needs empty phrases or not—plays such a large role in the opposition at the heart of *Irrungen, Wirrungen*. Lene, one will recall, is characterized by her "Unredensartlichkeit" (10:124, lack of empty talk, 114), which stands in sharp contrast to Käthe's style of speaking. The qualities that Botho admires in Lene are the very same qualities that Fontane admires in von Wildenbruch's characters. One thus finds in Fontane's theater reviews the same opposition between a simple, straightforward, serious manner of speech and a language of forced, frivolous phrases.[30] In the theater reviews, however, this opposition occurs within the purpose of aesthetic evaluation and judgment, and in this context, Fontane's preferences are much easier to discern. His reviews consistently plead for a turn away from stilted, overwrought language and consistently praise the unadorned simplicity of a more lapidary style.

The review of von Wildenbruch's *Die Quitzows* provides but one example of that tendency, but it is worth noting that this particular review appeared in 1888, the same year that saw the publication of *Irrungen, Wirrungen*. The temporal proximity of the novel and the review suggests that issues of language use occupied Fontane in various fashions in the late 1880s. It suggests furthermore that the novel uses its characters to dramatize the kind of rhetorical and aesthetic opposition that Fontane was observing at the same time in other areas of Berlin cultural production. In this sense, the theater reviews from this period reinforce in plainer language the opposition between Lene and Käthe and make clear that Fontane's aesthetic sensibility favors Lene's straightforward style over empty, ornamental language. If one wants to claim that Käthe embodies Fontane's journalistic feuilleton

---

[30] Blomqvist, too, identifies the parallel contrast in *Irrungen, Wirrungen*, though she does not devote much attention to the novel. She concludes her discussion of *Irrungen, Wirrungen* by saying that "the novelist's preference for simplicity and truthfulness in language as well as in character is obvious." Blomqvist, "Realism on Stage," 345.

style, one has to ignore the more obvious and explicit ways in which Käthe's speech overlaps with an artistic style to which Fontane was flatly opposed. The excesses of language and tone that make Botho cringe in his wife's company are the same excesses that make Fontane the reviewer cringe in the theater.

The distinction that Fontane draws in his novel as well as in his theater reviews calls to mind the terms of his earlier attempt to define the nature of realism in art. Writing in 1853, he says of realism, "er will das *Wahre*. Er schließt nichts aus als die Lüge, das Forcierte, das Nebelhafte, das Abgestorbene" (*NA* 21.1:13, it wants what is *true*. It excludes nothing but what is false, forced, nebulous, dead). With a word like "das Forcierte," one sees that Fontane's theater reviews, written decades later, still rely on the same terms that he uses to define realism, at least negatively. Even "das Nebelhafte" points forward to the muddled, cloudy language of stilted dramas. Most important, though, is the overriding concern with truth and falsehood, with the reliability of language and representation. This same concern resurfaces in *Irrungen, Wirrungen* and in the theater reviews. Given the overlap in terminology, perhaps what these writings share in common is a fundamental anxiety that the current fashion for banter, irony, and empty, artificial talk clashes with the language and aesthetics of realist representation. In the 1850s, Fontane was able to assert, "Was unsere Zeit nach allen Seiten hin charakterisiert, das ist ihr Realismus" (*NA* 21.1:7, Realism is what characterizes our time in all respects). Jump forward two or three decades, and the assertion is no longer so self-evidently true. One can perceive in *Irrungen, Wirrungen* the concern that the contemporary culture is no longer characterized by a desire for realism. Indeed, the latest developments in idiom and tone suggest a fetishizing fashion for everything that is antithetical to realism. What happens when truth no longer matters, when language no longer need be reliable, and when irony takes precedence over substance and sincerity? These are questions that drive Fontane's narratives, not only in *Irrungen, Wirrungen* but throughout his work.

It is thus not enough to recognize in *Irrungen, Wirrungen* the conflict between serious and unserious talk. To draw the proper lesson from the novel, the lesson, that is, that would allow one to pursue this thread through Fontane's other works, one must recognize two further points. These points are, first, that the novel presents Käthe's way of speaking as excessive and harmful, and, second, that it also presents her idiom as the result of a series of cultural developments, fashions, and choices— not merely as the unfortunate side effect of rapid modernization or historical upheaval. The distinction matters because if the shortcomings of communication truly reflect a broader crisis of meaning in a confusing world, then there is nothing that one could do to alter that state of affairs. There is no way out of the dilemma when "language merely reflects existing social conditions."[31] But Fontane does not mean merely to diagnose a turn of events or to present his characters as being churned by historical forces over which they have no control. Instead, he presents the departure from honest, straightforward communication as a deliberate choice.

It is important to see Käthe's style of speaking as something that she intentionally cultivates because such a view allows for a political element, an element of human agency. If speaking ironically, flippantly, and emptily is a choice, then one could choose to do otherwise. This aspect of will lies at the heart of Lene's comment early in the novel, when she says, "wenn es alles so redensartlich ist, da wundert es mich, dass ihr solche Gesellschaften mitmacht" (10:28, I'm surprised you go to entertainments like that if it's all just empty talk, 28). If a particular social group requires idle banter or stilted language, why belong to that group? It is a question that Fontane asks in various keys throughout his oeuvre. Why belong to the group of dramatists who write in affected and muddled language? Why belong to the writers who lean on forced, unnatural prose? Why be a lover who says the opposite of what he means, or an officer whose oath is not given in earnest? Why be a politician whose word is unreliable and therefore ineffectual? In all these guises, Fontane pursues not just the tension between two opposed modes of communication. He explores how the intentional misuse of language—how infidelity to one's word—leads to cynicism, decadence, and insidious harm.

---

[31] Orwell, *In Front of Your Nose*, 137.

Two The Broken Word: On the Rhetoric of Trust and Honor in *Schach von Wuthenow*

The 1883 novel *Schach von Wuthenow* provides another opportunity to explore the relationship between language use and historical change, as it presents further evidence for the insidious effects of disingenuous speech. In this novel, too, the way one speaks and the reliability of language constitute central concerns. Although the problem of empty language might not appear here as explicitly as it does in *Irrungen, Wirrungen*, the issue is no less pressing and its consequences are, if anything, more extreme. The curious case of Schach von Wuthenow revolves around a series of broken promises after Victoire von Carayon finds herself pregnant with Schach's child. When Victoire's mother confronts Schach with this news, he accepts all her stipulations, agrees to announce his engagement with Victoire shortly, and promises to marry her within a few weeks. And when Schach fails to make good on any of these promises, the king, Frederick Wilhelm III, brings the state's power to bear to insure the efficacy of language and the fulfillment of Schach's promissory oath. Schach, however, finds a way both to fulfill and to break his obligations in the same moment: on the day of the wedding, on his way home from the reception, he kills himself.

If the problem in *Irrungen, Wirrungen* was superficial social chatter, such that nothing mattered and people seldom meant what they said, *Schach von Wuthenow* gives the problem higher stakes through the concepts of trust and honor. When Botho asserts that at high-society parties, "yes" is just as good as "no," or when Käthe's amusing statements are not dependable, the damage is mitigated because those around them understand the rules of the game and are playing it too. On the other hand, when Schach's word is not dependable, when he promises to marry Victoire and then skips town, it causes real harm. Those around him expect, incorrectly, that Schach has made his promises in good faith, in the sense that he will make good on his word and the faith that Victoire and her mother have placed in him.

In sum, the novel's plot revolves around Schach's infidelity, not marital infidelity but linguistic infidelity, infidelity to his own word and to the trust that he has been given. It is ultimately, in Frau von Carayon's formulation, a case of "Wort- und Treubruch" (6:121, breach of promise and faith).[1] On a personal level, then, the reliability and efficacy of language are central concerns in this novel too. But here, perhaps more decisively than anywhere else in Fontane's oeuvre, the personal gets mapped onto the political and the historical. After Schach's suicide comes to light, the character Bülow writes a letter that makes the historico-political nature of Schach's deed plain.[2] He remarks that Schach is entirely a symptom of his time, a pure "Zeiterscheinung" (6:153, sign of the times, 185). The time in question is the summer of 1806. By setting his novel at the start of the nineteenth century, Fontane homes in on a key moment in the development of the Berlin idiom—the moment at which the Sanssouci tone tips toward excess—and thereby presents an explanatory or archeological account of how Wilhelmine Germany has become what it is. It is not that broad historical forces have eroded language and communication such that people no longer speak in reliable ways. It is, rather, that people have deliberately chosen not to mean what they say and not to say what they mean. These culturally contingent tendencies render language unreliable, which then becomes an historical force in its own right. Or, as Frau von Carayon puts it early in the novel, "was Ursach scheint, ist meist schon wieder Wirkung und Folge" (6:31, what seems to be cause is for the most part just as much effect and consequence, 33). Using her terms, one could say that the instability of the modern world—political instability, for example—*appears* to be the cause of unstable communication. In fact, however, it is the other way around. Fontane's text suggests that political instability results from destabilizations that begin in the linguistic sphere. Orwell coined a quip for both the 1880s and the current era when he wrote that "political chaos is connected with the decay of language, and [...] one can probably bring about some improvement by starting at the verbal end."[3] Fontane, I think, would agree, and he might add that emotional chaos, social chaos, and interpersonal chaos are also connected to the erosion of frank, reliable language.

---

[1] English from Theodor Fontane, *A Man of Honor*, trans. E. M. Valk (New York: Frederick Ungar, 1975), 146. Further references in this chapter to this translation are given parenthetically.

[2] On the allegorical nature of Fontane's narrative, see Gerhart von Graevenitz, *Theodor Fontane: ängstliche Moderne* (Konstanz: Konstanz University Press, 2014), especially 382–94.

[3] Orwell, *In Front of Your Nose*, 139.

Schach as Symptom

As a coda to the story of Schach's demise, the novel concludes with two letters that attempt to interpret the suicide and make it legible for their respective audiences, including the audience to the novel itself. Bülow writes to Sander, his friend and publisher, that Schach's case is symptomatic, and he concerns himself in the letter with unpacking its implications. The point of Bülow's letter is that the fatal flaw in Schach's character is the same flaw that will bring down the Prussian state, and a key crux in the secondary literature has been the attempt to discern precisely what that flaw is. Of what, exactly, is Schach a symptom? What malady presents via his decision to take his own life?[4] In my view, the novel ultimately identifies the deliberate departure from straightforward and reliable language as the root of political failure and historical decline.

Others explain Schach's suicide and hence the novel's central concern through the Prussian notion of honor. They have good reason to, for Bülow's letter dwells at length on the issue of false honor. Even contemporaneous reviews identified Schach as "the most apt expression of that emptied-out concept of honor that brought the state to the edge of the abyss."[5] Here, then, is a social concept that has been deformed and reflected in its deformity through Schach's actions, so that one finds in a false understanding of honor a road into Schach's status as a sign of the times. But what exactly is the nature of "einer falschen Ehre" (a bogus honor) and what is "die richtige Ehre" (6:153, the real thing, 186)? It would be easy, in the context of this work, to misunderstand honor simply as that which is injured by insult, or to conflate being honorable with being admirable. The novel makes clear that Victoire, having been scarred by smallpox, is no longer seen as attractive. And

---

[4] Szukala reads Schach as a symptom of Prussian decadence. Ralph Szukala, "Victoire 1806, Preußen. Zur Spiegelschrift der Bildmotive in Theodor Fontanes *Schach von Wuthenow*," in *In Bildern denken*, ed. Giovanni Scimonello and Ralph Szukala (Bielefeld: Aisthesis, 2008), 138. Franzel sees the symptoms of decline more specifically in the tropes of vanity and egoism. Sean Franzel, "'Alles ist eitel.' Flüchtigkeit und Dauer in *Schach von Wuthenow*," in *Herausforderungen des Realismus: Theodor Fontanes Gesellschaftsromane*, ed. Peter Uwe Hohendahl and Ulrike Vedder (Freiburg: Rombach, 2018), 61. Turk contends that Schach's downfall results from the collision of two contradictory systems, social validation and obedience to the state. Horst Turk, "The Order of Appearance and Validation: On Perennial Classicism in Fontane's Society Novel *Schach von Wuthenow*," trans. Eric Schwab, in *New Approaches to Theodor Fontane: Cultural Codes in Flux*, ed. Marion Doebeling (Columbia, SC: Camden House, 2000), 18–19.

[5] Contemporary review by Wilhelm Lübke, cited in Graevenitz, *Theodor Fontane*, 374.

Schach, repeatedly described as handsome and vain, worries that his fellow officers will ridicule him for marrying her. Indeed, he becomes an object of public ridicule when caricatures depict him struggling to choose between Frau von Carayon and her daughter. Those who know Schach understand that, for him, everything comes down to aesthetics, in the sense of beauty and outward impressions. Thus, to marry a woman who is no longer viewed as aesthetically pleasing would be a blow to his reputation and sense of self.

This is all true, but it does not begin to plumb the depths of honor in this novel, nor in Bülow's interpretation. Victoire's closing letter, too, doubts that the prospect of ridicule is what really drove Schach to ruin (6:156). If Schach is to be understood properly as a symptom, then it must be as the manifestation of a kind of sickness within language and communication. He reflects a certain tone that has metastasized in the upper registers of Prussian society, one that diminishes the reliability of the word one gives and makes language less effective. This diagnosis can even be located in Bülow's commentary. If one examines the novel carefully, one finds that his commentary does not come only at the end in epistolary form. In fact, Bülow's observations also open the novel on the first evening in Frau von Carayon's salon. And what he says on that first evening is remarkably similar to what he writes in his final letter. Essentially, then, Schach's entire story of sex and betrayal, promise and prevarication, is framed on both ends by Bülow's consistent commentary. Bülow has been saying the same things about Schach and Prussian society throughout the story, and when we look closely, we see that he repeatedly brings his critique back to a flawed and inadequate way of speaking, to a language that is fashionable but untrustworthy.

There is a degree of uncertainty and unreliability built into language, especially into language that makes promises about future deeds. Ever since humans began using language in more sophisticated ways—to speak, for example, about imagined, counterfactual, or future situations—they have probably also been complaining that others' words are not worth very much. Giorgio Agamben, looking back at Georges Dumézil's study of Indo-European texts, describes a "scourge" that surfaces repeatedly in ancient sources—namely, "the repudiation or disavowal of obligations one has assumed," which is to say "infidelity to the word one has given."[6] Promissory language is notoriously unreliable because it is easy to abuse. It is always possible that vows, oaths, and promises will never be realized in deed, and the faith one places in another person based on his or her words might never be

---

[6] Agamben, *Sacrament of Language*, 6.

made good upon. The abuse of language and the flimsiness of one's word are not only ancient concerns; they are also issues that were felt acutely in nineteenth-century German society and continue to be today. This is the social ill that presents through the symptom of Schach, and when Bülow sees Schach as a sign of the time, this is the warning he means to give: Schach represents a language of hollow appearances, one whose words cannot be depended on to speak truthfully. The more widespread this unreliable language becomes, the more dire a threat it poses to the stability of the state.

When one compares Bülow's letter with his remarks on the first evening in Frau von Carayon's salon, several recurrent ideas emerge. It is instructive to examine how Bülow introduces the distorting role that honor plays in contemporary society. He writes, "Ich habe lange genug dieser Armee angehört, um zu wissen, daß 'Ehre' das dritte Wort in ihr ist; eine Tänzerin ist scharmant 'auf Ehre', eine Schimmelstute magnifique 'auf Ehre'" (6:153, I was a member of this army long enough to know that its every other word is "honor"; a dancer is charming—"on my honor"; a white steed, fabulous—"on my honor," 186). Note that the issue is not so much honor itself but rather how people talk about honor, or the function it has assumed in language. It resembles in his description the proverbial coin that has been passed around for so long that it no longer has any discernible value. He confirms this suspicion when he concludes, writing, "Und dies beständige Sprechen von Ehre, von einer falschen Ehre, hat die Begriffe verwirrt und die richtige Ehre tot gemacht" (6:153, And this endless chatter about honor, a bogus honor, has turned the concepts upside down and destroyed the real thing, 186). Again, what is harmful is the constant talk of honor. Bülow directs his criticism at a mode of speaking that has the ability to distort and indeed destroy its object.

Attentive readers might also note that this section of the letter essentially reiterates a critique that Bülow voices in the opening salon gathering. "Unsere Herren Offiziere, deren drittes Wort der König und ihre Loyalität ist, [...] gefallen sich plötzlich in einer ebenso naiven wie gefährlichen Oppositionslust" (6:10, Our gentlemen officers, whose every other word is of the King and their loyalty [...], all of a sudden yield to a taste for opposition as naïve as it is dangerous, 7–8). With the repeated complaint about "every other word," he observes in both instances that certain words and ideas have become ubiquitous in the speech of military officers: honor, the king, and loyalty. His point is that the frequent appeals to ideals such as honor and loyalty are disingenuous. All their invocations of loyalty to the monarchy are belied by their desire for political opposition. Their rhetoric of loyalty cannot be trusted or relied upon because it is disconnected from an actual bearing of loyalty. And so it is with honor. By incessantly invoking honor, these officers serve only to cheapen it, to whittle it down to a meaningless expression.

There is a second expression that occurs in both Bülow's salon disquisition and his letter, the Latin saying "Hannibal ante portas" or "Hannibal before the gates" (6:155). The expression harks back to the Punic Wars and the Roman public's fear of the Carthaginian general. It suggests in its abstracted sense that a community faces a great calamity, a powerful enemy, or an imminent downfall. The saying is germane to Bülow's remarks on state politics as it refers in this context to the ongoing international conflicts and negotiations with France, as well as to the fear that Prussia's army could not hold its own in a direct battle with Napoleon's troops. It works especially well because of the parallels between the Punic Wars and the Coalition Wars of the early nineteenth century, including the accusations from both sides of the breaking of treaties.[7] The expression furthermore conveys Bülow's approval for Haugwitz's politics of avoiding belligerent ultimatums and instead negotiating with France, the very political position that Schach and the Regiments Gensdarmes oppose.[8] Bülow makes this remark both at the beginning of the novel and at the end, in September 1806, once war has been declared and shortly before Prussia's disastrous military defeat at Jena and Auerstedt.

In *Schach von Wuthenow*, the personal and the political are deeply intertwined, and a second Latin saying that derives from Hannibal and the Punic Wars lurks in the background—"Punica fides," which refers to the trustworthiness or reliability of a Carthaginian (a Punic). The stereotype is that the Carthaginians were not at all trustworthy or reliable, so that *Punica fides* connotes treachery, perfidy, and deception.[9] Hannibal provides the primary exemplar of the Carthaginians, and his reputation for treachery belonged to the general knowledge of Roman history during Fontane's time. An encyclopedia entry from the early 1900s, for instance, notes that Roman writers accused Hannibal of "perfidy [Treulosigkeit], deceit and brutality."[10] If this connotation of deception and treachery was active in the contemporaneous understanding of Hannibal, then Bülow's repeated reference to "Hannibal at the gates" subtly introduces issues of trustworthiness, duplicity, and

---

[7] For background on the causes of the Punic Wars, see Erich Gruen, *Rethinking the Other in Antiquity* (Princeton: Princeton University Press, 2010), 123.
[8] For a brief, lucid summary of the political situation that underlies these conversations, see Szukala, "Victoire 1806, Preußen," 141–4.
[9] Gruen, *Rethinking the Other*, 115.
[10] *Meyers Großes Konversationslexikon*, 6th ed. (Leipzig and Vienna: Bibliographisches Institut, 1905–9), 6:778.

reliability. With Hannibal comes the question of *fides*, the Latin term for trust, faith, or personal loyalty, *Treue* in German. It suggests that the threat Prussia faces might not be just a foreign conqueror but also something more insidious, something that is already inside the gates of the dominant discourse community—a lack of reliability, a lack of trustworthiness.

To be unworthy of *fides* is a serious charge and deficiency. As the same 1900s encyclopedia notes, *Fides* was for the Romans "the goddess of fidelity (in keeping promises and oaths)."[11] But failing to keep his promises or oaths in any meaningful way is precisely what Schach does to Victoire and Frau von Carayon. Even at the king's command, his ostensible obedience is little more than a ceremonial deception. Schach, like Hannibal, is a figure of treachery and deception. He breaks the Carayons' trust, a breach that is not technically a case of *Ehebruch*, or marital infidelity, but rather *Wortbruch*, infidelity to the word he has given (6:121). Agamben writes, "The object of the *fides* is, in every case, as in the oath, conformity between the parties' words and actions."[12] Schach's actions rarely conform to his language; his deeds repeatedly diverge from his ostensibly sincere promises. His language gives the appearance of sincerity to something he does not actually feel or mean sincerely, a discrepancy that becomes clear through the absence of action. By breaking his promises and repudiating his obligations, Schach also breaches the faith that others have placed in him.

Honor plays an important role within this dynamic of trust, promissory language, and faithfulness. It is precarious to place one's faith in another person, to trust their words and promises. To trust someone means, in a significant sense, to be at that person's mercy until the promise has been fulfilled. How can one decide whose words are reliable? Honor in its deeper sense serves as a barometer of trustworthiness, so that honor and trust operate as complementary concepts. To be honorable is to have earned the trust of others, to have demonstrated a scrupulous correspondence between words and deeds. It denotes a moral integrity that is dependent on the credibility of one's language. Honor, in this context, has the same function of guaranteeing and stabilizing language that Agamben observes in the oath. Like the oath, honor "does not concern the statement as such but the guarantee of its efficacy"; honor provides "the assurance of [language's] truthfulness and

---

[11] *Meyers Großes Konversationslexikon*, 6:550.
[12] Agamben, *Sacrament of Language*, 27.

its actualization."[13] It thus names that quality in a person that vouches for promises and guarantees that one's words are worthy of respect.

This function of honor is readily apparent in *Schach von Wuthenow*, especially when Schach is summoned to an audience before the king and queen. Because Schach has failed to make good on his promise to marry Victoire, the king admonishes him in terms of "honnêteté," a French word that encompasses the semantic field of honor, faithfulness, and honesty. The king presents his demand, saying, "Was mich angeht, das ist die honnêteté. *Die* verlang ich, und um dieser honnêteté willen verlang ich Ihre Heirat mit dem Fräulein von Carayon" (6:137, What does concern me is *honnêteté*. And for the sake of this *honnêteté* I insist on your marriage with Fräulein von Carayon, 166). Similar to the English *honesty* and the German *Ehrlichkeit*, *honnêteté* brings together senses of honorability, integrity, and truthfulness. That semantic convergence stands to reason, since one earns honor (and hence trust) by demonstrating one's integrity and honesty. In order to satisfy the demands of *honnêteté*, Schach must marry Victoire and align his actions with his words.

Ludgera Vogt, drawing on the work of Pierre Bourdieu, conceives of honor as a form of "symbolic capital." She writes, "Honor capital can be accumulated and, corresponding to the structures of a credit system, one can be in debt or can be a creditor of honor."[14] If honor functions like capital, it accrues through consistent fidelity to one's word, and this capital, once amassed, pays dividends in the form of trust and confidence. A person who consistently keeps her word accumulates honor in the sense that, having proven her credibility, she will be seen as more likely to keep her word in the future as well. Hence, the subtle wordplay that Fontane constructs through Aunt Marguerite, when she refers to the wedding day, now finally set, as "den Ehrentag," or day of honor (6:145), for this is the day on which Schach will presumably demonstrate his honorability and will repay the loan of confidence that the Carayons extended to him.

The queen only reinforces this impression when she reminds Schach that he is a "Mann von Ehre" (man of integrity [honor], 168) and asks him to keep in mind "*das*, was Pflicht und Ehre von Ihnen fordern" (6:139, *that* which duty and honor demand of you, 168). Honor functions here like a promise, or rather like a meta-promise: not only has Schach vowed to marry Victoire, his status as a man of honor, as a kind

---

[13] Agamben, *Sacrament of Language*, 4.
[14] Ludgera Vogt, *Zur Logik der Ehre in der Gegenwartsgesellschaft: Differenzierung, Macht, Integration* (Frankfurt am Main: Suhrkamp, 1997), 293. See further pages 121–52.

of secondary promissory overlay, has also implicitly promised that Schach would keep his word. His honor always adds the promise that his promises are credible. This is why both the king and queen admonish Schach in terms of honor and its connection to honesty.[15] They are willing to deploy the power of the state to enforce the demands of honor and thus protect the reliability of language. And if Schach refuses to make good on his word, the king insists that he relinquish his military position. The monarchy demonstrates in this instance its willingness to make Schach's service to the state contingent on his observance of his promises. All of this suggests that the state has a vested interest in dependable and efficacious language. Fontane underscores the strategic importance of linguistic fidelity by having the king, at the start of their meeting, reviewing maps from the Battle of Austerlitz. Graevenitz adds another good point: when Frau von Carayon goes to see the king, the bells play the song "Üb immer Treu und Redlichkeit" ("Always Practice Loyalty and Integrity"), which only reinforces the symbolic overlap between state power and fidelity to one's word.[16] In some important, though unseen, sense, the functioning of Prussia as a state and military power depends on *honnêteté* and its ability to guarantee the reliability of language.

This constellation of honor, honesty, and trust brings us back to Bülow's letter and its critique of false honor in the Prussian military. He complains that every third word out of the officers' mouths is "honor." The deployment of honor as a catchphrase to vouch for one's assertions reveals the difference Bülow perceives between true and false honor. In its true sense, honor is the trustworthiness one accumulates through the consistent correspondence between words and actions and the evidence of good faith. It vouches for the promises one makes because past performance can, if not guarantee, at least make more likely future results. Even the formulaic expression "on my honor" in the officers' speech serves a similar purpose. It is meant to guarantee that the statement in question is truthful and dependable. But in these instances, it functions as the most perfunctory oath.

Agamben writes that what matters in giving an oath "is not the semiotic or cognitive function of language as such but the assurance of its truthfulness and its actualization."[17] This passage captures nicely the purpose of "on my honor" as an addendum to a statement. First,

---

[15] Georg Simmel describes honor's social function similarly as "a peculiar guarantee for correct behavior" in areas where law and morality do not provide effective guarantees. Cited in Vogt, *Zur Logik der Ehre*, 175.
[16] Graevenitz, *Theodor Fontane*, 385.
[17] Agamben, *Sacrament of Language*, 4.

one asserts something, that dancer is charming, for example. Then, one adds the assertative oath "on my honor," which contributes nothing to the statement's content; it merely assures the listener that the connection between subject and predicate is truthful. If genuine honor reflects a thoroughgoing conformity between word and deed, the formulaic oath "on my honor" presents the word without any corresponding deed to support it. It is in this sense that Bülow derides false honor as a tendency to deploy words that have no corresponding referent in action, emotion, or reality. In a paradoxical way, one attempts through these invocations of honor to assure the referential reliability of language through a formula that is itself referentially unreliable.

In Bülow's characterization, then, false honor refers to an empty rhetoric of honor. The cultural trend in upper-class Prussian society is to invoke honor without any attachment to the institution of honor. One sees here how Schach could exemplify the tendencies of his era, for he too has the habit of engaging in the ritual expression of agreement or acquiescence, only to fail to follow up with the actions to which he has obligated himself. As Bülow puts it, Schach "löst sich feige von Pflicht und Wort" (6:154, beats a cowardly retreat from his obligation and commitment, 187). In a more concrete sense, he detaches himself—by fleeing to his Wuthenow estate, by committing suicide—from his word and from the obligations it entails. When he repeatedly breaks his promises and agreements, Schach violates the faithfulness he owes to *fides*. His willingness to give his word in bad faith signifies, as a symptom would, the deeper illness of a pervasive unreliability and insincerity in the prevailing tone of early nineteenth-century Prussia.

Words without Deeds

Long before Bülow interprets these events as a problem within Prussian language and communication, the novel underscores as a fundamental concern the question of whether language is dependable. It sets in contrast two competing ideas about the connection between words and referents. In this context, Schach personifies an alarming discrepancy between phenomenon and essence. On the surface, he expresses nothing but obedience and reconciliation, while in his heart he remains bent on disobedience. His disavowal of his obligations occurs as a form of irony, because the phenomenon of his speech is characterized by earnestness and sincerity, although his assurances are essentially insincere. He thus comes to embody a cynical, disingenuous style of speech that Fontane elsewhere identifies among the Prussian military elite around 1800—namely, the tendency to say "alles in einer zynisch-rücksichtsloser Sprache" (NA 19:749, everything in a cynical, heedless language). It is in this way that Schach functions as a case study for the diagnosis of an epidemic of undependable language in Prussian society.

Behind all the political debates, Bülow consistently criticizes empty, inflated rhetoric from the Regiment Gensdarmes and from Schach in particular. His quarrel with Schach is as much about language and rhetoric as about Prussian politics. When Bülow disparages Schach in this vein, the narrative establishes a classic Fontanean contrast between, on the one hand, what is genuine, natural, and reliable, and, on the other, what is not. In this case, the same sort of opposition that Lene and Käthe embody in *Irrungen, Wirrungen* now falls on Frau von Carayon and Schach. Bülow, speaking in terms reminiscent of Lene's charms, says of Frau von Carayon, "Sie hat den ganzen Zauber des Wahren und Nätürlichen" (6:25, all the magic of the true and natural, 26–7). Once again, in good realist fashion, what is laudable is the true and the natural. He goes on to characterize the other side of the dichotomy, saying of Schach, "mir ist er nichts als ein Pedant und Wichtigtuer, und zugleich die Verkörperung jener preußischen Beschränktheit" (6:25, to me he's just a pompous prig and at the same time the embodiment of that Prussian parochialism, 27). From Bülow's perspective, Schach personifies the shortcomings of Prussian culture, and he portrays the primary shortcoming—here as at the end of the novel—in terms of disingenuous speech and an overreliance on empty platitudes. One of the oft-repeated articles of faith he sarcastically cites is, "die Welt ruht nicht sichrer auf den Schultern des Atlas, als der preußische Staat auf den Schultern der preußischen Armee," a bit of bluster that, set in the summer of 1806, portends hubris and defeat (6:25, the world rests no more securely on the shoulders of Atlas than the State of Prussia rests on the shoulders of the Prussian army, 27).

It is humorous, then, that when Schach disparages Bülow to Frau von Carayon, he does so with recourse to this very dictum: "*ich* aber halte zu dem fridericianischen Satze, daß die Welt nicht sicherer auf den Schultern des Atlas ruht, als Preußen auf den Schultern seiner Armee" (6:39, *I* stand by the Frederickian axiom that the world rests no more securely on the shoulders of Atlas than does Prussia on those of her army, 43). With only the slightest variation in wording, Schach voices precisely the kind of hollow jingoism that Bülow has caricatured in his scathing critique of Schach's Prussian narrow-mindedness. Schach fulfills the expectations of Bülow's caricature by earnestly voicing such platitudes as if they constituted an unimpeachable conclusion. Embedded in Schach's assertion is a kind of promise—a promise regarding the outcome of hypothetical future military conflicts—but given Napoleon's recent victories, there is no guarantee that this promise could be made good. As Bülow says, "Ich verabscheue solche Redensarten, und der Tag ist nahe, wo die Welt die Hohlheit solcher Rodomontaden erkennen wird" (6:25, I loathe this kind of rhetoric, and the day isn't far off when the world will see through the sham of rodomontades like these, 27). It is worth emphasizing that the primary object of critique in this passage is, again, a reliance on *Redensarten*, empty phrases or figures of speech that, under scrutiny, mean much less than they appear to say. Mecklenburg puts it well when he writes that "Fontane's critical attention to language pertains primarily to contemporary speech communication and the prevalence of the hackneyed 'phrase' in it."[18] The crucial point in Bülow's critique is its forward-looking orientation. The Prussian officers have adopted a communicative posture that no longer accords with what is simple, true, natural, and credible. He predicts a day of reckoning on which their rhetoric's emptiness and cynicism will be revealed as a liability.[19] The passage reflects a narrative stance that consistently associates political and military defeat with the failure of language that is deliberately unreliable.

Peter James Bowman argues, however, that Bülow misinterprets Schach and that his diagnosis of false honor and empty rhetoric overlooks Schach's "reservations about fluent but callous verbal display."[20] If Schach ever harbored reservations about speaking callously or insincerely, he manages to overcome them splendidly by the time he professes his love for Victoire and agrees to move forward with the wedding plans. The passages cited above suggest further that Bülow is a relatively good judge of Schach's character and a sharp critic of the dominant manner of speaking in Prussian society. Although Bowman sees in Schach "the independence of spirit needed to defy the tone of conversation adopted and set by the Prince of Prussia," the narrative provides strong counterexamples of Schach parroting the hollow speech that has come to characterize the upper strata of Prussian society.[21]

While I disagree that Schach constitutes an exception to the dominant tone, it is an important point to dwell on, for Bowman has a case to make. When Bülow charges Schach with inauthenticity and empty talk, other figures step in to defend him. They see instead a model of sincerity and authenticity: "alles an ihm ist echt" (6:26, everything about him is sincere, 27). Furthermore, Bowman is correct that Schach does not always conform to the characteristic tone of the Regiment Gensdarmes. Most of the officers resemble Käthe from *Irrungen, Wirrungen*:

---

[18] Mecklenburg, *Theodor Fontane*, 158.
[19] Examining how language and dialogue construct social reality, Brandstetter and Neumann also pursue the novel's subversion of Prussian political mythology. Brandstetter and Neumann, "Le laid c'est le beau," 250–2.
[20] Peter James Bowman, "*Schach von Wuthenow*: Interpreters and Interpretants," in *Theodor Fontane and the European Context*, ed. Patricia Howe and Helen Chambers (Amsterdam: Rodopi, 2001), 55.
[21] Bowman, "*Schach von Wuthenow*," 55.

"Sie sahen alles ausschließlich auf seine komische Seite hin an" (6:85, They only had an eye for the comical side of it all, 101). Where others want to debate religion and morality, they find only "einen unerschöpflichen Stoff für ihren Spott und Übermut" (2:332, inexhaustible material for their sarcasm and levity, 101). One feels here a parallel to Fontane's genealogy of the Berlin idiom, to that moment around 1800 when the primary goal was to deliver clever, witty repartee (NA 19:748). The novel follows Fontane's account further when it suggests that the officers of the Regiment Gensdarmes constitute a primary motor of linguistic change. As Nostritz, addressing his fellow officers, puts it, "wir haben nicht nur der Schlacht die Richtung, wir haben auch der Gesellschaft den *Ton* gegeben" (6:86, we haven't only set the trend in combat, we've also set the *fashion* [*tone*] in society, 102). The military elite determine society's dominant tone, and their tone sounds like a precursor to the frivolous, unserious banter that characterizes Käthe's social circle in *Irrungen, Wirrungen*. It grows out of the witty, pointed, and ironic tone that developed in the literary salon milieu of Sanssouci, a setting that finds its echo here in the circle surrounding Prince Louis Ferdinand.[22]

Schach differs from this tone in significant ways. He refuses, for example, to participate in the bawdy, farcical sleigh ride that the others organize, and he resists some of the prince's statements about the Carayons. So the narrative does present evidence that Schach's style of speech is not always like that of others. But if Bowman is right on this point, how can I argue that Schach is nonetheless symptomatic of a prevalent and harmful trend in Prussian speech patterns? While it is true that Scach defies the dominant tone in some respects, his defiance is limited to the most overt ways in which language has become frivolous, unserious, and unreliable. In contrast to other officers, Schach will not banter. Nor will he play for laughs or cheap ridicule, because it would offend his sense of decorum and propriety. In these most obvious respects, Schach resists the sort of speech that has become fashionable in upper-class Prussian society. But this is the key point: Schach's surface-level resistance only makes his fundamental unreliability more insidious and more dangerous. When Käthe, for instance, speaks in a stream of amusing but meaningless remarks, her language announces

---

[22] Garland notes the contrast in speaking styles between Prince Louis Ferdinand and Frederick Wilhelm III, as the novel portrays them. Whereas the prince engages in long, abstract discussions, the king is "barely articulate." Henry Garland, *The Berlin Novels of Theodor Fontane* (Oxford: Clarendon Press, 1980), 34. On the depiction of the king as reserved and inarticulate, see further Bade, *Fontane's Landscapes*, 53.

its own unseriousness. Her small talk never presents itself in the guise of meaningful communication and seldom deceives anyone into taking it seriously. The same holds true for the jocular, bantering tone of the officer corps. Much of what they say is neither serious nor sincere, but then again, their humorous, even ridiculous tone underscores its own insincerity.

Schach, however, is different. His language is no more reliable than anyone else's. Indeed, in the end, his word is worth next to nothing. Not only is Schach happy to repeat empty platitudes of Prussian loyalty and exceptionalism, he is also willing to break his promises and breach the trust that others have placed in him. In Bülow's view, Schach's duplicity and the inability to rely on what he says place him squarely within the dominant discourse of Prussian society. Speaking eloquently but without sincere feeling, speaking cynically and heedlessly, is Schach's calling card in the novel's second half. The difference is that Schach *conceals* his insincerity. He hides the emptiness of his speech behind a mask of integrity, sincerity, and genuine feeling. Schach's earnest attitude dissimulates by giving the impression that everything he says is reliable and spoken in good faith. And this attitude comes through in his use of language. At his most duplicitous, Schach writes to the Carayons and asks for forgiveness "in anscheinend aufrichtigen Worten" (6:141, in ostensibly sincere words, 171). This surely qualifies as a fluent but callous verbal display. His disingenuous language projects earnestness and sincerity, but it is nothing more than a façade to conceal the lack of feeling in his heart, and it is perhaps here that the ironic discrepancy between phenomenon and essence becomes most severe. Schach wears his solemnity like a mask, and his false sincerity is calculated to deceive.[23]

Schach's apparent resistance to the dominant social tone—his attitude of earnest propriety, his antipathy toward lighthearted witticism—only makes the underlying hollowness and unreliability of his own language that much more pernicious. It seems to me that Fontane, through his depictions of characters like Käthe and Schach, is working toward a deeper insight into the nature of language use and social communication. Fontane portrays in various settings modes of speaking that are playful, unserious, and unreliable. But his concern is not merely with unserious forms of language as such, with irony, badinage,

---

[23] Kieffer finds in the novel a similar "concern with the disjunction between the inner and the outer person," though he connects this concern to Nietzsche's reflections on history. Bruce Kieffer, "Fontane and Nietzsche: The Use and Abuse of History in *Schach von Wuthenow,*" *The Germanic Review* 61, no. 1 (1986): 30.

small talk, and so on. Rather, his novels concern themselves with the question of whether one can control or contain that unreliable element within language, especially once it has become an established form of social interaction. To take Schach as a symptom and extend the metaphor of disease, the novel suggests that unreliable forms of language can spread rapidly, infecting contexts that depend on sincerity, transparency, and credibility.

The narrative presents early on Schach's tendency to produce promissory language that will never be realized in action. During the excursion to Tempelhof, Schach and Victoire's conversation about the Knights Templar looks ahead to the dynamic of promise and prevarication that will define their relationship. As Schach explains his respect for the Knights Templar, Victoire jokingly suggests that maybe he actually admires their clothing, which is to say, the aesthetics of outward appearances. Schach, as humorless as ever, counters her assertion by insisting on a core of idealism and fidelity: "Sie verkennen mich. Glauben Sie mir, es lebt etwas in mir, das mich vor keinem Gelübde zurückschrecken läßt" (6:45, You misjudge me. Believe me, there's some vital spark in me that won't let me shrink from any vow, 49). Schach indicates that he is not afraid of obligating himself by taking a vow or saying an oath. He presents himself, in other words, as a stalwart model of *fides*, as innately trustworthy and loyal.

It is furthermore odd that Schach needs to preface this assertion of trustworthiness with the formulaic assurance "believe me." It functions like an oath meant to guarantee the reliability of what he says, and yet it is merely a command. "Believe me when I say that I'm believable." The tautological reformulation points up the impossibility of guaranteeing language's efficacy through the use of more language. An oath is not made more reliable through the utterance of an additional oath. Far from controlling the unreliability in promissory language, supplemental oaths only redouble the unreliable element that is already present.[24] Schach possesses no force by which he could actually compel Victoire's belief; the best he can do is assert that his words are worthy of trust.

The first indication of unreliability comes in the next moment. Following Schach's earnest speech about his readiness to take a vow, Victoire asks, "'Um es zu halten?' Aber eh er noch antworten konnte, fuhr sie rasch in wieder scherzhafter werdendem Tone fort" (6:45, "And hold to it?" But before he had a chance to reply, she quickly continued in a more playful tone, 49). For all Schach's talk of fondness for vows, he is silent on the question of whether he means to keep what he promises. It

---

[24] On the oath's inadequacy in preventing perjury, see Agamben, *Sacrament of Language*, 6–8.

is true that Victoire does not afford him much opportunity to respond, but the absence of a response in this instance nonetheless foreshadows future encounters. Schach is frequently silent when others confront him with the obligations his solemn promises entail. Victoire's question splits the notion of the vow into its two component halves, word and deed. One can take a vow (or give a promise), but more importantly, one must also keep one's vow and make good on the word one has given. Schach's silence in this moment indicates that his appetite for vows might extend only to the linguistic act of taking a vow. Schach would never shy away from making a promise, but whether he intends to fulfill it is another question entirely. *Fides*, however, is the Roman goddess of *keeping* promises and oaths, not merely giving them. The *fides* Schach believes himself to embody is actually just *Punica fides*, the treachery of empty promises.

It is less surprising that Victoire drops her question, changing the topic (and the tone) before Schach replies. One sees this rhetorical situation more than once in Fontane's works, and Käthe's interrogation regarding the ashes of love letters provides a good model. Right at the moment of a high-stakes question, an avowal, or a deep insight into another person's nature, the speaking character retreats from the rhetorical precipice back to lighthearted banter, to the more comfortable mode of not meaning to be taken seriously. Victoire does the same thing, and by changing the topic, she lets her question go unanswered. The uncertainty in this exchange nonetheless captures in miniature a pattern that will repeat itself throughout the story: Schach is quick to give assurances, and then the other characters are suspended in the gap between word and deed, left wondering whether he will honor his promises. In the end, Schach's talk of vows and fidelity leaves his audience with a sense of uncertainty and a dark presentiment of infidelity.

This dynamic (promise–uncertainty–infidelity) begins in the very moment when Schach retreats from his intimate evening with Victoire. He departs with the words, "Bis auf morgen" (Until tomorrow), an implicit promise with an explicit deadline. The narrator highlights here the discrepancy between word and deed: "'Bis auf morgen,' war Schachs Abschiedswort gewesen, aber er kam nicht. Auch am zweiten und dritten Tage nicht" (6:80, "Until tomorrow," had been Schach's parting words, but he did not come. Nor did he on the second and third day, 94). Victoire has Schach's word but no corresponding deed, and she is left in the dark as to when, or whether, he will keep his promise. She finds herself in the vulnerable position of being dependent on another person's faithfulness.

As she struggles to account for Schach's sudden absence and aloofness, she recalls her friend Lisette's words, "daß Du ganz einfach vor einer Alternative stehst, und entweder Deine gute Meinung über S., oder aber Dein Mißtrauen gegen ihn fallen lassen mußt" (6:80, that you are simply faced with a choice and will have to rid yourself either of the high opinion you have of S. or of your distrust *toward him*, 94). The two alternatives that Lisette proposes correspond to the two possible answers to Victoire's question about vows. Either Schach will keep his word, in which case her positive impression of him can stand; or he will break his promise, in which case her mistrust is justified. At this moment, however, Victoire cannot decide between these two positions, because Schach has not yet fulfilled his promise, nor has he completely broken it. While it is clear that his word about "tomorrow" was not reliable, a belated visit would still make good on the most important element of his promise. Schach's tarrying strands Victoire between trust and mistrust and leaves her with the same uncertainty as her unanswered question about keeping a vow.

This minor prevarication is but the first in a series of escalating betrayals. The next one begins when Frau von Carayon confronts Schach with Victoire's pregnancy and presses him to legitimize the relationship with an engagement and a wedding. Schach, who has spoken so earnestly about his hunger for vows, now replies with such an alienating and distanced tone that he undermines his acquiescence. He assures her, "daß er wohl wisse, wie jegliches Ding im Leben seine natürliche Konsequenz habe. Und solcher Konsequenz gedenk er sich nicht zu entziehen" (6:97, that he was well aware that every action in life brought its logical consequence in its train. And he had no intention of evading such a consequence, 116). Several elements of Schach's speech in this instance make it strange and off-putting. First, his words are given in quotation marks, indicating that they are direct, quoted speech. And yet the entire passage is rendered in the subjunctive of indirect speech. Fontane's text thus presents Schach's speech as both direct and indirect at the same time, so that the speaking agent remains difficult to pin down. These might be Schach's words, or Schach might simply be parroting words that do not actually belong to him. This odd stylistic choice has the effect that even when Schach's speech is meant to be direct, intimate, and reassuring, it remains marked by indirection.

Second, Schach assumes in this passage an abstracted register of things, consequences, and steps to be taken. He thereby manages to avoid any mention of affection, regret, or Victoire herself. Both the narrator and Frau von Carayon note the absence of feeling in Schach's language. Frau von Carayon in particular is wounded by his aloof, businesslike tone. Schach's speech ultimately lacks any satisfactory act of avowal. He never makes a heartfelt declaration of love, nor does he declare himself to be the guilty party, now convicted and facing punishment. He merely concurs that things have consequences, and that certain steps need to be taken. Though his words are polite and obliging, they also reveal that his acquiescence is not attached to any heartfelt affection. And as Frau von Carayon spells out the terms of his obligations—quiet engagement, gala wedding with all that entails—Schach responds with his customary reticence.

Readers of the novel know that Schach does not keep his word to Frau von Carayon. Despite assuring her that he does not intend to evade the consequences of his actions, he does exactly that. By the time he is supposed to announce his engagement to Victoire, he has already left the city for his Wuthenow estate. Once again, a deadline passes without satisfaction, and everyone is left wondering whether Schach ever means to make good on his word. But before we get to the keeping and breaking of words, it is worth dwelling on Schach's eagerness to give his word, to enter into obligations by saying what the other party wants to hear. This is precisely what Schach does when he writes a letter that means to correct everything that went wrong in the previous day's conversation. In the letter, Schach produces the avowal that was absent from his spoken reaction. "Er bekannte sich darin in allem Freimut schuldig" (In it, he unreservedly pleaded guilty [avowed his guilt]), and he speaks "von seiner Liebe zu Victoiren" (of his love for Victoire) because he realizes that the situation requires "das einfache Geständnis einer herzlichen Neigung" (6:99, a simple avowal of affection, 118). The language in this passage points self-consciously to a register of confession and avowal. Schach candidly declares—and thereby appears to accept—sincere feelings of both guilt and love. Most importantly, he manages to strike throughout the letter "einen wärmeren Ton, eine herzlichere Sprache" (6:99, a more cordial tone and more warmhearted words, 118), so that all his assurances seem to be endowed with an aura of genuine affection. In this instance as throughout the novel, the narrative registers minor fluctuations in tone and language. Schach agrees to all demands, as well as to a specific timeframe for fulfilling his obligations, but there is reason for concern, even as he goes through all the motions of doing what honor and social convention demand of him.

Already as he writes his letter to the Carayons, the narrator applies a brake of caution: "Ja, sein Rechtsgefühl [...] ließ ihn vielleicht mehr sagen, als zu sagen gut und klug war" (6:99, his sense of rectitude [...] made him say more than was prudent and wise, 118). Schach's compliance stems not from love but from a sense of justice. He writes with uncharacteristic warmth in order to satisfy an abstract ideal. Here again one sees how Schach exemplifies the hollowness of his age. Just like officers regurgitating the catchphrases of honor and loyalty, Schach is moved by a sense of duty to speak but not to act. A confirmed bachelor who says more than he feels and more than he means, Schach resembles the fickle Prussian officers who nonetheless preach loyalty to the king. It is an odd sense of justice indeed that compels him to profess his love to Victoire and then subsequently allows him to abandon her and their unborn child.

Moreover, the situation demonstrates again the difficulty of controlling the unreliable element in language once one begins dissimulating and abusing trust. Schach's error in the letter is saying too much. He is unable, it seems, to stop producing language, even when the words are no longer reliable. He avows his guilt and confesses his love, but these acts of avowal turn out to be further instances of irony, because he professes in earnest what is not meant in earnest. At this point, the unreliability of irony, and of unserious speech in general, is no longer confined to the salon, the fashionable soiree, or the officers' club. Even in the most intimate and important settings, in crucial moments of avowal, there is an ambivalent fluctuation between what one professes and its opposite. In *Schach von Wuthenow*, Fontane crafts high-stakes scenes in which trust and honesty are of the utmost importance, and he repeatedly shows that, even under these circumstances, even backed by the social collateral of honor and duty, Schach's promissory language has become at best undependable and at worst an instrument of deception. Liselotte Grevel, looking ahead to the Lord Chandos letter and a fin-de-siècle crisis of language, sees the novel depicting "a world in which expressions threaten to lose any binding meaning."[25] Her formulation is too passive, though, because it does not identify the agent that has brought about that loss. It is not that words just happen to be broken, but rather that Schach repeatedly and deliberately chooses to break his word.

Of course, Schach cannot go on evading his promises indefinitely. When his conscience fails to ensure the fulfillment of his obligations, Frau von Carayon persuades the king to intervene. Up to this point, the Carayons are the vulnerable party to the informal contract with Schach. With nothing but their faith and trust, they are dependent on Schach's good will as they have no means by which to compel his compliance. The king, however, has the full authority of the state at his disposal, and he presents Schach with a simple ultimatum. He must either live up to the expectations of *honnêteté* or surrender his position in the military. Schach must demonstrate honor through honesty, *Ehre* through *Ehrlichkeit*, and come through with the marriage he has promised. Schach indicates further that he submits to the state's authority by assuring

---

[25] Liselotte Grevel, "Die 'sanfte Vergewaltigung' im Wort. Der Held im Kräftespiel zwischen Wort und Handlung in Fontanes Erzählung *Schach von Wuthenow*," in *Theodor Fontane am Ende des Jahrhunderts*, ed. Hanna Delf von Wolzogen and Helmuth Nürnberger (Würzburg: Königshausen & Neumann, 2000), 2:62.

both the king and the queen that he is at their command (6:138). What they command is the keeping of words and honoring of vows.

This ultimatum is where *Schach von Wuthenow* really gets interesting. Schach indicates through his bearing and demeanor—through his deference to hierarchy—that he intends to obey, to marry, and to set things right. And yet the fundamental discrepancy between appearance and reality remains operative in this exchange. Externally, Schach is all obedience and reconciliation; internally, he remains bent on evading his obligations. The narrative portrays his state mind as follows: "Er wußte, was er dem König schuldig sei: *Gehorsam*! Aber sein Herz widerstritt, und so galt es den für ihn, etwas ausfindig zu Machen, was Gehorsam und Ungehorsam in sich vereinigte" (6:140, He knew what he owed the king: *obedience*! But his heart rebelled, and he therefore had to devise a scheme that would combine obedience and disobedience in one, 169). Schach seeks to combine two courses of action that cancel each reciprocally. He wants to find a way to obey without really giving in. Thus, when Schach tells the king and queen that he is at their command, this constitutes another example of empty rhetoric. If meant sincerely, to be at someone's command means to do without question whatever that person requires. But from Schach, it is just another formulaic expression, a *Redensart* or empty phrase, since he always intends to follow the dictates of his own heart. As he realizes, suicide affords him the opportunity to both fulfill and break his promise on the same day. As long as he goes through with the wedding ceremony, he will have satisfied every debt of obedience owed to the Carayons and the king. And if he kills himself as soon as the ceremony is over, he can still avoid the reality of being married to Victoire.

Bülow's astute interpretation of Schach's act comes closest to the narrator's portrayal. He says that, when the king reminds Schach of his duty and demands his compliance, "da gehorcht er, aber nur, um im Momente des Gehorchens den Gehorsam in einer allerbrüskesten Weise zu brechen" (6:154, he obeys, but only to be guilty at the very moment of obeying of the most brusque refusal to obey, 187). Schach, who has already broken his word and the Carayons' trust, now manages to break his obedience in the very moment that he supposedly demonstrates that obedience. There is something in Schach's actions that borders on irony. In an ironic verbal expression, one typically says something but in the same moment negates, undercuts, or reverses what was said. The act of expression nullifies the effect of what was expressed. Imagine, for example, a child forced to apologize against his or her will. One solution would be to use irony, that is, to go through with the ritual expression of what has been demanded, but to express it in such a way that the expression takes back the apology in the same breath that it is given. The child thereby adheres (grudgingly, barely) to the letter of the demand but certainly not to its spirit. This, in essence, is what Schach does by finally consenting to marry Victoire. He goes through the motions of a wedding ceremony, a ritual expression of commitment and fidelity, only to nullify the ceremony's effect before it ever has a chance to take effect. The act that would fulfill his word cancels itself in the last moment. Schach's apparent obedience is thus nothing but a duplicitous mask. The narrative grants Victoire a vague presentiment of Schach's unreliability: when he describes a honeymoon excursion to Malta, she can think of nothing but "*Fata Morgana*," a mirage or optical illusion (6:146). Schach's promises are like mirages, something beautiful and reassuring on the distant horizon, but something that continuously recedes or simply disappears as one approaches.

In the end, the earlier exchange about the Knights Templar turns out to be prescient. Schach again takes a solemn vow, but not with the intention of honoring it. One feels the gap between word and deed acutely in Frau von Carayon's final conversation with Schach. She pulls him aside during the wedding reception to remind him that he must live up to Victoire's love: "Und so verlang ich kein Versprechen von Ihnen. Ich weiß im voraus, ich hab es" (6:150, And so I won't extract a promise from you. I know I have it in advance, 181). Frau von Carayon is correct, in a way: she *does* have Schach's promise. Unfortunately, that is all she has—his promise that he will honor his agreements, obey the king's orders, and take Victoire as his lawfully wedded wife. She has his word, to be sure, but his word is wholly unreliable. In point of fact, Schach will not show himself worthy of Victoire's love and will be dead within the hour. Here as elsewhere in the novel, the fidelity he has promised turns out to be *Punica fides*. Schach can sit silently with his half-mile stare because there is nothing left to say. Frau von Carayon does not require any further promises, although Schach would likely be happy to produce more promises, if necessary. And when she refers to honoring his marriage vows, Schach is just as silent as he was when Victoire asked him if he intended to keep the vows he was so eager to take. He is comfortable in the gap between word and deed.

The Politics and Aesthetics of Empty Language

When Bülow describes to Sander an act of obedience that negates itself, he presents it as an exemplary instance of false honor (6:154). He extrapolates from the cautionary tale of Schach's death and presents as a pressing social concern the communicative impulse toward cynicism and hollow rhetoric. If Schach is indeed symptomatic of a broader, decadent trend in Prussian society, then they inhabit an era in which it is distressingly difficult to distinguish obedience from disobedience, sincerity from insincerity, a solemn vow from the opening gambit of betrayal, or honor from treachery. In short, Schach is symptomatic of a post-truth age, and the novel clearly means to introduce resonances between Schach's time and the 1880s.[26] Sean Franzel, for example, points to "structures of repetition" in the novel and to the danger that the cult of false honor could persist into the *Gründerzeit* and the late nineteenth century.[27]

Irony introduces a kind of uncertainty principle into language: one cannot tell, without unpacking the black box of intention, whether the sentiment it contains has been left intact or transformed into its opposite. This element of uncertainty might be relatively harmless in the realm of amusing banter, but Fontane's novel suggests that irony and unreliability are invasive rhetorical species. Cultivated in the hothouse of literary salon culture, disseminated by the military, they now spring up where they are not wanted and choke out healthier forms of communication. In this respect, *Schach von Wuthenow* provides further evidence that Fontane does not identify political or economic upheaval as the root cause of communicative instability. In fact, the novel flips this image of cause and effect on its head. When Bülow characterizes Schach as a symptom of cultural decline, he points to the unreliability of disingenuous language as a factor in creating political upheaval. Societies that prioritize, as Schach does, hollow appearance and fashionable tone over the straightforward expression of truth will find themselves unable to respond to crisis.

Bülow makes this point through the downfall of the Ming Dynasty:

> Als es mit der Mingdynastie zur Neige ging und die siegreichen Mansdschuheere schon in den Palastgärten in Peking eingedrungen waren, erschienen immer noch Boten und Abgesandte, die dem Kaiser von Siegen und wieder Siegen meldeten, weil es gegen 'den Ton' der guten Gesellschaft und des Hofes war, von Niederlagen zu sprechen. Oh, dieser gute Ton! (6:154–5)

When the Ming dynasty was at the last gasp and the advance of the victorious Manchu armies had already engulfed the palace gardens of Peking, messengers and delegates kept appearing

---

[26] Although *Schach* is based on actual events, those events occurred in 1815. Geppert contends that Fontane shifted the timeframe to 1806 to emphasize the resonances between Berlin in 1806 and in his own era of the 1880s. Hans Vilmar Geppert, "Prussian Decadence: *Schach von Wuthenow* in an International Context," in *Theodor Fontane and the European Context*, ed. Patricia Howe and Helen Chambers (Amsterdam: Rodopi, 2001), 111. Those parallels are why *Schach* functions as both an historical novel and a society novel.

[27] Franzel, "Alles ist eitel," 74.

on the scene to regale the emperor with reports of victory after victory, because it was contrary to "good form [tone]" in high society and at court to speak of defeats. Oh, this business of good form [tone]! (187–8)

The remarkable part of this passage is that it attributes the downfall of the Ming Dynasty to a rhetorical rather than a military failure. Social expectations and cultural conventions warped communication such that it was impossible to speak forthrightly about an incontrovertible truth. The cynical and empty talk of victory paralyzed the state and blinded its leadership to impending disaster. This analogy reiterates *in nuce* Fontane's model of linguistic evolution and historical development. A certain tone or style of speech develops in the royal court and the upper classes. The fashionable style of speech then migrates through various levels of society, shaping throughout the forms of communication that are expected and acceptable. Ultimately, this tone becomes an historical agent in its own right, as it contributes to the success or failure of the nation from which it emanates.

When we connect this analogue to Prussia in 1806, the parallels run both backward and forward. Backward: the officer corps to which Schach belongs prides itself on setting the tone and style of speech for contemporary Prussian society. This is an alarming prospect, since the novel has offered numerous examples of empty expressions that seem just as cynical as the assurance of victory in the Ming Dynasty. In the historical example, a hollow rhetoric of victory concealed imminent defeat. In Berlin of 1806, a hollow rhetoric of loyalty and obedience conceals a posture of disloyalty and disobedience. Empty talk of honor conceals perfidy; empty talk of military superiority conceals the possibility of inferiority. Looking forward, it is not difficult to connect this flawed and ineffective language to an impending military defeat.[28] The "Hannibal ante portas" is Napoleon, whose troops are prepared to press into Prussian territory just as surely as the enemy hordes had already penetrated the Ming palace gardens, and all the officers can do is repeat clichés that compare the Prussian military to the shoulders of Atlas. This emphasis on the consequences of a predominant tone and an indifference to the truth helps to explain the extensive research that Fontane conducted before writing the novel. He gathered cultural documents in order to

---

[28] Brandstetter and Neumann see in the name "Victoire" an irony directed at cultural decadence and an unfounded optimistic belief in progress. Brandstetter and Neumann, "Le laid c'est le beau," 259. My point is that Fontane's critique directs itself at a dissimulating, unreliable, ironic tone that contributes to social decline.

capture, in his words, the "Colorit" (atmosphere), the "Stimmungen" (moods), and "Anschauungen" (opinions) of 1806.[29] He even pored over contemporaneous newspapers "wegen des Lokaltons" (for the sake of the local tone), as he put it in an 1878 letter.[30] The novel is intent on reproducing a certain attitude and rhetorical bearing that was especially prominent in Prussia in the early nineteenth century and then on showing how that tone contributes to a societal calamity.

The diagnosis for which Schach provides a key symptom is clear: when cultures are overtaken by unreliable and ineffectual forms of communication, they face the possibility of military and political decline. Matthew D'Ancona, explaining the erosion of trust in post-truth culture, writes that "all successful societies rely upon a relatively high degree of honesty to preserve order, uphold the law, hold the powerful to account and generate prosperity."[31] But when social discourse is dominated by empty, unreliable modes of speaking, this leads to a low degree of honesty and credibility, trust collapses, and society cannot function effectively. Bülow writes similarly of the Ming Dynasty, "Eine Stunde später war ein Reich zertrümmert und ein Thron gestürzt. Und warum? Weil alles Geschraubte zur Lüge führt und alle Lüge zum Tod" (6:155, An hour later an empire was in ruins and its monarchy dethroned. And why? Because every pose leads to a lie and every lie to death, 188). This passage expresses a strong hypothesis about language and history. Why was an empire laid to waste? The answer to this question follows Fontane's established pathway of linguistic and cultural change from affectation to deception to death.

The process begins with stilted, affected speech, one of the objects of Botho's disdain in *Irrungen, Wirrungen* when he wants to turn his back on sophisticated salon culture. Recall that in that novel "das Geschraubte" described a mode of social interaction that was forced, affected, and artificial. What follows in Bülow's critique is the truly critical piece of the argument—namely, the claim of a slippery slope, or of a contagion from one rhetorical sphere to another. It might be harmless enough to tolerate affected, artificial communication in certain contained social settings. But Bülow's point, which is essentially the novel's point as well, is that such containment is impossible. The disingenuous use of language will find its way into settings where it is not at all harmless, settings where one must act on the assumption of

---

[29] Fontane, August 11, 1878, *Der Dichter über sein Werk*, 2:293.
[30] Fontane, October 5, 1878, *Der Dichter über sein Werk*, 2:293. On Fontane as a media compiler who assembled his novels from contemporaneous sources, see Petra McGillen, *The Fontane Workshop: Manufacturing Realism in the Industrial Age of Print* (New York: Bloomsbury, 2019).
[31] D'Ancona, *Post-Truth*, 36.

accurate, straightforward language. Peter Pfeiffer offers one example of such a contagion with the prince's categorization of beauty, including the *beauté du diable* that he attributes to Victoire (6:68). On Pfeiffer's reading, the novels shows, "how the men's aestheticizing system of description and thus control destroys itself when it is no longer a pure language game but is rather applied to the reality of social life."[32] For the sake of their amusement and conversation, it does not really matter whether these men actually find Victoire attractive according to the prince's abstract system of beauty. But once Schach acts out that premise and realizes it in deed, this affected bit of philosophizing turns into a harmful deception.

Bülow does not mince words when he asserts that affected speech leads to lies. The difference between affectation and prevarication is that the latter occurs under the expectation of accurate, dependable language. Contracts, formal agreements, treaties, political negotiations—all these situations depend on the accuracy and reliability of the parties' language. They cannot operate in the absence of trust and good faith—hence the need for honor, oaths, and vows to guarantee the efficacy of language. But the argument of rhetorical contagion says that a society that spends its free time speaking in artificial, unreliable ways will find it hard to return to an unadorned language of honesty, even when it matters most. This is the situation in which Prussia finds itself in 1806, which Franzel describes as "a time of crisis, in which most contemporaries are blind to the impending catastrophe."[33] Like Schach after impregnating Victoire, like the Ming Dynasty in its final hours, Prussian society finds it impossible to speak forthrightly, in this case about its military prospects and its position vis-à-vis France. In post-factual fashion, it continues to lie to itself through a series of empty phrases about loyalty, superiority, and exceptionalism.

Bülow's final point is that this discrepancy between words and truth, this departure from a reliable language of realism, leads to death. To continue linking Schach's personal situation to the political situation, Prussia will continue deceiving itself and those around it right up to the point that it commits suicide. The way one speaks and one's relationship to language thus represent important political acts, and not just for figures such as Haugwitz, Napoleon, or Frederick Wilhelm III. The historical analogy makes clear that the accuracy of the underlings' language, the speech of anonymous messengers and emissaries, is just as important to the state's survival as that of the emperor. Agamben's

---

[32] Peter Pfeiffer, "Tod, Entstellung, Häßlichkeit: Fontanes *Schach von Wuthenow*," *Zeitschrift für deutsche Philologie* 113, no. 2 (1994): 270.
[33] Franzel, "Alles ist eitel," 61.

archaeology of the oath argues that the connection between words and things is not simply cognitive; it is also an ethical and political connection. For the human being constituted in language, "decisive is the problem of the efficacy and truthfulness of his word, that is, of what can guarantee the original connection between names and things, and between the subject who has become a speaker—and, thus capable of asserting and promising—and his actions." Attempts to articulate speech and actions do not present only cognitive challenges; they "above all pose problems of an ethical and political order."[34] It is this ethical aspect of the subject's relationship to language that Fontane's novel pursues on both a personal and political level.

Because modes of communication have the power to shape politics and the historical course of nations, it would be politically expedient for the officer corps and the educated classes—all those who set the tone in Prussian society—to reclaim a more serious and dependable form of language. They should reintroduce a true sense of honor, one based on *honnêteté* and the integrity of one's language. If only it were fashionable to say what you mean and to mean what you say, Prussia might not find itself in such dire straits. Of course, Schach's suicide indicates that it is likely too late to choose a different course, a different relationship to language and truth, at least for Prussia in 1806. But the novel suggests that the way one speaks is indeed a choice, not a side effect of historical change, and that the wrong choices can lead down a slope of decadence to ruin.[35] The novel's concluding letter, from Victoire to Lisette, is dated August, 1807—well after French troops have marched into Berlin—and thus includes that ruination within its narrative scope. In a letter that Victoire describes as "mein Bekenntnis" (6:157, a frank account of my views [my avowal], 191), she speaks directly of the misery and casualties of war.

Bülow's letter casts Prussia's predicament in terms of truth and lies, life and death. The parallel dichotomies point to an aesthetic dimension as well, for Fontane's programmatic statements about the nature of literary realism employ a similar vocabulary. In that key passage from 1853, he writes that realism wants "das *Wahre*" (what is *true*), that it eschews "die Lüge" (*NA* 21.1:13, the lie). The lie, the empty promise epitomized by Schach, the oath given in bad faith—all these are antithetical to

---

[34] Agamben, *Sacrament of Language*, 68.
[35] Neumann, examining Fontane's depiction of Prussian society and its manner of speaking, touches on the theme of decadence in *Schach von Wuthenow*. Gerhard Neumann, "Das Ritual der Mahlzeit und die realistische Literatur. Ein Beitrag zu Fontanes Romankunst," in *Das schwierige neunzehnte Jahrhundert*, ed. Jürgen Barkhoff, Gilbert Carr, and Roger Paulin (Tübingen: Max Niemeyer, 2000), 305–7.

realism and its reliable connection of words to referents. What Bülow presents as an inevitable decline—artifice–falsehood–death—Fontane casts rather as a fork in the road. One can choose the path of truth, honesty, and realism, or that of prevarication and uncertainty, and *Schach von Wuthenow* demonstrates where one of those paths leads.

Fontane, commenting on the return to realism, furthermore writes, "Der unnatürlichen Geschraubtheit *Gottscheds* mußte, nach einem ewigen Gesetz, der schöne, noch unerreicht gebliebene Realismus *Lessings* folgen" (*NA* 21.1:9, According to an eternal law, *Gottsched's* unnatural affectation had to be followed by *Lessing's* unrivaled realism). For Fontane, the word "Geschraubtheit" thus denotes not only a decadent style of speech in Prussian Berlin or the Ming Dynasty, but also the literary style to which his conception of realism opposes itself. Fontane underscores the sense of artificiality by describing Gottsched's affected style as "unnatural." It makes sense that he would define both a manner of speaking and a literary style with the same terms, for they share something fundamental in common. From Fontane's perspective, both have turned away from honest, unadorned, dependable communication. Both have become unhealthy. The depiction of bad literary sensibility could just as easily apply to some of the more extreme examples of unserious communication in Fontane's novels. The reason for this similarity is clear: Fontane's novels stage the conflict between falsehood and truth, irony and avowal, and play out the effects of this tension in various registers. The roman à clef aspect of Fontane's society novels is not just connecting his fictional characters to contemporaneous newspaper reports but rather connecting them to aesthetic and rhetorical positions that Fontane aims to juxtapose. Pfeiffer notes, for example, that Schach's aestheticism—his concern with surface and social image—stands "in opposition to the poetological premises of realism."[36] Because Schach privileges appearance over essence, because he willingly deploys words and phrases that turn out to be empty, he stands in opposition to what Fontane would characterize as the truthfulness and sincerity of realism.

For all the pessimism of *Schach von Wuthenow*, Fontane's pronouncements in 1853 are much more optimistic about the return to responsible language. He portrays his current age of realism as "eine Periode ehrlichen Gefühls und gesunden Menchenverstandes" (*NA* 21.1:9, a period of honest feeling and healthy common sense). The passage's modifiers link honesty and health, a connection that accords with Fontane's broader discourse of rhetorical decadence, illness, and contagion—with certain extreme examples such as Schach manifesting as symptoms of a

---

[36] Pfeiffer, "Tod, Entstellung, Häßlichkeit," 268.

deep-running disease. In fact, he casts the return to realism here as "die Wiedergenesung eines Kranken" (NA 21.1:9, the recuperation of a sick patient). In the realm of literature, at least, the prognosis is good. The disease of unhealthy, unreliable language is curable. But even if realism has eradicated the prevaricating, unhealthy impulse from literary language, it is far less clear how one could stamp out the same impulse in society at large.

Fontane can proclaim confidently in 1853 that his contemporary age is an era of unqualified realism (NA 21.1:7). The later novels from the 1870s and 1880s suggest a far more doubtful outlook. These works fret that, literary victories notwithstanding, it might be impossible to get the genie of urbane dissimulation back in the bottle. They acknowledge the possibility that literature might not be the standard bearer for a new era of realism. It is just as possible that realist literature will prove to be an outlier, the last facet of cultural life that insists on honesty and fidelity when the rest of the world propagates a post-truth style of hollow phrases and ironic artifice. *Schach von Wuthenow* casts the decadence of language in terms remarkably similar to those of Fontane's 1853 essay. The difference, however, is that the novel does not cast that relationship to language as a temporary perversion, as a rhetorical winter about to give way to the rejuvenating spring of common-sense realism. The novel gives us no comforting sense of cyclicality, no eternal law of a pendulum swinging between opposed poles. What we get instead is a bleak scene of cultural entropy and decline, one in which the rhetorical choices of innumerable individuals add up to a society that lets tone take precedence over truth.

Three Graf Petöfy and the Empty Vow

He was such a laugher, such an ironist, such an artist of unseriousness, that he didn't even recognize what was happening to him: he, too, was starting to cry.[1]

—Jonathan Franzen

Graf Petöfy (1884) seems to receive less critical attention than Fontane's other novels of society or adultery. Without drawing on quantitative evidence for support, one can still claim with a reasonable degree of confidence that commentators remain more occupied with the stories of broken relationships in *Irrungen, Wirrungen*, *Effi Briest*, or *Frau Jenny Treibel*. The less-robust critical reception has been attributed to various perceived shortcomings. Some claim that Fontane was not familiar enough with the Hungarian context to integrate it successfully into the novel; others fault the plot for running along entirely predictable lines.[2] The novel's predictability is beyond dispute, but this is surely by design, as Fontane's works typically avoid anything that smacks of suspense or sensationalism. Lene predicts that the relationship with Botho won't last, and it doesn't; Effi's parents fret that she'll get bored with Innstetten, and she does. In this case, Graf Adam Petöfy, a 70-year-old Austro-Hungarian count and theater enthusiast, wants to marry Franziska Franz, a 25-year-old Prussian Protestant actress. Friends and family discourage the union, pointing out all the

---

[1] Jonathan Franzen, *Purity* (New York: Bond Street Books, 2015), 95.
[2] On the reasons for *Graf Petöfy*'s second-tier status in the critical literature, see, for example, Detlef Haberland, "Theodor Fontanes Roman *Graf Petöfy*—ein 'ungarisches' Drama?" *Zeitschrift für mitteleuropäische Germanistik* 4, no. 2 (2014): 108, 110; Paul Irving Anderson, "Austro-Hungarian Camouflage: Theodor Fontane's *Graf Petöfy*," *Seminar* 47, no. 3 (2011): 324–5; and Maja Razbojnikova-Frateva, *Jeder ist seines Unglücks Schmied. Männer und Männlichkeiten in Werken Theodor Fontanes* (Berlin: Frank & Timme, 2012), 210–11.

reasons—differences in age, class, religion, and culture—that it is likely to end badly. Advice from all sides is ignored; they marry; it ends badly. When Franziska falls in love with the count's nephew, Graf Egon, her husband learns of their relationship and takes his own life.

So, yes, the plot follows fairly predictable lines. As is so often the case in Fontane, the bad outcome foretold in the novel's beginning comes to pass by the novel's end. I submit, though, that *Graf Petöfy* is not after an insight as banal as "age difference can make a marriage more difficult," and that we can better isolate the novel's most significant dynamic when we approach it from the perspective of unreliable language, empty promises, and infidelity to one's word. In this sense, we can take *Graf Petöfy* as a companion volume or follow-up to *Schach von Wuthenow*, which appeared as a book in 1883, just one year before the publication of *Graf Petöfy*. If *Schach* explores the ethical and political dilemma of the inadequation of speech and actions in an "age of the eclipse of the oath,"[3] *Graf Petöfy* proposes a radical but flawed solution to that dilemma—namely, to empty the vow, promise, or oath of any content or obligatory force.[4]

To be clear: all the concerns about the count's age and the actress's youth boil down to one caveat, the likelihood of marital infidelity. She is young, pretty, and charming, and she is not sexually attracted to a septuagenarian count. The novel thus uses age differences to create a situation in which there is a significant possibility that Franziska will break her marriage vow, will betray the Graf, and will take another lover. None of that, in and of itself, is particularly interesting. What is interesting, rather, is how the characters fully expect Franziska's vow to be broken, her words to be unreliable, and her actions to deviate from what she swears to in the sacrament of marriage. Petöfy is not naïve; he proposes the marital union with his eyes open to all these possibilities. The particularly interesting aspect is how the novel depicts the anticipation of a broken vow and the implementation of an unconventional solution. That experimental solution is to tolerate discrepancy and infidelity by asking only for an empty vow. Petöfy aims to craft a marriage contract that is blank, with a vow that cannot be broken because it is inherently ruptured in advance. If promises in a post-truth age are hollow, then one way to countenance and shield oneself from the risk of

---

[3] Agamben, *Sacrament of Language*, 71.
[4] Vows and oaths are not identical. They are sometimes differentiated according to purpose: oaths can be assertative, whereas vows are typically oriented toward future performance. Oaths also tend to appeal to a higher authority, such as a god or monarch. In the Catholic sacrament of matrimony, however, the vow and the oath have much in common. I focus on the overlap between oaths and vows in order to draw out the similarities to Petöfy's oath of service to the Kaiser.

betrayal is to allow for a hollow promise. Petöfy thus proposes to Franziska by making clear that her vow by itself will suffice; her words will not obligate her to fidelity. All that he requires is discretion, the maintenance of appearances, such that she does not flaunt the gap between oath and action.[5]

The novel retains an element of unpredictability by letting the characters initiate a marriage that is ironic in the sense that it is only half serious and is marked by the freedom to deviate from the obligations that an oath would otherwise entail. It implements this alternative response to unreliable language as a kind of experiment, and the results show that anticipating and tolerating verbal infidelity by means of an empty vow is really no solution at all. A lighthearted attitude of ironic detachment and cynicism plays well at the count's gala parties, but *Graf Petöfy* shows how quickly ironic detachment crumples when confronted with matters of real import. It seeks out the boundaries beyond which irony no longer functions and situations in which even the most committed ironist yearns for sincerity and authenticity. The idea that one is sophisticated enough to do without sincerity entirely is a dangerous self-delusion. Petöfy's ironic, cynical marriage of convenience evinces an element of naiveté when it turns out to be more earnest than he ever could have anticipated. He believes that detachment and discretion will see him through, but, as Fontane puts it in a summarizing note to his wife, "*an diesem Rechenfehler geht er zu Grunde*"[6] (*this miscalculation is what does him in*). Fontane describes his protagonist's undoing as a miscalculation, and I seek to demonstrate in what follows that the error has to do primarily with misjudging the efficacy of an empty vow as a prophylactic measure against unreliable language. The effort to tolerate and simultaneously contain the discrepancy between word and deed proves to be unsustainable.

The character of Franziska Franz extends Fontane's fundamental interest in how people speak and the ethical implications of their relationship to language. The novel goes out of its way to portray Franziska as a skilled narrator and conversationalist, as the master of a particular style of speech. Indeed, her renown as a storyteller serves as the basis of her attractiveness to Petöfy (7:192). When he explains to his sister Judith his reasons for pursuing the marriage, Petöfy insists that what he really wants is someone to talk away his boredom and to fill the void of his

---

[5] On discretion as a mode of social interaction, see Ulrike Vedder's "Ringe, Glocken, Tränen. Theatralität und Diskretion in Theodor Fontanes Roman *Graf Petöfy*," in *Herausforderungen des Realismus: Theodor Fontanes Gesellschaftsromane*, ed. Peter Uwe Hohendahl and Ulrike Vedder (Freiburg: Rombach, 2018), 85–105.

[6] Fontane, June 15, 1883 (original emphasis), *Der Dichter über sein Werk*, 3:322.

later years with entertaining language. From his perspective, Franziska is ideally suited to the position because "das kann Niemand besser als sie. Sie [...] übt die Kunst der Erzählung und Causerie wie keine Zweite" (7:84, no one can do that better than she can. She practices the art of storytelling and causerie like none other). Petöfy envisions a marriage that will consist solely—for he lists no further requirements—of conversation, chitchat, and idle talk.

His conception of a workable marriage revives a familiar topic in Fontane's society novels—the question of whether unserious banter provides a tenable basis for human relationships. The French term "causerie"—"chatting" or, in German, "Plauderei"—implies a lack of seriousness or depth. This is why later in the novel Franziska, now as the Countess Petöfy, will refer to it as "die bloße Causerie" (7:133, mere causerie) and claim decisively that it does not suffice for a satisfying life. Other novels such as *Irrungen, Wirrungen* suggest too that amusing banter alone is not up to the task of rounding out human life. Recall how Botho finds something lacking in his wife's steady stream of quips and jokes and yearns for something more natural, authentic, and sincere. Petöfy wants to marry because of an existential void that he feels more acutely in old age. But he sets out to fill that emptiness with conversation that is itself essentially empty, since he imagines it operating in the absence of any underlying essence of love and intimacy. Fontane shows through Petöfy's marriage that empty rhetoric and an empty vow can only compound the existential emptiness that they mean to counteract.

Fontane's novels so often focus on how people talk, and the point here is that Petöfy is drawn to Franziska precisely for her conversational talent, a talent that the narrative takes pains to capture.[7] The narrator as well as the other characters portray her as a charming, ideal conversationalist, a view that the novel reinforces by giving over so much space to her entertaining anecdotes about her hometown, her childhood, and her impressions of Hungary. The narrative voice speaks positively of "den leichten Ton ihres [...] Geplauders" (7:21, the light tone of her chatting), while the participants in Judith's salon circle unanimously find her to be "charmant," "pointirt," and "klug" (7:28, charming, pointed, smart). In sum, the narrative presents a glowing portrait of Franiska as a gifted conversationalist, an actress

---

[7] Petra Kabus's afterword to the *GBA* edition of *Graf Petöfy* notes of Franziska that "her narrative talent" and "her conversational talent" are what captivate the count (7:237–8).

who, even under the bright lights of aristocratic social scrutiny, can play her role and deliver her lines with aplomb.[8]

Although the novel attends carefully to Franziska's conversational skill and manner of speaking, it is worth pointing out that it never lays the consequences of unreliable language at her feet.[9] She is not excessively unserious like Käthe in *Irrungen, Wirrungen*, nor mortifying like van der Straaten in *L'Adultera*, nor relentlessly flippant like Ebba in *Unwiederbringlich*. Rather, the attention to her conversational and especially *narrative* talents locates her closer to a rhetorical ideal to which Fontane might have aspired in his own social life. I see *Graf Petöfy* as the first of Fontane's novels in which the issue of empty language and unfulfilled vows gets shifted away from the individual and depicted in more situational or structural terms. Unlike the negative rhetorical portraits mentioned above, where the individual makes a conscious choice to speak in affected and off-putting ways, unlike Schach, who chooses to make promises he has no intention to fulfill, Franziska appears sympathetically as someone whose sacred word is likely to be broken through little fault of her own. In fact, shortly before his suicide, Petöfy attributes her infidelity to "den natürlichen Gang der Dinge" (7:210, the natural course of things). Fontane will further develop this theme of transgression without blame—and present it with unparalleled finesse in the late novel *Effi Briest*—but it makes its first appearance here in *Graf Petöfy*, in the guise of a vow so likely to be broken that it is better left empty in the first place.[10]

The novel's characters recognize that the proposed marriage will be predicated on nothing but conversation and talk. When Petöfy meets with Franziska to finalize the arrangement, the first thing she brings up is his "Vertrauen zu meinen Erzählungskünsten" (trust in my narrative talents). She characterizes the nature of his proposal, saying that what he really wants is "eine Märchenerzählerin, eine Redefrau" (a fairy-tale teller, a conversational partner), someone like Scheherazade, or even more bluntly "eine Plaudertasche" (7:90, a chatterbox). The allusion to Scheherazade and fairy tales suggests that the talk he seeks could be

---

[8] Liebrand writes that Petöfy wants Franziska "ostensibly as a wife but actually as an actress and entertainer." Claudia Liebrand, *Das Ich und die andern: Fontanes Figuren und ihre Selbstbilder* (Freiburg: Rombach, 1990), 100. See further Vedder, who emphasizes the theatricality inherent in this arrangement and argues that it allows for a self-reflexive realism. Vedder, "Ringe, Glocken, Tränen," 90.

[9] See again Fontane's letter to his wife of June 15, 1883, in which he describes how he tries to reflect subtle fluctuations in Franziska's manner of speaking, depending on her audience. Fontane, *Der Dichter über sein Werk*, 3:322.

[10] Kabus's afterword outlines several parallels between *Graf Petöfy* and *Effi Briest* (7:241–3).

entirely detached from any corresponding reality, while the reference to his desire for a "chatterbox" suggests that he simply wants someone who can generate language, regardless of its content, to such an extent that his ideal spouse would exist exclusively in the form of conversation—as evidenced by the impossible-to-translate word "Redefrau," a discursively constituted woman. It is odd that Petöfy initially disputes this characterization of the marriage he desires, since the terms Franziska uses are essentially the same ones Petöfy used when describing it to Judith. But I believe that what he objects to is the idea that, for him, any form of language will do to pass the time. What he really wants is a particular, perfected tone, one that is clever, insouciant, and amusing without tipping into excess and absurdity. He explains, "Ich […] liebe Licht und Lachen und Esprit und Witz. Das ist Alles, und nur darauf bin ich aus" (7:91, I love light and laughter and esprit and wit. That's all, and that's all I'm after). Petöfy means to narrow the field of his expectations, but with the stipulations of humor and quick wit, he also narrows the sort of conversation he seeks to a particular idiom and manner of speaking. He wants to be surrounded by the Sanssouci tone that Fontane identifies as a precursor to the distinctive Berlin idiom. Fontane's essay on the *Berlinertum* explains that late in the eighteenth century, during Frederick the Great's reign, the upper classes acquired a cosmopolitan, literary esprit and became "Repräsentanten des Witzes, der Pointe, der Antithese" (*NA* 19:748, representatives of wit, pointe, and antithesis). Petöfy is attracted to that pointed, witty style of speech, and Franziska, a Prussian-born actress, is well suited to deliver it. It is telling that, when she responds, "mit Geflissentlichkeit einen halb scherzhaften Ton anschlagend" (7:91, deliberately striking a half-facetious tone), she forgoes earnestness for a tongue-in-cheek disquisition on gender differences. Her reply thus adopts and performs exactly the lighthearted, clever conversational tone that Petöfy desires.

Their marriage then will base itself on mere causerie, on conversations made up of language that need not be serious, nor tethered to an external reality. The production of talk, in and of itself, will suffice. It is fitting that the couple will consecrate a union of superficial chatter with a marital arrangement or vow that is itself superficial, even empty, mere words without ensuing deeds. For when Petöfy explains his designs to Judith, she cautions that he will be purchasing his happiness at the price of Franziska's. Her point returns to the issue of age difference: Franziska is young and will naturally be attracted to people her own age. Locking her into a promise of fidelity and marital monogamy with a much older man would take away her independence and happiness, and moreover (she leaves this bit unsaid) it is a vow that the young bride would struggle to uphold over time. Countenancing the potential for broken words and betrayal, Petöfy proposes to obviate the issue of infidelity with an unconventional arrangement. He envisions a relationship, "das sich auf vollkommener Freiheit aufbaut, ein Ehepakt, der statt der Verklausulirungsparagraphen ein einziges weißes Blatt hat. Carte blanche" (7:85, established on absolute freedom, a marriage pact that has, instead of paragraphs of intricate clauses, a single white page. Carte blanche). It is of course fair to wonder what the point is of a contract that lacks any statement of obligation or promise of performance. A marriage is typically predicated on fidelity and monogamy, so to remove that predicate empties it of a primary thing that differentiates it from other relationships. Ulrike Vedder puts a somewhat finer point on the issue, writing that Petöfy wants sociable companionship, "while sexuality is obviously not a part of it."[11] The key point from my perspective, though, is not that Petöfy proposes a sexless marriage, but rather that he attempts to anticipate and tolerate the non-correspondence of word and deed, to fold that very discrepancy into a ritual designed to guarantee the credibility of fidelity.

Despite Petöfy's vision of a hollow relationship, devoid of the obligation of fidelity, when he and Franziska marry in Vienna, they nonetheless go through a Catholic rite of marriage. In the Catholic Church, the celebration of matrimony requires the bride and groom to respond affirmatively to a series of questions, and these affirmations function as the vows or oaths of matrimony. Affirmations such as "I take you to be my wife" or "I do" constitute the crucial enunciation of matrimonial consent, by means of which the marriage is formed.[12] The participants in the rite of marriage give themselves to one another and vow to maintain lifelong fidelity. The declaration of marital consent is thus a speech act whose performative force is intended "to guarantee the truth and trustworthiness of the *logos*."[13] In other words, the wedding vow is not simply a denotative statement of love and honor. It is, rather, a form of veridiction, through which, as Agamben (following Foucault) writes, the subject "puts itself in play as such by linking itself performatively to the truth of its own affirmation."[14] By promising "inviolable fidelity," the "I" of the "I do" binds itself to its vow and reconstitutes itself through its obligation to act in accordance with its promise.[15] So essential is this vow to the religious institution of marriage that Catholics call

---

[11] Vedder, "Ringe, Glocken, Tränen," 91.
[12] *Catechism of the Catholic Church*, 1627.
[13] Agamben, *Sacrament of Language*, 59.
[14] Agamben, *Sacrament of Language*, 57.
[15] *Catechism of the Catholic Church*, 1646. Although see again Austin on promises made in bad faith, without the intent to fulfill them. Austin, *How to Do Things with Words*, 40.

the union it seals "the matrimonial covenant" and recognize it as a sacrament because they believe it to reflect God's fidelity to his covenant and Christ's relationship to the Church.[16]

This essential vow of fidelity, *Treue*, or *fides*, however, is precisely the one from which Franziska has been released in advance. Petöfy has already indicated that he would not object to her having lovers, or at least suitors: "es würde mich glücklich machen, sie von unseren besten Kavalieren umworben zu sehen" (7:86, it would make me happy to see her courted by our best gentlemen). Herein lies the essential emptiness of the vow of fidelity. Although Franziska has vowed her faithfulness to the count, she is not expected to uphold that vow through her actions. Agamben writes, "In order for something like an oath to be able to take place, it is necessary, in fact, to be able above all [...] to articulate together in some way, life and language, actions and words."[17] And yet Petöfy aims for the exact opposite, for the disarticulation of life and language, and for actions unencumbered by promissory words. It is a disconnect that "makes marriage vows/As false as dicers' oaths," to borrow words from Hamlet.[18] Fontane's novel indicates that, over the long run, such an arrangement is untenable and unsustainable. Petöfy reflects a society that believes it can operate comfortably with a high degree of detachment, discrepancy, and disarticulation. It is a society that believes it can do without reliable, efficacious language, but the novel reveals that tolerance to be a grave miscalculation.

Although Petöfy abrogates Franziska's obligation of fidelity, it turns out that their marital agreement is not entirely blank. He insists on one stipulation—namely, that she maintain discretion and propriety, that she not flout her vows in an open, humiliating way. What he wants is "Decorum. Nichts weiter. [...] Diskretion also, Decorum, Dehors" (7:86, Decorum. Nothing more. So discretion, decorum, appearances). The last term, *dehors*, proves crucial for Petöfy's expectations. It refers to outward appearance, to *Schein* as opposed to *Sein*, used here in the sense of maintaining the appearance of conformity to what is socially acceptable. Petöfy thus waives the obligation of fidelity, but he demands that his future wife maintain via discretion a façade of fidelity and monogamy. From the very beginning, he proposes a marriage constituted over a discrepancy between phenomenon and essence, as one finds in irony. As long as the outward phenomenon of fidelity is preserved, the

---

[16] *Catechism of the Catholic Church*, 1661.
[17] Agamben, *Sacrament of Language*, 69.
[18] William Shakespeare, "Hamlet, Prince of Denmark," in *The Complete Works of Shakespeare*, ed. David Bevington (New York: HarperCollins, 1992), 1096 (III.4, 45–6).

essence of their marriage can be anything but undying faithfulness.[19] Petöfy thus asks only for the empty shell of a vow, for words without corresponding deeds. He comes to grips with the unreliability of promissory language by building the premonition of betrayal into the vow itself—which actually entails hollowing out the vow and the ensuing relationship.

The empty vow is a fitting corollary for a society that finds itself in a post-truth condition. As noted in the introduction, Petöfy himself evinces a post-truth skepticism. When Judith appeals to the importance of truth, he responds derisively: "Ach, die Wahrheit? Glaube mir, Judith, die Welt bleibt ewig in der alten Pilatusfrage stecken" (7:200, Oh, the truth? Believe me, Judith, the world is forever mired in Pilate's old question). In context, Petöfy's point is that the truth cannot really matter because there is no consensus on what is true. He attacks Judith's notion of fixed, eternal truth with a Nietzschean, perspectivist version in which "truth" is the result of continual debate and negotiation.[20] Fontane thus depicts a world in which it is easy to dismiss truth as a quaint, outdated conceit. At the same time, he also asserts an ethical and indeed political dimension to the connection between language and the world, as well as to the subject's relationship to language. The danger of a thoroughgoing, post-truth skepticism is that it breaks (or at least radically loosens) those bonds. Instead of practicing an ethics of efficacy and credibility, the speaking subject now has no expectation that language will be reliable, that oaths will be upheld, and that words will be matched by actions. In this environment, the proliferation of haphazard words, hollow promises, and empty vows is a predictable development.

One sees something similar when the Oeslau outing passes through a fairground, and they come upon a fortune teller's tent promising, for the low, low price of fifty Kreuzer, the "Einzige Verkündigung der Wahrheit" (7:57, sole annunciation of the truth). There is a post-truth aspect to this moment—the ironic assertion that the only place one can hear the truth pronounced is at a shabby regional amusement park. The knowability and pronounceability of truth have been transformed into a cheap carnival act, an entertainment commodity worth nothing more than a few coins and undertaken with an ironic wink. Although

---

[19] Hence Michael White's reference to "an artificial marriage." White, *Space*, 84. Grawe also notes that Petöfy's characterization of the French as "a people of the theater" functions well as a self-portrait. They value style over substance, phenomenon over essence. Grawe, "*Graf Petöfy*. Roman," in *Fontane-Handbuch*, ed. Christian Grawe and Helmuth Nürnberger (Stuttgart: Kröner, 2000), 551.

[20] Ferraris, "Was ist der Neue Realismus?" 55.

Phemi's interest in the fortune teller is obviously ironic, not earnest, Franziska takes it quite seriously and refuses to let her go in. She objects to the cheapening or commodification of truth and especially to "die Neugier, die nicht einmal ernsthaft gemeint ist" (7:58, curiosity that is not even earnestly meant). A merely ironic curiosity serves to ironize and thus diminish the notion of truth and violates the ethical connection between language and the world. This is why, when Egon asks whether such feigned curiosity is permissible when it is carried out in jest or as a game, she still opposes it. She explains her opposition, saying, "Denn es ist ein Spiel mit Dingen, die nicht zum Spielen da sind" (7:58, For it is a game with things that aren't there for playing). It is important that the fortune teller has billed herself as the "sole annunciation of the truth," for the ability to speak truth through language, to link words and future actions, is what Franziska wants to preserve as serious and earnest. It is essential that there remains a space within language reserved for earnestness and truth-telling, and she wants to prevent that space from being enfolded in a flippant, unserious, ironic relationship to language and truth. Her efforts are in vain, though, since her marriage to Petöfy will do exactly that, turning the vow of fidelity and the credibility of language into a mere plaything that need not be taken seriously.

There are several ways in which the novel's imagery draws attention to the discrepancy between appearance and reality that underlies their relationship, as well as to a covenant that is broken in the very moment that the couple enters into it.[21] The bells of Castle Arpa constitute one of the novel's most prominent motifs. One of the bells cracks at the moment of Franziska's arrival; it gets repaired but does not ring again until Petöfy's burial back in Hungary at the novel's conclusion. The image of the broken bell practically begs to be interpreted as a forward-looking omen, portending a broken vow and a broken marriage. The plausibility of that tenor is only reinforced by the bell's return upon the count's burial: it cannot ring again until "death do us part" releases Franziska from the vow that she could not uphold. The narrative certainly pushes the reader to see the bell as an image of something broken both within Franziska and within her relationship to the count. When Father Feßler reassures Judith, for example, that Franziska would not be such a bad match for the count, he writes that "die Seele der jungen Dame [ist] von einer Legirung, aus der eine Glocke werden kann, die

---

[21] On the discrepancy between appearance and reality as a figure for the marriage, see White's nice reading of the fairground scene and its inherent theatricality, as well as of the Hungarian toponyms that sound exotic but are actually mundane. White, *Space*, 88–90.

klingt" (7:71, the young lady's soul is of an alloy that can produce a bell that rings). And when one of the bells promptly *stops* ringing upon her arrival as a new bride, Franziska wants to interpret it along similar lines, symbolically and ominously, as pointing toward a personal flaw and a tragic outcome.

Hannah, however, puts an end to the game of reading portents, assuring her that the bell was already cracked before she arrived. Hannah's anodyne explanation is meant to console Franziska, but focusing on the empty vow and the unconventional marriage arrangement allows us to read Hannah's explanation against the grain. She tells Franziska, in essence, not to worry because the broken bell is not an omen that points toward a future misstep or bad outcome. In fact, its brokenness points backward to a preexisting structural flaw, or, to borrow Feßler's words, to a flawed alloy, such that the bell cannot ring as intended. To put it plainly, the bell was already broken, just as the vow of fidelity was already inherently broken before their marriage had even begun. The crack in the bell's frame reflects a preexisting structural flaw in the marriage arrangement and, more specifically, a gap or fissure that has been opened between word and deed. Finally, Hannah takes her backward-looking interpretation and gives it a forward-looking twist. The flaws may have been there all along, but it is the newlyweds' arrival in Arpa that will now bring everything flawed and broken to light. Her words of solace predict the novel's subsequent course of events with unintended prescience. The structural flaw in their relationship and in Petöfy's calculations will indeed come to the fore during their time in Arpa, even if its consequences will not be fully revealed until they are back in Vienna. Other fissures come to light too. Petöfy presents himself as someone unconcerned with sincere affection or actual monogamy, but over the course of the novel, cracks appear in his façade of ironic detachment.

A final point on the broken bell: Feßler has compared Franziska's soul to a high-quality alloy, but of course an alloy is not a single metal but rather a compound mixture. In the context of considering a possible marriage match, it presents a mixed metaphor. Franziska, by herself, cannot be a good or bad alloy; the alloy comes about only when two things are melted into one another and joined together as one, as when tin and copper are joined together to form bronze, or when husband and wife are joined in matrimony. Moreover, the German term for alloy that Feßler uses derives from the Latin verb *ligare*, meaning to tie, bind, or unite. Feßler's statement ostensibly pertains to Franziska and her unique, individual soul, but one hears a perhaps unintended suggestion that the metaphor of the ringing bell refers not to the quality of an individual but rather to the quality and soundness of the union (the alloy) that underlies its construction. And when the bell then fails to ring as Feßler predicts, the flaw rests not with Franziska's individual faults but rather with a faulty union, one that allowed too much space and freedom for two things to be joined in an enduring bond. The broken bell thus represents the vow that is already broken by design.

The issue of a hollowed-out vow provides the lynchpin that connects the characters' personal outcomes to the novel's historico-political background. To borrow Franziska's words, it provides "eine Brücke" (a bridge) to questions, "die wie politische Fragen aussehen und doch schließlich keine sind, sonder nur allerpersönliche Fragen und Lebensfragen dazu" (7:130, that look like political questions but ultimately aren't, that are rather highly personal questions, even vital questions). Her statement provides a roadmap for how to understand the chapter's subsequent conversations. The characters will ostensibly be talking about Hungarian history and politics, but all those conversations, as a kind of historical allegory, will at the same time evoke and pertain to their personal dynamic. It is frequently said that the personal is political, but the cited passage reverses the equation such that the political dimension reveals itself to be deeply personal. When the couple retires to Castle Arpa, much of Franziska's introduction to Hungarian politics and culture involves discussing the Hungarian Revolution of 1848–9, which occurred about twenty-five years prior to the events depicted in the story. As it turns out, the novel's portrayal of that revolt against the Austrian Empire, as well as Petöfy's relationship to it, revolves around a series of empty oaths. For example, after Franziska views a painting of Hungarian revolutionary troops and generals, Petöfy explains why those martyrs for independence were hanged: "Bloß weil sie's Ungarland mehr geliebt, als den Eid, den sie dem Kaiser geschworen" (7:132, Just because they loved Hungary more than the oath they had sworn to the Kaiser). They swore loyalty to the Kaiser, but it turns out that they loved something else more, and they violated their oath by joining the fight for Hungarian independence. It is telling that, in Petofy's view, they were executed "merely" for violating their oath, which, from the imperial perspective, entails treason and treachery. This is essentially the same sort of betrayal and broken oath that Petöfy's empty marriage arrangement means to avoid.

But the broken oath is an issue not only for long-dead Hungarian military leaders; it also plays a role in Petöfy's account of his own political pathway through the revolutionary era. Petöfy was also an officer in the Kaiser's army, but unlike the Hungarian generals who broke their oath of fidelity, he chose a different course. Anticipating an ineluctable discrepancy between his oath and his future actions—he could never take up arms to suppress Hungarian independence—he requests instead his demission, the relinquishment of the obligations to which his oath binds him.[22] He recounts what he said at the time to the Kaiser, "Ich habe [...] eh' ich Eurer Majestät schwur, Ungarn geschworen; das ist der ewige Blutschwur, den Jeder seinem Lande schwört, dem Stück Erde, darauf er geboren" (7:133, Before I swore an oath to Your Majesty, I swore one to Hungary; that is the eternal blood oath that each person swears to his country, to the piece of earth on which he was born). In order to avoid violating his oath, he asks to be released from the duties that it entails. When he foresees a divergence between word and deed, his solution is to countenance that divergence and ask that it be tolerated. In the end, Petöfy reveals how little duty and obligation he attaches to an oath. His vow to fight for the Kaiser's interests turns out to mean merely that he will not take up arms *against* the Kaiser's interests. The oath he swore to his beloved fatherland means only that he will not fight *against* his own country. In this conflict between nation and empire, in this tangle of split loyalties and allegiances, he will not do anything on behalf of either side. In neither instance does he take any positive action to fulfill his oath of loyalty and make good on the obligation of fidelity.

The themes of freedom and independence (Hungary's, Franziska's), loyalty and fidelity (Petöfy's, Franziska's), duty and betrayal (of the service oath, of the marriage vow) provide the bridge between political history and personal intimacy. Despite the dearth of commentary on this aspect of the novel, the parallels are not difficult to discern: Petöfy anticipates that the Hungarian Revolution (and his implicit blood oath) will put him in an untenable position vis-à-vis his oath of loyalty and service to the Kaiser, so he asks to be released from the obligations to which he swore. And because the Kaiser has a noble, lenient heart, he tolerates his officer's demission. In similar fashion, everyone anticipates that the marriage (and her young blood) will put Franziska in an untenable position vis-à-vis her vow of fidelity. Petöfy now takes on the role of the Kaiser and releases Franziska from the obligations that she will pledge to fulfill. On both a personal and political level, the characters grapple with the problem of "infidelity to the word one has given," and "the repudiation or disavowal of obligations one has assumed."[23] In both cases, the attempted solution is to avoid the threat of perjury or betrayal by emptying the vow of its obligations. This of course does

---

[22] Note that demission is the same price that Schach would pay if he did not uphold his promises to Frau Carayon.
[23] Agamben, *Sacrament of Language*, 6.

nothing to improve language's efficacy and reliability, nor to curb the scourge of infidelity. To accept a hollow vow is to resign oneself to unreliable language, and to let others break the referential function within promissory language such that words will no longer credibly indicate future deeds.

On the topic of neglected oaths and the Hungarian fight for independence, one should not overlook the literary allusion evoked by the novel's title and its eponym, Graf Petöfy. His name resonates with that of Sándor Petöfi, the nom de plume of the revolutionary poet who composed the Hungarian national anthem, a poem said to have helped inspire the 1848 revolt. When the secondary literature discusses the link between Petöfy and Petöfi, it tends with good reason to emphasize the incongruences between the character and the literary figure, pointing out how the poet Sándor Petöfi is too different to provide a road into a better understanding of the eponymous character and the novel's dynamic. Indeed, the two figures could hardly be more different: the young proletarian firebrand and the elderly nobleman, the patriotic martyr for the cause of Hungarian independence and the ex-patriate officer who abandons his country in its moment of need. Such differences lead Detlef Haberland to conclude that the allusion to Petöfi "actually means next to nothing for the analysis of the marital and existential problem at the novel's center." The only thing it shows is "that the current case is not a matter of 'telling names' ['sprechende Namen']."[24]

Such readings are certainly correct that Sándor Petöfi will not provide the skeleton key to unlock Fontane's novel. It would be a mistake to assume, based on the similar names, that Fontane means to refract the revolutionary literary figure of Petöfi through the mind of a septuagenarian nobleman, just as it would be another mistake to assume that the evocation of Petöfi brings out similarities that would illuminate the nature of the fictional character. The two figures are far too different for a fruitful interpretation by analogy. That lack of similarity does not mean, however, that the allusion to Petöfi has no bearing on our understanding of the novel. Rather, the allusion matters precisely because of the glaring differences between the two figures. Fontane uses the contrast between Petöfy and Petöfi to bring the emptiness of Graf Petöfy's oath to the fore. Via the revolutionary martyr, he underscores the ethical

---

[24] Haberland, "Theodor Fontanes Roman *Graf Petöfy*," 109. See also Anderson, who points out the class and ideological differences between the two figures, "Austro-Hungarian Camouflage," 325.

and political consequences of dissolving the connection between words and deeds and loosening the bonds of promissory language.

Sándor Petőfi composed the *Nemzeti dal*, the "National Song" of Hungary, a work that both grew out of and contributed to the revolutionary fervor of 1848. It is noteworthy that the most famous composition by Petőfy's literary namesake repeatedly insists on the necessity of swearing an oath. Each of its six stanzas concludes with the same vow, "By the Magyar's God above,/We truly swear,/We truly swear the tyrant's yoke/No more to bear!"[25] This is the last line of each stanza, and the repeated word "Esküszünk" in the original is typically translated into English as "we vow" or "we swear," and into German as "Schwören wir." ("Eskü" is the Hungarian word for "oath," while "esküvő," building upon the root form for taking a vow, means "wedding" or "marriage."[26]) The English and German translations of that line are furthermore consonant with the semantic field that Petőfy employs to assert his own patriotism and fidelity to his homeland—"schwur" (swore), "Ungarn geschworen" (sworn to Hungary), "Blutschwur" (blood oath), "schwört" (7:133, swears). The allusion thus resonates not only in Petőfy's name. His patriotic rhetoric evokes the most famous lines of the most famous work by the most famous poet of the Hungarian Revolution. And if the intertextual allusion here feels too far afield for some readers, recall that Franziska has been learning numerous songs from the revolutionary period, any collection of which would necessarily include the *Nemzeti dal*, and that she takes it upon herself to translate a Hungarian ballad (of infidelity and violent retribution, no less) into German. In these ways, the narrative pushes readers to consider the intertext of Hungarian revolutionary literature, and when one does, one cannot avoid the prominent theme of vows, oaths, and sworn fidelity.

Haberland dismisses the literary allusion on the grounds that Petőfy is no Petőfi, but perhaps that is exactly the point of the allusion, especially with regard to upholding one's oath. Within the context of the 1848 revolutionary era, Petőfi's sincerity and commitment to a cause stand in stark contrast to Graf Petőfy's relative aloofness. When Petőfi swears on his ancestor's god—and exhorts an entire community to do the same—his oath evinces a truthful and reliable relation to actions. He takes up arms, enters the fight for Hungarian independence, and goes missing, likely killed in action, in the Battle of Segesvár. He invokes the

---

[25] Sándor Petőfi, "National Song," in *Gems from Petőfi and Other Hungarian Poets*, trans. William Loew (New York: Paul O. D'Esterhazy, 1881), 6–7.
[26] Tamás Magay and László Országh, *Concise Hungarian-English Dictionary* (Oxford: Oxford University Press, 1990), 264.

name of god to guarantee the credibility of his oath, and he upholds that credibility with actions. Petöfy's relationship to language, to his oath, and to the cause of Hungarian independence is quite different. Although he deploys a similar rhetoric of oath and national fidelity, he never takes decisive action on behalf of his country's independence. His commitment to the cause exhausts itself in the refusal to fight against his country's cause, in the decision to go instead into exile. Petöfy gives the signifier of loyalty and commitment but not the signified, the word but not the thing itself.

Interestingly enough, Petöfi's "National Song" addresses precisely this case of the cowardly patriot who will not align word and deed, who will not make good on his solemn oath. "A miserable wretch is he,/Who fears to die my land for thee!/His worthless life who thinks to be,/More worth than thou, sweet liberty!"[27] First, these lines highlight the ultimate degree of commitment required of the patriot: in swearing an oath of fidelity to the nation, the subject puts its very existence at stake. Second, they use a word like "wretch"—another translation renders it as "villain"—to bring out the ethical dimension inherent in upholding the oath of fidelity. To disavow one's obligations constitutes not just a political betrayal but also a violation of ethical norms. This is essentially how Petöfy says he negotiated his reciprocally cancelling obligations to both Hungary and the Kaiser. He would not take a side, choosing instead to save his skin by walking away from his opposed duties and fleeing the fight.

Franziska herself perceives that Petöfy lacks constancy, that he wavers, and she finds that inconsistency reflected in his exaggerated declarations of loyalty to Hungary: "Selbst sein prononcirt ungrischer Patriotismus […] war doch schließlich nicht ganz das, wofür er ihn ausgab […]. Es ging eben ein Bruch durch sein Leben und seine Denkweise" (7:140, Even his pronounced Hungarian patriotism was, in the end, not quite what he tried to pass it off as. There was simply a fracture that ran through his life and his way of thinking). The rupture or fracture that she identifies is the cleft between his words and his actions. The term "Bruch" evokes a semantic field in German that includes related words such as *Treuebruch* (perfidy, breach of trust), *Ehebruch* (adultery), and the *Wortbruch* (breach of promise) that occurs in *Schach von Wuthenow*. We call it a *Wortbruch*, or breaking one's word, because the unfulfilled pledge disrupts the reliable connection between words and things. It is the same breach that Petöfy anticipates and builds into their marriage vows, and it is also the breach represented by the broken bell in Arpa.

---

[27] Petöfi, "National Song," 6.

This is not a case of language being inherently broken, nor an early articulation of a *Sprachkrise* ahead of Wittgenstein and Hofmannsthal. It is, rather, another instance of human behavior and deliberate infidelity to one's word undoing the ethical link between signifiers and signifieds.

In sum, the historical depiction of the Hungarian Revolution demonstrates how Petöfy produces all the expected signifiers (words, oaths, vows, promises) of service and fidelity, but he never produces the actions signified by his promissory language. As a sign without corresponding substance, he represents the erosion of credibility and the loosening bond between words and things. In a sense, that is exactly how the literary allusion of the name "Petöfy" operates in the novel. Scholars have cautioned that, while it looks like a telling name (or *sprechender Name*), the deeper one digs, the less one finds in the way of substantive correspondences. The differences only accumulate, so that the minor orthographic divergence in the semiotic field becomes a chasm of discrepancy in the semantic field. The overlap between Petöfy and Petöfi thus occurs only at the level of signification, not between the things that those names designate. By putting forward an apparent allusion that turns out not to go anywhere, the novel plays out in discourse the dissolution of the connection between language and world. The name "Petöfy" carries an implicit promise, that it alludes in some meaningful way to the poet Sándor Petöfi and that there is a significant connection between the two figures. But Fontane's novel never delivers on that promise. Instead, it crafts a Petöfy character so diametrically opposed to its namesake that it frustrates—even betrays—that hermeneutic impulse at every turn. Readers must accept the unfulfilled promise of the novel's eponym and tolerate the inadequation of name and referent.

In their opposition, Petöfi and Petöfy represent two contrasting possible outcomes—the upheld oath and the broken oath. They reflect an opposition that Agamben describes as a "double possibility inscribed" in language: oath and perjury, blessing and curse, "bene-diction and male-diction."[28] Here, the fulfilled oath is a blessing or a benediction, in the sense that one has spoken well; one has produced words that correspond to things or actions. If, in contrast, one's words are empty, if there is a discrepancy between the words and the things they signify, then it is a curse in the sense of a malediction; one has spoken badly, has spoken evil, or one is, in Petöfi's version of the curse, a miserable wretch. Graf Petöfy's central flaw in the novel is to assume that malediction is not really that *mal*, that a broken connection between words and things

---

[28] Agamben, *Sacrament of Language*, 70.

is not really a curse. In fact, when he explains his notion of a free, open marriage to Judith, he casts the concerns about vows, fidelity, monogamy, and duty as something petty with which only philistines could occupy themselves. Dismissing them as "Alltagsbegriffe" (mundane concepts) or "Feierlichkeitsbetrachtungen" (ceremonious considerations), he asserts that society's upper stratum should be exempt from the ethical strictures of narrow-minded prudery (7:85). He fails to see, however, that his unconventional arrangement disavows not only the morality of traditional marital fidelity; it disavows the very necessity of credible language.

By extending the flippancy of causerie and social banter into the realm of matrimony, Petöfy's empty vow turns the marital blessing (benediction) into a curse (malediction). Through the story's events, it becomes apparent that he has deluded himself into thinking that superficial talk and conversation would suffice to fill out his marriage, his wedding vows, and the void at the center of his existence. Franziska diagnoses that self-delusion but without yet spelling out its deleterious side-effects: "darin täuscht Du Dich, Petöfy, die bloße Causerie reicht nicht aus für unser Leben, ebensowenig wie das beste Feuilleton für eine Zeitung nicht ausreicht; es muß noch etwas Ernsthaftes hinzukommen, sonst wird das Scherzhafte bald schal und abständig" (7:133, that's where you're fooling yourself, Petöfy, mere causerie isn't enough for our life, just as even the best feuilleton isn't enough for a newspaper; there also has to be something earnest too, otherwise the playful [tone] quickly becomes vapid and withered). Franziska distills here a sentiment that one finds repeatedly in Fontane's society novels. There may be a time and a place for unserious, superficial chatter, but there is also a danger in letting that become the dominant manner of speaking. Petöfy thinks, like other of Fontane's characters, that empty talk is enough for life, and that things can always be blithe, flippant, and ironic. But Franziska delivers the counterpoint that there has to be something beyond banter and inconsequential talk. There has to be a space for earnestness and matters of consequence, in other words, for a language of avowal. Petöfy's flaw is to pretend that there is no such space and that it is a mark of sophistication to treat what is serious (love, marriage, fidelity) as if it were not, with a degree of ironic detachment.

Petöfy might be satisfied with mere causerie, but Franziska is not, and she has to look outside her marriage for the kind of fulfilling conversation that her husband does not provide. This is right about when Egon arrives in Arpa, and it is remarkable how much his manner of speaking contributes to the attraction between the two. In social settings, he and Franziska maintain a teasing, jocular banter. Their interactions conform to social expectations by being superficial and unserious, carried out merely for the sake of laughs and amusement. But when they go out riding together, the conversational tone changes. "Egon zeigte sich dann sehr anders als im Kreise daheim. Er ließ den spöttischen Ton fallen, sprach ernst und einfach und vermied Fragen, die für ihn ohnehin so gut wie beantwortet waren" (7:172, Egon presented himself very differently from in the circle at home. He dropped the ironic tone, spoke earnestly and simply and avoided questions that in any case were already as good as answered for him). Egon succeeds where others fail: he can set aside the pose of ironic, mocking banter. Just imagine if Käthe in *Irrungen, Wirrungen* were able, at least in private, to take a break from witty quips and to speak with the seriousness, simplicity, and authenticity that mark Lene's speech. She cannot, much to Botho's chagrin, but Egon can; he retains the capacity to speak earnestly and forthrightly, without irony or affectation. He thus demonstrates the possibility—lacking in her marriage to Petöfy—of a mode of speech that transcends empty talk.

It's funny, in a way: everyone predicted, with their talk of age differences and young blood, that Franziska would be unsatisfied in her marriage and would have to seek satisfaction from people her own age. Petöfy, after all, has rescinded "all possible emotional or sexual claims on Franziska."[29] They assumed that she would stray in order to satisfy sexual desire, when in fact her initial attraction to Egon grows out of a rhetorical desire. His seriousness and attentiveness appeal to her in a way that her husband's need for a constant stream of entertaining causerie never can.

Petöfy thought he could take the vow of fidelity ironically, but he gradually begins to take it more seriously than he ever thought he would. Vedder argues along similar lines that the marriage pact is unsustainable, "because Graf Petöfy, contrary to his self-image, does not stand above it all."[30] Or, as Razbojnikova-Frateva puts it, he proposes a "marriage of convention" that ultimately reveals itself to be a traditional "marriage of love."[31] Both readings identify a movement from irony to earnestness, even though they do not cast it in those terms. The façade or hollow shell of a marriage—an ironic marriage—gradually becomes earnest as an unintended consequence. Looking back at the "künstliche Situation" (artificial situation) he created, Petöfy sees its flaws: "daß wir, sie wie ich, das Leben ernsthafter zu nehmen anfingen, als es geplant war, das entscheidet nun über mich und vielleicht auch über sie" (7:215, the fact that we, she as much as I, began to take life more earnestly than was planned, that now determines my fate and

---

[29] Razbojnikova-Frateva, *Jeder ist seines Unglücks Schmied*, 237.
[30] Vedder, "Ringe, Glocken, Tränen" 86.
[31] Razbojnikova-Frateva, *Jeder ist seines Unglücks Schmied*, 234.

perhaps hers as well). He laments an uncertainty that centers on the artificiality of the marriage arrangement, its hollow union and empty vow. He is confused, in essence, about whether his marriage is to be taken ironically or earnestly. Is their marriage truly artificial, unserious, detached from any real-world obligations? Or could it perhaps, in spite of its tongue-in-cheek formulation, nonetheless be taken seriously? Readers know by now that, in Fontane, the typical counterpart to "ernsthaft" is *scherzhaft*, something that is facetious, ironic, or said only in jest. We thus have a marriage that starts off as *scherzhaft*, since both parties to the agreement plan to take their vows with a degree of ironic detachment. But that plan goes awry as their facetious marriage quickly becomes earnest.[32] In this way, the novel probes the border or limit beyond which detachment, irony, and sophisticated cynicism are no longer possible. He proposed that they get "married," in air quotes to indicate that they were not passé or old-fashioned enough to take earnestly all the trappings and obligations of matrimony. Over time, though, the air quotes fade, and the longer they are together, the more they shift from being "married" to simply being married.

The point is that *Graf Petöfy* depicts a set of confusions and delusions that revolve around the indeterminacy of irony and earnestness. The categories are unstable, so that what one believes to be merely ironic could always turn out to be deadly serious, whereas things one takes as reliable and earnest might have been said ironically. Moreover, Petöfy himself locates the decisive factor for his fate in the invisible slippage from irony to earnestness. They gradually began to take their unserious marriage more seriously, and at some moment in the previous year, they crossed an unseen tipping point, beyond which the empty vow became full and infidelity would be seen as a consequential betrayal. He realizes belatedly that he cannot even blame Franziska for what has transpired. In a moment of self-flagellation, he asks himself, "Ihre Schuld? [...] Hab' ich ihr nicht selber im Voraus den Ablaßzettel in die Hand gegeben? Bin ich nicht das Kind, das etwas wieder haben will, das es zuvor weggeschenkt hat?" (7:212, Her guilt? Didn't I myself put the ticket of indulgence in her hand in advance? Aren't I like a child who wants something back after it has already given it away?). Petöfy says in Catholic terms that he granted her an indulgence, but the unconventional aspect is that the indulgence was granted in advance of the sin and was built into the marriage vow. He cannot renounce the obligation

---

[32] Razbojnikova-Frateva observes a similar dynamic in Petöfy's proposal to Franziska. What begins with "chatting" and "downplaying [Verharmlosung]" shifts toward a "passionate avowal." Razbojnikova-Frateva, *Jeder ist seines Unglücks Schmied*, 236.

of fidelity and then insist on it later. He cannot, he now realizes, tolerate unreliable language and then belatedly insist on a credible connection between words and actions. The gap that he introduced—into the vow, the marriage, and symbolically into the bell's frame—cannot be made whole until his death dissolves the corrupted bonds.[33]

The novel thus presents the process of rhetorical contagion from a different angle of vision. *Schach von Wuthenow*, for example, shows how unreliable language and infidelity to one's word infect communicative spheres in which one would normally insist on honesty, fidelity, transparency, and earnestness. *Graf Petöfy* does this too, by letting unserious, ironic language contaminate marriage vows. But it also shows earnestness creeping back into situations that were designed to be unserious or ironic. It demonstrates how the reality of significant matters snaps back against the pose of ironic detachment. Petöfy's central lament is that his bearing of ironic detachment, of not taking things seriously, proves to be untenable. It does not even last a year. And like Andreas the ironist in Franzen's *Purity*, Petöfy does not even recognize the slippage from irony to earnestness until it is too late, until his lighthearted laughter has already turned into bitter injury. The story comes full circle as he commits suicide on the day of their opening ball, the same event the year before that occasioned Franziska's first visit to the Petöfy residence.

One could say that Petöfy's suicide brings things full circle for a second reason: it echoes the suicide that occurred prior to last year's opening ball, when his friend Gablenz took his life. On the anniversary of Gablenz's suicide and the day of his own death, Petöfy cannot resist linking his fate to his friend's: "War es eine Vorahnung? Jedenfalls ist es mir lieb, damals nicht anders gesprochen zu haben" (7:218, Was it a premonition? In any case, I'm glad not to have spoken differently at the time). The words to which he refers were spoken in defense of Gablenz. Petöfy means essentially that he is glad to have defended Gablenz's

---

[33] Petöfy's final words to Franziska occur in response to an inscription that reads "Entsage!" (7:213, Forsake!). The verb "ent-*sagen*" implies an aspect of formal declaration (as does the related word "renunciation"), which situates the act of relinquishment in the realm of language. One hears that note clearly in other equivalents, such as "to swear off" or "forswear." This loaded word reiterates the point that all the issues of trust, fidelity, and betrayal occur within the speaking subject's relationship to language. It suggests that she might be able to "say away" her infidelity and thus correct her relationship not only to Petöfy but to language itself. There is little reason to believe, however, that more language will repair the breach that they have already inscribed in language. It merely perpetuates the double possibility inherent in the experience of language—oath and perjury, benediction and malediction.

suicide as a courageous rather than cowardly deed, but as with the Petőfy-Petöfi allusion, it will be instructive to examine his words more closely and to explore the parallel he suggests. At last year's opening ball, he defended the suicide as an act of honor and integrity: "Er war ein vollkommener Kavalier und hielt es mit dem Wort: 'Ich marchandire nicht.' Und an dem Festhalten an diesem Worte ist er zu Grunde gegangen" (7:13, He was a perfect gentleman and was true to the expression: "I don't negotiate." And sticking to this word was his demise). In other words, Gablenz's death results directly from his honor and credibility, from his refusal to deviate from the word he has given. He sounds here like a poor model indeed for Petöfy, who has spent most of the novel insisting that there is no need to hold fast to one's word. If Gablenz's cardinal principle is that he will not negotiate or compromise in matters of *fides*, Petöfy's sole strategy throughout has been to trade away honor and fidelity for the sake of companionship, to accept decorum as a sufficient substitute, and to tolerate infidelity in its various forms.

Despite these glaring differences, Gablenz's suicide nevertheless foreshadows Petöfy's demise, because the two are far more similar than Petöfy's self-presentation would suggest. After all the concessions and compromises he is willing to make to win Franziska's hand, Petöfy moves, over the course of the novel, closer to Gablenz's position of a tight ethical bond between words and deeds. He comes to ruin precisely as a result of his holding true to an expression, his clinging to the fullness and credibility of Franziska's vow, even though he himself emptied that vow of its obligations. At the novel's outset, he says of his departed friend Gablenz, "Hätte er mit dem Ehrenpunkte marchandiren können, er lebte noch" (7:13, If he could have bargained with the issue of honor, he would still be alive). The same holds true for Petöfy at the novel's conclusion. He miscalculates when he acts as if trust and fidelity are insignificant things that can be bartered away without consequence. But the upwelling of unanticipated earnestness and sincere affection flows into the otherwise arid environment of unmeant promises and unserious language. Petöfy sets out to establish an empty vow with the illusion of fidelity. Instead, he ends up with the illusion of an empty vow and the ongoing need for fidelity and sincerity. The attempt to craft a hollow vow does nothing to shield him from the scourge of unreliable language.

After Petöfy's death, no one outside the family is quite sure why he killed himself. But people talk as people will, and the gossip that the narrative recounts reflects back on the story in interesting ways. According to one rumor, Petöfy committed suicide over a vacant court position that he had hoped to receive, "der Kaiser aber hab' es nicht gewollt, entweder wegen der jungen Gräfin oder noch von Neunundvierzig und der Revolution her" (7:219, but the Kaiser was against it, either because of the young countess or from back in '49 and the revolution). The mention of 1849 and the Hungarian Revolution attempts to explain Petöfy's suicide through recourse to his other empty oath, his oath of loyalty to the Kaiser. The rumor suggests that Petöfy did not receive a choice post due to lingering resentment from the time of the Hungarian revolt: perhaps the Kaiser is still upset that Petöfy walked away from his service and the obligations of his oath. Of course, the Kaiser granted Petöfy his demission and released him from his service oath. He granted him the same ticket of indulgence that Petöfy gave Franziska, but maybe he cannot fully accept the discrepancy between the oath and the resulting actions. According to the popular wisdom of gossip, it is entirely plausible that the façade of noble tolerance for a broken vow conceals a reservoir of intolerance and resentment. In this version of events, the Kaiser believed he could countenance and accept Petöfy's infidelity, but in the end, he cannot. He remains aggrieved by his indulgence of infidelity. In this instance, the wisdom of the *Volksmund* has identified the correct dynamic, even though it misattributes the roles.

As for Franziska, she retreats to Castle Arpa as the widowed countess and refuses to consider a second marriage with Egon. She is also prepared to convert, not only from Protestantism to Catholicism, but also from the side of empty words and vows to the side of duty and deeds. She tells Hannah, "Ich will nun Pflichten leben," (I now want to live by my obligations) or as Judith puts it, "den guten Werken leben" (7:223–4, living by good works). Now a widow, she is intent on fulfilling with actions the obligations of fidelity and monogamy that she could not uphold as a wife, obligations that now manifest in the form of isolation, celibacy, and charitable deeds. The novel concludes with Franziska trying to compensate for the scourge of unreliable language and repair the damage of an empty vow, not by applying more promissory language but rather by reestablishing the ethical connection between words and deeds.

Four L'Adultera, Adulteration, and Avowal

First published serially in 1880 and then as a book in 1882, *L'Adultera* is the first of Fontane's society novels. It tells the story of the wealthy financier Ezechiel van der Straaten and his younger wife Melanie, who, after ten years of marriage, falls in love with a house guest, Ebenezer Rubehn, leaves her husband and children behind, and starts a new life. Both a novel of Berlin society and an adultery novel, *L'Adultera* represents something of an outlier in Fontane's works for the way in which the female protagonist is able to extricate herself successfully from an unhappy relationship and then rehabilitate herself after the transgression of infidelity.

In the present chapter, I aim to show that, in addition to being a novel (or, initially, a novella) of contemporary society and adultery, it is also a text that revolves around portraying a certain *Redeweise*, a particular manner of speaking, that has been taken to extremes. Fontane's inaugural society novel is at heart a portrait of an excessive idiom and its disruptive effects. How van der Straaten speaks constitutes the story's central focus. It is the prism through which the main characters get introduced and the driving force of conflict between him and Melanie. It is also a catalyst for her attraction to Rubehn and plays an important part in her justification for leaving. In short, Fontane's first attempt to portray contemporary Berlin society is in large part an attempt to portray an extreme version of the tone and idiom that characterize his Berlin.

One gets a sense of van der Straaten's manner of speaking when Christel the maid tries to persuade Melanie not to leave him: "Un daß er immer so spricht un solche Redensarten macht, [...] ja, Du himmlische Güte, warum soll er nich? [...] Er is nu 'mal für's Berlinsche. Aber is er denn nich einer?" (4:111, And him [always] talking like that [and spouting phrases], [...], well, for heaven's sake, why shouldn't he? [...] He likes Berlinese, that's all. After all, he is a Berliner).[1] Christel's

---

[1] Translation from Fontane, *The Woman Taken in Adultery and the Poggenpuhl Family*, 87. Further references in this chapter to this translation are given parenthetically.

characterization revisits the formulaic turns of phrase so familiar from *Irrungen, Wirrungen*, and she emphasizes that he *always* talks this way, without exception. Her statement furthermore ties van der Straaten's speech mannerisms to that tone particular to Berlin, the tone that Fontane has described in other venues: witty, trenchant, ironic, ambivalent, and suggestive, and in van der Straaten's case, frequently offensive and in poor taste. Van der Straaten is a Berliner, and he talks like one. Or rather, he takes this style of speech so far that even other Berliner are put off by it. Fontane's knack for capturing dialogue and natural speech has long been recognized,[2] but it is important to acknowledge, at the same time, that *L'Adultera* does not paint a flattering portrait of sophisticated causerie or lighthearted social banter. Van der Straaten's often mortifying manner of speaking is, for example, nothing like the open-minded humor and humanity of a conversationalist such as Dubslav von Stechlin. To the contrary, *L'Adultera* casts van der Straaten's predilection for a mannered style of speech—one that is cynical, ironic, and humiliating—as a disruptive, malignant force. It is telling that Christel's attempt to dissuade Melanie from leaving focuses on how van der Straaten talks and tries to diminish its contentiousness.

To this first point—about the central role of speech mannerisms in *L'Adultera* and in the society novels in general—the story adds a second: namely, it makes visible the porous border between social speech and private, intimate speech. A major source of conflict in the novel is that different realms of discourse do not remain separate and demarcated. To the chagrin of those around him, van der Straaten in particular tends not to distinguish between what is appropriate in a public versus a private setting. Eva Geulen identifies the issue as one of tact and refers to van der Straaten as Melanie's "notoriously tactless first husband."[3] To be sure, van der Straaten lacks discretion, but his tactlessness is also meant to embody a more general concern—the tendency for modes of speaking to proliferate beyond the settings in which they originally

---

[2] Praise for this aspect of Fontane's work runs all the way back to his contemporaneous reviewers. For more recent examples, see Barabara Naumann, "Schwatzhaftigkeit. Formen der Rede in späten Romanen Fontanes," in *Theodor Fontane am Ende des Jahrhunderts*, ed. Hanna Delf von Wolzogen and Helmuth Nürnberger (Würzburg: Königshausen & Neumann, 2000), 2:13–26; and Walter Jens, *Über Fontane* (Stuttgart: J.B. Metzler, 2000), 26, in which he notes that Fontane always portrays his characters via their "Sprachduktus" or characteristic style of speech.

[3] Eva Geulen, "Realismus ohne Entsagung. Fontanes *L'Adultera*," in *Herausforderungen des Realismus: Theodor Fontanes Gesellschaftsromane*, ed. Peter Uwe Hohendahl and Ulrike Vedder (Freiburg: Rombach, 2018), 51.

developed and to contaminate settings for which they are unsuitable. *L'Adultera* documents how the glib, ambivalent banter of Berlin society does not remain relegated to social settings; this way of speaking seeps into the most serious and intimate discussions. From the other side, what should be serious, intimate, and private migrates into the social realm to become just more fodder for pointed, ironic banter at dinner parties. The novel thus brings to the fore the difficulty of containing rhetorical forms such as irony or ambiguity.

Many of Fontane's society novels are also novels of adultery, and the issue of rhetorical contagion could help to explain Fontane's fondness for the genre of the adultery novel. The format of the society novel as adultery novel allows Fontane to work out the consequences of social speech in a personal setting. A couple like Melanie and van der Straaten provides a case study for the corrosive effects of a *Redeweise* that is unstintingly coy about whether it should be taken seriously or ironically and that refuses to distinguish between the small talk of social gatherings and the "big talk" of marital intimacy. If other works such as *Schach von Wuthenow* have depicted the political and historical consequences of a society in the thrall of empty, fatuous talk, *L'Adultera* plays out its effects in the realm of personal, emotional life. It demonstrates how a fashionable idiom, taken to extremes, can disrupt interpersonal communication and interfere with human relationships.

Finally, *L'Adultera* is an outlier among Fontane's society and adultery novels for a second reason. Unlike other works, *L'Adultera* envisions an alternative—one might even say an antidote—to the unserious, ironic banter that has become ubiquitous in Berlin society. Fontane at this point appears to be still optimistic enough to imagine a different kind of speech—namely, avowal—that could counter and cut through the emptiness and ambivalence of social banter. It is precisely through the force of avowal—that straightforward, confessional, high-stakes form of truth-telling—that Melanie is able to end her marriage and refashion her existence and identity.

In a Manner of Speaking

The novel's initial pages already establish the central themes of speech patterns and rhetorical contagion. They open with a painstaking effort to specify the details of speech mannerisms, with the introduction of Ezechiel van der Straaten, a caricature of excessive devotion to the Berlin idiom that Fontane would continue to characterize in *Irrungen, Wirrungen* and in the article on the *Berlinertum*.

Van der Straaten is not universally admired in Berlin society. The opening paragraph reports that he lacks worldly polish and instead retains "seinen spezifisch localen Stempel" (typically Berlin manner, 3), which includes "seine Vorliebe für drastische Sprüchwörter und heimische 'geflügelte Worte' von der derberen Observanz" (4:5, his fondness for vigorous locutions and local proverbs of a somewhat uncouth nature, 3). Van der Straaten is a bit too obviously and emphatically a Berliner, a fact evident in his penchant for local sayings, aphorisms, and turns of phrase. Moreover, the modifiers "drastisch" and "derb" suggest that there is something extreme and coarse about his particular manner of speaking. The narrative further specifies his speech, remarking, "er liebte das Einstreuen lyrischer Stellen, ganz besonders solcher, die seinem echt-berlinischen Hange zum bequem Gefühlvollen einen Ausdruck gaben. Daß er eben diesen Hang auch wieder ironisierte, versteht sich von selbst" (4:6, he liked to throw in a little verse, especially if it allowed him to express his especially Berlin predilection for a cozy kind of sentimentality. It goes without saying that he [ironized precisely this trait], 4). Van der Straaten is self-satisfied, sentimental, ironic, and at ease. The emphasis falls, once again, on how his speech patterns reflect an idiom that is particular to Berlin. Not only does van der Straaten display a weakness for catch phrases, literary references, and local color; he also tends to distance himself from his own language through irony. By ironizing his feelings, van der Straaten suggests that their expression is not meant to be taken seriously. And the narrator remarks that such an ironic disposition should be self-evident—*of course* he speaks ironically. It practically goes without saying that a member of Berlin's upper class at this time would adopt an ironic tone. Because *L'Adultera* is both a society novel and a novel of adultery, van der Straaten's irony acts as a window onto patterns of Prussian social interaction and, at the same time, as a factor in the demise of his marriage.

Van der Straaten's position in society—wealthy yet not entirely embraced or respected—also reflects his status as an assimilated Jew with a diasporic background. It is possible that the type of language he employs is not just personal preference, but rather that Fontane uses speech mannerisms to expose or perpetuate cultural stereotypes. There is, of course, a long anti-Semitic tradition that derides the Jewish use of German as awkward and inauthentic. Mecklenburg, commenting on the ubiquitous discourse of anti-Semitism in Fontane's time, finds reflected in his works the stereotype that Jews have a tendency toward flowery language and other forms of pompous showiness.[4] In a reading particular to *L'Adultera*, Franziska Schößler sees van der Straaten's

---

[4] Mecklenburg, *Theodor Fontane*, 91–2.

tactlessness and indiscretion as depictions of anti-Jewish topoi.[5] The evidence of anti-Semitic impulses in Fontane's writing is clear, but I am not sure that van der Straaten's ironic, mortifying manner of speaking can be linked definitively to his Jewishness. For one thing, the novel repeatedly identifies his speech mannerisms as typical of Berlin. He appears to caricature not a Yiddish-inflected *Maulschen*, but rather the Berlinese tone that was fashionable at the time, especially among the upper classes. Leo Poggenpuhl, one notes, is just as fond of Berlinese expressions as van der Straaten is (16:41). For another, it is difficult to read van der Straaten as a pardoy of Jewish assimilation when Ebenezer Rubehn, another assimilated Jew, functions as a contrasting figure. His reliability undercuts whatever rhetorical dichotomy one might try to establish between Jews and other Germans in the novel.[6]

As the attention to ways of speaking continues, the narrator notes that van der Straaten loves "Berolinismen und Cynismen" (Berlinisms and cynical remarks, 4). And in lines reminiscent of Käthe's character description in *Irrungen, Wirrungen*, the narrative declares that "es gab nichts in der Welt zu dem er allezeit so beständig aufgelegt gewesen wäre, wie zu Bonmots und scherzhaften Repartis" (4:6, there was nothing in the world for which he was so constantly in the mood as witticisms and repartee, 4). This sounds quite a bit like Käthe, who always has a humorous retort at the ready, and the passage's language, with its bons mots and witty repartee, reflects practically word for word the details of the Berlin idiom that Fontane outlined in his essay on the *Berlinertum*. We are, at this point, only a page or two into the text, but its primary focus in these opening lines is on trying to convey the way van der Straaten speaks and to specify what is so particular and potentially off-putting in his speech. I dwell here on the description of van der Straaten and his language only because the narrative itself dwells on them. Fontane, describing the structure of another of his works, once

---

[5] Franziska Schößler, "Der jüdische Börsianer und das unmögliche Projekt der Assimilation. Zu Fontanes Roman *L'Adultera*," in *Poetische Ordnungen. Zur Erzählprosa des deutschen Realismus*, ed. Ulrich Kittstein and Stefani Kugler (Würzburg: Königshausen & Neumann, 2007), 98. See further Nicolas von Passavant, "Performing the Philistine. Gossip as a Narrative Device and a Strategy for Reflection on Anti-Semitism in Theodor Fontane's *L'Adultera*," in *Fontane in the Twenty-First Century*, ed. John B. Lyon and Brian Tucker (Rochester, NY: Camden House, 2019), 48–62, who connects van der Straaten's depiction as an outsider and a philistine to anti-Semitism in the *Gründerzeit*.

[6] On the depiction of Jewishness in *L'Adultera*, see further Michael Fleischer, *"Kommen Sie, Cohn." Fontane und die "Judenfrage"* (Berlin: Michael Fleischer, 1998), 110–12. Fleischer comments that *L'Adultera* shows how cautiously Fontane approached the "Jewish question" (112).

wrote in a letter, "Der Anfang ist immer das entscheidende; hat mans darin gut getroffen, so muß der Rest mit einer Art von innerer Notwendigkeit gelingen."[7] (The beginning is always the decisive thing: if you do that well, then the rest of it will come off successfully, by a kind of inner necessity.) The remark was occasioned by his initial progress on *Schach von Wuthenow*, but the general import of Fontane's declaration applies just as well to *L'Adultera*. Here, too, the introduction is decisive, because van der Straaten's manner of speaking is decisive not only for his personal characterization; it also provides the engine that drives the entire story. Fontane's epistolary passage speaks to an internal structural necessity, as the entirety of the work grows out of the introduction, like a plant from a seed. In similar fashion, the events in *L'Adultera*—Melanie's infidelity and the demise of their marriage—all stem from the manner of speaking that the opening pages introduce in meticulous detail.[8]

At the outset, the novel also points to the overlap between the private-personal and the social. It indicates that even van der Straaten's relationship to Melanie is shaped by his ironic, trenchant tone. The narrative reports, for example, that he is fond of referring to Melanie with the ironically elevated term "Gemahlin" (spouse). "Und dies Wort," the narrator says, "sprach er dann mit einer gewissen Feierlichkeit, in der Scherz und Ernst geschickt zusammenklangen" (4:7, This last word he uttered with a certain solemnity in which seriousness and jest were neatly harmonized, 4). This instance exemplifies van der Straaten's ironic attitude in the novel in two ways. First, he delivers the word "Gemahlin" with a solemnity that is both genuine and artificial. The passage's wording recalls Schlegel's fragment on Socratic irony: "Everything in it should be jest [Scherz] and everything should be earnest [Ernst], ingenuously open and deeply feigned."[9] The fragment is fitting because so much of van der Straaten's speech comprises a self-contradictory mixture of earnestness and jest, so that it is difficult, if not impossible, to pin down the extent to which he means in earnest what he says.

Second, this balancing act between irony and serious expression pertains even when talking about his wife. The narrator asserts that "der Ernst überwog, wenigstens in seinem Herzen" (4:7, seriousness was dominant, at least in his heart), which implies that, in the act of

---

[7] Fontane, June 3, 1879, *Der Dichter über sein Werk*, 2:294.
[8] Norbert Mecklenburg, attending to erotic subtexts in Fontane's works, writes similarly that the "decisive turn" is precipitated by a series of double entendres. Mecklenburg, *Theodor Fontane*, 244–5.
[9] Schlegel, *Kritische Ausgabe*, 2:160.

expression, irony has the upper hand. It severs the link between his words and whatever sincerely held emotions lie behind them. The passage speaks to a discrepancy between the degree of sincerity in his heart and in his language, so that not even his marriage is exempted from a tone that ironizes and distorts—and thereby diminishes—its object. The faux solemnity with which he refers to Melanie represents one of those introductory seeds, a portrait *en miniature*, that will set the course of events in the novel. A tone and manner of speaking that habitually disrupt van der Straaten's social relationships will also come to disrupt his most intimate relationship.

In all these ways, the novel's opening presents van der Straaten as an exemplar of Berlin speech patterns and an ironist. Jonathan Lear, in a series of lectures on ironic existence, says, "We tend to think casually of 'the ironist' as someone who is able to make certain forms of witty remarks, perhaps saying the opposite of what he means, of remaining detached by undercutting any manifestation of seriousness."[10] This is clearly the sort of ironist that van der Straaten represents; he loves witty replies and is certainly skilled at using irony to undercut serious or sentimental expressions. Lear contends, however, that this kind of ironist embodies a derivative or superficial form of irony. Following Kierkegaard and the model of Socrates, he is after a deeper form of irony, an ironic existence, which, for Lear, represents a positive, humane form of irony.

This same distinction—between the derivative irony of expression and a deeper irony of existence—can also be observed in Fontane's text, though in a more pessimistic light. Van der Straaten exemplifies the ironist in Lear's casual sense, but Fontane asks what happens when this derivative form of irony encroaches on other realms of being, when existence itself becomes ironically tinged—not in a positive sense, but rather in a nihilistic sense in which the negative force of irony cancels meaning and emotion. Kierkegaard, following Hegel, designates this deeper irony "infinite absolute negativity," an irony that "no longer directs itself against this or that particular phenomenon […] but that the whole of existence has become alien to the ironic subject, that he in turn has become estranged from existence."[11] Through characters such as Käthe, Schach, and now van der Straaten, Fontane's novels trace a movement from derivative irony to deep irony. Irony might begin as a lighthearted form of social banter, as a means to undercut solemnity *in particular expressions*. One finds repeatedly, though, that

---

[10] Lear, *Case for Irony*, 9.
[11] Kierkegaard, *Concept of Irony*, 276.

irony's negative force cannot be contained. It alienates phenomenon from essence so thoroughly that, as Kierkegaard puts it, it estranges the ironist from existence itself. In *L'Adultera*, one observes the beginnings of this estrangement in the first interactions depicted between Melanie and van der Straaten.

Alienation Affects

L'Adultera makes clear that the fondness for ironic expression is not particular to van der Straaten but rather represents a prominent aspect of Berlin society in the late nineteenth century. One sees van der Straaten's irony as symptomatic of broader social tendencies when he bursts out in laughter over a newspaper article. The scene alludes to the work of Ludwig Pietsch, a well-known society reporter for the *Vossische Zeitung* who had a sharp, ironic bent. Fontane himself wrote theater reviews for the *Vossische Zeitung* and was well acquainted with Pietsch. He even found himself on more than one occasion to be the object of Pietsch's writing, so he evokes here a world of which he was very much a part.[12] Reading a report on the latest society ball, van der Straaten chuckles and says, "Er schreibt *zu* gut [...] Und was mich am meisten freut, sie nimmt es Alles für Ernst" (4:9, He really does write [too] well [...] And what gives me the most pleasure is that she takes it all so seriously, 6). First, van der Straaten identifies a degree of excess in Pietsch's society reportage. Whatever van der Straaten admires in this writing, that element is present in abundance; it is *too* good. Fontane himself remarked in a more critical tone on the excesses of Pietsch's style: "Manchmal übertröpfeln Sie sich und überwürzen den Wein."[13] (Sometimes you lay it on too thick and over-spice the wine.) If one of Fontane's concerns is a decadent rhetorical excess, then introducing a main character through his amusement over such writing (these are van der Straaten's first spoken words in the novel) serves to locate that character on the continuum of language use—toward the extreme end of decadence, empty banter, and irony.

Second, van der Straaten's remark illustrates a key point about irony, about its abyssal nature. The danger of verbal irony, of turning away from straightforward expression, is that it renders illegible the distinction between what is earnest and facetious. What van der Straaten admires in press reports on recent social events is the same contradictory

---

[12] Roland Berbig, *Theodor Fontane Chronik* (Berlin: de Gruyter, 2010), 3:1811.
[13] See Helmuth Nürnberger's notes to the dtv edition of *L'Adultera*, 161 (note 10). The metaphor of "overspicing the wine" recurs in Chapter 9, when van der Straaten's banter humiliates Melanie and creates the circumstances under which she acknowledges her attraction to Rubehn.

mixture of earnestness and jest that his own speech displays. He feels himself to be on the inside of irony; he is in on the joke and can laugh at those who take ironic expressions seriously. Irony serves here to draw the boundaries of Berlin society's discourse community. It separates outsiders from insiders, and the quickest way to make a fool of oneself is to speak plainly or to mistake ironic banter for plain-spoken truth. But the darker possibility lurking in the background is, to use Schlegel's terminology, one of "permanent parabasis"—it could become impossible to distinguish between what is meant seriously and what is not.[14]

Now, I want to be careful not to push a line of reading that makes Fontane into too much of an alarmist reactionary. Fontane, a writer widely held in high regard for the lighthearted, ironic tone of his narratives, is not really out to warn about the dangers of irony in the gossip pages of the *Vossische Zeitung*. But the novel has already emphasized (through the ironically delivered term "spouse") that a rhetorical mixture of earnestness and jest can be difficult to read, a point reiterated by the reception of Pietsch's article. Fontane is attending, in various ways, to a self-cancelling trope, an indeterminable oscillation between sincerity and flippancy, that speakers deliberately employ. The problem is not so much a lack of meaning in speech, but rather the ability to overlay its ostensible meaning with ironic, contradictory meanings—to twist it into its opposite. And the important thing is that, while van der Straaten can laugh now at readers who take Pietsch's unserious prose too seriously, this breakfast scene serves to introduce two tense conversations between Melanie and her husband, both of which involve a spouse trying to weigh the degree of earnestness and jest in the other's speech—and misjudging it. The point, then, is not that an ironic, emptied-out tone in the society pages is a bad thing in and of itself. It is, rather, that the ironic tone has become pervasive. It has come to characterize a wide swath of human interaction, such that one is always unsure whether it is safe to take another's speech seriously, or whether taking things seriously will expose oneself as the butt of an ironic joke.

The first of these conversations is occasioned by the delivery of the copied Tintoretto painting "L'Adultera," which gives the novel its title. As van der Straaten presents the painting, the conversation takes a high-stakes, confessional turn. Melanie wants to know why, exactly, her husband wanted a copy of this Tintoretto: "sie wollte wissen, was in seiner Seele vorging. Und er wollt' es auch nicht länger verbergen" (4:14, she wanted to know what was going on in his mind. Nor did he wish to hide it any longer, 10). It is important to Melanie's theory

---

[14] Schlegel, *Kritische Ausgabe*, 18:85.

of mind that van der Straaten express what he truly feels; the phenomenon of his speech must accord with the essence of his emotions. According to the narrative voice, van der Straaten also wants to end the masquerade and have a confessional moment of avowal. What follows is a serious and intimate dialogue about jealousy and fidelity, in which van der Straaten reveals both a deep-seated insecurity and a fatalistic view of his marriage.[15] He says that he wants to have the painting as a kind of "Memento mori," as a constant reminder that someday his wife will betray him, as if it were an ineluctable fate. One might pause here to note that van der Straaten's viewpoint and indeed the entire conversation are profoundly weird, serious, and personal.

But just as the discussion arrives at this deep and thorny point, they both creep back from the precipice and return to something like casual banter. It begins with a retreat to platitudes and trite expressions: "Zeit gewonnen, alles gewonnen" (Gain time, gain all), "die trivialsten Sätze simmer immer die richtigsten" (The most banal sayings are always the truest), and "Dann vergiß auch nicht *den*, daß man den Teufel nicht an die Wand malen soll" (4:15, Well, then, don't forget "speaking of the devil," 11). Shortly thereafter, Melanie shrugs the entire conversation off as unserious banter. "Und ich war eigentlich eine Thörin und ein Kindskopf, daß ich alles so bitter ernsthaft genommen und dir jedes Wort geglaubt habe! Du hast das Bild haben wollen, c'est tout" (4:15, And I was really a fool and an idiot to take it all in deadly earnest and to believe every word you said. You wanted the picture, *c'est tout*, 11). She chastises herself for having made the same foolish mistake as the newspaper reader who takes ironic prose too seriously. She decides to discount everything van der Straaten just revealed as another ironic disquisition, not meant in earnest. With the expression "c'est tout," she strikes all the anxiety about infidelity and predestination from the record. It is a baffling end to a serious conversation. She gets up, laughs (like her husband reading the newspaper), and leaves; and van der Straaten never bothers to tell her that he means what he said. But hers is a severe misreading of the situation, as the narrative voice has already remarked that van der Straaten in this moment is inclined "angesichts dieses Bildes einmal aus sich heraus zu gehen" (4:14, the painting for once drew him out of his shell, 10). He is prepared to expose his most profound vulnerabilities, but Melanie professes to take it all as a bit of unserious talk, so that irony becomes a way to avoid what is serious and what needs to be said. We observed a similar dynamic in *Irrungen*,

---

[15] Geulen, too, notes the shift in tone in this conversation, as they discuss without bantering the prospect of infidelity. Geulen, "Realismus ohne Entsagung," 55.

Wirrungen when Käthe jokingly interrogated Botho about the existence of love letters and then dismissed his confession as an ironic reply. In both cases, irony comes to function as an escape hatch or eject button to get out of difficult exchanges. "Oh, you were just kidding," the characters seem to say, "you didn't mean any of that in earnest, so we can just forget it."

Wayne Booth, in *A Rhetoric of Irony*, takes up the practical critical task of determining how one could identify irony in literary texts. In Paul de Man's characterization, Booth wants to know "by what markers, by what devices, by what indications or signals in the text we can decide that a text is ironic or not."[16] De Man, of course, will go on to say that what seems like an entirely sensible project—simply deciding whether or not a given text is ironic—is actually an impossible one. In Fontane, too, one repeatedly finds a profound skepticism vis-à-vis the critical ability to identify and pin down irony. People are not good at reading irony and earnestness, he suggests, nor at telling the difference between them. A deeper, implicit consequence is that the speakers might no longer know the difference either because their speech is never purely one or the other. In a rhetorically decadent, post-truth age, practically every utterance is an alloy of irony and earnest sentiment.

At the same time, I want to point out that Fontane remains enough of a practical rhetorical critic (or, more succinctly, enough of a realist) that he sees the endless, hall-of-mirrors regress of irony as a bad thing. Booth himself calls irony "an infinite chain of solvents" and argues that a rhetoric of irony, that is, a proper understanding of irony, "is required if we are not to be caught [...] in an infinite regress of negations."[17] Whereas de Man sees irony as the foundation of all literary language, Booth believes that, if taken too far, irony becomes a trap from which one cannot escape. Fontane's nuanced approach to irony partakes of both positions and is suspended somewhere between them. When it comes to diagnosis, Fontane is de Manian to the extent that he presents the potential impossibility of deciding whether a given expression, text, or attitude is ironic. When it comes to treatment and prognosis, however, Fontane remains Boothian enough to want to put a stop to that infinite chain of negations. Rather than celebrate the abyssal nature of irony, Fontane worries about what happens when irony metastasizes from a

---

[16] Paul de Man, "The Concept of Irony," in *Aesthetic Ideology*, ed. Andrzej Warminski (Minneapolis: University of Minnesota Press, 1996), 165. For a lucid introduction to the dominant understandings of irony in the twentieth century, see Richard Bernstein, *Ironic Life*, especially the introduction and first two chapters.

[17] Wayne Booth, *A Rhetoric of Irony* (Chicago: University of Chicago Press, 1974), 59, n 14.

figure of speech to a mode of existence. And, like Booth, he wants to find a way to bring irony to a halt, to contain it within boundaries—not through a rhetoric of irony, as in Booth's conception, but rather through a countervailing rhetoric of avowal.

The second conversation occurs later that same morning, and it involves the same uncertainty about whether something is said in earnest or in jest. It begins when van der Straaten comes to Melanie's room to convey a message. He enters in an excited, jovial mood, but more important is the way in which his joking manner colors the performance of formality: "Die Feierlichkeit, mit der dies alles geschah, machte Melanie lachen" (4:17, He did all this with so much solemnity that Melanie began to laugh, 13). Van der Straaten delivers an air of solemn ceremony but in a humorous, self-deprecating way that undermines the very formality he performs. It is a moment of either solemn tomfoolery or tongue-in-cheek solemnity. In a word, it's ironic. Melanie, for her part, plays on van der Straaten's tone with her own mixture of seriousness and jest: "Ist es doch, als ob Du Dich auf eine ganz besondere Beichte vorzubereiten hättest. Ich will es Dir aber leicht machen. Ist es etwas Altes? Etwas aus Deiner dunklen Vergangenheit ... ?" (4:18, You look as though you were preparing to make a very special confession. But I shall make it easy for you. Is it an old sin? Something from your murky past?, 13). With the term "confession," the passage lays the groundwork for avowal and veridiction, but Melanie's playful, unserious tone both reflects and deflates the inflated solemnity of van der Straaten's behavior. The passage resembles, once again, Käthe's demand in *Irrungen, Wirrungen* that Botho confess to burning old love letters. The demand for avowal—but delivered in an ironic, unserious way—is something of a rhetorical tic among the characters of Fontane's society novels.

When she presses him to tell her finally what it is, he replies that it is "Eine Bagatelle" (4:18, A mere trifle, 13), just a trivial matter, nothing really. Van der Straaten duplicates here the mixed or ambiguous message of his previous behavior—the implication that something is very serious but also trifling, the suggestion that he has an important message to convey but also that it is nothing of import. When he finally reveals that they will be hosting a long-term house guest, Melanie reacts with consternation. "Und das nennst Du eine Bagatelle? Du weißt recht gut, daß es etwas sehr Ernsthaftes ist" (4:18, And you call that a trifle? You know very well it's a very serious [earnest] matter, 13). The crux of their disagreement lies in the question of whether the matter is serious or trivial. When the reader first encounters this couple, van der Straaten is laughing as he imagines a newspaper reader who takes all too earnestly a flippant bit of society reportage. He laughs at the expense of the ignorant person who does not know when to take something seriously, and more importantly, when not to. And yet the subsequent encounters with his spouse underscore that these two continually struggle with the same issue. When he bares his heart and reveals his most profound anxieties, she dismisses it all as causerie, not meant to be taken earnestly. And when she takes the prospect of a house guest very seriously, he dismisses it as a mere trifle. There thus exists a good deal of dissonance, alienation, and uncertainty as this couple tries to negotiate what is serious and what is trivial.

The degree of uncertainty, even undecidability, on display in these scenes recalls de Man's unpacking of an Archie Bunker quip in the 1973 essay "Semiology and Rhetoric." When Archie's wife says that he's tied his bowling shoes the wrong way, he replies, "What's the difference?" The joke is that he delivers it as a rhetorical question, not meant to be answered, but his wife misreads the rhetorical import and begins patiently explaining a difference and answering a question that Archie never meant to ask. She takes his question seriously, literally, according to its grammatical illocution: "There is a difference, and I would like you to explain that difference to me." The rhetorical expression, however, erases the basis of the very question that grammar poses, asserting instead, "There is no difference." What the television show plays for a laugh, de Man takes as a serious example of the relationship of grammar and rhetoric, of the work of the trope, and of the abyssal dilemma that arises from attending to rhetoric. One cannot even tell whether a question is being asked or not, whether a difference is being asserted or denied. One cannot tell, that is, whether a statement means what it says (grammatically) or rather the opposite of what it says.

These early exchanges between Melanie and van der Straaten play out a similar dynamic of uncertainty and miscommunication, but again with a key difference. Whereas de Man sees the "the rhetorical, figural potentiality of language" as the *Urform* of literature, Fontane's exploration of uncertainty and rhetoric leads him to a more pessimistic appraisal.[18] To be fair, de Man locates a powerfully negative potential in the work of rhetoric as well. As long as it is just a matter of how to tie shoes, he says, "the consequences are relatively trivial." But there remains the broader point that cannot be avoided: "Rhetoric radically suspends logic and opens up vertiginous possibilities of referential aberration."[19] It does so whether the topic is something trivial (such as the proper method of tying shoes, or the latest high-society ball) or something with much higher stakes (marital infidelity, promissory

---

[18] Paul de Man, "Semiology and Rhetoric," in *Allegories of Reading* (New Haven: Yale University Press, 1979), 10.
[19] De Man, "Semiology and Rhetoric," 10.

oaths, political decisions, and so on). This captures a key aspect of the novel's opening and indeed of its central conflict: van der Straaten deliberately blurs the distinction between the earnest and the ironic, and as a result, those around him can no longer distinguish between them. The dilemma reflects de Man's essential point. A question becomes rhetorical, he says, "when it is impossible to decide by grammatical or other linguistic devices which of the two meanings (that can be entirely incompatible) prevails."[20] In the case of *L'Adultera*, van der Straaten comes to Melanie and says in essence, "What I need to tell you is just a trifle, a *Bagatelle*, nothing really." The statement's grammar presents a straightforward meaning, "This matter is not important," while its rhetorical import suggests just the opposite, "it actually *is* important; it is not trifling at all." When the narrative voice says that van der Straaten "bewegte sich gern [...] in Gegensätzen" (4:16, oscillated [...] between one extreme and the other [or: liked to dwell in antitheses], 11), or that his bearing evinces a mixture of *Scherz* and *Ernst*, it says in essence that the unresolvable tension between contradictory meanings operates in most of what he says and does.

From the two conversations examined above, it appears that this admixture of the serious and the unserious has crept into all of van der Straaten's interactions. It has migrated from the gossip pages and the society soiree to the boudoir. It interferes in his communication with Melanie because the question is always open as to whether van der Straaten actually means what he says. To put it differently, his mode of speaking has *adulterated* his marriage and his ability to communicate efficaciously with his wife. The kind of glib, ironic banter he employs in social situations has contaminated, infected, or polluted—all of which are signified under the term "adulteration"—his most serious and intimate conversations. Indeed, this dynamic of rhetorical contamination and adulteration constitutes a central point in the novel entitled *L'Adultera*.

In correspondence with publishers, Fontane was adamant that the titular "Adultera" referred not to the female protagonist but rather to the Tintoretto paining and, furthermore, that it was essential to the story's structure.[21] If one takes "Adultera" not as pointing to a particular woman but rather in a broader, figurative sense, one could understand it not only as the "adulteress" but also as the "adulterant," as that which adulterates. Gerhard Neumann makes a similar point about the title referring not to a person but rather to a cultural medium, to a

---

[20] De Man, "Semiology and Rhetoric," 10.
[21] See Fontane's letter to Julius Grosser, April 4 or 5, 1880, *Der Dichter über sein Werk*, 2:263–4.

copied, "cited" image. He sees in the copied painting a reflection of a Prussian "culture of citation," a society "that is constructed [...] from citations, well-known sayings, clichés, and platitudes."[22] It is important to remember that the primary exemplar of this culture of citation is van der Straaten himself and his manner of speaking. He is the "homme copie" who embodies an entire "société copie,"[23] so that here, too, the object of inquiry remains the same: the proliferation of empty, unreliable speech. In its stringent sense, to adulterate a product means to debase or taint it by contaminating it with ingredients of inferior quality. This is essentially what van der Straaten's manner of speaking does to marital communication: it contaminates the openness of intimacy with the emptiness of social banter; it infects plainspoken veridiction with the ever-present threat of ironic contradiction. The result is an inferior, adulterated alloy. Reading the title's connotations in this way allows one to take the arrival of the Tinoretto painting in their home not only prophetically—as pointing forward to the outcome of Melanie's infidelity—but also analytically, as isolating and identifying a root cause (adulterated, unreliable speech) in the breakdown of their relationship.

L'Adultera depicts the dynamic of rhetorical adulteration moving in two directions at once—both from the public-social to the private-personal and vice versa. In the former, as the above examples demonstrate, the empty, ironizing tone of social chatter impinges upon attempts at serious and intimate conversation. In the latter instance, however, it is not that the serious tone of private conversations migrates into social settings. Rather, van der Straaten takes topics that ought to be private and discreet and deploys them in social settings as more fodder for his rollicking banter.

This tendency is already in evidence at the novel's outset, during the first dinner party that the couple hosts. It isn't long before van der Straaten starts to move in the direction of coarser and more sexually suggestive comments. True to form, he hijacks the table conversation with monologues that are ostensibly about art criticism but become more and more openly opportunities to make crass remarks about sexuality, religion, women's bodies, and his wife's faults. For instance, discussing the Spanish painter Murillo and different types of Madonna figures, van der Straaten professes to prefer a "warm" Madonna to a "cold" one. He describes a typical depiction of a Madonna sitting on a

---

[22] Gerhard Neumann, "Speisesaal und Gemäldegalerie. Die Geburt des Erzählens aus der bildenden Kunst: Fontanes Roman *L'Adultera*," in *Roman und Ästhetik im 19. Jahrhundert*, ed. Tim Mehigan and Gerhard Sauder (St. Ingbert: Röhrig Universitätsverlag, 2001), 142.
[23] Neumann, "Speisesaal und Gemäldegalerie," 141.

sickle moon, saying, "Und so blickt sie brünstig oder sagen wir lieber inbrünstig gen Himmel" (4:32, And there she is, passionately—or perhaps we'd better say fervently—gazing toward heaven, 25). This is van der Straaten's kind of humor. Instead of describing the Madonna as "inbrünstig," as looking devout or religiously reverent, he says that she looks "brünstig," which is to say, sexually excited, like an animal in heat.

Remarks like this one are not merely irreverent or inappropriate; they are crass in a way that seems designed to be maximally offensive at a dinner party. The outburst exemplifies van der Straaten's unrestrained rhetorical tendencies, and the narrative indicates it is not an isolated occurrence. The anticipated catastrophe comes to pass when van der Straaten, sensing at the table an implicit rebuke to his speech, drops all pretense of worldly, ironic detachment and defends himself: "Ich bin erzogen" (I am quite sufficiently educated, 28). The narrative emphasizes how serious he is in this moment by noting that he speaks in a trembling voice (4:37). Van der Straaten wants to banter and make witty wordplays, seem flippant, and act like he remains above the fray, but he reveals himself, at base, to be all too serious and defensive; he demands to be taken seriously.

Something similar happens at the novel's turning point, when the group makes an outing to Stralau. Over a bowl of mulled wine, van der Straaten begins commenting on the waitress's looks, specifically on her body. With flailing references to Goethe and art history, he compares her to the goddess Aphrodite, to a "Venus Spreavensis," a Venus from the Spree, and a "Venus Kallipygos," or callipygian Venus (4:72). Again, van der Straaten wants to come across as learned and clever; he wants to be a Sanssouci sort of wit who can banter all night long with ironic detachment and grand theories about everything. But he fails, appearing instead as an unpolished jerk with no sense of propriety and none of the lightness that sophisticated, ironic talk requires.

Worse still, he tries to get Melanie to recite a sexually suggestive distich about a "divine peach," something he claims they laughed about in private. Goading her into joining in with him, he reminds her, "ich sagte noch 'man fühl' ihn ordentlich.' Und Du fand'st es auch und stimmtest mit ein" (4:72, I said you could really feel it. And you thought so too and agreed with me, 56). Not only does van der Straaten in this instance objectify the waitress and pontificate to his assorted guests on the attractiveness of her figure, he also drags what he and Melanie have shared in private out into the open and shames her in public. Lacking tact or discretion, he recognizes no clear distinction between what is intimate and what can be shared openly. Whatever Melanie said to him in a private setting about handling divine peaches, it was said with the tacit understanding that it would not be recycled as part of a wine-fueled social conversation. Norbert Mecklenburg, noting the asymmetrical power of gendered relationships, points out another insulting aspect to this moment, "In the consciousness of the—male—listeners, [...] the spark could of course easily leap from the erotic allure of a Venus Kallipygos to that of Melanie van der Straaten."[24] His sexually charged rhetoric has crossed an invisible boundary, so that it is no longer an abstract, slightly salacious disquisition on art history and women's bodies. It now impinges on Melanie's own body, her own sexuality, and her marital relationship, and it exposes them in the harsh, potentially derisive light of ironic social speech. A good analogue for van der Straaten's manner of speaking is how Count Haldern (Sarastro) speaks to and about his out-of-wedlock lover Pauline in the novel *Stine*. At dinner, he too repeatedly makes "halb scherzhaften, halb huldigenden" remarks (11:24, half joking, half reverent), but always with a derisive, humiliating undertone. One sees by analogy that van der Straaten treats Melanie here less like a spouse than a courtesan. The alienating effects of his manner of speaking thus become apparent from the other side. Just as no conversation is so serious or intimate that it cannot be adulterated by an ironic tone, nothing is so serious or intimate that it cannot provide material for his mortifying banter.[25]

The narrative voice, summarizing Melanie's state of mind, attributes her embarrassment and indeed shame again to her husband's particularly off-putting style of speech, "Ihres Gatten Art und Redeweise" (4:71, her husband's manner and speech, 55). Here, too, the repellant aspect of van der Straaten's manner of speaking is only exacerbated by his fondness for a form of verbal irony in which the tone or manner of expression undermines a statement's ostensible sentiment. At one point, van der Straaten conveys the effect of tone through an alcoholic metaphor. He says, "Glühwein ist diejenige Form des Weines, in der der Wein nichts und das Gewürznägelchen alles bedeutet" (4:70, mulled wine is that form of wine in which the wine itself signifies nothing, and the cloves everything, 54). The figure's key point is that the addition of something small (note the diminutive emphasis of "Nägelchen") can transform the effect of the whole. A tinge of irony is, for example, enough to transform the meaning of a statement. The metaphor recalls an aphorism that Thomas Mann occasionally attributed to Goethe: "Irony is the kernel [das Körnchen] of salt that makes everything

---

[24] Mecklenburg, *Theodor Fontane*, 249.
[25] My summary of these two scenes samples only the most egregious examples of van der Straaten's tactlessness. Mecklenburg's helpful chapter on "Zweideutigkeiten" examines in greater detail the thicket of wordplays, allusions, and double entendres. Mecklenburg, *Theodor Fontane*, 244–51.

served palatable."²⁶ Whether it is a "Körnchen" or a "Nägelchen," irony decisively flavors everything it touches, though van der Straaten's tone tends to render everything at the table unpalatable.

In subsequent passages of dialogue from the same evening, one finds repeatedly that the addition of one small element—a certain tone of voice, or an interjected word—radically alters the meaning of a statement. Melanie, for instance, puts a stop to van der Straaten's bawdy indiscretions when she interrupts him and indicates that they have had enough to drink. His response reflects perfectly the process of ironic flavoring: "'Ich bin es zufrieden,' entgegnete van der Straaten, aber in einem Tone, der nur allzu deutlich erkennen ließ, daß seine gute Stimmung in ihr Gegenteil umzuschlagen begann" (4:72, "That's all right with me," said van der Straaten, but it was all too clear from his tone that his humor was beginning to change into the opposite, 56). His tone twists the sentence's ostensible sentiment into its opposite. While the logic of his statement expresses satisfaction, the rhetorical form overlays it with a contradictory expression of *dis*satisfaction.

This self-nullifying movement within van der Straaten's statement provides a clear example of irony as a figure of speech. In Kierkegaard's words, "the phenomenon is not the essence but the opposite of the essence," and this is certainly evident in van der Straaten's faux expression of satisfaction.²⁷ He delivers a sentence that is unmistakably clear, terse, and straightforward, but irony transforms the sentiment's straightforward expression with another layer of opposed meaning. Van der Straaten's irony suggests a language that presents too many meanings at the same time, a language that could always cancel and contradict itself. If his statement can simultaneously indicate both satisfaction and dissatisfaction, this instance demonstrates irony's ability to add a surfeit of contradictory meaning to even the simplest statements.

It is important to recognize that these two phenomena—van der Straaten's ironic ambivalence and his tactless indiscretion—are two sides of the same coin. Melanie complains to Rubehn of her husband, "er kennt kein Geheimniß, weil ihm nichts des Geheimnisses werth dünkt. Weil ihm nichts heilig ist" (4:77, he knows no secrets because nothing seems worth keeping secret to him. Because he holds nothing sacred, 60). She identifies a core issue: nothing is sacred, nothing is worth taking seriously. This malady presents through both the ironic contamination of serious conversations—so that one cannot know

---

²⁶ Andreas Blödorn and Friedhelm Marx, ed., *Thomas Mann Handbuch: Leben, Werk, Wirkung* (Stuttgart: J.B. Metzler, 2015), 306.
²⁷ Kierkegaard, *Concept of Irony*, 264.

whether to take the other person in earnest—and van der Straaten's tendency to expose in public what should remain private and intimate. His entire tone is marked by a failure to distinguish between the frivolous and the serious-intimate. This, Melanie confesses bitterly to Rubehn, is "der Ton unsres Hauses. Ein bischen spitz, ein bischen zweideutig und immer unpassend" (4:76, that's the tone of our house. A little sharp, a little ambiguous, and always inappropriate, 59). Snide, suggestive, and unseemly: the middle term "zweideutig" in Melanie's complaint links van der Straaten's irony to his tactlessness in social settings, for, as the terms itself suggests, it can be understood in more than one way. On the one hand, van der Straaten has just subjected his wife to public embarrassment (for the how many hundredth time?) with a series of sexually suggestive double entendres that culminated in the exposure of their intimate, erotic repartee. On the other hand, something is "zweideutig" in a literary sense when ambiguity arises from language that lends itself to multiple, often contradictory, interpretations. Van der Straaten's statement of (dis)satisfaction and Riekchen's "O, er gefällt mir" (4:74, Oh, I like him, 57), are ambiguous in the sense that they ironically present two contradictory meanings at the same time. In both ways, van der Straaten's manner of speaking is unreliable, capricious, and potentially volatile. It is precisely this disingenuous discrepancy or misalignment between the essence of meaning and the phenomenon of speech that Melanie points to in her decision to end her marriage. Her decision to leave, her act of avowal, functions primarily as an attempt to realign essence and phenomenon.

Before continuing on to the novel's moment of avowal, it is worth pausing to consider a potential incongruity. That is, Fontane himself was well known in his personal life as a conversationalist who loved bons mots and the witty, exuberant banter of a dinner party. Nor was he one to shy away from double entendre and erotic subtext. He details in a letter all the conversational indiscretions he has indulged in with women in polite company, "Kleine Frivolitäten, Anzüglichkeiten, selbst Zynismen."[28] (Little frivolities, lewd remarks, even cynical remarks.) Fontane seems to step back here and marvel at all the indiscretions he has gotten away with. This is, after all, a writer who once gravely offended Theodor Storm by expressing to Storm's wife over dinner, as Storm put it, "relentless double entendres and naked remarks [Nuditäten]."[29] The insult generated by Fontane's table talk with the

---

[28] Cited in Jens, *Über Fontane*, 19.
[29] Cited in Jens, *Über Fontane*, 19. Also recounted in Mecklenburg, *Theodor Fontane*, 242–4.

Storms sounds unfortunately similar to van der Straaten's dinner party offenses. Doesn't this overlap between Fontane the person and van der Straaten the character undermine any attempt to argue that the novel presents van der Straaten as a personification of harmful rhetorical tendencies?

The best way to square Fontane's personal proclivities with his depiction of van der Straaten (and, by extension, characters such as Käthe and Schach) is by differentiating them. One can differentiate a speaker like van der Straaten from Fontane the conversationalist and from his Berliner peers by the degree of his enthrallment to a particular idiom. For van der Straaten is, at base, a portrait of excess, a caricature of fashionable rhetorical tendencies run amok. Even Melanie, who despises van der Straaten's tone, engages occasionally in playful banter (4:82). A character like Melanie demonstrates that small talk and lighthearted social chatter are not problematic in and of themselves—a view that aligns better with what we know of Fontane's personality. His society novels are concerned rather with questions of rhetorical limits and boundaries, and with what happens when they are crossed or in fact turn out to be illusory. His works stage experiments that explore what occurs when someone consistently fails to distinguish between the serious and the unserious, the earnest and the frivolous, when one's entire bearing is capricious and unreliable. He examines, that is, what happens when a rhetorical disposition of superficial, ironic detachment becomes a mode of existence. This is why a remark like Christel's—"daß er *immer* so spricht" (4:111 [my emphasis], him [*always*] talking like that, 87)—is so important and why it does more harm than good when it comes to persuading Melanie to stay. For this maximalist tendency, this ability of a flippant rhetorical stance to choke out all other forms of communication, this is a root problem in *L'Adultera* and other society novels. Van der Straaten *always* recites empty platitudes and says things he does not really mean; Käthe *never* thinks to set aside her prodigious talents in the realm of meaningless banter. Both represent particularly severe instantiations of rhetorical contagion.

When one sees these characters as the limit cases that they are, it is easier to recognize the difference between Fontane's personal life and those that he depicts in his fiction. That difference is one of degree, of severity and acuteness. Whatever fondness Fontane exhibited for witty repartee, subtext, and bons mots, he was not known to be mired in superficial platitudes. Nor did he have the reputation of someone with whom one could not have a serious conversation, someone unable to be earnest or take others seriously. Mecklenburg, writing on this very issue, says of the resemblance between Fontane and van der Straaten, "The fact that Fontane artistically objectified his own tendencies in this direction makes his texts that much more believable and does nothing to lessen the substance of their critique."[30] Mecklenburg's point is that the details of Fontane's social life do not undermine his literary critique of rhetorical decadence and contagion. I would add that this is so because Fontane the author takes speech patterns that he himself employed, speech patterns that were indeed prevalent and popular among Berlin's educated classes, and magnifies them through figures such as Käthe, Schach, and van der Straaten. Not that he enlarges these traits to the point of absurdity; what he is after, rather, is the danger of language controlling and crafting the subject more than the subject can control and craft language. Those who believe, for example, that they have mastered an ironically detached air find that their ironic detachment actually has mastery over them.

In his apology, if one can call it that, to Storm, Fontane makes a sort of confession: "Ich habe hinsichtlich meiner Taten und Worte eine große Unbekümmertheit, und von meinen Worten möcht ich gelegentlich sagen: sie haben mich."[31] (I have with regard to my actions and words a large degree of carelessness, and of my expressions I sometimes want to say: they have me.) He confesses here to a remarkable lack of control and concern when it comes to language. His words and utterances have him in their grip, rather than the other way around. Though this might be true of the desire to whisper off-color remarks at a dinner party, Fontane's prose, and his knack for dialogue in particular, demonstrates a masterful control of language that mitigates against a far-reaching or existential understanding of this passage. Note that he describes the feeling as occurring from time to time, as opposed to the relentless rhetorical enthrallment of his fictional characters. Nonetheless, this propensity toward being captured by one's own language is precisely what Fontane explores in works such as *L'Adultera*. Despite the lack of concern expressed in his correspondence with Storm, Fontane's novels are not nearly so blithe with regard to a language that takes control of the subject and shapes existence. Fontane's society novels suggest that a fashionable rhetorical stance, a particularly heedless relationship to language and truth, if adopted too often and enthusiastically, can stick.

Avowal, Irony's Antidote

In addition to worrying about the erosion of reliable communication, the novel also presents an alternative in the form of avowal. This could represent another advantage to the genre of the adultery novel as society novel. In works such as *L'Adultera* and *Unwiederbringlich*, irony and adultery eventually lead to moments of avowal, to lover's confessions

---

[30] Mecklenburg, *Theodor Fontane*, 262.
[31] Cited in Mecklenburg, *Theodor Fontane*, 243.

that could not be more earnest. The ironic characters in these novels believe that it does not matter what one says, that truth is passé, and that yes is as good as no. They believe this right up until the moment when they need to know whether their love will be requited, or whether their spouse has taken another lover. Intense conflicts such as these force the ironist's hand and demonstrate that there is a limit beyond which the negative freedom of irony no longer applies. Adultery is thus a vehicle by which Fontane pursues the topic of avowal and truth-telling in an environment of ubiquitous irony. The overlap of adultery and social realism allows him to juxtapose the private and the public, the earnest and the ironic.

L'Adultera's highpoint of domestic drama comes when Melanie reveals to van der Straaten her intention to leave him for another man. Here, the fundamental conflict between irony and avowal becomes acute. On the one hand, van der Straaten's ironic attitude reveals itself in this moment to be not just a form of frivolous social interaction but rather a mode of being, a thoroughgoing cynicism and lack of principle. Melanie, on the other hand, insists finally on an act of avowal, not just to her husband but to the world at large. Both her language and the narrator's in this instance point to juridical and religious registers of avowal and confession, to a speech act that will bring real-world consequences. As Melanie puts it in her most direct and emphatic statement, "ich will wieder klare Verhältnisse sehen" (I want my position [my relationships] to be clear, 92), which is only possible, she says, "wenn ich gehe, wenn ich mich von Dir trenne und mich offen und vor aller Welt zu meinem Thun bekenne" (4:117, if I go, if I leave you and acknowledge [avow] my acts before the world, 92). She insists on openly and publicly avowing, admitting, or confessing to a deed that she now accepts as her own.[32] The desire to avow, to state clearly how things stand, is precisely what necessitates her departure. When she wants to restore clear relationships, she refers not just to romantic relationships but also to relationships between phenomenon and essence, between the phenomenon of her public attachment (e.g., marriage) and the essence of her desire and affection. As long as she stays together with van der Straaten, those two remain misaligned.

In order to understand the depth of conflict in this scene, it is important to see Melanie's avowal as a counterpoint to van der Straaten's

---

[32] Melanie's avowal is the functional opposite of a speech act more frequently found in novels of adultery—namely, the excuse. She does not seek, as one typically does with an excuse, to refute or evade an accusation; rather, she openly accepts her guilt. On the excuse, see Fritz Breithaupt, *Kultur der Ausrede* (Berlin: Suhrkamp, 2012), particularly the chapter on "Selbstausreden," 193–211.

fundamental irony. When Melanie confesses to van der Straaten her intention to leave him, even when she insinuates that the child she is expecting is not his, he responds with forgiveness and understanding. Above all, he wants her to stay. He argues, in essence, that her affair is not serious enough to destroy their life together, and that he is willing to trade passion for stability. "Bleib," he says, "Es soll nichts sein" (4:115, [Stay.] It won't matter, 91). At first, Melanie finds herself deeply affected by her husband's words, but the more he speaks, the more his speech undoes itself. The narrator describes this internal contradiction, "Es war eben immer dasselbe Lied. Alles, was er sagte, kam aus einem Herzen voll Gütigkeit und Nachsicht, aber die Form, in die sich diese Nachsicht kleidete, verletzte wieder" (4:116, It was always the same old song. Everything he said came from a generous heart, but the tolerance took a form that wounded her, 91). The passage identifies an opposition between the logic of van der Straaten's statements and the rhetorical form in which they are couched. He means to speak to his wife in ways that are comforting and reassuring, and yet his form of expression contorts the most obvious sentiment into its opposite: goodwill comes to seem mean-spirited, while charity turns into cynicism. In short, the fatal flaw in van der Straaten's attempt to dissuade his wife is an irony in which expression turns away from the essence of what is meant. And the narrative underscores that there is nothing new or surprising in the self-canceling effects of his language. His words operate detached from the feeling that gives rise to them and engender an effect opposed to that which he feels. Even when so much is at stake and van der Straaten's language is calculated for maximum effect, it still overflows with contradictory meanings.

There is a second and more fundamental sense in which van der Straaten's attitude is ironic. By proposing that they stay together, regardless of how Melanie feels, he essentially recommends to her a cynical irony of behavior: there is no obligation to live, speak, or behave in a way that conforms to the truth of one's feelings. It is as if he proposes an ironic marriage. Even though they do not love each other in earnest, they can profess the opposite to Berlin society. In van der Straaten's eyes, there is no need for the phenomenon of marriage to reflect a core of love and affection; indeed, the two can be polar opposites. His proposed solution is of a piece with his other expressions of irony—the same old song—since here too he wants to treat serious things as if they were not serious at all. "Er behandelte das, was vorgefallen, aller Erschütterung unerachtet, doch bagatellmäßig obenhin und mit einem starken Anflug von cynischem Humor" (4:116, In spite of his deep emotion he treated the incident as a trifle, with contempt and a definite streak of cynical amusement, 91). Van der Straaten has arrived at the point of irony as a way of being. Fontane achieves in this conversation a striking incongruity between the gravity of the situation and the frivolity of van der Straaten's response. Nothing is so serious that it cannot be treated as trivial.

In the narrator's words, the sticking point in his expressions of leniency and forgiveness is his tendency to treat Melanie's announcement "bagatellmäßig" as a fleeting trifle rather than a devastating rupture. The choice of term is significant, since the first time he mentions Rubehn's visit, he asserts that it is merely a bagatelle. Melanie, however, senses that the ostensibly trivial matter is actually "eine ganz besondere Beichte" (4:18, a very special confession, 13), so that even in that early scene, as well as in their arguments about whether something should be taken seriously, Fontane plants the seeds of their irreconcilable conflict between irony and avowal. Melanie sees her affair and her change of heart as essential to her being, whereas van der Straaten wants to treat it all as trivial, as something that might even be humorous in a cynical way.

The narrative reflects the depth of their conflict as it conveys Melanie's thoughts. Even though society will judge her harshly, "Das Geschehene [...] war doch auch zugleich ihr Stolz, dies Einsetzen ihrer Existenz, dies rückhaltlose Bekenntniß ihrer Neigung" (4:116, at the same time she took pride in putting her whole life on the line, in the unreserved confession [avowal] of her love, 91). Van der Straaten wants to treat her affair as inconsequential: they can continue to put forward the appearance of marital union, even though the underlying relationship has fallen apart. It is this fundamentally ironic discrepancy between phenomenon and essence that Melanie can no longer tolerate. Her avowal aims to bring back into alignment the outward form of her relationships and the inward substance of her attachments, regardless of what it costs her—hence the language of unqualified confession, a full-throated acknowledgment of her deed that holds nothing back. Her forthrightness interrupts the chain of ironic negation. Whereas van der Straaten aims to perpetuate that ironic chain, avowal counters irony and closes the discrepancy by realigning language with what it signifies.

What Melanie professes in this moment is serious, reliable, and efficacious. In a word, it is realistic. She intends to present to the world a more accurate and faithful picture of where her affections lie. At the beginning of their conversation, she explains her intention to leave, saying, "Es soll klar zwischen uns werden. Ich habe diese schnöde Lüge satt" (4:114, I want things to be straight between us. I'm sick of this vile lie, 90). Her counterpoint to irony seeks clarity as opposed to ambiguity, truth as opposed to falsehood. The sentiment accords with Fontane's early programmatic statements regarding realism, when he writes that realism wants "das *Wahre*" (the *true*) as opposed to "die Lüge" (*NA*

21.1:13, the lie). According to the terms that Fontane outlines in 1853, Melanie is a realist whose avowal is carried out in the spirit of that movement. She will no longer tolerate hazy ambiguity, the forced performance of an insincere marriage, nor the lie of empty words that do not correspond to deeds. As Neumann puts it with slightly different emphasis, "It is the conventionalized discourse of the others, contaminated by well-worn sayings and figural patterns, that the novel's heroine refuses."[33] In the face of all that contaminated, empty chatter, she speaks the truth. This speech act—whether one calls it avowal, confession, *l'aveu*, or *Bekenntnis*—is the recourse of realism in an insincere age. It is the language one turns to as a counter to the unreliable speech and ironic detachment that proliferates in contemporary society.

This is why it is so important to Melanie that she follow up her declaration with a punctual departure. "ich will mein neues Leben nicht mit einer Unpünktlichkeit beginnen. Unpünktlich sein ist unordentlich sein. [...] Es soll Ordnung in mein Leben kommen, Ordnung und Einheit" (4:118, I don't want to begin my new life by being unpunctual. Unpunctuality is a kind of disorder. [...] I want order in my life, order and unity, 93). This might seem at first glance like an extraneous bit of fastidiousness or a convenient way to end a difficult conversation. But punctuality takes on an outsized role in this moment because it returns to the question of whether one means what one says, whether one's language is reliable, and whether one's words and deeds are aligned. Melanie has promised Rubehn that she would arrive to meet him at a certain time. This is a recurring theme in Fontane's explorations of unreliable language—recall, for example, the ramifications of Schach's betrayal when he promises Victoire that he will return the next day but then breaks his word. So it is important to Melanie that she keep her word by being punctual. She has just explained that she can no longer abide a fundamental disjunction of word and deed. If avowal represents her attempt to realign those two elements, then the first step in acting upon her avowal is to make good on her promise by turning words into action. Thus, the orderliness to which her statement refers is not just a matter of being organized and on time. It refers, rather, to bringing phenomenon and essence back into order and harmony— hence the closing word "unity," as she means to unify word and deed and undo the disorder that van der Straaten's irony has introduced. Dirk Baecker, writing from a systems theoretical perspective, asserts that earnestness "makes it possible to enact the unity of communication and consciousness," where irony "lets consciousness experience its

---

[33] Neumann, "Speisesaal und Gemäldegalerie," 153.

difference."[34] In his formulation, phenomenon and essence are replaced by communication and consciousness, but the unifying power of earnestness (e.g., of avowal) remains the same.

Melanie's defiant speech act in this scene is not a simple declaration of fact; it is an avowal, and it conforms with the main components of avowal that Foucault outlines in his lectures. First, there is "a certain cost of enunciation" to Melanie's avowal.[35] Through this verbal act, Melanie leaves behind her children, her home, her social circle, and the comfortable upper-class life to which she was accustomed. These consequences constitute the most obvious way in which Melanie's avowal differs from more mundane affirmations of truth. Second, through the avowal, the speaker binds herself to her declaration; she constitutes herself as the thing she says she is, be it a lover, a criminal, or a madwoman. She obligates herself willingly to the role referred to in the book's title, that of the adulteress, and she takes it on as part of her being. In a passage cited above, the narrative equates her wholehearted avowal with "das Einsetzen ihrer Existenz" (4:116, putting her whole life on the line, 91). It is remarkable that Melanie and the narrator perceive her act of truth-telling in almost Foucauldian terms as putting her very life at stake, as the implementation of a new kind of existence.

Third, in Foucault's model of avowal, one must subjugate oneself to the authority of another person. It could certainly seem that Melanie does not follow the Foucauldian model in this instance, at least not vis-à-vis her husband. She does not give in; she does not submit to the nineteenth-century norm of male authority. Indeed, she rejects all of van der Straaten's entreaties, such that the husband appears here to be the one avowing himself as a lover and submitting to *her* authority. And yet, in a broader sense, Melanie's avowal does take place within a power structure, Prussian society in the late nineteenth century, which exercises its authority over her through moral condemnation and social shunning. This is a theme that one finds both early and late in Fontane's literary career, for Melanie suffers under the same force of denunciation and exclusion that Effi Briest must endure when her affair comes to light. Effi's mother describes a situation that applies as much to Melanie as it does to Effi, when she writes, "Die Welt, in der Du gelebt hast, wird Dir verschlossen sein" (15:301, The world you have lived in will be closed to you).[36] In both novels, society exacts a heavy price from those

---

[34] Dirk Baecker, "Ernste Kommunikation," in *Sprachen der Ironie—Sprachen des Ernstes*, ed. Karl Heinz Bohrer (Frankfurt am Main: Suhrkamp, 2000), 398.
[35] Foucault, *Wrong-Doing, Truth-Telling*, 15.
[36] Translation from Fontane, *Effi Briest*, 187.

who go against its standards of behavior, and in Melanie's case, this consequence contributes to the costliness of her avowal.[37]

There is a fourth aspect to Foucault's definition of avowal, and it is the most important for illuminating *L'Adultera*. Foucault says that the defining feature of avowal is its ability to change one's relationship both to oneself and to what has been avowed. He elaborates on this idea, saying, "To avow one's love means to begin to love in another way;" it "qualifies [the subject] differently with regard to what he says." These quotations focus on the subject's relationship to what has been avowed, but Foucault eventually shifts the emphasis and restates this point as an investigation into how avowal modifies "his [the subject's] relationship to himself."[38] It goes without saying that Melanie's avowal changes the way in which she loves. No longer forced to lie and conceal, she can now, by dint of her avowal, openly acknowledge her relationship with Rubehn. But it is also important to Melanie that her verbal act modifies her relationship to herself. As she tells van der Straaten, "Ich will fort [...] um mich vor mir selber wieder herzustellen" (4:117, I want to go in order to rebuild my self-respect [myself], 92). When Melanie identifies the purpose of her decision to leave, she refers not only to her relationship with Rubehn. She focuses also on her relationship to herself. The necessity of her departure is a matter of self-perception, and her choice of words is noteworthy. A term like "herstellen" evinces a surprisingly modern notion of subjectivity as a construct or work in progress. She intends to reconstitute or reassemble herself in her own eyes, which involves reestablishing a continuity between outward presentation and inward essence.

In all these ways, one finds a significant degree of overlap between *L'Adultera*'s depiction of avowal and its theoretical elaboration in Foucault's lectures. My aim, though, is not merely to engage in the sterile critical exercise of imposing Foucault's terminology on Fontane's novel. By reading these scenes through a Foucauldian lens, I seek, rather, to gain new purchase on the function of avowal in Fontane's works. Through the novel's marital conflict, avowal emerges as a possible antidote and alternative to irony. It represents the potential for a different way of speaking and a different relationship to language and truth. In this way, Fontane steps beyond the diagnosis of modern communication being corrupted by irony and unreliability. He suggests

---

[37] On power relations, the male gaze, and *la société disciplinaire* in *L'Adultera*, see John Osborne, "Vision, Supervision, and Resistance: Power Relationships in Theodor Fontane's *L'Adultera*," *Deutsche Vierteljahrsschrift für Literaturwissenschaft und Geistesgeschichte* 70, no. 1 (1996): 67–79.

[38] Foucault, *Wrong-Doing, Truth-Telling*, 17.

a way to break free from the game of irony, from the *société copie*, and to find a way back to serious, authentic speech. To be sure, Fontane also presents avowal as a perilous alternative—sometimes liberating, sometimes devastating, and always costly. The point remains, though, that this narrative is invested in the idea that there is something beyond irony, that it is still possible, in a post-truth world, to speak clearly and dependably.

This assertion—that the novel presents avowal as an alternative, even an antidote, to empty speech—goes against the grain of some recent interpretations of *L'Adultera*. Scholars who attend to rhetorical contamination or unreliable language in the novel tend to see Melanie's resistance as failed; they tend to take the story's final third as a perpetuation of the very rhetorical entanglements from which she has tried to extricate herself. I have profited from Neumann's work on the Prussian culture of citation, copy, and cliché in the novel, and I agree with his conclusion that Fontane's novels are interested in "the construction of reality through the social act of communication."[39] But our readings part ways, for example, when he sees Melanie's speech act as leading her back into the same rhetorical trap (empty, iterative inauthenticity) from which she had hoped to escape. He points to Melanie's own words in the decisive scene, "es gibt keine Lebenslagen, in denen man aus der Selbsttäuschung und dem Komödienspiele herauskäme" (4:117, there's no situation in which we don't deceive ourselves and play act, 92), and reads them as evidence "of the intractability of this dilemma of authentication, of the indissolubility of a copied existence."[40] Authentic speech is, in other words, impossible, because conventional forms of empty rhetoric adulterate every attempt to talk one's way beyond them.[41] There is nothing beyond the copies and citations, no authentic original, to which one could retreat.

Without yet outlining my argument for seeing avowal as a viable alternative in the novel, I want to note the context in which Melanie delivers these lines. She catches herself talking about shame and guilt and reciting platitudes about feeling remorse that she does not sincerely believe. Her statement thus acknowledges from a position of critical

---

[39] Neumann, "Speisesaal und Gemäldegalerie," 156.
[40] Neumann, "Speisesaal und Gemäldegalerie," 153.
[41] The interpretation also highlights a performative dilemma in properly reading rhetoric: if Melanie is correct that there is no way out of inauthentic play-acting, then it is problematic to take her statement as an authentic, reliable depiction of that predicament. Should one construe this particular statement as somehow exempt from the ineluctable self-delusion that it diagnoses? Or is it rather a further manifestation of delusional masquerade, something that cannot be taken at face value?

distance the danger of slipping back into recited clichés, but it pivots away from them to a forthright language of avowal and reconstruction of the self. Immediately after the complaint of rhetorical futility, she undermines that pessimism with a clear-eyed statement of verity: "Wie steht es denn eigentlich? Ich will fort, nicht aus Schuld, sondern aus Stolz" (4:117, What is the real position? I want to go, not because I feel guilty, but because I am proud, 92). Melanie cannot really mean that there is *no way out* of inauthenticity. Her demonstrated ability to recognize inauthentic speech and to state plainly and truthfully how things actually stand belies the pessimism embedded in the prior statement. What the narrative does here, though, is speak to the persistent danger of rhetorical contagion. She says that there are no special circumstances, no situations that are solemn enough to turn back the tide of empty, ironic talk. As van der Straaten amply demonstrates, even a profoundly serious conversation about infidelity and separation runs the risk of being adulterated by platitudes and ironic detachment ("it's nothing"). The circumstances alone—even circumstances as grave as the ones in which Melanie now finds herself—won't save her; they are not enough to interrupt the seemingly infinite chain of delusion and negation. Instead, the turn from lie to truth, from obscurity to clarity—a turn that Melanie executes precisely in the above cited lines—requires an act of will and subjective agency. As Melanie's departure and her subsequent life with Rubehn demonstrate, it is only by saying what she means and living out what she says that the subject can use a different mode of speech to construct a different mode of being.

Geulen takes Neumann's argument about the narrative's unresolvable dilemma a step further by highlighting all the repetitions in the book's final third. Noting that the novel's end is much like its beginning—it famously closes with another copy of the Tintoretto painting—she argues, too, that the culture of copy, citation, and empty phrases cannot be so easily escaped. From the perspective of narrative design, if Melanie's ostensibly new life is depicted via a series of citations and repetitions from her old life, then the narrative blurs any distinction between the old and the new and thereby suggests that she is stuck in the same inauthentic rhetorical culture that she thought she had left behind. Geulen writes, "The theater of citation perpetuates itself even behind the characters' backs." And she concludes that the narrative ultimately renders itself suspect, "because it acts as if there were an alternative within the system, an alternative that the narrative voice cancels through reference to repetitions."[42] The passage puts its

---

[42] Geulen, "Realismus ohne Entsagung," 48–9.

finger on the crux of the issue: are Melanie's avowal and subsequent new beginning meant to be taken as a legitimate alternative to the rhetorical culture that van der Straaten embodies? Or are they merely an "as if" alternative, couched in the subjunctive, one that the narrative puts forward only to undercut subtly via its discursive presentation?

It will not go lost on readers that this latter possibility would represent a higher potentiation of irony in the novel, another link in the chain of ironic solvents. The narrative, then, would propose an alternative to irony (i.e., avowal), but it would present that alternative in a way that cancels and reverses the content of the proposition, putting it in air quotes, *as if* there were any alternative to the prevailing conventions of non-communication. In a pristine reflection of irony's discrepancy between phenomenon and essence, the form of narrative discourse would rescind the very alternative that the story presents. There is a seductive aspect to this line of argument. It makes Fontane an ironist in the mold of infinite instability, aligning him with both the German Romantic tradition of "permanent parabasis" and twentieth-century critical theories that see in the work of rhetoric "vertiginous possibilities of referential aberration."[43] It makes him more of an early modernist than a late realist, and it rescues the novel's relatively happy ending from the tarnish of affirmative sentimentality. On this view, the final gesture of reconciliation—van der Straaten giving Rubehn and Melanie the gift of a miniature Tintoretto copy—represents not a smoothing-out of prior conflicts but rather another involution in the novel's reflections on irony and authenticity. It returns to the novel's conclusion an edge of uncertainty and ambivalence.

The attractiveness of such arguments notwithstanding, Fontane is representationally more conservative than the above readings would allow. He does not in *L'Adultera* write Melanie into an abyss of ironic inauthenticity; nor does the narrative rescind the viability of avowal as an alternative to forms of fatuous talk. In fact, it insists via repetition that the rhetorical stance of avowal is sustainable and capable of functioning in the world. Geulen is correct to point out how the book's final third harks back to and echoes earlier events. But rather than enfold Melanie back into a rhetoric of inauthenticity and empty phrases, such repetitions actually reiterate the fundamental opposition that has emerged between Melanie and her ex-husband, between avowal and irony. Take, for instance, the Christmas gift, the miniature of *L'Adultera*, that van der Straaten has delivered to Melanie and Rubehn. On one level, yes, this gesture perpetuates a culture of copy, citation, and repetition. But it also

---

[43] De Man, "Semiology and Rhetoric," 10

reiterates that curious admixture of *Scherz* and *Ernst* that typifies van der Straaten's ironic bearing. The package is labeled simply "Julklapp," which situates it within the Scandinavian tradition of humorous, anonymous gift-giving. The point of *Julklapp* is that there should be something funny or joking about the gift, and that comedic aspect is often added through excessive packaging, or the addition of a humorous verse that pokes fun at the recipient and hints at the sender's identity.[44] The novel thus closes with van der Straaten taking the most serious and devastating occurrence in his life—his premonition of infidelity, the affair, the divorce—and repackaging it in the form of something lighthearted and humorous. It reiterates his ironic incongruity to such an extent that the gift is less a Tintoretto *en miniature* and more a portrait of van der Straaten's entire rhetorical bearing *en miniature*, the very bearing that Melanie left behind when she separated from him.

The unnecessarily frustrating packaging of the *Julklapp* gift is also noteworthy. At the bottom of the crate, they find a large apple, which feels like a bit of heavy-handed symbolism of female guilt. Melanie cannot figure out how to get at the gift inside the apple, "als sich durch eine zufällige Bewegung ihrer Hand *die geschickt zusammengepaßten Hälften* des Apfels auseinanderschoben" (4:163 [my emphasis], when a chance movement of her hand dislodged the two halves, which had been carefully fitted together, 128). The passage's language evinces another echo from the novel's beginning. One will recall that, according to the narrative voice, van der Straaten speaks of his wife with a certain "Feierlichkeit, in der *Scherz und Ernst geschickt zusammenklangen*" (4:7 [emphasis mine], solemnity in which seriousness and jest were neatly harmonized, 4). Like the two halves of the apple, van der Straaten's faux solemnity skillfully fits together the earnest and the unserious. And if the closing passage's language repeats that formulation, it is because here, too, van der Straaten blurs the line between what is serious and what is not and forces those opposites together in a volatile form of irony. He continues to treat with cynical humor what is actually serious.

But the crucial point is that the novel ends with Melanie pulling those two halves apart. No matter how skillfully van der Straaten has fitted together the ironic and the earnest, Melanie is able to separate them. In a highly symbolic gesture, she reasserts the distinction between what is serious and what is frivolous and insists on a difference that irony sought to erase. She emerges as the character who is able to deconstruct a false, pieced-together façade in order to arrive at the essence or core, at the "Stelle des Kernhauses" (4:163, the core, 128). Her bisecting of

---

[44] Martina Eberspächer, *Der Weihnachtsmann: zur Entstehung einer Bildtradition in Aufklärung und Romantik* (Stuttgart: M. Eberspächer, 2002), 72.

the apple is akin to her cutting the chain of ironic negation. She accomplishes this through a rhetorical bearing that holds apart the poles of the serious and the unserious, in short, through avowal, by speaking earnestly of what is serious and by meaning what she says.

The narrative in the last third in fact insists on the sustainability of Melanie's new way of speaking and new way of being. Far from undermining the efficacy of avowal, the narrative depicts her ongoing commitment to aligning word and deed and to enacting the person she presents herself as in language. When Rubehn's finances take a turn for the worse, Melanie brushes aside his despair and insists that she can do without luxuries and adapt to a modest lifestyle. For her, it is another opportunity to avow. Foucault says that "avowal is not simply an observation about oneself. It is a sort of engagement [...]. It implies that he who speaks promises to be what he affirms himself to be."[45] This sense of avowal provides a fitting description of Melanie's attitude. In this moment, she affirms that she is committed to Rubehn, for better or for worse, that her vows were not impulsive, and that she will continue to live out her word by adjusting to the reality of deprivation. It is only from this perspective that her earnest declaration makes sense: "Und nun kann ich mich bewähren und will es und werd' es, und nun kommt *meine* Zeit. Ich will nun zeigen, was ich kann" (4:155, And now I can prove myself, and I shall and I will; my time has come. Now I will show what I am capable of, 122). By adapting to modest circumstances, she will demonstrate her fidelity to Rubehn but also her fidelity to her word.

Their conversation revolves around an issue that has proved central to the novel—whether one can be taken seriously, whether language is reliable, whether one actually means what one says. Rubehn, for his part, replies in essence that talk is cheap. It is easy for Melanie to speak of belt tightening and doing without, but since she has never experienced deprivation, she does not understand what it would mean to transform those words into practice. Her words are nice, but they are naïve and therefore insincere. His rebuttal hinges on a discrepancy between appearance and reality, so that he sees in her declarations an unintended irony. Without first-hand experience of the conditions to which she commits herself, she does not understand what her words entail and thus cannot mean them sincerely. They are, in the long run, not dependable.

In the end, Rubehn is wrong. He underestimates Melanie, who makes good on her word and fulfills everything to which she has obligated

---

[45] Foucault, *Wrong-Doing, Truth-Telling*, 16.

herself. Although Rubehn was initially inclined, "den Eifer Melanie's für eine bloße Opfer-Caprice zu nehmen" (4:158, to regard Melanie's eagerness as a capricious show of sacrifice, 125), he must eventually concede that she is true to her word. What he took to be merely capricious turns out to be in earnest. The key line comes when the narrative voice says, "Und Melanie nahm es ernst mit jedem Worte, das sie gesagt hatte" (4:157, And Melanie meant [earnestly] every word she had spoken, 124). The statement applies as much to Melanie's avowal to van der Straaten as it does to her promises to Rubehn; it summarizes her entire disposition. By meaning what she says and saying what she means, by maintaining the distinction between avowal and unserious banter, Melanie reveals herself as the antithesis to van der Straaten's manner of speaking. In her new life with Rubehn, Melanie continues to align word and deed, and it is her ongoing fidelity to her word that steers her out of problems.

The numerous repetitions in the book's final third thus reiterate the fundamental opposition between van der Straaten and Melanie, between irony and avowal. The repetitive design of *L'Adultera*'s narrative does not demonstrate Melanie's ongoing entrapment within a culture of mindless recitation, nor does it mark as futile any attempt to get beyond the rhetoric of irony and empty talk. Rather, those repetitions restate Melanie's commitment to a different way of speaking and different way of being. The book's conclusion is affirmative, but not so much in the sense of overwrought sentimentality. What it affirms, at least at this point in Fontane's literary career, is the power of avowal to cut through irony and to speak in ways that are meaningful and reliable, free from pretense or dissimulation. If anything, the numerous repetitions toward the end of novel show that Melanie is able to maintain this culturally idiosyncratic relationship to language and truth even within a society devoted to empty phrases and the recitation of platitudes. *L'Adultera* thus makes a strong case for the efficacy of avowal. Within Fontane's oeuvre, it provides the strongest statement of belief in an antidote to pervasive irony. *L'Adultera* remains an outlier among the adultery novels precisely because of the protagonist's success in breaking with the past and refashioning her life, all of which is necessitated and made possible by her rhetorical bearing of avowal.

Five *Unwiederbringlich*, or the Impotence of Being Earnest

Ernst ist das Leben, heiter ist die Kunst.[1]
—Friedrich Schiller

We should treat all the trivial things of life seriously, and all the serious things of life with sincere and studied triviality.[2]
—Oscar Wilde

Unwiederbringlich presents a fitting counterpoint to *L'Adultera*. When we juxtapose them in terms of avowal and its efficacy, it appears to be the earlier novel's functional opposite: avowal emerges in *Unwiederbringlich* not as a noble act of reclaiming rhetorical authenticity and efficacy but rather as a laughable display of pathos. Now it seems that he who avows makes a fool of himself. The gender roles are reversed— here it is the husband who wants to leave and start a new life with a new lover—and the outcomes are reversed as well. Melanie's successful avowal is mirrored, darkly, by Helmuth Holk's humiliating and unrequited declaration of love. Unlike *L'Adultera*, *Unwiederbringlich* sharply circumscribes the power and promise of avowal.

In several respects, the circumstances of the two adultery plots are similar. Holk, a wealthy Junker from Schleswig–Holstein, has been married for many years now and has two children, though he is not entirely satisfied with his pious wife and her overly serious manner. Divergent rhetorical bearings and speech mannerisms lead to conflict in this novel, as well. Partly as a result of these frictions, when Holk travels to Copenhagen in his role as gentleman-in-waiting to Princess Maria Eleonore, he falls in love with another woman, Ebba von Rosenberg, a member of the princess's court. He then returns to Schleswig, to his

---

[1] Friedrich Schiller, *Werke und Briefe*, ed. Klaus Harro Hilzinger (Frankfurt am Main: Deutscher Klassiker Verlag, 1988–2004), 4:17.
[2] Cited in Sylvan Barnet, "Introduction," in *The Importance of Being Earnest and Other Plays*, ed. Oscar Wilde (New York: New American Library, 1985), xxxi.

wife Christine, to make the kind of declaration that Melanie makes to van der Straaten, but this is where the similarities end. Holk's attempts to avow—to the princess, to Christine, and finally to Ebba—all fail miserably and leave him a laughingstock of Copenhagen and persona non grata back home in Holkenäs. The question for the present chapter is: what does this outcome mean for the depiction of irony and avowal in Fontane's works? Does it in fact undermine the affirmative portrayal of avowal in *L'Adultera*?

In what follows, I argue that *Unwiederbringlich*'s depiction of failed avowal does not directly contradict the import of *L'Adultera*, but it certainly constricts the range of avowal's efficacy. The later novel presents avowal as fraught and precarious, as dependent not only on the will and pleasure of another person but also on the reliability of her language. And that language turns out not to be reliable at all. Holk's avowal ultimately fails because it does not aim to counteract irony with forthright truth-telling. It seeks instead to rely upon and to build upon ironic speech, to transform inconsequential play with language into something serious, solid, and reliable. Holk mistakes Ebba's wanton, flirtatious banter—which is never meant in earnest—for her version of avowal, for a declaration of love, and he then seeks to reiterate that ostensible avowal to others. *Unwiederbringlich*, sometimes classified as the first example of Fontane's mature novelistic output, thus portrays from a different angle of vision the age-old dilemma in the society novels, the inability to distinguish between what is meant to be taken seriously and what is not.³ In this instance, irony and its misreading have the power to enervate avowal before a single earnest word is spoken.

Like other of Fontane's novels, *Unwiederbringlich* revolves around the difficulty of determining whether particular utterances should be taken seriously or ironically. Also like other Fontane novels, this one establishes that concern in its opening paragraphs. The narrative begins with a description of its initial setting, with the sea, the dunes, and the Holkenäs estate. Commenting humorously on its Italianate architectural style and neoclassical Greek references, Holk's brother-in-law Arne calls it a "nachgeborenen 'Tempel zu Pästum'" (*latter-day temple of Paestum*).⁴ Here the narrator steps in to clarify, or not: "Natürlich

---

³ On the inclusion of *Unwiederbringlich* among Fontane's mature novels, see, for example, Helen Chambers, "The Inadequacy of the Wife-and-Mother Model: Female Happiness in Theodor Fontane's Unwiederbringlich," *Seminar* 47, no. 2 (2011): 286.
⁴ English from Theodor Fontane, *Irretrievable*, trans. Douglas Parmée (New York: New York Review Books, 2011), 3. Further references in this chapter to this translation appear parenthetically.

Unwiederbringlich, or the Impotence of Being Earnest 149

Alles ironisch. Und doch auch wieder mit einer gewissen Berechtigung. Denn was man von der See her sah, war wirklich ein aus Säulen zusammengestelltes Oblong" (13:5, Ironically, of course, yet with some justification, for seen from the sea it looked like an oblong cluster of columns, 3). The comparison is completely ironic, but it is also in a certain sense justified and reasonable. On the one hand, the narrative voice asserts that the comparison is facetious, overblown, and not to be taken seriously. And yet, on the other hand, that same commentary blurs the distinction between the earnest and the ironic. It suggests that perhaps one should take the comparison seriously, despite the facetious, joking tone. The narrative voice dwells in this moment in the tension between two incompatible readings—between dismissing someone's speech as an ironic joke and taking it seriously. Should one chuckle at the comparison? Or does it deserve serious consideration? Or both at once?

Arne's comment could be overlooked as a superfluous bit of dialogue, and I do not want to make too much hay out of an off-hand remark. But Fontane has an affinity for precisely this sort of iconic detail that captures in miniature the central themes and conflicts of his narrative. So it is in *Unwiederbringlich*, as the issue of whether to take others' speech as serious or flippant becomes an urgent, high-stakes question. The rhetorical ambiguity that the narrative voice highlights in Arne's comment is the very same ambiguity to which Holk falls prey in his dealings with Ebba. And it isn't just Holk. Rapid oscillations between the serious and the ironic characterize many of the novel's interactions. For example, when Holk and Ebba skate dangerously close to the ice's edge (when they've gone *too far*, when they're on *thin ice*), the princess somewhat jokingly expresses her misgivings about their risky behavior. The narrator traces the oscillation in her words, saying, "Dies Alles war am Kaffeetisch so halb scherzhaft hingesagt worden [...]; aber hinter dem Scherze hatte sich offenbar ein Ernst versteckt" (13:220, She made these remarks half-jokingly when taking coffee [...], but in spite of her jocular tone she was obviously serious, 192). The majority of the novel's dilemma is captured by the vexing term "half-joking," which denotes a familiar amalgamation of the serious and the unserious. The very choice of verbs—*[da]hinsagen*—indicates that her remarks are not meant to be taken in earnest, for it suggests saying something without having given it a great deal of thought or consideration. And yet, once again, there is obviously an element of earnestness concealed behind that façade of humor. This sort of language confronts one with the dilemma of adulterated, ironic speech all over again. If one takes the princess's words as earnest, one risks taking them *too* seriously; after all, it is clear that she is speaking to some extent in jest. But if one dismisses it all as joking, unserious banter, one risks missing the serious import of her misgivings. After all, there is clearly something earnest buried under her facetious tone. This fundamental uncertainty with regard to language and its reliability lies at the heart of the conflicts between Holk and Christine and between Holk and Ebba. In short, it lies at the heart of the narrative's central tensions.

The opposition between *Ernst* and *Scherz*, between the earnest and the unserious, constitutes the central conflict in Holk and Christine's marriage. Initially, their differences are introduced in broader terms of character or temperament. One the one hand, Christine is presented as dour, pious, melancholy, condescending, and serious to a fault. On the other, Holk appears in contrast as less devout, as more easygoing and lighthearted. He would rather think about new infrastructure for his livestock than questions of religious dogma. Despite the different labels used in this novel (e.g., the devout Pietist versus her happy-go-lucky husband), it is important to recognize that the marital conflict depicted at the outset follows a familiar Fontanean pattern. It is essentially the same conflict as in *L'Adultera*, when Melanie and van der Straaten cannot agree on whether something is worth taking seriously, or in *Irrungen, Wirrungen*, when Käthe lacks the capacity to distinguish between serious and unserious matters. For among all the different ways that the narrative portrays Christine as excessively morose, earnestness is the dominant, most frequently recurring term. Her relentless habit of taking everything as deadly serious is precisely what exasperates Holk. Conversely, his habit of not taking things earnestly enough, in her eyes, is his primary flaw. The marital conflict centers on the same ambiguity and uncertainty that is evident in the language of Arne, the princess, and the narrative voice.

Take Arne's characterization of Christine as indicative of her tendencies toward earnestness. Evoking her Pietism with literary references, Arne says she is "ganz schöne Seele, nachgeborene Jean Paul'sche Figur, die sich [...] mit dem Ernste des Lebens den Kopf zerbricht" (13:36, some soulful figure straight out of the works of Jean Paul Richter, someone perpetually worrying about the fact that life is real, life is earnest, 30–1). It is telling that Arne describes her not just as earnest but as being overwhelmed and consumed by earnestness. Living according to Schiller's dictum that "life is serious," she cannot help but treat it as such and agonize over it. Recalling a tense conversation between Holk and Christine, he continues, "meine Schwester nahm die mehr oder weniger scherzhafte Sache wie gewöhnlich wieder ganz ernsthaft und antwortete halb gereizt, halb sentimental" (13:39, My sister took what was intended more or less as a joke with deadly seriousness and replied half in anger and half sentimentally, 32–3). This is a key passage for describing Christine's character, and the language of "partially," "entirely," and "more or less" plays an important role. Something that is "more or less" facetious or tongue-in-cheek resembles the half-serious, semi-facetious words that the princess delivers. But Christine has no ear for that complex, alloyed tone that means to be earnest and unserious at the same time. She tends to take even things that are said flippantly or ironically as entirely earnest.

Within the marriage, the spouses hold similarly binary views of each other. Holk piles on, telling Christine, "Es glückt mir nicht, [...] Dich aus Deinem ewigen Brüten und Ernstnehmen herauszureißen" (13:52, I see that I've failed to put you in a better temper or prevent you from brooding and being so serious all the time, 45). This is the flaw in her virtue, that she is relentless in her insistence on taking everything seriously, and it is interesting to look ahead and see that taking things too seriously is essentially the same mistake that Holk will make in Copenhagen. From the other side, Christine faults Holk for taking things too lightly and being insufficiently earnest. She tells Arne that her husband has a well-known "Neigung, ernste Dinge leicht zu nehmen" (13:65, tendency to take [serious] things lightly, 55).[5] Whatever other differences exist between the spouses, these passages establish the terms of their primary disagreement. Unlike in other novels, the conflict here is not so much about one's manner of speaking, although Holk has in fact manifested a shift in tone as he becomes more "ungeduldig, anzüglich, ironisch" (13:38, impatient and touchy and sarcastic [ironic], 32). It is rather about how one takes things, how one reacts to and interprets the language of others. It centers more on the effects of irony and earnestness than on their production.

One sees this conflict in action when Christine revisits the topic of the children's education. Holk's impatience shows through in the ironic, dismissive tone of his response, and the narrative reports on his tone's unintended consequence: "Aber gerade diese spöttische Behandlung, die der Gräfin zeigen sollte, daß sie das Alles mal wieder viel zu wichtig nähme, steigerte nur ihren Ernst" (13:44, This mocking tone should have warned the countess that she was once again taking things too seriously; instead it merely made her more serious, 38). Christine clearly takes such questions quite earnestly, but Holk employs ironic mockery to signal that choosing the most dogmatically correct boarding school is, from his perspective, not an issue of primary importance

---

[5] Peter Uwe Hohendahl, writing on reciprocal observation both within the novel and as part of its narrative structure, notes that character descriptions in *Unwiederbringlich* frequently come not from the narrator but from other characters' judgments and observations. Hohendahl, "Eindringliche Beobachtung. Zur Konstitution des Sozialen in *Unwiederbringlich*," in *Herausforderungen des Realismus*, ed. Peter Uwe Hohendahl and Ulrike Vedder (Freiburg: Rombach, 2018), 169–71.

for the children's well-being. Of course, this rhetorical gambit backfires. Rather than temper her earnestness, the trivializing mockery only exacerbates it. She responds with a rebuke of her own, "Ich bitte Dich, Helmuth, verzichte doch endlich darauf, eine ernsthafte Sache ins Scherzhafte zu ziehen" (13:44, I beg of you, Helmut, to stop taking this serious matter as a joke, 38). If Holk's complaint is that his wife relentlessly takes even trivial, amusing matters in an overly serious way, her complaint is just the opposite, that he drags what is serious into the realm of trivial amusement. It is an intractable conflict over what is earnest and what is not, over the extent to which one can treat something lightly, ironically, jokingly.

Despite the apparently dichotomous marital conflict presented in these scenes, the binary opposition in *Unwiederbringlich* is not quite the same as in *L'Adultera*, where the conflict was primarily between the two spouses. Instead, *Unwiederbringlich* locates the opposed positions in two radically different women, Christine and Ebba von Rosenberg, and two radically different places, Holkenäs and Copenhagen. The novel establishes a contrast between the earnest, isolated world of Holkenäs and Copenhagen, a city of pleasure, gossip, and wit.[6] The Danish city figures in the novel as a space of incessant badinage and banter, where it would be a faux pas to take anything too seriously. The geographic contrast carries over to and encompasses the two central female characters. Whereas Christine, who stays home in Holkenäs while Holk travels to Copenhagen, broods earnestly about life's serious matters, Ebba von Rosenberg is well versed in the urbane art of taking everything lightly and never meaning what she says.[7] She is risqué, flirtatious, unserious, and ironic. Her ironic disposition reflects the atmosphere that Holk finds throughout Copenhagen's courtly life. Its motto could well be, "wer die Kunst des Leichtnehmens versteht, *der* lebt, und wer alles schwer nimmt, der lebt nicht" (13:262, someone who has the art of taking them lightly knows how to live and anyone who always takes things seriously, does not know how to live, 228). Better, then, to be ironic and frivolous than to get worked up over questions of truth, morality, or justice.

And when Christine refuses to accompany Holk to Copenhagen, her refusal rests not only on the city's dissolute lifestyle, but also on its manner of speaking. "Ich kann diesen Ton nicht recht leiden" (I cannot

---

[6] On the contrasts associated with these two places, see further Christian Grawe, "*Unwiederbringlich*. Roman," in *Fontane-Handbuch*, ed. Christian Grawe and Helmuth Nürnberger (Stuttgart: Kröner, 2000), 609–10.

[7] See again Chambers for a discussion of the contrasting female roles in the novel, "The Inadequacy of the Wife-and-Mother Model."

bear that tone), she says, referring to exactly the sort of ironic, unserious tone that Ebba embodies, "es ist der Ton, der nach meinem Gefühl [...] immer einer Katastrophe vorausgeht" (13:51, I think that it is heading straight for disaster, 43–4). Christine intuits, correctly as it turns out, that a frivolous, ironic tone can lead to ruin. Her prophetic (and earnest) statement works both on the level of personal catastrophe (Holk's humiliation, their failed marriage, her suicide) and on the level of a political and military catastrophe. Just as *Schach von Wuthenow* was set in an era of impending military disaster, so *Unwiederbringlich* presents Copenhagen in the years directly before the Second Schleswig War of 1864 and Denmark's loss of Schleswig and Holstein.[8] Both novels suggest—*Schach* explicitly, *Unwiederbringlich* more subtly—that a certain ironic, unserious tone often precedes and indeed hastens political and military downfall.

As the novel establishes this contrast between the two women and two locations, it presents both as extreme poles on the continuum between absolute irony and absolute earnestness. Michael White notes similarly that the novel "may be said to operate around two opposing poles," Christine and Ebba, and that alongside "these two incompatible alternatives, two antithetical realms are constructed," Holkenäs and Copenhagen.[9] The novel then suspends Holk in the tension between these two irreconcilable positions, and it is worth noting that neither side is valorized at the outset. The narrative does not, for example, push the reader to take Christine's side, to see her serious demeanor as the necessary corrective to Holk's excessive frivolity. Quite the contrary, the narrative signals collectively suggest that the excess lies on Christine's side, in her unstinting, devout earnestness, and that Holk is somewhat justified in chafing against her rhetorical discipline.

At the same time, though, Ebba's exuberant frivolity also does not appear as the proper antidote to Christine's earnestness. It feels, rather, as if the pendulum has swung too far in the opposite direction, toward ironic emptiness, or, to avoid mixing metaphors, as if the antidote in this instance might be as bad as the sickness it was meant to cure. Holk, traveling between Holkenäs and Copenhagen, chatting with Ebba and corresponding with Christine, is located in the middle, and this situation constitutes the novel's central tension. Holk's ambivalent position is reflected in his perpetual half-ness and partiality (13:154). With one

---

[8] Hohendahl agrees that this historical background is important in assessing the novel, and he points in particular to the narrator's ignorance of future events. Hohendahl, "Eindringliche Beobachtung," 177–82.

[9] White, *Space*, 113. White eventually exchanges the binary oppositions for "journeys around a central point" (117).

foot in Copenhagen and the other in Holkenäs, he is truly at home in neither place. He's too much the happy-go-lucky cosmopolitan at home and too much the severe rural German at court. The novel began with a minor, local uncertainty regarding Arne's mostly ironic—but also partially justified—characterization of Holk's estate. But this minor uncertainty turns out, in a broader sense, to be Holk's existential dilemma. Once again, one finds that the uncertainties inherent in particular expressions or turns of phrase grow beyond all bounds to render one's very mode of being uncertain.

Once Holk arrives in Copenhagen and in the princess's service, the polarities are reversed. No longer the lighthearted foil to Christine's earnest piety, he now provides the earnest foil to Ebba's exuberance and frivolity. Indeed, he appears generally as the earnest man out in a metropolis that is already well on its way to inhabiting a post-truth age. The minor character Pentz provides a secondary embodiment of the dominant idiom. He cannot be bothered to take anything seriously, "Er bekannte sich vielmehr zu 'ride si sapis' und nahm Alles von der heiteren Seite. Dem alten Pilatus Wort 'Was ist Wahrheit' gab er in Leben, Politik und Kirche die weiteste Ausdehnung" (13:79, He believed above all in *ride si sapis* and saw everything from its funny side. In life, politics, and religion he gave the broadest possible interpretation to Pontius Pilate's words: "What is truth?" 68). Pentz lives by two maxims: *ride si sapis*, or "Laugh, if you are wise," from Martial's *Epigrams* and Pilate's profoundly skeptical question regarding the nature and existence of truth. With the verb "bekennen," the irony folds back on itself: the only thing he will avow is irony. At the base of this detached, ironic attitude is a deep-seated relativism and anti-realism. In contrast to somber Christine and her "Wahrheitsliebe" (13:199, love of the truth, 173), the cosmopolitan attitude sees the notion of truth as a passé conceit or a culturally contingent construct. Like Pilate's bearing in the biblical account, the attitude in Cophenhagen suggests that language cannot be a reliable vehicle for communicating the truth because there is no such thing as a reliable truth to be communicated. Lee McIntyre, writing on the twenty-first-century condition, identifies in the current post-truth era "a challenge not just to the idea of *knowing* reality but to the existence of reality itself."[10] This challenge, however, is not unique to the contemporary era. One finds in the nineteenth century a similarly cynical attitude that if the truth is unknowable or non-existent, one might as well laugh about it.

---

[10] McIntyre, *Post-Truth*, 10.

The depiction of Cophenhagen as a society in the thrall of ironic detachment is bolstered by the fact that *Unwiederbringlich* alludes at least twice to the Danish philosopher Kierkegaard. For instance, the ballad that so upsets Christine and plays an important role in the novel is Wilhelm Waiblinger's "Kirchhof," whose title translates the word "kirkegården" or "graveyard."[11] This point might seem trivial, except that when Holk travels to Cophenhagen, the ship that takes him there belongs to "Rheder Kirkegard" (13:68), which reinforces the sense that Kierkegaard's writings are lurking in the background of this novel. Such allusions have set scholars to work looking for ways in which Fontane's works engage with Kierkegaard's thought.[12] There is not much evidence to suggest that Fontane was deeply influenced by those works of Kierkegaard that had been translated into German by the 1880s, but perhaps the texts available to Fontane in German—primarily *Either/Or* and *Fear and Trembling*—are the wrong place to look for Kierkegaard's presence in *Unwiederbringlich*.

In fact, given the novel's sustained concern with irony, with language that, in Kierkegaard's words, "is not serious about its seriousness,"[13] it is possible to read the novel's allusions as gestures toward a Kierkegaardian notion of irony. While it is true that the thesis on irony was not available in German until 1929, long after Fontane's death, it is also true that in the late nineteenth century, Kierkegaard was widely regarded as the epitome or embodiment of modern irony. Philipp Schwab, describing Kierkegaard's early reception in Germany, acknowledges the lack of close engagement with the work on irony. But he writes, "*On the other hand* one should note that hardly any depiction of Kierkegaard can get by without a reference to his 'subtle irony' or to the title 'master of irony.'"[14] Kierkegaard was so closely associated with the concept of irony that the mere mention of his name would suffice to situate this topic within the reader's horizon of expectation. Moreover,

---

[11] Paul Irving Anderson, *Ehrgeiz und Trauer. Fontanes offiziöse Agitation 1859 und ihre Wiederkehr in Unwiederbringlich* (Stuttgart: Franz Steiner, 2002), 170.

[12] In addition to Paul Irving Anderson, see also Erwin Kobel, "Theodor Fontane—Ein Kierkegaard-Leser?" *Jahrbuch der deutschen Schillergesellschaft* 36 (1992): 255–87, who focuses more on the reception of *Stages on Life's Way*, and Julie Allen, "Theodor Fontane: A Probable Pioneer in German Kierkegaard Reception," in *Kierkegaard's Influence on Literature, Criticism, and Art. Tome I: The Germanophone World*, ed. Jon Steward (Burlington, VT: Ashgate, 2013), who notes that Fontane was acquainted with authors who contributed to the early German-language reception of Kierkegaard's works.

[13] Kierkegaard, *Concept of Irony*, 265.

[14] Philipp Schwab, "Der 'ganze Kierkegaard im Keim' und die Tradition der Ironie. Grundlinien der deutschsprachigen Rezeptionsgeschichte von Kierkegaards *Über den Begriff der Ironie*," *Kierkegaard Studies Yearbook* (2009): 391.

the association with irony underscores the novel's geographic contrast. It is fitting that the ship that takes Holk from his home to Copenhagen belongs to someone named Kirkegard—this aptly named vessel removes Holk from the earnest people around him and delivers him to a city where almost everyone is a master of irony.

In this context, Holk appears far less lighthearted, risqué, and ironic than he did back in the drab isolation of Holkenäs. Ebba's first impression is that he is excessively "nüchtern" (13:110, sober), a disparaging term that Holk will apply regularly to Christine, and Ebba complains to the princess, "Er steht da mit der Feierlichkeit eines Oberpriesters und weiß nie, wann er lachen soll" (13:109, He stands there as solemn as a high priest and has no idea when to laugh, 93). Holk, with his misplaced solemnity, comes across in the world of courtly banter as wooden and awkward. He errs on the side of being too earnest and taking things too seriously, which is why he does not know when to laugh—he cannot discern when things said in all ostensible seriousness are nonetheless meant to be taken lightly.

In stark contrast to Christine, as well as to Holk, Ebba is described as sarcastic, sardonic, sassy, and brash (13:150, 152, 189). She makes sexually suggestive insinuations and has a tendency, "alles auf die Spitze zu treiben" (13:189, exaggerating everything [to carry everything to extremes], 164). But the term used most often to describe Ebba is "übermütig," as when the narrative voice reports that she is becoming with each passing day "kecker und übermüthiger" (13:152, more and more impertinent and mischievous, 131). It is not the easiest term to translate—no single English equivalent really does it justice—but "übermütig" suggests a disposition that is wanton, exuberant, and frivolous. It designates a lightheartedness that expresses itself in careless or reckless behavior. In short, she is flippant and unserious in ways that could always migrate from careless talk to reckless action—precisely the sort of rhetorical contagion with which Fontane's work often concerns itself.

What is more, this manner of speaking accounts for much of Ebba's attractiveness in the novel. Claudia Liebrand, discussing the rhetorical performance of gender and attraction, writes that Ebba generates seductive power "with her speech, with her desire to talk. Seductive femininity is not Ebba's 'nature' but rather an effect of her rhetoric."[15] Liebrand has it right: seduction and attraction occur in *Unwiederbringlich* as a result of rhetorical performance. The novel plays out Holk's growing infatuation with the seductive power of a particular manner of

---

[15] Claudia Liebrand, "Geschlechterkonfigurationen in Fontanes *Unwiederbringlich*," in *Theodor Fontane am Ende des Jahrhunderts*, ed. Hanna Delf von Wolzogen and Helmuth Nürnberger (Würzburg: Königshausen & Neumann, 2000), 166.

Unwiederbringlich, or the Impotence of Being Earnest   157

speaking—light, ironic, frivolous, and unserious.[16] Ebba attracts Holk through the rhetorical counterpoint she offers to his wife. She speaks with ironic detachment; she reacts to others' speech with ironic detachment; and in both these respects, she differs sharply from Christine.

Hohendahl describes the Danish court along the same lines as Fontane's portrait of the Sanssouci tone: "In courtly conversation, the clever, sharp-witted thought [Einfall] counts for more than does showing consideration for other people."[17] Ebba epitomizes this sophisticated, courtly tone, and the passage points to both the attraction and the danger of Ebba's rhetorical bearing. She always has something witty, risqué, or provocative to say, but her way of speaking evinces a distinct lack of regard for other people. Those with whom she interacts, especially those with whom she flirts, cannot rely on what she says or take her seriously. She flirts, which is to say, she gives indications of amorous desire but without earnest intent. Her amorous behavior always occurs in the mode of irony rather than that of avowal. And the dilemma presented by the ironic mode is that one cannot know whether it is serious about its seriousness.

One observes that uncertainty in the first full conversation between Holk and Ebba. As they discuss genealogy and family history, Holk delivers a detailed portrait of a branch of the Rosenberg family, to which Ebba responds with the ambivalence typical of ironic speech. "'Wovon ich leider nie gehört habe,' sagte das Fräulein in anscheinendem oder vielleicht auch wirklichem Ernste" (13:114, "And I am afraid that I have never even heard of it," said Fräulein von Rosenberg, seemingly, or perhaps really, in earnest for a moment, 97). It is not only Holk who is befuddled. Even the narrative voice cannot discern whether her apparent earnestness is authentic or merely feigned. Hohendahl makes the point that Fontane's novel employs "not an omniscient but rather an observing narrator, one who accompanies the characters through the plot's progress."[18] The narrator's limitations are evident in this moment, when confronted with the task of deciding whether Ebba's seriousness is meant in all seriousness. Crucial here is not so much the narrator's limited knowledge, nor pinning down whether the apparent earnestness is facetious; it is rather that the narrative once again draws

---

[16] The character Brigitte Hansen constitutes the flip-side to Liebrand's argument. Though attractive, she is statuesque, practically mute. She lacks Ebba's conversational talent and thus the seductive effect of rhetoric. Her sexuality is constructed via spectatorship, not conversation. Liebrand, "Geschlechterkonfigurationen," 164.
[17] Hohendahl, "Eindringliche Beobachtung," 168.
[18] Hohendahl, "Eindringliche Beobachtung," 177.

attention to a continual fluctuation between irony and earnestness, as well as to the fundamental uncertainty that such fluctuation generates. By repeatedly musing on whether to take characters seriously or ironically, the narrator duplicates at the level of narrative discourse the same uncertainty that plagues Holk within the story.

Despite the differences in setting and details of description, *Unwiederbringlich* essentially plays out the same familiar conflict between earnestness and irony. In a reading informed by the work of Mikhail Bakhtin, Peter James Bowman identifies in the novel four discourses: the righteous, the sentimental, the mischievous, and the courtly.[19] And yet underneath the proliferation of labels, characters, and details lies a core polarity between the serious and the unserious, *Ernst* and *Scherz*. Reading in this way reframes the novel according to its central rhetorical conflict and reveals its coherence with other Fontane novels in working through the social implications of ubiquitous irony. *Unwiederbringlich* traces the ambivalence in ironic rhetoric—a continual rhetorical fluctuation translates into an existential fluctuation.

Just as the trope can turn an expression from seriousness to jest (and back again), one observes Holk in the princess's company twisting back and forth between irony and earnestness. When Ebba and the princess, for instance, put him on the conversational spot, this is his flailing response: "er [fuhr] unsicher hin und her [...] während er abwechselnd einen ernsthaften und dann wieder ironischen Ton anzuschlagen versuchte" (13:196, He [...] hummed and hawed a little and tried to adopt a half serious, half ironical attitude [tone], 169). This highlighted moment reiterates Holk's half-ness—he's neither the libertine ironist nor the earnest Pietist—but it also illustrates his conflicted position in the novel, which suspends him between the poles of extreme earnestness and excessive irony. His rhetorical uncertainty in this moment reflects a deeper, existential uncertainty, as he alternates between two reciprocally canceling alternatives.[20] The novel brings to the fore the overlap between speaking and being; it reveals how a mode of speaking not only reflects but also inflects a mode of being.

In an oft-noted passage, the princess says, "das Menschlichste, was wir haben, ist doch die Sprache, und wir haben sie um zu sprechen" (13:108, the most human attribute is speech and we are given it in order to be able to talk, 92). Her outlook identifies language as a species

---

[19] Peter James Bowman, "Fontane's *Unwiederbringlich*: A Bakhtinian Reading," *German Quarterly* 77, no. 2 (2004): 172.

[20] Bowman also notes that Holk "fluctuates wildly between competing impressions." He attributes the condition to what he labels "discursive overload." Bowman, "Fontane's *Unwiederbringlich*," 178.

marker, as constitutive of what differentiates human beings from other animals. Remarks like this one in Fontane tend to get interpreted in quantitative terms as the more speech, the better.[21] If speaking makes one human, and if there is something inhumane in silence, then speak up, the thinking goes. But such pronouncements should also be considered from a qualitative perspective. Important is not only the quantity of language generated but also the quality of that language. After all, the princess also says that the capacity to speak requires a concomitant "Unterscheidungsvermögen" (sense of tact) to discern "was gesagt werden darf und was nicht" (13:108, what can and what cannot be said, 92). In addition to that faculty of discernment, the truly essential differentiation required in the society novels is the ability to distinguish between what is serious and what is not. If the characters repeat the truism that "language makes one human," the novel at large suggests a finer differentiation: language determines not just whether you are human, but also what kind of human you are, what kind of existence you lead.

Holk fluctuates for a while between two rhetorical modes, but he eventually succumbs to the seductive power of Ebba, irony, and Copenhagen's cynical post-truth relativism. When Ebba finally seduces Holk, she is at her most wanton, exuberant, and ironic. When she encounters him alone later that evening, she cannot drop the ironic tone of the soirée's banter. She bids him good night with "einer scherzhaft feierlichen Verbeugung" (13:230, with a mock-solemn bow, 200). Her tongue-in-cheek solemnity recalls van der Straaten's rhetoric and behavior in *L'Adultera*. Fontane turns repeatedly to "ceremoniousness" as a vehicle for expressing irony. The term implies the public performance of gravitas, and delivering a facetious performance is the surest way to undercut the effect of earnestness. Kierkegaard would call such a performance ironic because "it is not serious about its seriousness."[22] Dirk Baecker would call it "the result of playing with earnestness," and he characterizes a new form of earnestness as "the experience of the indistinguishability of earnestness and play."[23]

It is precisely this indeterminacy that confuses Holk and to which he wants to put a stop. Confronted with an ambiguous, ironic gesture that merely reiterates the irony and ambiguity of her entire rhetorical bearing, he aims to break the chain of ironic negation and cut through empty chatter. "Aber Holk ergriff ihre Hand und sagte: 'Nein, Ebba, nicht so; Sie müssen mich hören.' Und miteintretend sah er sie verwirrt

---

[21] See Jens, *Über Fontane*, 5–9.
[22] Kierkegaard, *Concept of Irony*, 265.
[23] Baecker, "Ernste Kommunikation," 402.

und leidenschaftlich an" (13:230, But Holk seized her by the hand and said: "No, Ebba, you mustn't go like that. You must listen to me." And following her into the room he gazed at her with eyes full of a turmoil of passion, 200). Holk's admonishment refers to her ironic attitude of facetious solemnity. Ebba plays with earnestness; she acts serious, but with a wink, so that her tone takes it all back and nullifies any expression of emotion. He wants to stop the undecidability and the playful negation of earnestness, which is why he counters with something that sounds a lot like a prelude to avowal. He wants to be serious, he wants to be heard, because he is about to say what he really means. This is the moment when irony should give way to avowal, when confusion should give way to the straightforward declaration of passion.

It does not go as planned. She twists herself out of his grasp, a gesture that also symbolizes her refusal to be rhetorically pinned down, to be bound to her words, and continues in the same ironic tone. She recasts his desire for avowal as nothing more than neoclassical play-acting and laughs as she does so. Holk should not require any more proof that Ebba takes nothing seriously and that her language is thoroughly unreliable. He had hoped in this encounter to dispel ambiguity and uncertainty, but her jocular exuberance "steigerte nur seine Verwirrung" (13:230, only increased Holk's confusion, 200). Of course he is confused. He wants to shift from irony to avowal; he wants to drop the game of flirtation and initiate the old-school earnestness of a serious declaration. But all he gets is "the new earnestness," in Baecker's sense of that term, an earnestness that is indistinguishable from ironic play. He is perplexed because she shows him "that all earnestness can be ironized."[24] His every attempt to be taken seriously gets folded back into the play of irony.

Following one of those classic Fontanean narrative gaps, an hour later there is a knock on the bedroom door because the castle tower has caught fire. The narrative is coy on whether the couple get interrupted *in flagrante delicto*, but it is clear that some degree of intimacy precedes the emergency and their escape from the fire. Taken together, these events constitute a key turning point in the plot, for from this point forward, Holk will interpret their escape from the flames as a divine sign and will set out on the serious business of ending his marriage and establishing a new life with Ebba. But even in this very night, while the castle still burns, the narrative indicates in subtle ways that the leap from irony to avowal has not been made successfully. It indicates, in short, that nothing has changed in courtly tone or courtly life. For example, no sooner have Holk and Ebba made it back to the

---

[24] Baecker, "Ernste Kommunikation," 402–3.

safety of firm ground than the king greets them with a sarcastic remark about Holk's chivalry. The narrative voice reports, "Und in die leicht hingeworfenen Worte mischte sich, trotz des Ernstes der Situation, ein Anflug von Spott" (13:234, And despite the gravity of the occurrence, there was a touch of mockery in the casually spoken words, 203). The passage packs a great deal of dissonance into that word "despite." Fontane does something important in these scenes. With the fire and the rescue, he creates not just a moment of gripping melodrama. Rather, he crafts a deadly serious situation, a matter of life and death, and he does so to bring out the incongruity between rhetoric and reality. The king's lighthearted, careless mockery in this moment reveals that there is no calamity severe enough to interrupt the ironic tone or the flow of amusing banter. Irony flourishes even in extremis.

That tone continues in the next exchange as well. The king's men report that the princess is already at the station, taking a specially arranged train back to Copenhagen, because, they explain, "Der Boden brennt ihr hier unter den Füßen" (13:234, she feels like a cat on hot bricks here [the ground is burning under her feet], 203). This idiomatic expression of haste and urgency, unfortunately chosen under the circumstances, gives Ebba the opening she needs to keep the stream of badinage going:

> Es war ein ganz unbeabsichtigtes Wortspiel und Niemand nahm es als solches. Nur Ebba, die selbst in diesem Augenblicke noch auf zugespitzte Worte gestellt blieb, hörte heraus, was gar nicht hineingelegt war und sagte: "Ja, der Boden unter den Füßen! Die Prinzessin darf es kaum sagen … aber Holk und ich." (13:234)
>
> The pun [wordplay] was quite unintentional and everyone took it as such. Only Ebba saw the unwitting humour of the remark and unable, even at a moment such as this, to resist a witticism, she said: "On hot bricks, indeed! The Princess has much less right to say that than Holk and I!" (203–4)

There are several points to make about this exchange. First, it drives home the kind of character Ebba is and the way in which she epitomizes a rhetoric of relentless banter. Even in this moment, having barely escaped death, she cannot help but continue to produce the sort of clever wordplays that make her a darling of the Danish court.[25] With

---

[25] See again Bowman, who remarks on courtly rhetoric's "desire to dazzle," as well as its "evacuation of content in favor of brilliant badinage." Bowman, Fontane's *Unwiederbringlich*, 174.

the world around her on fire, she still feels compelled to respond with a clever quip, in a facetious tone.

But there is more going on in this passage. One finds a significant amount of foreshadowing packed into the witty reply. For one thing, the narrator says that she reads something into another's words that was never intended. Teasing out a meaning that no one meant to express in the first place, this is exactly how Holk will make a fool of himself over the next couple of weeks. Furthermore, her response takes as its point of departure a conventional phrase, an idiomatic expression, something never meant to be taken in a literal sense, and yet it insists on taking it seriously. It literalizes the figure of "burning ground" and tethers rhetoric to reality in a way that cancels any degree of detachment or casual expression. Her witty reaction is, in a certain sense, also an overreaction because it attributes to the expression a degree of deliberate intent and consideration that was never there. Again, this is the error Holk will make when he takes Ebba's unreliable words too seriously and ascribes to her flirtation an earnestness that was never intended. In the aftermath of the conflagration, the narrative thus signals, first, that the ironic banter will continue unabated, regardless of the circumstances, and, second, that the characters are prone to errors of misreading, to taking empty turns of phrase more seriously and literally than they are actually meant. Neither is a good omen for Holk or his attempt to create avowal from the cloth of irony.

Over the course of the novel, as Holk slowly succumbs to Ebba's charms, he adopts more and more the tone and disposition of the Copenhagen court. When it suits his purposes, he even begins to espouse a deep-seated skepticism with regard to truth. Under the influence of Pentz and Ebba, he comes to assert a post-truth perspectivism, assuring himself, "Christine war in Allem so sicher; was stand denn aber fest? Nichts, gar nichts" (Christine was always so certain of everything: but what, in fact, could be considered entirely beyond question? Nothing, absolutely nothing, 139). He continues in this vein, "Alles war Abkommen auf Zeit, Alles jeweiliger Majoritätsbeschluß; Moral, Dogma, Geschmack, Alles schwankte" (13:160, Everything was provisional, everything a mere majority decision of the moment: morals, dogma, taste, everything was uncertain, 139). Holk comes close to Pentz's cynical "what is truth?" attitude. His subordination of truth and fact to ideology—remarkable for its casual nihilism—reflects the degree to which he has absorbed Copenhagen's post-truth atmosphere.[26] Nothing is fixed, everything is in flux; what gets sold as unassailable truth is

---

[26] On the constitutive elements of a post-truth age, see McIntyre, "What Is Post-Truth?" in *Post-Truth*, 1–15.

really just the capricious whim of cultural consensus. And this skepticism is directly related to irony for it extrapolates from the unreliability of language. If the first step in adapting to irony is to doubt the existence of any stable truth-content within linguistic expression, the next step is to doubt the existence of stable truths, regardless of whether one tries to express them in language.

As Holk's intentions vis-à-vis Ebba become earnest, however, as he begins to take her flirtatious banter seriously, he drops the radically skeptical perspective. He is prepared once again to believe in certainty, in stable truths, and in the reliability of language. His change in outlook derives from his eagerness to switch from one mode of speaking to another. Done with facetious banter, he wants to get at the core of earnestness that he believes was there all along, concealed beneath irony and unserious talk. In short, he is ready to avow. "Er wollte zu Ebba, diese Stunde noch, und dann wollt' er mit ihr vor die Prinzessin treten und Alles bekennen und erst ihre Verzeihung und dann ihre Zustimmung anrufen" (13:241, He would go and see Ebba this very minute and then take her to the Princess, confess [avow] everything to her and then beg first for forgiveness and then for her consent, 210). The object of his avowal will be the princess, not Ebba, who he believes (without a shred of reliable evidence) is just as committed to this course of action as he is. Note also the Foucauldian aspects of avowal at work here: the avowal is a confessional act that submits to the power relation and "enables the exercise of that power relation over the one who avows."[27] The higher authority in this instance is clearly the princess, whose pardon and consent are required before the relationship could ever be seen as legitimate. What Holk has in mind is a true act of avowal, and once he sets himself on this course of action, he is repulsed by perspectivism, by empty phrases, by Copenhagen and its ironic tone. Ticking through a list of the city's attractions, he finds nothing of interest, and "wenn er gar an Pentz dachte, befiel ihn ein Grauen" (13:243, when he thought of Pentz, he felt a shudder run down his back, 212). One will recall that Pentz is the novel's primary embodiment of post-truth cynicism and, next to Ebba, the second most gifted practitioner of ironic banter. Fittingly, Holk admits to himself that "das Letzte, was er aushalten konnte" (the last thing that he could bear) are "die Pentz'schen Bonmots und Wortspiele" (13:243, Pentz's puns and *bons mots*, 212). In sum, Holk is put off by everything associated with Copenhagen, with its cynicism and ironic tone, because it is antithetical to the straightforward truth-telling that he feels compelled to carry out. Eager now to speak

---

[27] Foucault, *Wrong-Doing, Truth-Telling*, 17.

forthrightly, Holk's demeanor swings back in the direction of earnest Holkenäs.

In the subsequent chapters, Holk will make three attempts at avowal, to the princess, to Christine, and finally to Ebba. All three attempts will fail. There is an element of redundancy inherent in the multiple scenes of avowal, but they each illustrate different aspects of avowal and, taken together, reiterate the novel's structural opposition between irony and earnestness. Each of Holk's attempts at avowal fails for a slightly different reason, but examining the scenes closely reveals a common thread: in each instance, Holk fails because he finds himself unable to avow, unable to say what he really means. When it comes time to lay it all on the line with a high-stakes act of truth-telling, he repeatedly finds himself rhetorically paralyzed and incapable of delivering his message. He defers his avowal to the princess because she confronts him with a discrepancy between rhetoric and grammar (i.e., irony); he says little of consequence to Christine because she overwhelms him with her own candor and earnestness (i.e., avowal); and finally, he never manages to make a proper proposal to Ebba because she preempts him by revealing his entire enterprise to be a grave misreading of ironic expression. In each case, Holk's earnestness turns out to be unable to translate itself into a firm declaration, much less into action. *Unwiederbringlich* stages a conflict between irony and avowal, and to the extent that it resolves that conflict, it does so by depicting Holk's earnestness as impotent in the face of ubiquitous irony. Avowal possesses no mysterious alchemical power in this novel. It finds itself incapable of transforming irony into reliable language with a stable meaning. This impotence lies at the heart of the novel's more circumspect depiction of avowal as an alternative to empty speech.

Holk's first attempt, during an audience with the princess, provides what would be the purest example of avowal, were he able to pull it off. He comes before a figure of authority to confess what he has done, declare who he really is, commit himself to a future course of action, and subordinate himself to her power. The audience gets off to an auspicious start, with the princess's words of gratitude providing an opening for the avowal that Holk is eager to deliver. The narrative situates us on the verge of avowal; it is already on the tip of his tongue. Indeed, the narrative voice reports that he has arrived at the point where he is ready, "sein Herz vor ihr auszuschütten und seine Pläne sie wissen zu lassen" (13:245, to unburden his heart to her and reveal all his plans, 213). Holk teeters on the brink of divulging his true attachments and revealing himself as the person he is, and it seems as if the princess's warm words propel him on that course. But the narrative's account hedges: her statements are auspicious "nach ihrem Inhalt" or "according to their content" (13:245), which is to say, there is some other element, beyond the content, that undercuts the apparent propitiousness of the moment.

Although his avowal is on the tip of his tongue, Holk senses that it would actually be an inopportune time to bare his heart to the princess: "Aber so sehr der Inhalt der Worte dazu auffordern mochte, nicht die Haltung der Prinzessin, nicht der Ton, in dem ihre Worte gesprochen waren. Alles klang beinah leblos" (13:245, But however encouraging the words, her attitude and the tone in which she uttered them were not so in the least. Everything about her was listless, 213). The passage depicts a dawning (and belated) realization that there can exist a discrepancy between what people say and what they actually mean. Holk awakens in this moment to the possibility of ironic difference, to the possibility that tone—or manner of expression—can hollow out, even cancel out, the primary meaning of an utterance. He thus opts to defer his avowal to a more opportune moment. It would be a mistake, however, to conclude that the primary reason for the delay is that the princess is tired, or out of sorts, or melancholy. She is those things, of course, and Holk realizes it. But Holk's realization, as Fontane captures it in this scene, is both deeper and darker. He gets a taste of the vertigo of irony, that queasiness of standing at the edge of an abyss, and looking into a bottomless pit where words do not necessarily mean what they denote, where signifiers are unmoored from any stable referent, and where earnestness is just another form of play. Put plainly: he has an epiphany, or *Einfall*, that language cannot necessarily be trusted. And if the princess's words can mean something other than what they ostensibly say—if their tone can negate their import—then Ebba's words might also mean something other than their bare content. Despite his desire for clarity and closure, he leaves with more confusion, "statt irgend welche Confessions zu machen" (13:246, instead of making his confession, 214).

The next stop is an unannounced visit back in Holkenäs, where Holk will once again fail to produce the avowal that he has come to deliver. Christine recognizes the reason for his visit. Although she paves the way for his avowal, he remains reticent: "er schwieg und spielte dabei mit dem Christkind" (13:252, he remained silent, playing with the figure of the Christ child, 218). Even though he has traveled to Holkenäs only to unburden himself of his true affections and intentions, he hardly has anything to say to Christine, beyond reiterating the familiar litany of complaints. This encounter should be the clearest parallel to the climactic scene of avowal and departure in *L'Adultera*, but to compare avowal's representation in the two novels, one must begin by noting that Holk's diffidence stands in stark contrast to Melanie's candor and honesty. He never says anything as direct as, "I'm leaving because I love someone else," even though this is the sort of truth-telling that he owes Christine and that he has come to carry out. It is not so much that avowal is impotent in this moment; it is, rather, that Holk lacks the power or force to deliver the avowal. Beset by fear, "Zweifel" (doubts), and "sein Gewissen" (13:249, the voice of conscience, 217), he cannot produce the sincere candor that avowal requires. It makes sense: his entire relationship with Ebba, which he intends to disclose and legitimize, has been based on frivolous, flirtatious banter. How can he bring that back to Holkenäs and Christine and translate ironic exuberance into an earnest confession and a statement of sincere intent? He cannot, so he sits there, silent, and lets Christine do the talking for him.

While Holk cannot comfortably inhabit the role of avower, Christine slips into it easily: "Was Du nicht sagen magst, *ich* will es sagen" (13:252, What you cannot bring yourself to say, I shall say for you, 219). This is the point at which Christine takes over the task of speaking forthrightly. It turns out that *Unwiederbringlich* does in fact include a powerful act of avowal. It just comes from an unexpected quarter, given all the narrative focus on Holk's infatuation and grand designs. Christine has been positioned throughout the novel as the epitome of earnestness, as one who speaks seriously, who means what she says, and who takes others seriously too. By all rights, if anyone in this novel is going to avow, it's Christine. And she does. She tells him directly that he can leave if he wants to, "denn ich bin nicht für halbe Verhältnisse [...] ich will einen ganzen Mann und ein ganzes Herz" (13:253, "because I can't bear half-heartedness in any relationship. [...] I want the whole of a man, the whole of his heart, 220). Just as Melanie in *L'Adultera* insists on clear relationships, so Christine insists on whole or total relationships. Her remark activates a sense of halfness and wholeness that has not been much commented upon in the novel. The halfness or incompleteness that Christine rejects refers both to sharing her husband's affection with another woman and to the phenomenal presentation of a marriage that no longer derives its legitimacy from a corresponding essence. The relationship between phenomenon and essence is a referential relationship, and Christine insists on making the reference whole, on completing the connection between phenomenon and essence. What she will not tolerate is the referential discrepancy that irony introduces. She cannot abide appearance without corresponding reality, *Schein* without *Sein*. In her insistence on earnestness, wholeness, and alignment, it is Christine—not Holk—who evinces the clearest correspondence with Melanie van der Straaten (Rubehn) and her act of avowal.

The desire for clarity and candor gives Christine the power to avow in a way that Holk cannot. She admonishes him, "Also sprich es aus, daß Du gekommen bist, um mit mir von Trennung zu sprechen" (13:253, So tell me openly that you have come to talk of separation, 220). She orders him to speak frankly, but one notes that the command already does much of the work for him—it names without reservation the reason for his visit. Through her candor, the heretofore silent center around which their encounter revolves "passes from the realm of the unspoken to the realm of the spoken."²⁸ The act of naming functions here as a speech act that brings about consequences outside of language. To give the reason for his visit a name—separation, divorce—is to actualize it, to make it real. It constitutes a tipping point, beyond which there is no going back to the prior state of affairs. From this point in the conversation forward, Christine, not Holk, will outline the terms of their separation and set the process in motion. She tells him, bluntly, that her brother will handle her side of the divorce proceedings and that he will not ask for custody of the children. And then she leaves.

Twice now Holk has sought out an opportunity to avow, and both times he has failed even to begin. If he deferred the first attempt at avowal because the rhetorical context appeared too ironic, self-contradictory, and unreliable, he fails to avow in the second instance because the context is too candid and plainspoken. Christine's unreserved sincerity silences him and overpowers his desire to avow. In the harsh light of earnestness, his certainty and resolve appear fragile, and the words he hopes to speak lose their force before they ever leave his mouth. Having just arrived from Copenhagen, Holk finds that he cannot avow from a position of irony and insincerity. These twin failures underscore Holk's position, stranded between two opposed poles in the novel's rhetorical field. Whereas the courtly tone was too ironic and unstable for his earnest declaration, here the atmosphere is too serious for him to say in all earnestness that he has fallen for facetious flirtation. He exchanges avowal for reticence.

The final attempt at avowal comes when Holk returns to Copenhagen, to propose to Ebba. He fails once again, however, as Ebba rejects him, preempting his proposition with a trenchant critique of his misreading of irony and his misplaced solemnity. Although the rejection comes as a devastating shock to Holk, most readers likely anticipate an unhappy outcome. *Unwiederbringlich* employs narrative irony when it presents Holk's state of mind. In addition to the repeated assertions of certainty that he and Ebba are of one mind, Holk also professes to have completely adopted the Copenhagen spirit of ironic detachment. Shortly before the climactic encounter with Ebba, the narrative quotes his inner monologue, as he assures himself, "Leicht nehmen, Alles leicht nehmen, dabei fährt man am besten […], und ein lachendes Gesicht ist der erste Schritt zum Siege" (12:263, Take things as they come [lightly],

---

²⁸ Foucault, *Wrong-Doing, Truth-Telling*, 16.

everything as it comes [lightly], that's the best way [...]. The first step to success is laughter, 228). Holk's musings reactivate the novel's central tension between taking things seriously or unseriously, and he professes to fall completely on the side of ironic detachment, opposed to earnestness. In an interesting twist, though, the narrative ironizes Holk's assertions. It is not that he delivers these words to himself in an instance of verbal irony—he is clearly trying to screw up his courage before setting off to bare his heart to Ebba. It is, rather, that the narrative has been working to open a gap between Holk's perspective and the reader's perspective. His entire course of action over the past week, his earnest response to flirtation, his repeated attempts to avow, his plan to leave his wife and children—all this belies any claim he could make to lighthearted detachment. The narrative thus opens a difference between the phenomenon of Holk's inner monologue (what he tells himself about himself) and the essence of his character. It lets his own bearing undercut the content of his utterance. And if ironic negation can twist an expressed sentiment into its opposite, then the ironizing of Holk's professed detachment results in a higher-order earnestness. The narrative detaches Holk from his own professions of ironic detachment. The result of this narrative maneuver is to highlight how Holk arrives at his earnestness via irony, via language that is unreliable because it can also mean the opposite of what it says. Part of Holk's rhetorical displacement derives from his attempt to resurrect earnestness upon an ironic field. He has built his house, so to speak, on the rhetorical sands of irony, an image that calls to mind Holk's "temple" perched upon the dunes.

Despite Holk's professions of taking it lightly and laughing it off, he proceeds to Ebba's quarters to make an entirely earnest proposal. Before he gets the opportunity to propose, though, he can tell that something has changed. Sensing Ebba's resistance, he both declares his feelings and attempts to justify them:

Sie wissen [...], daß ich alles, und vielleicht mehr als ich durfte, darangesetzt habe, Sie zu besitzen. [...] Jedes Ihrer Worte hat sich mir in die Seele eingeschrieben. Und Ihre Blicke sprachen es mit, beide, Worte und Blicke, sagten es mir, daß Sie's durch alle Tage hin beklagen würden [...], wenn ich Sie verließe. Leugnen Sie's Ebba,—das waren Ihre Worte. (13:265)

You know [...] that I have staked everything—perhaps more than I should—on winning you. [...] Every word you uttered went straight to my heart and your eyes spoke the same language, and they both said, your words and your look, that you would be unhappy for the rest of your days [...], if I were ever to abandon you. Deny that, Ebba—those were your very words. (230)

Unwiederbringlich, or the Impotence of Being Earnest 169

One observes, first, just how earnestly Holk has taken everything that occurred between him and Ebba. Her words inscribed themselves upon his very soul; to him, they unequivocally conveyed true love and enduring affection. Even though Holk and Ebba have been flirting in Copenhagen, that city of irony and frivolous banter, he allows no space for irony, ambivalence, or distance. Instead, he lets everything go straight from her mouth to his heart. He is far indeed from taking things lightly when he tells her, in all earnestness, that he took her words as earnest too. Second, Holk hints here at the high stakes that separate his avowal from a mere declaration. He has staked everything on winning Ebba, he says, and this is not exaggeration. Having already walked out on his wife, children, and home, Holk has committed himself to a future with her. Third, the closing verb "leugnen" is telling. He essentially dares her to disavow her words, which suggests that he takes (mistakes) her previous utterances for serious, binding speech, for an avowal that would now have to be disavowed or abnegated to lose its force.

Holk's precarious position in this instance illustrates another of Foucault's central points about avowal—namely, that it necessarily entails submitting to a power relation. When Holk comes to propose a shared life, he subjugates himself to the authority of Ebba's response. Her response, it turns out, is devastating. Instead of leaping into his arms, she sneers at his misplaced earnestness, just as Lady Montagu does in the Frith painting that Fontane reported on. She accuses him of being a Don Quixote figure, a fitting literary reference. Don Quixote makes a fool of himself by trying to literalize the tropes of romance and chivalry. He takes literary language far too seriously and tries to realize it in his own life. She says, in essence, that Holk has made a similar error. A quixotic knight errant, he seeks to literalize and live out the tropes of flirtation, even though he should recognize their fictional, or at least facetious, status. He is being too earnest now, she argues, because he has been too earnest all along and has failed to play the game of irony correctly.

"Worte waren Worte; so viel mußten selbst *Sie* wissen" (Words are only words; that much, even you must have known, 231), she says in a scathing rebuke, and now "wollen Sie mich einschwören auf ein einzig Wort oder doch auf nicht viel mehr und wollen aus einem bloßen Spiel einen bittern Ernst machen" (13:267, you want to make me swear everlasting love on the strength of a single word, or not very much more, and turn a mere game into bitter earnest, 231). Holk cannot hold Ebba to her word when irony allows her to dismiss the substance of any statement through its means of expression. Words are just words; language is just a meaningless game, and woe unto the fool who would try to transform playful banter into earnestness, or irony into avowal. The language is again telling. She casts Holk's earnest rhetorical aim as "einschwören."

She means that he wants to obligate her to a course of action purely on the basis of a few heedless statements, but "einschwören" also carries the sense of a swearing in, of taking an oath that initiates a new role and a new set of responsibilities. Holk's error lies in reinterpreting heedless words as a solemn vow or an oath of office. Holk does not just react too earnestly to blithe speech; he wants to transform that speech itself into something as serious and obligating as an oath, confession, or avowal.

Irony is a trope of fluctuation and indeterminacy, and hence of uncertainty, but Ebba's rejection puts all uncertainty to rest. The two possible bearings put forth in the novel—taking things lightly or taking things seriously—correspond to at least two possible meanings in a potentially ironic utterance, "of which the one asserts and the other denies its own illocutionary mode."[29] To use Holk's example, one approaches a statement such as "I couldn't bear for you to leave me" according either to its literal meaning, as an earnest statement of undying affection, or to its figural meaning, as an unserious bit of ironic exuberance that cancels the very sentiment it asserts. De Man writes that, through irony, the interlocutor is "confronted with a structure of linguistic meaning that he cannot control and that holds the discouraging prospect of an infinity of similar future confusions, all of them potentially catastrophic in their consequences."[30] The novel's denouement ends the vertiginous uncertainty of rhetoric when Ebba intervenes and sets Holk straight: nothing she said was meant to be taken seriously, and he has been misinterpreting her language all along. Lighthearted, ironic banter becomes a mean-spirited farce "nur *dann*, wenn Ihre deplacierte Feierlichkeit das, was leicht war, schwer genommen haben sollte" (13:266, only if by being too solemn [...] you try to take something seriously which should be taken lightly, 231). This is the moment when the ironic self-delusion of Holk's take-it-all-lightly attitude fully comes to light.

Ebba's rebuttal rests further on the assumption that Holk should have known better; he should have been sophisticated enough to realize that her flirtatious words were not meant to be taken as more than a momentary game. She seems here to follow Quintilian's clues to irony, which he says is "evident to the understanding either by the delivery, the character of the speaker or the nature of its object."[31] She argues that any words of devotion were not in keeping with her character, and thus Holk should never have imposed his earnestness on them. This is why Ebba can assert so decisively that Holk is neither a proper courtier nor a proper bon vivant. His earnestness and his inability to engage properly

---

[29] De Man, "Semiology and Rhetoric," 10
[30] De Man, "Semiology and Rhetoric," 10
[31] Quoted in Booth, *Rhetoric of Irony*, 49.

with irony expose his unsuitability for the role. Holk, for his part, submits to the authority of her rejection, and through this submission, he furthermore accepts the costliness of his attempted avowal. Not only is his personal life in tatters, the whole escapade ends for him in public humiliation. The world laughs at him, just as Lady Montagu laughs at Pope, and just as van der Straaten does at the earnest simpleton who takes it all too seriously.

Through Holk's rejection, Fontane dramatizes the high cost of avowal and the vulnerability that comes with speaking plainly. Avowal does not appear here to be an effective antidote to irony; in fact, it comes across as impotent. It is essential to consider how and why the novel circumscribes avowal's force. How can we differentiate Melanie's avowal from Holk's? To what can we attribute the power and success of the earlier avowal, and to what can we attribute the latter's failure? It is not that Fontane has simply changed his mind about avowal or the danger of relentless irony, nor that his views have evolved significantly in the intervening ten years or so between *L'Adultera* and *Unwiederbringlich*. Rather, his 1891 novel depicts avowal as precarious and vulnerable because it emphasizes the extent to which the communicative efficacy of avowal depends upon other interlocutors, upon the reliability of their language and the proper understanding of their speech. Why does Holk's proposal to Ebba fail? Because he has misinterpreted her words, has mistaken her insincere flirtation for earnestness, and has attributed to her a state of mind that she does not in fact share. In short, what Holk's avowal lacks is theory of mind, which Lisa Zunshine describes in both literary and cognitive terms as the ability to "ascribe to a person a certain mental state on the basis of her observable action" or to "intuit a complex state of mind based on a limited verbal description."[32] Throughout the novel, Holk tries—and fails—to read Ebba's mind to ascertain her thoughts, feelings, and beliefs. But if theory of mind is an important precondition for the efficacy of avowal, the unfortunate news is that irony works against precisely this ability to intuit another person's state of mind. Irony severs the link between language and mind, such that it renders mental states opaque.

The narrative reveals Holk's flawed theory of mind as he sets out on his quest to avow his love and start a new life. There is a reason why he starts with the princess and with Christine: he does not believe it necessary to avow his love to Ebba because he feels certain that they are of one mind on this point. The narrator conveys his confidence, saying, for example, "daß Ebba dieselben Gedanken habe, stand ihm fest"

---

[32] Lisa Zunshine, *Why We Read Fiction: Theory of Mind and the Novel* (Columbus, OH: Ohio State University Press, 2006), 6.

(12:242, he was convinced that Ebba had the same idea, 211). Indeed, he is so certain that she will accept his proposal that his initial plan is to go before the princess *with Ebba*, to confess and avow their love together, as a couple. As time passes without a resolution, the narrative gently shades his confidence with doubt: Holk is anxious for "Aussprache mit Ebba, so sehr er ihrer Zustimmung sicher war" (12:246, A meeting with Ebba—although he was sure of her agreement, 215). Passages such as these make clear that Holk grounds his course of action in a state of mind that he has, rightly or wrongly, ascribed to Ebba.

Moreover, the narrative goes out of its way to point out the ongoing social practice of empathic mind-reading. The first time Holk tries to see Ebba after the fire, Karin alludes to their affair in a whisper, "weil sie sich nicht versagen mochte, Holk ihre Gedanken erraten zu lassen" (12:243, loth to deny herself the pleasure of letting Holk guess her thoughts, 211). Fontane experiments here with a literary version of theory of mind *avant la lettre*. These scenes from *Unwiederbringlich* indicate, first, that intuiting others' states of mind is an essential and ongoing social practice; second, that language is the best basis one has for intuiting another person's mental state; and third, that language is a thoroughly flawed and unreliable window onto others' thoughts, feelings, and beliefs. The capacity to ascribe a state of mind to another person depends, as Karin's diffidence shows, on the person's willingness to let her mind be read. The spigot of language can be turned on and off; the signal can go silent. And when irony is involved, even strong signals can become utterly unreliable as a means to intuiting an other's state of mind. Language can provide a window onto complex states of mind, but irony can pull down the shades and render that interior world opaque.

Zunshine argues that this mind-reading capacity is a crucial cognitive adaptation that enables human beings to navigate through their social world; she also argues that it is one of the reasons why we read fictional narrative, "because it engages, in a variety of particularly focused ways, our Theory of Mind."[33] Zunshine's cognitive approach to novels such as *Clarissa* attends to the instabilities of reading—and misreading—states of mind, but she cites other theorists who attribute the pleasure of literature to the respite it provides from the hard work of intuiting others' interior states. Novels provide "direct access to fictional minds," which is "a relief from the hard work of daily life, much of which requires the ability to decode accurately the behavior of others."[34] The point is that mind-reading in real life is complicated,

---

[33] Zunshine, *Why We Read Fiction*, 162.
[34] Alan Palmer, cited in Zunshine, *Why We Read Fiction*, 19.

taxing, and fraught with uncertainty. By giving the reader direct access to characters' thoughts and feelings, fictional narrative eases that burden; it creates a world in which theory of mind is direct and effortless.

Needless to say, Fontane does not provide strong evidence for that critical view. Despite its glimpses into Holk's state of mind, a novel like *Unwiederbringlich* provides no break from the hermeneutic work of intuiting others' mental states. Quite the contrary, the novel dramatizes the instability and uncertainty that go along with relying on language as a means to intuit mental states. With its emphasis on ambiguity and misreading, it makes the reader a spectator to the confusion that attends reading language as a means to reading minds. When we attend to irony and avowal, we see that many of Fontane's society novels aim to show how fashionable modes of speaking make the already difficult work of mind-reading that much more complicated and strenuous. Käthe and Botho in *Irrungen, Wirrungen* fail to intuit the other's state of mind; Melanie in *L'Adultera* cannot tell whether van der Straaten's solemn words reflect earnestly held beliefs; Schach's letters and promises give no reliable indication of what he actually feels or intends. And in the present instance, Holk's calamity stems from a thorough misreading of irony and the misattribution of a state of mind. This trail of misunderstanding and misery that runs through Fontane's works results from a single rhetorical affectation—the talent for speaking flippantly and facetiously, for concealing the self behind a façade of irony.

The society novels demonstrate, in various guises, how the tendency to blur the rhetorical boundaries between the ironic and the earnest disrupts the semiotic link between language and interior states. Kierkegaard describes this effect in terms of "subjective freedom" and finds a deep insight expressed in Talleyrand's remark "that man was given speech not in order to reveal his thoughts but to conceal them."[35] For Kierkegaard, irony labels the discrepancy between the phenomenon of speech and the essence of thought. But for those who rely on language as an expression of mental states, irony renders that language anti-realistic. Theory of mind operates on the perhaps optimistic belief that a person's words and actions will deliver an undistorted reflection of her interior life, that the phenomenon of language will be a realistic and reliable expression of thoughts, feelings, and beliefs. But irony's negative subjective freedom introduces the constant threat of distortion and disruption. Irony undercuts the semiotic link between self and language.

---

[35] Kierkegaard, *Concept of Irony*, 270–1.

Here, in a nutshell, is Holk's fundamental error in the novel. He operates as if irony did not sever that link between phenomenon and essence, language and self, and make theory of mind, at best, a shot-in-the-dark conjecture. He reads for truth and realism in a world that is post-truth and cynically perspectivist. The people in the Copenhagen court do not speak *sub specie aeternitatis*, under the aspect of the eternal, but rather *sub specie ironiae*, under the aspect of irony. Holk, however, blind to irony's effects, misattributes earnestly felt affection to Ebba, hence his misplaced solemnity and his ineffectual avowal. This is why their encounter ends not with a proposal but with an argument over the reliability of language. Just as Ebba cannot accept Holk's earnestness, so Holk cannot accept Ebba's irony. He concludes their conversation by saying, "ich kann nicht erkennen, daß mir eine Pflicht vorlag, den Ernst Ihrer Gefühle zu bezweifeln; im Gegenteil, ich glaubte den Glauben daran haben zu dürfen" (13:268, I refuse to recognize that it was my duty to doubt the genuineness [earnestness] of your feelings; on the contrary, I felt [believed] that I could believe in them, 232). He is mistaken, for a culture of irony and a post-truth age demand precisely that the recipient doubt the substance and sincerity of everything that is said. Instead, Holk speaks to a kind of meta-conviction, a belief in the believability of her words.[36] He insists on treating as credible a sincerity that in fact never existed.

Consider for a moment a bit of alternative-history speculation: if Ebba had been speaking sincerely and forthrightly, then Holk's intuitions regarding her state of mind would have been accurate. If his theory of mind had been correct, then his avowal—his attempted marriage proposal—would have turned out much differently. He would never have made a fool of himself and would instead have been successful in ending his unsatisfying marriage and in starting a new relationship. The chain of errors traces back to the ambiguity of ironic speech. What, ultimately, is the difference between Melanie's forceful avowal and Holk's failed avowal? Rubohn is a reliable interlocutor with earnest intentions, whereas Ebba is not. Where Rubehn declares, Ebba dissimulates.

Although this outcome does not eliminate avowal as a viable alternative to irony, *Unwiederbringlich* should certainly be read as a cautionary tale for those invested in the efficacy of plainspoken candor. The novel reveals avowal to be precarious and unpredictable in its effect. Its efficacy is contingent on the language and state of mind of those to whom it is addressed, and because Holk has premised his avowal on

---

[36] Agamben has described the function of the oath in similar terms to encourage belief in the believability of words and make credible their correspondence with actions. Agamben, *Sacrament of Language*, 21.

ironic chatter, he is bound to fail. Whereas *L'Adultera* shows that avowal can cut through empty, ironic banter, *Unwiederbringlich* adds a note of wariness: it cannot transform irony into serious conviction; it has no alchemical power to make earnest what was never meant in earnest. The pessimistic view here has to do with irony's potentially insidious effects: in this instance, it preempts avowal, enervates it, and condemns it to failure before a single word is spoken. Fontane shows that, in a society of relentless irony, it becomes ever more difficult to engage in truth-telling and avowal. The concern is that there comes a saturation point for irony, beyond which any expression of earnestness or solemnity would be misplaced. Or, to switch metaphors, it returns to the notion of irony as an invasive species. If allowed to take over, it could drive extinct other rhetorical modes (e.g., earnestness, ingenuousness, guileless candor). This is the atmosphere surrounding the Danish court in the novel, where any sincere declaration exposes one to ridicule. In the absence of reliable interlocutors, Wilde's "studied triviality" would become the only possible response.

But Fontane's society novels remain unsatisfied by—indeed, troubled by—the prospect of an entirely trivial, glib bearing. There are characters who adopt such a bearing, to be sure, but they are presented more as a symptom of decline than an artful adaptation to the demands of contemporary culture. One need look no further than Käthe in *Irrungen, Wirrungen*, a master in the art of studied triviality and ironic detachment. She speaks in the clever, superficial tone of a character from one of Wilde's farcical comedies, someone who will "never talk anything but nonsense."[37] The novel indicates that she embodies both the pinnacle of glib social banter and the nadir of authentic, effective communication. In short, Käthe's affected, empty talk offers no solution to the culture of rampant irony. Her critical presentation in the novel captures the feel of George Bernard Shaw's critique of *The Importance of Being Earnest*, which premiered in 1895, the same year that saw the publication of *Effi Briest*. Despite "the force and daintiness of its wit," Shaw calls it Wilde's "first really heartless play."[38] The criticism is equally true, *mutatis mutandis*, of Käthe's bearing in *Irrungen, Wirrungen* and Ebba's in *Unwiederbringlich*. Though their studied triviality is witty and amusing, there is ultimately something empty and heartless at its core. Botho does not celebrate his wife's verbal dexterity; he resigns himself to it. And through a character like Lene, the narrative holds out the hope for an alternative mode of communication beyond the levity of idle banter.

---

[37] Wilde, *The Importance of Being Earnest and Other Plays*, 141.
[38] Cited in Karl Beckson, ed., *Oscar Wilde: The Critical Heritage* (New York: Routledge, 2003), 221–2.

The society novels are thus invested in the importance of being earnest—if not in the stern and steadfast sense of Victorian morality satirized by Wilde's most famous play, then at least in the sense of retaining a capacity for sincere expression in a world that tilts toward irony and empty banter.[39] While they are invested in the importance of being able to speak earnestly, they are also aware of the precarious nature of earnestness and avowal. Through Holk's unrequited passion, *Unwiederbringlich* points out the potential impotence of being earnest in a culture that appears to have left sincerity behind. I say "precarious" and "potential impotence" because the outcome of avowal is never certain in advance; it depends, ultimately, on the other person's authority and their language's reliability. The outcome in *Unwiederbringlich* does not abrogate avowal as a potential alternative to irony, but it marks its efficacy as deeply uncertain. Because avowal is essentially dialogic (it requires an interlocutor), and because it is contingent on an other's language, the uncertainty of avowal is a further reverberation of the ambiguity and indeterminacy inherent in ironic speech. The uncertainty with regard to how to take others' statements (either earnestly or facetiously) gets reflected in a fundamental uncertainty about how our own language will be received by others. If avowal represents the attempt to produce declarations that are maximally earnest and reliable, the novel demonstrates how even that rhetorical act can get enfolded back into irony's uncertainty and unreliability.

Unwiederbringlich does not conclude, however, with Holk's failed avowal. Following his rejection, he leaves Copenhagen, travels, and fashions a life for himself in exile, in London. Friends and family do their part to try to reconcile Holk and Christine, and after a separation that lasts around a year and a half, the hoped-for reunion takes place back in Holkenäs in 1861, where the estranged spouses renew their vows. This chapter concludes by considering briefly the novel's final section—the attempt to revive the marriage and Christine's suicide—as well as the Second Schleswig War, which begins in early 1864 and which leads to Denmark's defeat and loss of the Schleswig and Holstein territories. Set alongside Holk's unrequited avowal, these further episodes establish a pattern of repeated failure and downfall, one of which gets narrated, while the other looms in the background, just beyond the horizon of the novel's depicted events.

The story ends fairly abruptly in dashed hopes and self-destruction. Though Holk and Christine try to renew their marriage, they are never able to reclaim the happiness and contentment that they had

---

[39] On the Victorian ideal of earnestness, see Walter Houghton, *The Victorian Frame of Mind, 1830–1870* (New Haven: Yale University Press, 1985), 218–62.

once enjoyed prior to the novel's outset. This second chapter in their shared life feels more like a ceasefire than a true alliance. Readings of *Unwiederbringlich* must necessarily take into account the failed marital reconciliation, Christine's suicide, and the tragic outcome of untenable resignation.[40] The revived marriage between Holk and Christine resembles nothing so much as the cynical, ironic marriage of outward appearances that van der Straaten proposes to Melanie in *L'Adultera*. It is a union that tries to treat everything that transpired as a bagatelle, a mere trifle, and that trades passion for the peace and stability of resignation. But as Melanie predicts and Christine experiences first hand, it is exceedingly difficult to treat grave personal injuries as if they were nothing and to take them lightly. The pessimistic verdict, "Christine will vergessen, aber sie kann es nicht" (13:286, Christine is trying to forget but cannot, 248), mirrors Melanie's prediction when she rejects van der Straaten's marriage of appearances, "Und keiner kann vergessen. Erinnungen aber sind mächtig" (4:117, And no one can forget. But memories are powerful).[41] The stubborn persistence of memory and injury leads to an irreconcilable gap between appearance and reality. They are trapped in the outward performance of a union over a fracture that has never healed.

The irony of their renewed vows—the discrepancy between word and state of mind—is already evident at the ceremony. The narrative signals in various ways that the celebratory atmosphere is tainted by melancholic foreboding. It speaks of "ein banges Gefühl" (an anxious foreboding, 245) and a "Gefühl der Trauer, das bei der schönen Feier vorgeherrscht hatte" (13:283, feeling of sadness that had dominated the splendid celebration, 246). The wedding ceremony evinces a funereal aspect, and the celebration feels more like an act of mourning for a loss that has already occurred but is not yet apparent. Holk and Christine do everything they can to maintain the façade of a happy marriage, "und nur wer schärfer zusah, sah deutlich, daß diesem Allen doch das rechte Leben fehlte" (13:283, and only the more observant noticed that one essential [life] was absent, 246). The language of perspicacity in this passage gets at the discrepancy between phenomenon and essence characteristic of irony. It is only by looking past the outward appearance of marital contentment that one can see through to the hollow, lifeless core of their relationship. (Note further that "lifeless" is how

---

[40] Chambers, for example, concludes that "the wife-and-mother model" cannot guarantee female happiness. Chambers, "Inadequacy of the Wife-and-Mother Model," 295.

[41] English from Fontane, *The Woman Taken in Adultery and The Poggenpuhl Family*, 91.

Holk describes the princess's speech when he first becomes alert to the divergence of grammar and rhetoric.) And the ongoing maintenance of that façade is more challenging than the couple would have guessed. Theirs is a relationship in which communication, ironic, earnest, or otherwise, must be highly regulated.

One can thus read the conclusion to *Unwiederbringlich* as an alternative-history pendant to *L'Adultera*—what might have happened, had Melanie accepted van der Straaten's proposal to forget about the affair and continue their relationship with reduced expectations? Holk and Christine's folly bears out the soundness of Melanie's principled rejection. The point is that this cynically ironic existence of discrepancy and contradiction is untenable, unsustainable. Holk, who is susceptible to ironic expression, can tolerate the discrepancy, but Christine, the epitome of earnestness, cannot. For her, the corrosive situation leads to ruin. Unable to make his ironic affair with Ebba a relationship in earnest, Holk instead makes his earnest union with Christine into an ironic tragedy.

Fontane sketches this story of a marriage in collapse onto the background of a deepening political crisis among Denmark, the German Confederation, and Prussia over the status of Schleswig and Holstein. It is well known that Fontane based the personal story on actual events but that he transposed the plot from Mecklenburg to Schleswig and Copenhagen and from the early 1840s to the years around 1860, closer to the boiling point of the Schleswig–Holstein conflict.[42] He was already well acquainted with the Second Schleswig War, having been stationed in Copenhagen in 1864 to report on it, but he also took care to learn the details of Danish politics in the lead-up to the conflict in the 1850s. The setting, then, is more than mere backdrop; Fontane takes pains to get it right.[43]

The specificity of the setting has led scholars to investigate how Fontane interweaves the personal and the political and how the historical context shapes the significance of the marriage story. Stefan Blessin, for example, maps the marital conflict between Holk and Christine onto different positions regarding the status of Schleswig–Holstein. Christine opposes letting Denmark annex Schleswig, but she also opposes a Prussian annexation. On her view, Schleswig and Holstein should

---

[42] Christine Hehle's afterword to the *GBA* edition of *Unwiederbringlich* includes a helpful summary of both the material on which the plot is based and the context into which Fontane embeds the story (13:299–312).
[43] For evidence of Fontane's concern for historical accuracy, see, for instance, the letter to Julius Rodenberg of November 25, 1888, *Der Dichter über sein Werk*, 2:415–16.

remain together as German territories, not Prussian, whereas Holk is more inclined to have them subsumed under the Danish monarchy.[44] Taking a different tack, Hohendahl sees the failed marriage as a figure for the collapsing monarchy as Denmark transitions to a modern nation-state. He writes, "Complex and broken reflections emerge, in which private fates become a symptom for a broad, historical process."[45] These readings draw significant parallels between the novel's events and the details of the Schleswig–Holstein question, showing where Fontane foregrounds that historical background and makes it an important part of the novel's fictional world. At the same time, though, the characters' personal lives never quite come together as a coherent allegory for the contemporaneous relationships among political actors and institutions. After all, the proposed union between Holk and Ebba, the novel's chief representatives of Schleswig and Scandinavia, respectively, gets rejected from the Scandinavian side, a plot point that turns the political impetus for the Second Schleswig War on its head.

I want to step back, though, from the level of character relationships to consider the setting from a wider angle of vision. The essential point is that Fontane takes the underlying adultery story and chooses to stage the story in a place that will soon have to face humiliating defeat and loss of territory. Unbeknownst to the narrator, Holk's time in Cophenhagen turns out to portray a society on the verge of disaster. As the preceding analysis has tried to show, the novel also depicts Copenhagen in 1859 as a society in the thrall of cynical irony and insincere speech. It recalls nothing so much as the political background in *Schach von Wuthenow*—namely, Prussia in 1806, about to be routed by Napoleon's troops.[46] Fontane has a tendency to set novels in periods that preface political and military downfall, and when he does so, he tends also to emphasize how those periods are beset by irony and empty rhetoric. *Unwiederbringlich*, for example, dwells at length on the ironic tone of Copenhagen society, especially among the members of the Danish court. Christine, whose earnest bearing is antithetical to the Copenhagen manner of speaking, delivers the portent early in the novel, "es ist

---

[44] Stefan Blessin, "*Unwiederbringlich*—ein historisch-politischer Roman? Bemerkungen zu Fontanes Symbolkunst," *Deutsche Vierteljahrsschrift für Literaturwissenschaft und Geistesgeschichte* 48, no. 4 (1974): 677–80. Blessin concludes that Fontane remains unsuccessful in the attempt to integrate the political context into the story of private infidelity and misfortune (690).
[45] Hohendahl, "Eindringliche Beobachtung," 184.
[46] Lohmeier draws a similar connection between the two novels, arguing that both use a private affair to highlight the fragility of social structures. Dieter Lohmeier, "Vor dem Niedergang. Dänemark in Fontanes Roman *Unwiederbringlich*," *Skandinavistik* 2 (1972): 44.

der Ton, der [...] immer einer Katastrophe vorausgeht" (13:51, I think that it [the tone] is heading straight for disaster, 43–4). Readers of Fontane's novels share that experience, since they see repeatedly how socially accepted forms of empty speech constitute a weakness that contributes to social decline.

Rather than pursue this argument deep into the details of Fontane's text, it will suffice to note the parallel settings and the parallel concerns with unreliable language in both *Schach von Wuthenow* and *Unwiederbringlich* in order to make the point that Fontane presents ironic, unreliable speech as a potential catalyst for political and military downfall. Recall how Bülow, in *Schach von Wuthenow*, draws an analogy between the Prussian situation in 1806 and the fall of the Ming Dynasty—in both cases, the prevailing social tone (empty, prevaricating, unreliable) deviates from the truth. *Unwiederbringlich* includes nothing so explicit regarding rhetoric and historical causality. But it is not hard to see how the novel's rhetorical dichotomy could present a cultural obstacle to Copenhagen's claim on Schleswig and Holstein. As much as Christine expresses contempt for Copenhagen's frivolous tone, members of the princess's court are just as quick to disdain the Germans' dour solemnity. All of this suggests that Schleswig and Holstein diverge culturally from Denmark, and that they could thus prove difficult to assimilate to the Danish monarchy. The novel's events, in which language proves unreliable and one can never tell whether the other person is speaking in earnest, furthermore imply that, when it comes to the possible annexation of Schleswig and Holstein, the Danes might not be reliable, good-faith negotiating partners.

Fontane traveled in Schleswig–Holstein and Denmark during the conflict, acting as a correspondent of sorts, and in 1866 he published *Der Schleswig-Holsteinische Krieg im Jahre 1864*. His reflections on the historical context and the lead-up to the Second Schleswig War provide some support for reading ironic decadence and political downfall as key factors in his choice of settings for *Unwiederbringlich*. For instance, although Fontane does not comment directly on Copenhagen or its manner of speaking, he describes the geography and culture of Schleswig–Holstein in ways that reinforce the novel's central dichotomy. He divides the territory into four sub-cultures, though he also draws out the similarities that make up the area's general cultural climate. Of the Dithmarschen in western Holstein, he writes, for example, "Man geht aufrecht und übt alle Tugenden des Aufrechtgehenden, man spricht die Wahrheit, weil es feig ist zu lügen, man setzt Gut und Leben an das gegebene Wort" (*NA* 19:289, They walk upright and practice all the virtues of the upright, they speak the truth because it is cowardly to lie, they will stake their property and their life on their given word). In this brief summary of a cultural character, Fontane underscores the virtues of honesty and fidelity. When they give their word, it carries a credibility on which they would stake their very lives. Needless to say, this stands in sharp contrast to the frivolity and facetiousness that one observes in Copenhagen. It aligns far more readily with Christine's love for the truth. One could object that Fontane actually differentiates among the different peoples of Schleswig–Holstein and that he sets Holkenäs in Angeln, not in Dithmarschen, so that this description of the Dithmarschen is at best tangentially relevant to the culture of other parts of Schleswig. But Fontane draws out the similarities among the regions, according to which, he writes, "könnte man die Angliter die Dithmarschen der Ostküste nennen" (*NA* 19:290, one could call the Angliter the Dithmarschen of the east coast). In other words, they share common virtues of honesty, forthrightness, and dependability. When *Unwiederbringlich* establishes the central rhetorical opposition into which Holk is cast, it recycles aspects of a cultural portrait that Fontane had already laid down in his reporting on the Second Schleswig War. For Fontane, one cannot comprehend the Schleswig–Holstein issue purely in political or military terms; it also has a cultural and indeed rhetorical dimension, one that the novel then exploits in order to draw its deepest tension and conflict.

Moreover, Fontane's history of the Second Schleswig War suggests that the failure to avoid military conflict could be attributed, at least in part, to a lack of candor and reliability in statements made by the Danish throne. He describes in particular the so-called Märzpatent of 1863, which dealt with the organization of Holstein's affairs in such a way that one could read the document as a precursor to the annexation of Schleswig. But Fontane explains how the declaration dissembles: Danish designs on Schleswig are never stated plainly or directly; it hides them instead under the false appearance of interest in Holstein. He writes:

> Das Patent sprach dies [the intention to incorporate Schleswig] zwar nicht unumwunden aus, es verschwieg sogar den Namen Schleswig, aber eben dies Verschweigen, weil es geflissentlich war, deutete darauf hin, daß man die Incorporation bereits als eine unausbleibliche Thatsache in Rechnung stelle. (*NA* 19:307)

> The edict did not state outright this intention to incorporate Schleswig. In fact, it never mentioned the name Schleswig, but this very concealment, because it was deliberate, indicated they had already factored in the incorporation as an inevitable fact.

Fontane finds nothing in the declaration to be candid or straightforward, two possible equivalents for his term "unumwunden," which derives from the verb "umwinden," to twist around or entwine—in other words, to trope. One would not necessarily label this an instance of irony, but it is certainly an example of deliberately saying something other than what one actually means. In fact, Fontane charges that the *Märzpatent* actively suppresses any reference to Denmark's true intentions. It dissimulates, seeking to conceal the country's collective, political state of mind under a false appearance. One must approach this document alert to the potential for discrepancy between grammatical content and actual import. While a reader like the hapless Holk might accept the declaration at face value, Fontane is far more astute. It is only by reading the document's gaps and omissions, what it leaves unsaid, that Fontane is able to discern its concealed meaning: for the Danes, the incorporation of Schleswig is a foregone conclusion.

The dissembling, unreliable rhetoric in this document is of a piece with the novelistic depiction of insincerity and facetiousness, of the widespread inclination not to say what one means. Just as Ebba conceals her true feelings and intentions under the pretense of genuine affection, so the Danish edict conceals its true designs under the pretense of attentiveness to Holstein. The entwinement of the personal and the political in Fontane thus can be seen to occur at the level of language and an ambiguous relationship to truth. The novel presents in the personal realm the same challenges of rhetoric, reading, and discerning states of mind that occur here in the realm of international diplomacy. The difference is largely one of scale and of consequence. When Ebba's empty flirtation engenders misunderstanding of her true intentions, it results in a personal catastrophe, a ruined marriage, and an individual death. When the Danish monarchy's dissembling declaration conceals its political intentions, it results in a national catastrophe, redrawn borders, and death on a much larger scale.

As is often the case in Fontane, the proximity of the personal and the political serves to highlight the potentially rapid and risky transmission of unreliable rhetoric from one sphere to another. The effects of irony and indeterminacy in the personal realm can be unpleasant, to be sure, but the potential for negative consequences increases exponentially when the influence of ironic, insincere speech begins to corrupt higher-stakes communicative realms of politics, diplomacy, and military affairs. It is once again an issue of contagion and exacerbation, of the inability to hold ironic forms of expression in check. The proclivity for ironic remarks morphs into an ironic existence; a culture of insincere social banter gives way to a culture of insincerity, without limitation. The spark of irony travels far and fast, and a novel like *Unwiederbringlich* plays out the difficulty of reasserting rhetorical control once the conflagration has been allowed to run rampant. Earnestness, sincerity, honesty without guile—these all come to seem passé and ineffectual in a society beholden to the tone of pervasive irony. When Fontane's readers encountered a story set in the Prussia of 1806 or the Copenhagen of

Unwiederbringlich, or the Impotence of Being Earnest   183

1859, it would not go lost on them that these are societies standing on the brink of a brutal defeat. Hohendahl, writing on the narrator's limited knowledge, notes that readers (especially Fontane's contemporaneous readers in the 1890s) approach the story fully aware of the course and consequences of history beyond the novel's frame. The historical background of the conflict over Schleswig–Holstein therefore impinges on readerly judgments and matters to a proper understanding of the novel.[47] Nor would it be lost on them that the most salient detail in the depiction of these societies is a ubiquitous tendency toward empty, insincere talk. The implied connection between rhetorical bearing and historical outcome would not have been difficult to deduce. Dieter Lohmeier remarks on the linkage of decadence and frivolity already in 1972: "Old Denmark is consigned to demise, but in its decline, it develops its more alluring charm [...]. They don't agonize over life's earnestness; they play with it."[48] While Lohmeier sees that fundamental unseriousness as a charming side effect of decline, Fontane presents it rather as a precipitating factor in cultural decline.

Kierkegaard writes that "there is as little social unity in a coterie of ironists as there is truly honesty among a band of thieves."[49] Fontane portrays the Danish elite in 1859 (not to mention the Prussian officer corps in 1806) essentially as a coterie of ironists. And the novel's historical setting suggests a real concern with the ability to maintain social cohesion and a unified diplomatic front within a culture of pervasive irony. The deliberate affectation of not saying what one means and not meaning what one says leads along a pathway whose further waypoints include dissembling, lying, and eventual downfall.

---

[47] Hohendahl, "Eindringliche Beobachtung," 178.
[48] Lohmeier, "Vor dem Niedergang," 41.
[49] Kierkegaard, *Concept of Irony*, 266.

Six Haunting Ambivalence: The Rhetorical Education of *Effi Briest*

The present study's attention to earnestness and irony, to avowal and uncertainty, pays off when we arrive at *Effi Briest*, widely regarded as Fontane's most accomplished and significant novel. The payoff is that the approach developed in previous chapters, through readings of other society novels, can cast familiar scenes from *Effi Briest* in a new light. It reveals an under-acknowledged rhetorical dimension to Effi's transition, as she assimilates to the norms and expectations of social discourse in late-nineteenth-century Germany. A sort of anti-bildungsroman, the novel traces her path as she adapts to ambiguity and insincerity, grapples with ironic ambivalence, and eventually repurposes the tools of dissimulation to serve her own ends. In other words, it follows her socialization into a particular kind of speaking subject as she becomes adept in the art of empty talk.

Reading from this perspective sheds new light on the purpose and effect of Innstetten's ghost story. One sees that the men surrounding Effi present her with parallel rhetorical uncertainties, twin dilemmas of deciding whether language has been delivered earnestly or merely in jest. Just as Effi must decide whether Innstetten's "belief" in the ghost is serious (*ernsthaft*) or rather a bit of fun at the expense of the gullible (*schorahaft*), so she must also determine whether Crampas's flirtations are sincere or harmlessly playful. The upshot is that *Effi Briest* revolves around themes of rhetorical uncertainty and disingenuous language in ways that the scholarly literature has not fully recognized. In some respects, *Effi Briest* has always appeared as the outlier tour de force in Fontane's oeuvre, the novel that differs from and transcends his other works. And yet reading for earnestness, irony, and uncertainty reveals how *Effi Briest* dwells on issues that bind it more closely than has previously been realized to the central concerns of earlier novels such as *Schach von Wuthenow*, *Graf Petöfy*, and *Unwiederbringlich*. The characters in *Effi Briest* employ ironic ambivalence as a deliberate form of dissimulation and rhetorical discipline, as a means to prevent the clear expression of meaning. But the novel seeks out flaws in the armor of rhetorical control and shows repeatedly how that discipline fails. Although the novel eschews any portrayal of intentional acts of avowal, it nonetheless depicts how meaning finds its way into expression unintentionally, despite the characters' best attempts to negate and repress it.

Hertha: "Come back Effi"

Much scholarly attention has been paid to the opening pages of *Effi Briest*, to its depiction of an adolescent Effi, charming, innocent, childlike, still playing with her friends in the yard, and to how abruptly she transitions into betrothal and adulthood.[1] That transitional introduction culminates in a threshold scene with Effi positioned between two worlds. On the one side stands Baron von Innstetten with his marriage proposal; on the other, the ongoing game of tag outside with her friends. Fontane himself identified this fraught moment, with the friends' simple command, "Effi, komm" (15:18, Come back Effi),[2] as the core from which the impetus for the rest of the novel grew. He writes in a letter to Friedrich Spielhagen that, once he had heard this detail of the Ardenne background story, he knew it could be turned into a novel. It made such an impression on him, "daß aus *dieser* Szene die ganze lange Geschichte entstanden ist"[3] (that the whole long story was developed from *this* scene).

It is of course a crucial scene because it reflects vividly Effi's liminal position on the cusp of adulthood, torn between childhood play and adult responsibility, friends and lovers, freedom and obligation. It thus captures in a miniature allegory what will become the novel's decisive tensions. To the above list of oppositional elements, one must add the classic Fontanean duality *Scherz* und *Ernst*, unserious and serious speech, or irony and earnestness. Note, for instance, how the narrative establishes that threshold moment with Effi pulled in two directions at once. When Effi's mother calls her in from playing in order to present her to their guest, Innstetten, she reveals to her daughter that Innstetten has just asked for Effi's hand in marriage. Effi's first reaction is to doubt the earnestness of the proposal: "Um meine Hand angehalten? Und im

---

[1] Irmgard Roebling, for example, details how the opening emphasizes, even exaggerates, Effi's childlike qualities. Irmgard Roebling, "'Effi, komm'—Der Weg zu Fontanes berühmtester Kindsbraut," in *Zwischen Mignon und Lulu*, ed. Malte Stein, Regina Fasold and Heinrich Detering (Berlin: Erich Schmidt Verlag, 2010), 268–71.
[2] Fontane, *Effi Briest*, 13. Further references in this chapter to this translation are given parenthetically.
[3] Fontane, February 21, 1896, *Der Dichter über sein Werk*, 2:460.

Ernst?" (15:18, Wants to marry me? Is he serious?, 13). When Effi calls the proposal's sincerity into question, this is not merely a throwaway expression, equivalent to a contemporary, "Really?" or "Seriously?" Consider that Effi has, just a few pages back, characterized to her friends another semi-serious marriage proposal. A young acquaintance suggests to her that they could well be standing at a wedding ceremony in less than a year, but she deflects—with feigned obtuseness— his designs from herself to her older friend Hulda. "Und dabei sah er mich ganz ernsthaft an," she reports to her friends (15:10, And he gave me a very serious look, 8). The point is that we have seen Effi encounter a marriage proposal before, and in her childlike innocence (or naiveté) she tends not to take male desire very seriously, even when it is apparently meant in earnest. So this most famous and significant scene in *Effi Briest* gets introduced under the banner of a familiar uncertainty— uncertainty regarding whether someone's words are facetious or meant to be taken seriously. Effi's questioning of Innstetten's earnestness aims to bend the proposal back toward the not-yet-adult and not-quite-serious realm of childhood with which she is well acquainted.

Effi's mother, however, quickly puts any uncertainty regarding Innstetten's proposal to rest, saying, "Es ist keine Sache, um einen Scherz daraus zu machen" (15:18, It's not the kind of thing to be joked about, 13). A marriage proposal, she insists, is no laughing matter, which means that it requires the rigorous alignment of language and meaning, words and deeds. It is precisely in this tension between *Scherz* and *Ernst* that Innstetten approaches Effi and her friends call to her from the window.[4] Embodied in this moment are thus two different relationships to language and truth. On the one hand, Hertha's appeal is the simplest, most straightforward kind of language. Consisting of nothing more than an address and an imperative verb, it means exactly what it says. It is honest and direct without being especially earnest. The chapter ends, after all, with the twins laughing and giggling as they disappear, which emphasizes the innocent playfulness attached to their way of speaking. Their *Scherz*, opposed to Innstetten's *Ernst*, is not the empty irony of adult society or the *Komödie* of deceptive language that will come to dictate Effi's discourse. It is instead the joyful exuberance of natural, uninhibited play. On the other hand, Effi is about to enter into an agreement that is completely in earnest, one in which there is no room for being unserious or for saying something other than what she means.

---

[4] Elisabeth Strowick interprets this scene as an *Urszene* of both interruption and repetition. Strowick, *Gespenster des Realismus* (Paderborn: Wilhelm Fink, 2019), 230–5.

Fontane was taken with this threshold moment in which Effi goes from being a girl to a woman, a playmate to a bride, in the blink of an eye. He saw it as the crucible in which the entire dynamic of his novel would be forged. It is important that he crafts this scene through the interaction of rhetorical elements that will by now be familiar—earnestness and unserious speech, in this case the unselfconscious language of adolescent play. The scene introduces a cascade of transitions and developments, not the least of which is Effi's development into a full-fledged adult speaker. Effi must learn how to negotiate adult social discourse and speak like the people around her. It will involve cultivating a hermeneutics of suspicion—already budding in the exchange with her mother—a skeptical bearing that assumes others do not necessarily mean what they say, that they might also mean something other than what they say.[5] It will require her to develop an ear for rhetorical artifice and then learn to wield that artifice herself in order to advance her own interests. On a rhetorical level, Effi Briest is a kind of bildungsroman, or rather an anti-bildungsroman. The eponymous heroine will receive an education in adult social discourse, but it will ultimately be an evolution into rhetorical decadence.

It is telling that, in this moment of competing interpellations, in which Effi is "hailed" by both her friends outside and the dominant ideology of gender and class, she remains silent.[6] Stranded between two discursive realms, she can speak neither in the playful, unserious mode of childhood nor in the earnest mode of adulthood. What she lacks in this moment is *Mündigkeit*, not only in the juridical sense of legal competence, nor in the Enlightenment sense of independent critical thought, but in the more prosaic sense of being able to speak for herself. Over the course of the novel, Effi becomes ever more *mündig* as she grows into the role of speaking subject within the discourse

---

[5] On interpretation as an "exercise of suspicion," see Paul Ricoeur, *Freud and Philosophy: An Essay on Interpretation*, trans. Denis Savage (New Haven: Yale University Press, 1970), 32.

[6] The terms "interpellation" and "hailing" are drawn from Louis Althusser's "Ideology and Ideological State Apparatuses," in *Lenin and Philosophy, and Other Essays* (New York: Monthly Review Press, 1972). An Althusserian reading of this scene could argue that the marriage proposal constitutes Effi as a bourgeois subject and that the friends at the window represent a vanishing opportunity to be outside of ideology. Christian Begemann, for example, reads the call as coming from "an elemental world beyond or prior to the social." Begemann, "'Ein Spukhaus ist nie 'was Gewöhnliches ... ' Das Gespenst und das soziale Imaginäre in Fontanes *Effi Briest*," in *Herausforderungen des Realismus: Theodor Fontanes Gesellschaftsromane*, ed. Peter Uwe Hohendahl and Ulrike Vedder (Freiburg: Rombach, 2018), 204.

Haunting Ambivalence: *Effi Briest* 189

community of the Prussian upper class.[7] But in an age of post-truth decadence, to become *mündig*, to become one's own mouthpiece, also means to acquire the tools of rhetorical discipline, artifice, and duplicity. Fontane once remarked that he loved characters like Effi for their "Echtheit und Natürlichkeit," "auch die Ehrlichkeit" (15:477, authenticity and naturalness, also honesty). There is clearly a rhetorical dimension to honesty, and novels such as *Irrungen, Wirrungen*, with Lene's unadorned, straightforward style of speech, remind us that authenticity and naturalness also carry rhetorical implications. The portrait of Hohen-Cremmen thus locates Effi within a vision of authentic, idyllic simplicity; it casts her as a Lene-type figure, natural, honest, innocent, and uninhibited. As Effi takes on the mantle of adult speaking subject, however, she sacrifices her authenticity for artifice, her directness for evasion, and her credibility for deception.

This opening differs from other of Fontane's introductions, especially those of other society novels, as it pays little attention to how characters talk in social settings. Compared to a novel like *L'Adultera*, it opens with very little commentary from the narrator about the characters' manner of speaking. Except for brief references to Briest's clichés and pronounced bonhomie, this is not a portrait of rhetorical affectation, outspoken irony, or antipathy to earnestness. But language is nonetheless important to the novel's opening. The prelapsarian feel of the introductory chapters also has to do with a transition into a different relationship to language, with Effi's reconstitution of herself as an adult speaking subject.

Her transition into a different rhetorical role is felt almost immediately after the engagement. Just before the engagement, her friends had called her to come. She does come to them, eventually, but after crossing the threshold to adulthood and to a different experience of language. When she returns to them, she speaks differently. She says, for example, "Wie mir ist? O, ganz gut. [...] Er heißt nämlich Geert, was ich Euch, wie mir einfallt, auch schon gesagt habe" (15:20, How do I feel? Oh all right. [...] He's called Geert by the way, but I've told you that already, I seem to remember, 14). It is the same information but presented now in a different tone. One hears, in addition to a note of ambivalence or resignation, a manner of speaking that has become a bit more formal, serious, and reserved. After a few more statements in this tone, Hertha remarks on the change: "Gott, Effi, wie Du nur

---

[7] A case in point regarding Effi's lack of *Mündigkeit*: even after the engagement, her mother continues to act as her *Vormund*, her guardian or spokesperson, speaking on her behalf whenever "es von ernsteren Dingen zu besprechen gab" (15:23, serious matters had to be discussed, 15).

sprichst. Sonst sprachst Du doch ganz anders" (15:21, My goodness, Effi, the way you talk. It's quite different from how you used to talk, 14). The juxtaposition of the past and present tenses brings to the fore a before-and-after difference in Effi's mode of speaking. Effi responds to Hertha's observation laconically and somewhat cryptically, "Ja, sonst" (15:21, Yes, used to, 14). "Sonst" here means as much as otherwise, at other times, or under different circumstances. It reflects Effi's awareness that the engagement has introduced a radical change of circumstance, a rupture in her life, and that she must now speak differently. Of course, she does not actually say any of that, because a significant part of her new manner of speaking entails a heightened degree of reticence and reserve. Effi has crossed the threshold into a new role and a new relationship to language.

Innstetten: "Up already?" ["Finally up?"]

Effi's engagement begins with her questioning of Innstetten's earnestness, and this sort of skepticism runs like a red thread through their relationship. Many of their conversations involve one spouse calling into question the sincerity or earnestness of what the other says.[8] The narrative foregrounds rhetorical skepticism and uncertainty by making it the centerpiece of the couple's first conversation on their first morning of married life in Kessin. Effi, disoriented in her new home and disturbed by strange sounds from the upstairs room, has overslept. And Innstetten, orderly as always, has been up for hours and is waiting on Effi to have breakfast together. When she finally joins him, he greets her with the question, "Schon?" (15:62, Up already?, 39). Having learned from both the narrator and Johanna that Innstetten is stringently punctual and an early riser, it is easy to read his greeting ironically, as suggesting the opposite of its ostensible import, which is exactly what Effi does: "Schon, sagst Du. Natürlich um mich zu verspotten" (15:62, Up already, you say. You're making fun of me of course, 39). She hears in his greeting a note of sarcastic, impatient taunting. This exchange does not present a strong example of ironic indeterminacy; it is fairly obvious that Innstetten is not actually caught off guard by how early Effi has arrived. In fact, he is remarking on the lateness of her arrival, so that his "already" actually means something closer to "finally."

---

[8] In addition to the passages discussed in this section, see further examples such as "Das sagst Du so hin […] und ist doch eigentlich alles nicht wahr" (15:142, You're just saying that […] but in fact it's not true at all, 89) and "Du sagst es nur so" (15:211, you're just saying it, 131). The spouses repeatedly express the perception of insincerity along the lines of "you're just saying that."

Effi's lateness this first morning extends via contrast the opening allegory of Innstetten showing up early, before she is ready. "Warum kommt er so früh?" she asks her mother in the opening scene (15:17, Why has he come so early?, 12), unconsciously pointing beyond the question of thirty minutes to larger issues of maturity and age difference. The allegory of this exchange is that Innstetten (with his proposal) has arrived before Effi has had a chance to prepare herself—to receive a guest, to be sure, but also to assume adult responsibilities. The converse continuation of that allegory occurs here, where Innstetten has been ready and waiting for a long time before Effi finally shows up. On both these levels, his remark "already?" expresses via irony his perception of temporal lag or delay; the Briest girls have kept him waiting, in more ways than one.

The odd aspect of this exchange is that Innstetten denies any degree of irony in his question. He shakes his head, disavows a sarcastic, derisive tone, and insists that his question was in earnest. Indeed, he produces multiple "Versicherungen [...], daß sein 'schon' ganz aufrichtig gemeint gewsen sei" (15:62, assurances that his "Up already" had been sincerely meant, 39). With the word "aufrichtig," he asserts that his remark was genuine and earnest. One sees him in this moment trying to control and constrain the range of meanings that could be attributed to his words. He refuses to acknowledge, let alone admit, that a trope such as irony could make his statement equivocal or ambivalent. He sticks to the ideal of a single, unequivocal meaning, however implausible that might be.

The exchange acquires extra significance through its proximity to a previous discussion of similar themes. The day before, as they are riding through the countryside into Kessin, Innstetten presents a cultural portrait in broad strokes that dwells on a discrepancy between phenomenon and essence: these people look pleasant and respectful enough, but they are unreliable. One cannot count on their word, as it is always uncertain whether they will actually follow through on what they say. This characterization forms one piece of a contrast with people (such as Effi) from the Mark: "Eure märkischen Leute sehen unscheinbarer aus [...], aber ihr Ja ist Ja und Nein ist Nein, und man kann sich auf sie verlassen. Hier ist alles unsicher" (15:50, Your people in the Mark are an unprepossessing and morose lot [...], but when they say yes they mean yes and when they say no they mean no, and you can rely on them. Here nothing is clear-cut, 32). His description of the Mark recalls Fontane's characterization of the "upright" or "upstanding" Dithmarschen people in Holstein (NA 19:289). What makes them upstanding is the credibility of their given word, something that people from the Kessin countryside lack and people from the Mark have. Innstetten describes people as reliable when they speak unequivocally, when there is no possibility of multiple meanings and no worry that a meaning might twist into its opposite, that "yes" might actually mean "no," or that "so soon" might in fact mean "finally." Of course, Innstetten's ethnic stereotypes about Slavic unreliability and märkisch forthrightness turn out to be wrong. So often in the society novels, the Prussian officers and nobility are the least reliable speakers. Unreliable language is a sickness diagnosed at the heart of Prussian society, not a symptom of foreignness or otherness. The steadfast reliability that Innstetten praises in other's language is not in evidence in his own, and the uncertainty and unreliability that he laments among the country folk operate in his language too; he just refuses to admit it. The conclusion to draw is not that Innstetten's language is broken or empty. It is, rather, brimming with polysemous possibilities that he struggles to control. This will turn out to be a central theme in the novel, as characters repeatedly try to discipline their language, constrain communication, and repress unwanted meanings. Innstetten does not want Effi to draw a credible connection between his words ("already?") and his feelings (impatience, primarily), but the fact that the ironic bent of his remark is legible to her suggests that rhetorical discipline is imperfect and that one cannot do much to prevent the revelation and apprehension of meaning.

As the conversation goes on, Effi continues to doubt and reinterpret what Innstetten says. When he tells her that her parents raised her well, here, too, she doubts that he really means it in earnest, and she interrogates the motivation behind the compliment. "Das sagst Du so, weil wir noch in den Flitterwochen sind" (15:62, You're just saying that because it's still our honeymoon, 40). Believing his compliment to be insincere, she accuses him of flattering and indulging her. Her point is that Innstetten's language is not as reliable or certain as he would have one believe; it should not be taken at face value. Even if only in a lighthearted way, Effi tends to question the sincerity of her husband's language. In each instance, she must decide how to take an utterance, and it is always a negotiation. Should his words be dismissed as so much ironic teasing or insincere flattery? Or are they genuinely meant? Exercising interpretive suspicion is Effi's first stage of development as she steps into the role of a social speaking subject. The learning curve is steep because she will be confronted from all sides by rhetorical uncertainty, by language that has multiple planes of meaning, and by the ambivalent fluctuation between irony and earnestness. Before the novel's conclusion, she will brandish all those tools in support of her own reticence and secrecy.

Once Effi and Instetten arrive in Kessin and begin their shared marital life, the novel begins more to resemble other examples of Fontane's society novels. It depicts similar marital conversations, similar navigations of meaning, and similar wrangling over the possibility of ironic insincerity. If there is a difference, though, it is that *Effi Briest* depicts decisively how this uncertainty is not merely a matter of interpreting stray equivocal remarks. It is, rather, a question of how to interpret and thus relate to an entire rhetorical bearing. It becomes less about the uncertainty of a potentially ironic statement and more about the uncertainty of a potentially disingenuous mode of being. Effi must figure out not just how to take Innstetten's ironic remark; she must figure out how to take Innstetten himself, and Crampas too. The challenges presented by this fundamental uncertainty become particularly acute in the face of Innstetten's ghost story and Crampas's advances. What they have in common is that, in both cases, the men present as facetious or ironic things that they might actually mean quite in earnest, while also presenting as serious things that they do not sincerely believe. They confront her with parallel uncertainties, with twin dilemmas of whether something is meant seriously or just in jest. Are Crampas's words earnest advances, or just ironically insincere flirtation? Does Innstetten sincerely believe in the ghost, or is it just a bit of ironic condescension? This reading of sincere and insincere speech thus opens a new perspective on the function of the ghost story in the narrative. In addition to all of its symbolic resonances with the story, the ghost's deployment itself is crucial for the way in which it foregrounds the indeterminacy of irony and earnestness. The ghost story reveals Innstetten as an equivocal, unreliable interlocutor, opening an abyss of uncertainty about whether he actually means what he says.

Effi: "Strange, [...] I thought you were just kidding about all that."

The house in Kessin appears to be haunted, and Innstetten is happy to provide the backstory, with its many gaps and indeterminacies. Their house was previously owned by a Captain Thomsen, who settled in Kessin with his niece or granddaughter—no one knows for sure—and a beloved Chinese servant. The niece eventually married a ship's captain, according to Thomsen's wishes, but she disappeared on the night of the wedding reception, and the Chinese man died fourteen days later (15:98–9). Whether the proximity of those two events is correlation, causation, or coincidence remains unclear. But this much is certain: several people attribute the nighttime disturbances that frighten Effi to the Chinaman's ghost continuing to haunt the house.

This ghost story has been the object of a significant amount of scholarly literature. Daragh Downes, summarizing the state of twentieth-century scholarship, writes that the commentary on the ghost story has been "intense, contentious, and multifaceted [perspektivenreich]," contentious because the appraisals range from disparaging to laudatory, and multiperspectival because the elusive indeterminateness of the ghost story allows for multiple connections between the content of the story and the narrative situation in which it occurs.⁹ Christian Grawe, for instance, describes "this symbol's ingenious ambiguity," which allows it to reflect so many of the novel's subjects—an arranged marriage, a desire to escape, a love triangle, guilt, and death.¹⁰ According to Frances Subiotto, the ghost story represents Fontane's narrative "sleight-of-hand," in which the ghost gives a refracted rhetorical presence to the extramarital affair that haunts the novel but is never depicted directly.¹¹

Even critics who are not enamored of the ghost story cannot dismiss it entirely, since Fontane himself emphasized its centrality to the narrative. He responds to a contemporaneous reviewer by wondering, "wie man daran vorbeisehen kann" (how one can overlook it) when the ghost story is in fact "ein Drehpunkt für die ganze Geschichte" (a fulcrum for the entire story).¹² Despite his identification of the ghost as a pivotal point in the narrative, the secondary literature has not entirely come to grips with the ghost story, as evidenced by the many conflicting interpretations. In short, commentary on the novel cannot quite decide how to take the ghost story. From my perspective, the lack of critical consensus is consistent with the function of the ghost story, which is designed to be ambivalent, equivocal, and difficult to read.¹³ Indeed, figuring out how to take the ghost story becomes one of Effi's main interpretive dilemmas in the novel, as well as an enduring source of discord in her marriage and a first point of connection between her and Crampas. Commentators cannot agree on how to take the ghost story because it is intended to raise precisely this question of how to take something. The ghost occupies a pivotal position in the secondary

---

[9] Daragh Downes, "*Effi Briest*. Roman," in *Fontane-Handbuch*, ed. Christian Grawe and Helmuth Nürnberger (Stuttgart: Kröner, 2000), 644.
[10] Cited in Downes, "*Effi Briest*. Roman," 644.
[11] Frances Subiotto, "The Ghost in *Effi Briest*," *Forum for Modern Language Studies* 21, no. 2 (1985): 137. Other interpretations read the ghost story as a self-reflexive model for Fontane's narrative strategies. See, for example, Sofia Källström, *Das Eigentliche bleibt doch zurück. Zum Problem der semantischen Unbestimmtheit am Beispiel von Theodor Fontanes Effi Briest* (Uppsala: Uppsala University Press, 2002), on the novel's semantic indeterminacies; Simone Arnold-de Simine, "'Denn das Haus, was wir bewohnen, [...] ist ein Spukhaus.' Fontanes *Effi Briest* und Fassbinders Verfilmung in der Tradition des Female Gothic," *Germanic Review* 79, no. 2 (2004): 83–113, on the gothic haunted house motif and narrative reticence; and Strowick, *Gespenster des Realismus*, 242, on Fontane's staging of the real as an incommensurable other.
[12] Fontane, November 19, 1895, *Der Dichter über sein Werk*, 2:454.
[13] Greenberg attends to the ghost story as incomplete and indecipherable and connects it to other narrative gaps and ambiguities. Valerie Greenberg, "The Resistance of *Effi Briest*: An (Un)told Tale," *PMLA* 103, no. 5 (1988): 773–4.

literature for the same reason that it plays a pivotal role in the novel—
it activates the grand subjects of unreliable language and rhetorical
uncertainty and dwells in an indeterminate space between irony and
earnestness.

Those themes are apparent in the remark that serves as this section's
header. Effi has been struggling for some time to determine whether
Innstetten sincerely believes that the house is haunted, or whether he is
just sharing folksy nonsense in an ironic, tongue-in-cheek mode. That
uncertainty haunts Effi from the very moment that she learns about the
ghost. On her introductory tour of the Kessin house, for instance, she
finds a small picture of a Chinese man stuck to a chair in an empty
upstairs room. Innstetten quickly assures her that it is just "Spielerei"
(Some kind of game, 44), which is to say, nothing that she should take
seriously. Yet how he stands in relation to the ghost's potential existence is never quite clear. "Effi [...] war nur verwundert, daß Innstetten alles so ernsthaft nahm, als ob es doch etwas sei" (15:69, Effi [...]
was only surprised that Innstetten was taking it all so seriously, as if it
really mattered [as if there were really something to it], 44). The reader
observes Effi in this moment observing her husband and trying to get a
read on his degree of earnestness. She struggles to do so, because Innstetten positions himself in ironic ambivalence, making it impossible
to determine whether he actually means what he says or says what
he means. Christian Bregemann summarizes that ambivalence nicely,
writing, "This dichotomy of nothing and something determines Innstetten's entire attitude, which oscillates in the various conversations
from denial to indecision and from there to affirmation."[14] It is a familiar dynamic in Fontane. On the one hand, Innstetten asserts that it's
just a bunch of playful nonsense that she shouldn't lose sleep over. On
the other hand, he undercuts that flippant stance with a solemnity that
suggests that he might in fact take the ghost story seriously.[15]

Effi and Crampas will eventually discuss Innstetten's penchant for
telling ghost stories, and the scholarly literature has tended to focus on
Crampas's assertion that Innstetten uses the ghost story as a didactic
instrument to control and discipline his young wife. But one should
note that Crampas identifies not only a didactic bent to the ghost story;
he begins by pointing out Innstetten's fundamental insincerity with

---

[14] Begemann, "Ein Spukhaus," 214.
[15] Mülder-Bach helpfully points out that Effi commands Innstetten to tell her "das Wirkliche," that which is real and true. And yet the extent to which the ghost story is real and true is precisely what he refuses to divulge. Inka Mülder-Bach, "'Verjährung ist [...] etwas Prosaisches.' *Effi Briest* und das Gespenst der Geschichte," *Deutsche Vierteljahrsschrift* 83, no. 4 (2009): 628.

regard to the ghost. Even back in his military days, Innstetten liked to share ghost stories, and Crampas observes that, even then, no one could tell whether he was telling them in earnest. Many people, Crampas reports, were under the impression, "daß er doch nicht ganz so dazu stände, wie er's uns einreden wollte" (15:153, that he wasn't quite so committed to it as he would have us believe, 95). In other words, there exists an ironic discrepancy between the phenomenon of Innstetten's narrative and the essence of his own belief. He wants to persuade others to take seriously something that he himself does not sincerely believe. His supernatural storytelling is, in Kierkegaard's words, perhaps "not serious about its seriousness."[16] That duplicity leads Crampas to assert that Innstetten's talk about ghosts is "ja alles bloß Komödie" (15:153, all an act, 95). "Komödie" is a noteworthy term. In this context, it has little to do with comedy and more to do with its idiomatic register of "putting on a show." To put on an act is to wear a mask, play a role, and present oneself as something other than what one actually is, to dissimulate. In *Effi Briest*, the word functions as a mark of duplicity, as it is the same term that the narrative applies to Effi's deceptions later in the novel.[17] Effi gradually comes to realize that her husband wears a rhetorical poker face of equivocation and disingenuousness, and she will eventually don a similar mask herself. The didacticism of the ghost story misses the mark that Innstetten intends when it corrals Effi not toward obedience but rather toward the production of deceptive language.

Innstetten is often described as a man of character and principle, but for all his solid Prussian virtues, he emerges in such scenes as a not particularly reliable or transparent speaker. One primary purpose of the ghost story is thus to bring to the fore the ambiguity surrounding Innstetten's rhetoric. Although he presents himself as solemn and earnest, it is not at all clear that his talk about the ghost is credible. As Effi writes to her mother, his attitude suggests to her that she should "das alles als alten Weiberunsinn ansehen und darüber lachen, aber mit einemmal schien er doch auch wieder selber daran zu glauben" (15:117, see all this as an old wives' tale and laugh at it, but then suddenly he seemed to believe in it all himself, 73). Effi's conundrum—vexing enough to warrant inclusion in a letter to her parents—reveals itself to be not so different from that of Holk in *Unwiederbringlich*, when he must interpret

---

[16] Kierkegaard, *Concept of Irony*, 265.
[17] See, for example, "ein verstecktes Komödienspiel" (15:199, duplicity and play-acting, 124), and "sie mußte wieder eine Komödie spielen" (15:232, some more play-acting, 144).

Haunting Ambivalence: *Effi Briest* 197

Ebba's flirtatious talk. Whereas Holk, a strong example of misreading, plunges headlong onto the wrong side of an either/or decision (either she loves him, or her talk is facetious), Effi comes across as a more sensitive and sophisticated interlocutor, alert to the both/and possibility of multiple, conflicting planes of meaning. She comes to realize that the most pressing question is perhaps not the extent to which Innstetten is serious about the ghost but rather why he would so steadfastly maintain a posture of equivocation and ambivalence. She characterizes this ambivalence-by-design succinctly, telling Crampas, "Er sagte nicht ja und nicht nein, und ich bin nicht klug aus ihm geworden" (15:154, He didn't say yes, he didn't say no, and I couldn't get any sense out of him, 96).

One might recall here Botho's report from Berlin's high-society soirees that, when it comes to superficial banter, the particulars of what one says are entirely inconsequential because "yes" means as much as "no." One should also recall, in contrast, Innstetten's praise for the upstanding people of the Mark, whose word is utterly reliable because their "yes" means "yes" and their "no" means "no." In those two references to "yes" and "no," one finds the primary rhetorical dichotomy that operates in Fontane's novels—the conflict between language that is unserious, unreliable and language that is serious and therefore credible. Innstetten refuses to come down squarely on one side or the other. Instead, he occupies an indeterminate middle ground between irony and avowal. Although he praises the earnest, transparent honesty of people from the Mark, he himself dwells in ironic indeterminacy. He deploys against Effi what Fontane elsewhere identifies as a tone that is "halb ernst-, halb scherzhaft" (15:144, half in earnest, half joking), and the novel depicts how this manner of speaking drives a wedge between the two spouses.

The remark cited as the header for this section occurs in a conversation that reflects both Effi's uncertainty and Innstetten's equivocation. The couple has just returned home from Effi's performance in the significantly titled play "One False Step," and Innstetten is reminding her that she needs to be careful around Crampas. At this moment, she claims to hear the sound of dancing—the ghost—from upstairs, and she says to Innstetten, "Sonderbar, daß es immer wieder kommt. Ich dachte, Du hättest mit dem allen nur so gespaßt" (15:173, Strange how it keeps coming back. I thought that you were only joking about all that, 107). The repeated occurrence of the haunting leads Effi to reassess her take on Innstetten's account of the ghost. Whereas Holk thought Ebba was serious and then found out she was not, Effi thought Innstetten was (mostly) joking but now thinks he might have meant it seriously after all. The point is that, deep into the novel, somewhere around its midpoint, Effi is still plagued by uncertainty surrounding whether Innstetten means what he says.[18]

More interesting, though, is Innstetten's response, which aims to perpetuate rather than alleviate her uncertainty.[19] To the suggestion that he was just kidding about the ghost, he replies, "Das will ich doch nicht sagen, Effi. Aber so oder so, man muss nur in Ordnung sein und sich nicht zu fürchten brauchen" (15:173, I wouldn't say that, Effi. But be that as it may, one just has to keep one's life in order and have no reason to be afraid, 108). He continues to produce language that fails to clarify his stance. In fact, his Bartleby-style response simply reiterates his refusal to take a clear side: he does not want to say that the ghost story is an ironic, unserious joke, nor will he state unequivocally that he means it in earnest. He would prefer not to say one way or the other, which is evident in the summarizing phrase "so oder so." His phrasing dismisses the very issue that has become a profound source of anxiety and consternation in Effi's life. It does not matter whether he means the ghost story to be taken earnestly or ironically; what matters is discipline and orderliness. In Innstetten's language, equivocation is a feature rather than a bug. He cultivates rhetorical ambivalence so that no one can pin him to a fixed meaning and wields it as a didactic instrument.

Effi's rhetorical education continues apace, and one observes her becoming ever more alert to subtlety and ambiguity. If Innstetten in fact uses the ghost story as an instrument of *Erziehung*, as a way of nurturing or educating Effi, the lessons she draws from it are not the ones he intended. She learns in particular to exercise suspicion and to be keen-eared when it comes to ambivalence and the possibility of multiple meanings.[20] Innstetten, for example, delivers another of his

---

[18] There is another way in which this exchange constitutes a pivotal point in the novel: there is no guarantee that Effi actually hears the ghost in this moment. It could be that she deploys the haunting here to divert Innstetten away from his lecture about Crampas. This would make it perhaps the first instance in which Effi intentionally says something she does not sincerely believe in order to deceive. This moment—occurring in the eighteenth of thirty-six chapters—would then represent a midpoint after which Effi now embraces the dissimulating rhetoric that was so foreign to her at the novel's outset.

[19] Begemann, too, sees Innstetten's ambivalence engendering "a far-reaching epistemological uncertainty." Begemann, "Ein Spukhaus," 214.

[20] Effi exercises a hermeneutics of suspicion vis-à-vis almost everyone around her. Even when Crampas instructs her to doubt the sincerity of Innstetten's ghost story, she applies her suspicion both to Innstetten and to Crampas. She asks herself, "Wer bürgt mir denn dafür, daß Crampas recht hat! Crampas […] ist unzuverlässig und bloßer Haselant" (15:157, What guarantee have I that Crampas is right! Crampas is […] unreliable, just a poseur, 98). The passage evokes an abyssal, hall-of-mirrors aspect to identifying irony and insincerity. When Crampas tells her that Innstetten's assertions are unreliable, she must now, in a higher-order reflection, decide whether that assertion is itself unreliable.

difficult-to-read pronouncements: "Zuletzt ist es doch so: was man empfängt, das hat man auch verdient" (15:174, It comes down to one thing in the end: what you get is what you deserve, 108). In context, the statement's obvious meaning is positive: Effi says that everyone is spoiling her and she feels like she does not deserve it. And Innstetten basically says, no, if people are pampering you, it's because you deserve it—you get what you've earned. But lurking in the background is a potentially more punitive suggestion: you get what you deserve, in the sense of an ominous warning, you're going to get what's coming to you. And Effi, who, before her marriage, might have been too innocent or naïve to hear how language could trope its way into extra, contradictory meanings, is now fully alert to the intricacies of ambiguity. "Effi hörte scharf hin, und ihr schlechtes Gewissen ließ sie sich selber fragen, ob er das absichtlich in so zweideutiger Form gesagt habe" (15:174, Effi listened intently, and her bad conscience prompted her to ask herself whether he had deliberately put it in such an ambiguous way, 108). One will recognize in this questioning the same conundrum that surrounds the reception of the ghost story. Just as Effi cannot decide whether to take the ghost as earnestly meant, so she also cannot decide whether to take intimations of her guilt as earnestly meant—or as hallucinatory apparitions of her own guilty conscience. What haunts Effi is not the ghost itself but rather the potential truth of its existence, the potential sincerity that Innstetten could attach to it. In similar fashion, her marriage is haunted by the potential existence of insinuations of guilt, by the possibility that Innstetten sincerely means what she hears in his words. The anxiety in *Effi Briest* derives from the haunting possibility of submerged meaning coming to the surface. The fear is that ostensibly empty turns of phrase or haphazard manners of speaking hold in reserve a meaning that is earnest and sincere and will eventually come to light.

Crampas: "all just quotation, or more precisely a *façon de parler*. And yet there was some sincerity in it."

Once we recognize that Effi's relationship with Innstetten revolves around familiar Fontanean questions of uncertainty, irony, and insincerity, it reveals a parallel between Innstetten and Crampas. They both confront Effi with the same dilemma—namely, whether to take what they say as earnest or ironic. In the case of Crampas, resolving this question is even more urgent, because his ambiguity threatens both her honor and her social standing. If she takes his flirtations too seriously, she appears vain and laughable to those around her. If she takes them too lightly, she risks exposing herself to the threat of infidelity. Crampas exploits this very uncertainty by blurring the boundary between irony and avowal. Fontane crafts in *Effi Briest* an adultery novel in which the affair is enabled by and grows out of the deft deployment of ironic ambiguity.

The passage heading this section highlights the instability of language that appears empty and haphazard but might conceal something earnest beneath its inconsequential surface. In a conversation with Effi and Innstetten, Crampas qualifies a turn of phrase that he has just delivered by saying that it is "alles bloß Citat oder noch richtiger façon de parler. Und doch steckt etwas Aufrichtiggemeintes dahinter" (15:145, all just quotation, or more precisely a *façon de parler*. And yet there was some sincerity in it, 90). His statement evokes Neumann's notion of a Prussian "culture of citation," a clichéd manner of speaking via empty repetition that should not be taken too seriously because it is not sincerely meant.[21] But then Crampas's "and yet" sets in motion the wobble of ironic indeterminacy that destabilizes so many interactions in Fontane's society novels. His manner of speaking is empty and yet meaningful, blithe and yet earnest. It is that familiar half-joking, half-serious tone that couches earnestness in irony and flippancy in feigned sincerity. In this instance, however, untangling what is in jest from what is serious becomes an especially pressing task, because Crampas uses precisely that ambiguity to advance his designs on Effi.

One can trace this interplay of empty citation and earnest import in Crampas's interactions with Effi. He is, for example, fond of citing poems such as Heine's "Deine weichen Lilienfinger" (15:160, "Fingers soft and lily-white," 100). She can hardly take umbrage at a high-brow literary reference—after all, he is merely citing canonical poetry—and yet in the same moment that he mentions the poem, he also touches her hand. He thereby suggests a situationally specific referent for those supple lily fingers and indicates that there is indeed, as his earlier statement asserted, a sincere sentiment tucked into what would otherwise be an innocuous reference. This indeterminate language that is both playful and serious at the same time continues during their morning outing in the dunes. He wants to keep the glass from their shared breakfast, which Effi recognizes as a performative allusion to Goethe's "König in Thule" and a winking reference to having a mistress. In each case of "mere" citation, his educated, literary manner of speaking both conceals and hints at the possibility of earnestly felt attraction. As Mecklenburg writes of a different citation in *Effi Briest*, "Citation means using a statement merely by invoking it. Its validity is left undecided."[22] The literary references allow Crampas to introduce themes of sensuality, erotic desire, and infidelity without ever indicating decisively the extent

---

[21] Neumann, "Speisesaal und Gemäldegalerie," 142.
[22] Mecklenburg, *Theodor Fontane*, 266. Mecklenburg focuses on Effi's citation of her father's gendered maxim, "Weiber weiblich, Männer männlich" (15:9, women should be womanly, men should be manly, 7).

to which the quoted material applies to the present situation. Subiotto notes that this kind of flirtation via language and double entendre is typical in Fontane's novels. He connects it to Professor Schmidt's manner of speaking in *Frau Jenny Treibel* and sees both Crampas and Schmidt exemplifying this aspect of the "Fontane tone."[23] In addition to literary references, Crampas also makes jokes and wordplays. When Effi apologizes for presenting him bread on a basket lid, he reaches for the pun, "Ein Korbdeckel ist kein Korb" (15:162, The giver, not the gift is what matters, 101). He makes a play on words that goes lost in translation because the term for basket (*Korb*) is also an idiomatic expression for rejection.[24] Crampas says that, whatever Effi is doing in this moment, at least she's not rejecting him—and this exchange follows closely on the heels of his touching her hand.

It is important that Crampas makes his advances under the mask of playful banter. Because it is just play, it diminishes the risk of offense. Ostensibly unserious speech provides a way to push the boundaries of socially acceptable expression without committing to a serious statement. There exists an established tradition of conceiving of jokes and wordplay as a means to evade cultural constraints and give voice to otherwise-taboo ideas. Sigmund Freud, for example, hypothesizes that the pleasure inherent in laughter and joking helps to override censorship, creating a brief exemption that allows one to express in polite society sexuality or aggression.[25] In *Effi Briest*, Crampas's wordplay and citations—all the facets of his playful banter—create an interval of permissibility, but it operates differently from Freud's theory of the joke. Here, the façade of joking and facetiousness allows Crampas to touch upon a serious topic as if it were not serious. It allows him, in other words, to ironize his attraction and attempts at seduction. He *is* making advances; he *is* out to seduce her, even though she is married, but he can present his designs on Effi as if they were just playful fun. It represents another one of these "halb scherzhaft" moments, but there is something quite serious and taboo behind it, something that he would not be able to say had he not couched it in a joke. This is why Effi labels him a "Humoristen, aber doch von ganz sonderbarer Art" (15:166, a humorist [with] an odd sense of humor, 103). He may be a humorist, but his humor falls into an indeterminate zone between joking and earnest expression. Crampas's ironic distance from his own work of seduction has one key purpose: it provides a cover of plausible deniability. If

---

[23] Subiotto, "The Ghost in *Effi Briest*," 142.
[24] For example, the narrative voice refers to Holk's rejection in *Unwiederbringlich* as "ein Korb" (13:268).
[25] Freud, *Standard Edition*, 8:103.

Effi (or Innstetten or anyone else) were ever to accuse him of a serious transgression, he could always retreat behind the facetiousness of his *façon de parler* and assert that they have simply taken too earnestly what was said in jest.

Lest one object that this do-I-really-mean-it-or-not? sort of duplicity should not qualify as an instance of irony in the strict sense, I point again to the description of irony that occurs at the beginning of *Der Stechlin*. There, the narrator describes irony as the act of putting "hinter alles ein Fragezeichen" (17:8, a question mark behind everything). This is essentially what Crampas does with Effi: rather than avow his desire, he expresses it in a way that undercuts the attribution of sincerity and shrouds in indeterminacy whether an earnest desire was ever expressed. Moreover, *Der Stechlin*'s narrator reports that Dubslav's irony routinely obscures, "ob er's ernsthaft oder scherzhaft gemeint habe" (17:9, whether he meant it seriously or ironically). The effect of self-ironization in these two novels is ultimately the same—interlocutors cannot determine whether to take a statement as earnest or in jest. There are two salient differences, though. First, what the narrator states as a straightforward fact in *Der Stechlin* only comes to light circuitously in *Effi Briest*, via Effi's self-questioning internal monologue. Second, Dubslav Stechlin's ironic bearing could seem innocuous, even charming. Although he is an old-school aristocrat, he is, to his credit, quick to undercut the appearance of arrogant self-regard. In Effi's case, however, there is nothing innocuous about ironic indeterminacy. The inability to say conclusively whether Crampas speaks earnestly or facetiously allows him to pursue a strategy of seduction under the cloak of irony. Ironic indeterminacy is the motor that drives the novel's major conflicts.

Seen in this light, the interactions with Crampas reactivate the most fundamental and vexing experience of language in Fontane's novels. How seriously should Crampas be taken? Is he sincerely courting Effi and putting her in a precarious position? Or is he just a friend who pushes the boundaries of decorum in a playful, unserious way? These are questions that haunt Effi in moments of solitary reflection. She agonizes over whether it was a mistake to joke with Crampas in that same bantering tone, and this represents the crux of the matter. If it is all just playful banter, then there is no harm in joking around with a friend of the family. In fact, it would be small-minded to scold a friend for every comment that could be taken as double entendre. On the other hand, there is always the potential disturbance of irony. If the playfulness is disingenuous, if it harbors a serious core of attraction, temptation, and willingness to betray, then Effi is engaged in a dangerous game indeed. Effi's reflections do not resolve this uncertainty but rather hold the dissonance of two conflicting possibilities in mind: "Nein, sie konnte sich nicht Tadeln, auf seinen Ton eingegangen zu sein, und doch hatte sie ganz leise das Gefühl einer überstandenen Gefahr" (15:167, No, she could not accuse herself of having responded to his manner [tone], yet she had just a slight sense of having escaped danger, 104). Effi's "and yet" reflects that core dissonance as a symptomatic reaction to irony, ambiguity, and uncertainty. It furthermore echoes the "und doch" from Crampas's statement about everything being mere citation *and yet* harboring a sincere meaning. Because Crampas speaks in the mode of *and yet*, Effi ultimately reacts to it with an *and yet*. Effi's responsiveness to that tone is innocent *and yet* dangerous.

Annie: "Yes, if I'm allowed."

When Effi marries Innstetten and leaves Hohen-Cremmen for Kessin, the transition thrusts her into a world of adult social discourse and a new relationship to language. It is a discourse that privileges reticence, reserve, calculated conversation, and the strict control of meaning. In short, Effi must learn to read and practice the art of rhetorical discipline. One sees that in the calculated interactions discussed above, when Innstetten, for example, tries to disavow the expression of sarcastic irritation or refuses to divulge his true stance on the ghost, or when Crampas deploys irony to conceal the earnestness of his advances. One sees it in the obligatory social visits that the couple must make around Kessin, where every conversation is a pretext proffered for the sake of scrutinizing the newly arrived Effi. And one sees it, furthermore, in a general attitude of caution and reserve; there is much in this novel that is better left unsaid. Effi, for instance, writes to her mother that she is sad and lonely, but "Innstetten darf es nicht sehen" (15:114, Innstetten must not see [it], 71). She hopes, after she has given birth, to take the newborn child for a long visit to Hohen-Cremmen, but "Innstetten darf nicht davon wissen" (15:115, Innstetten must know nothing of it, 72). So it is with discussions of the ghost and many other matters. And it's not just Effi; it's everyone around her. Her father discourages Effi from repeating certain comments, even to her mother (15:141), and Crampas forbids her from sharing his "König von Thule" allusion with her husband (15:166). Crampas is committed to having his flirtatious, semi-joking double entendre read as harmless, unserious banter. Innstetten, however, would see it much differently—as a too-forward expression of desire and a serious threat to marital fidelity. Thus, in order to exert rhetorical discipline and control the meaning that will be derived from his statements, he asks Effi to keep the details of their conversation from her husband.

In this environment, Effi develops an acute ear for artifice, privative rhetoric, and duplicity. But one can go a step further and say that the initiation into adult social discourse leads Effi herself to develop into an evasive, duplicitous speaker. This is especially true once the affair with Crampas shifts from the hypothetical to the tangible. In the book's second third, Effi leaves behind the authenticity, honesty, and openness of her childhood existence and adopts instead a different way of speaking and comporting herself—not just reticent but secretive, even deceptive. It is under the power of the taboo and the unspeakable, "daß sie sich, von Natur frei und offen, in ein verstecktes Komödienspeil mehr und mehr hineinlebte" (15:199, that she, by nature frank and open, slipped further and further into duplicity and play-acting, 124). She goes from being naïve, honest, and authentic—in a word, childlike—to being someone who can navigate irony and dissimulation, and from there to being someone who will wield deception to protect her own secrets. The cited passage calls to mind Fontane's epistolary remark about loving characters such as Effi for their "Echtheit und Natürlichkeit," as well as their "Ehrlichkeit" (15:477, authenticity and naturalness, honesty). Effi grows up, or gets educated, precisely by sacrificing the authenticity and honesty that Fontane took pains to depict at the novel's outset. Later in the novel, Effi summarizes this sacrifice and her transition to a different kind of speaker, reflecting, "immer war es mein Stolz, daß ich nicht lügen könne und auch nicht zu lügen brauche, [...] und nun habe ich doch immer lügen müssen, vor ihm [Innstetten] und aller Welt" (15:258, I was always proud that I couldn't lie, and also that I didn't need to lie [...], and now I've had to lie all the time, to him and the whole world, 160). What Fontane values in Effi's character is also something that he has her value in her own character. It is telling that here, back at her childhood home, she feels most acutely her departure from her prior mode of speaking. Against her own values, she has exchanged honesty for deception and credibility for unreliability. The extramarital affair once again has a rhetorical function: it necessitates an intensification of Effi's departure from an authentic relationship to language and pushes her toward an extreme of disingenuous, duplicitous speech, until she is enthralled in a comedy of lies.

This shift represents the arc of Effi's rhetorical education, which begins in earnest with Innstetten's employment of the ghost story as a didactic, disciplinary tool. Its purpose is probably to enforce her marital fidelity. But the ghost story educates Effi according to its form rather than its content, according to its discursive presentation rather than the story itself. What Effi learns, in effect, is how to deploy things one does not really believe in order to engender belief in others. In earlier works such as *Quitt* and *Unterm Birnbaum*, Fontane already explores more concrete and criminal forms of deception; with Effi he pursues a similar topic within the realm of everyday rhetoric. She learns to speak duplicitously, to produce words that conceal rather than reveal, and to use language in a way that breaks its ethical and indexical relationship to the world. The fact that this practice of rhetorical discipline represents her coming into adulthood becomes clear when the affair begins and lying becomes a necessity. When Innstetten returns from a trip to Berlin, he remarks on her change, saying, "Du hattest so 'was von einem verwöhnten Kind, mit einemmal siehst Du aus wie eine Frau" (15:211, Before you could sometimes look like a spoilt child, and now all of a sudden you look like a woman, 131). One obvious implication is that, in his absence, Effi has consummated the affair with Crampas. But there is also the suggestion that she becomes an adult woman, or becomes *mündig*, through this new experience of language—by exploiting the discrepancy between her statements and her actual intent.

The attempt to discipline discourse and control the proliferation of meaning reaches its apotheosis during the devastating reunion between Effi and her daughter, Annie, who responds to every suggestion of further meetings with the rote reply, "O gewiß, wenn ich darf" (15:324, Yes, if I'm allowed, 201). The conditional statement, infuriatingly evasive and non-committal, allows her to respond without promising anything definite. Clearly, Innstetten has prepared her for the meeting and armed her with this memorized sentence, as it bears the hallmarks of his predilection for ambivalence. It is essentially an elaborate way of saying neither "yes" nor "no," of avoiding side-taking, just as Innstetten did with his stories about the ghost. Effi recognizes his hand at work, complaining to herself, "ehe er das Kind schickt, richtet er's ab wie einen Papagei und bringt ihm die Phrase bei" (15:325, before he sends the child, he trains her like a parrot and teaches her [the phrase], 202). The comparison with a parrot reinforces the sense that Annie's words are mechanical and unthinking. Indeed, Fontane's novels occasionally identify language as a species marker that distinguishes humans from other animals (for example, 17:24), so that likening Annie's speech to that of a parrot would suggest that what she produces are not signifiers but rather sounds stripped of meaning. Note further that the German word for parrot—*Papagei*—includes the word "Papa," as if by parroting a string of empty words, she demonstrates that she has internalized her father's ambivalent voice. Annie's training—her *Eziehung*, or upbringing—thus succeeds in suppressing meaning. These are words without any credible connection to thoughts, feelings, or deeds. As the furthest thing possible from the unreserved, unself-conscious speech of Effi and her friends at play at the beginning of the novel, it represents the victory of artifice over nature and discipline over free expression.

I am certainly not the first to comment upon this element of rhetorical control in Fontane's works. It has been discussed from various perspectives and under various designations, including "tact," "discretion," and an intentionally generated "semantic indeterminacy."[26] Katharina Engler-Coldren, drawing from the text's own vocabulary, refers to it as maintaining the "right measure," which the novel presents as a comportment that is consistently balanced and proportionate,[27] whereas Berman calls the "systematic prohibition of certain classes of speech" a form of "linguistic disciplining."[28] Such readings often make the sophisticated move of connecting the characters' rhetorical reserve to an element of reserve at the level of narrative discourse. The gaps, interruptions, and omissions in the characters' language get reflected by a narrative voice that omits key events or leaves, say, the beginning and extent of the affair shrouded in ambiguity.[29] In short, they draw out a congruence between the story and its discursive presentation, between the characters' evasive, unreliable speech and a narrative that is also, at key junctures, unforthcoming.[30] The present reading builds upon those insights but it also differs from them in an important respect. I am interested primarily in how that discipline or reticence fails. The following section explores how language and gestures continue to signify in ways that exceed, and even undermine, what was intended. In *Effi Briest*, the expression of meaning keeps happening, despite the characters' best efforts to prevent it.

---

[26] On tact, see Minden, "*Effi Briest* and 'Die historische Stunde des Takts,'" *Modern Language Review* 76, no. 4 (1981): 869–79; on discretion and ellipsis: Vedder, "Ringe, Glocken, Tränen," 101–3; on semantic indeterminacy: Källström, *Das Eigentliche bleibt doch zurück*, a title that cites the novel's characterization of Effi's reserve (15:253); and on gestures of interruption: Strowick, *Gespenster des Realismus*, 237. Minden's take on tact and its pattern of constraints gets closest to my reading of irony and earnestness when he interprets one of Effi's tactful statements, writing, "There is a fine complexity behind this image of a formula, tacitly accepted in its nature as insincere, tactful and polite, within which [...] we know that a very intense sincerity lurks, at some undefined level of articulation." Minden, "*Effi Briest*," 871.

[27] Katharina Adeline Engler-Coldren, "On the 'Right Measure' in *Effi Briest*: Ethics and Aesthetics of the Prosaic," in *Fontane in the Twenty-First Century*, ed. John B. Lyon and Brian Tucker (Rochester, NY: Camden House, 2019), 121.

[28] Russell Berman, "*Effi Briest* and the End of Realism," in *A Companion to German Realism, 1848–1900*, ed. Todd Kontje (Rochester, NY: Camden House, 2002), 339–40.

[29] On the "inevitably fragmentary character" of storytelling, see Greenberg, "The Resistance of *Effi Briest*," 771; on "measure" as both a behavioral and aesthetic ideal, Engler-Coldren, "On the 'Right Measure,'" 136–8; and on indeterminacy as constitutive of the narrative design, Källström, *Das Eigentliche bleibt doch zurück*, 9.

[30] For a reading that connects these gaps to the narrative design and depiction of boredom, see Brian Tucker, "Performing Boredom in *Effi Briest*: On the Effects of Narrative Speed," *German Quarterly* 80, no. 2 (2007): 185–200.

Effi: "Thank God!"

Effi Briest is, without question, a story about fragmentary processes of storytelling, about the strategic deployment of omission, indeterminacy, and insincere speech. At the same time, though, it is also a story about how the strategies of rhetorical discipline fail and how meaning nevertheless comes to light. Late in the novel, when Effi feels trapped in a web of lies, she describes her conscience wracked less by guilt than by fear. She calls it "die ewige Furcht: es kommt doch am Ende noch an den Tag" (15:258, the constant fear that I'll be found out [or: that it will ultimately come to light], 160). The passage of course signifies in the acute sense the worry that her affair will be revealed, but it also signifies in a broader sense the inability to control and suppress meaning.[31] As Innstetten asserts to Wüllersdorf in their discussion of societal obligation and the passage of time, "es giebt keine Verschwiegenheit" (15:279, there's no such thing as confidentiality, 174). Whether one translates that term as reticence, confidentiality, or discretion, the passage indicates the failure of rhetorical discipline and the inability to contain the expression of meaning. Less than a decade later, Freud, reflecting on the treatment of hysteria, would write similarly that "no mortal can keep a secret. If his lips are silent, he chatters with his finger-tips; betrayal oozes out of him at every pore."[32] Despite the radically different contexts, the passages share one of modernity's central insights into human nature—namely, that signification cannot be fully repressed, that meaning will always find its way, perhaps via detour or disguise, into expression.[33] In *Effi Briest*, people try to control and direct how they communicate, but they often fail, experiencing a lack of control over their own language. What they say and do communicates in ways they never intended, do not understand, and often do not even realize.

The first instance exemplifies both the attempt to suppress meaning with irony and the failure of that rhetorical device. It occurs when Gieshübler tells Effi that she will play the female lead in the community play "One False Step," which sounds ominous indeed. Effi immediately worries that Crampas might play the male lead, a Don Juan-type character, thus creating a dramatic pairing that could signify to the local audience in ways other than intended. Effi realizes, that is, that playing

---

[31] Mülder-Bach connects this passage to the fear of a past that has never actually passed. Mülder-Bach, "Verjährung," 629.
[32] Freud, *Standard Edition*, 7:77.
[33] For a more detailed attempt to establish points of contact between *Effi Briest* and the psychoanalytic theory of hysteria, see Edith Krause, "Eclectic Affinities: Fontane's Effi and Freud's Dora," *Women's Studies* 32, no. 4 (2003): 431–54.

alongside Crampas in a dramatization of adultery would add overlays of meaning beyond her control. When Gieshübler assures her that Crampas will not be acting but rather directing, it opens a crack in her reserve. She lets slip the observation, "Desto schlimmer" (So much the worse, 105), which only puzzles her interlocutor. Effi then tries to repair this momentary lapse of self-censorship with recourse to irony: "O, Sie dürfen das nicht so feierlich nehmen; das ist nur so eine Redensart, die eigentlich das Gegenteil bedeutet. Auf der anderen Seite freilich, der Major hat so 'was Gewaltsames" (15:169, Oh you mustn't take me so seriously, it's just a manner of speaking and I really mean the opposite. On the other hand of course there is something overpowering about the major, 105). The passage presents in its clearest form an example of verbal irony, something that means not what it says but rather the opposite of what it ostensibly says. "Even worse" should apparently be understood to mean "even better." Effi insists on being taken seriously but not literally.

The remark's ambivalence generates uncertainty. Gieshübler tries to read it as straightforward and earnest but cannot make sense of it. His uncertainty in this moment reflects in miniature Effi's rhetorical dilemma throughout the novel. Just as Gieshübler struggles over whether to take her remark seriously or ironically, so Effi struggles with whether to take Crampas's advances seriously and whether to take Innstetten's ghost story seriously. But the point here is that Effi must work to suppress the apprehension of that literal, earnest meaning, because it would force her to reveal things about her relationship with Crampas that must be kept secret. So irony becomes the tool to empty her words of unwanted meaning. By dismissing her language as merely an ironic turn of phrase, she vacates the expression of anxiety that slipped past her rhetorical control. Moreover, declaring it an empty figure of speech accords with Crampas's recourse to empty citation and a *façon de parler*. In both cases, the postulation of irony and insincerity conceals a core of something sincerely felt and sincerely meant.

For Effi, that core of sincerity continuously finds its way into expression. Even though she has clarified her remark, asserting that it means the opposite of what it seems to say, she then goes on to negate that meaning as well, by spelling out reasons why it actually *is* worse that Crampas will be directing the play. Her argument with herself runs: Oh, that's even worse. By which I mean, that's better. But here's why it's actually worse. As the narrator puts it, she "verwickelte sich immer mehr in Widersprüche" (15:169, [tied] herself up in one contradiction after another, 105). There is a point to this back and forth, as it illustrates an oscillation between rhetorical discipline and its failure. Effi cannot successfully repress unwanted meaning; the best she can do is generate contradictory or self-canceling meanings. But the overarching issue is that the two possible meanings do not necessarily cancel each other out. They operate simultaneously, in all their obvious contradiction. It is correct to speak here of indeterminacy because one cannot determine which meaning is correct or intended. The categories on which the differentiation would be based collapse on themselves so that it is always both at once—meant and unmeant, serious and insincere, earnest and ironic. And this doubleness or duplicity returns to the heart of Effi's dilemma, because it is exactly how Innstetten treats the ghost story and how she should relate to it, and it is exactly why she cannot feel entirely sanguine about the tone Crampas strikes when they are alone. The only difference is that in Effi's case the indeterminacy appears to result from an involuntary slip.

Another slip of the tongue gives rise to one of the novel's tensest moments. When Innstetten surprises Effi with the announcement that they will soon be leaving Kessin and moving to Berlin, she almost gives away her secret. Her relief is so palpable and intense that something must be afoot. The narrator describes her reaction in a passage worth citing at length:

> Effi sagte kein Wort, und nur ihre Augen wurden immer größer; um ihre Mundwinkel war ein nervöses Zucken, und ihr ganzer zarter Körper zitterte. Mit einemmale aber glitt sie von ihrem Sitze vor Innstetten nieder, umklammerte seine Knie und sagte in einem Tone, wie wenn sie betete: "Gott sei Dank!"
> (15:214)

> Effi said nothing, her eyes only grew wider; there was a nervous twitch at the corner of her mouth and her whole delicate frame quivered. Suddenly she slid down from her seat in front of Innstetten, hugged his knees and in a tone as if she were praying said, "Thank God."
> (132–3)

The passage begins with the established theme of rhetorical control. Effi remains tight-lipped. She cannot express to Innstetten her relief at escaping from her predicament in Kessin, so she chooses to say nothing. The disciplined maintenance of reticence conceals her relief, her distress, and ultimately her affair. But as Innstetten would tell us, there is no such thing as perfect secrecy, and Effi confirms his assertion with a set of physical symptoms that could have been drawn from a Freudian case study. Her widening eyes, twitching lips, and shivering body all run counter to her enforced reserve and composure. Just as Freud will predict, even though her lips are silent, her somatic symptoms chatter away and "betrayal oozes out of [her] at every pore."[34]

Those physical manifestations already look suspect, but the damning slip is when she falls to the ground, as if praying, with an exclamation of gratitude. Overwhelmed by feelings of relief, Effi loses all rhetorical control and gives voice to the prospect of liberation that was supposed to remain below the surface.[35] Put another way, this is the moment when Effi's irony—in the sense of her calculated discrepancy between phenomenon and essence—fails. The slip thus entails saying what she actually means in a direct and earnest manner. And that turn from irony and insincerity to earnest expression puts Effi, for the first time, in the mode of avowal. The narrator describes her involuntary slippage, reporting, "Sie hatte sich durch ein schönes Gefühl, das nicht viel 'was andres als ein Bekenntnis ihrer Schuld war, hinreißen lassen und dabei mehr gesagt, als sie sagen durfte" (15:214, She had been swept away by a noble sentiment that was little short of a confession [avowal] of her guilt and had said more than she should have, 133). She intends to control language and resist signifying anything, but she is overcome, and her expression of relief, the narrator says, is more or less a confession of guilt, an involuntary act of avowal. Through this inadvertent outburst, Effi comes a step closer to revealing who she truly is and reconstituting herself through a new mode of existence. It is important that her avowal only occurs against her will, despite her efforts to suppress the truth. It represents the obverse of Melanie's volitional and self-assured act of avowal in *L'Adultera*.

This contrast brings to the fore the general dearth of avowal in *Effi Briest*. There are no scenes of high-drama marital conflict, no moment when Effi deliberately confesses to her husband, nor any moment when he confronts her with the accusation of infidelity. In this novel, written words typically supplant the necessity of face-to-face speech, and when letters do not suffice, the protagonists communicate through intermediaries, through parents, servants, or seconds. The affair thus comes to light not through avowal but through a trove of old letters. Effi's divorce and ostracization will also be communicated to her in epistolary form—now doubly removed from its origin, since Innstetten sends a letter to Effi's parents, who then send another letter on to her.

In this instance, too, one sees that there is no intentional act of avowal, since Effi immediately tries to negate the involuntary signals

---

[34] Freud, *Standard Edition*, 7:77.
[35] Engler-Coldren cites this scene as an example of failing to maintain the right measure and points to Effi's attempt to "re-balance" ("wieder ausgleichen") her reaction. Engler-Coldren, "On the 'Right Measure,'" 132.

of confession. The narrative voice says, "Sie mußte das wieder ausgleichen, mußte was finden, irgend einen Ausweg, es koste, was es wolle" (15:214, She had to counteract that again, had to find something, some way out, whatever the cost, 133). "Ausgleichen" is a loaded word in this context. Though it has a casual sense of smoothing things over, it means in a technical sense to offset something with a counterbalance so that two sides cancel each other out (for example, profits that suffice to balance against expenditures). One must recognize, though, that in the realm of rhetoric, to annul one utterance through the suggestion of its opposite veers into the territory of ironic negation. Indeed, locating oneself in the balance between two contradictory, self-canceling propositions is the hallmark of ironic ambivalence, especially as practiced by Innstetten and Crampas.[36] It is clear in this instance that Innstetten provides a model for dissimulating ambivalence, as she turns to the ghost story for cover. "Es ist ein Spukhaus" (This house is haunted, 133), she says to justify her exclamation, "und ich habes auch glauben sollen, das mit dem Spuk—denn Du bist ein Erzieher" (15:215, and I was meant to believe that business about the ghost—for you're a pedagogue, 133). The statement negates her involuntary avowal—sincere and revealing—with something insincere and deceptive. It demonstrates again that the didactic instrument of the ghost story has educated Effi according to its form rather than its content. She too can say things she does not actually believe in order to engender belief or trust in others. In this way, she reasserts rhetorical control, but it continues to evince gaps, as in this case when a citation of Crampas's manner of speaking sneaks into Effi's defense. She inadvertently gives voice to the very identity that her statement means to conceal.

Innstetten greets all this with a healthy dose of suspicion, but he shrugs off his concerns with the skeptical axiom that "alle Zeichen trügen" (15:216, all signs are deceptive, 133). This radical semiotic skepticism harks back to post-truth retorts such as "What is truth?" If all signifiers deceive, then signification can never be trusted, and there is no way to get at meaning or truth, no way to move from language to the signified world. He's right, in a way, but not in the way he thinks. He means that Effi's behavior *looks* suspicious, but because he's wise enough to know that appearances or signifiers can be deceptive, he won't take it too seriously. What he fails to realize is that Effi's signifiers are deceptive because she speaks in ways designed to deceive. Innstetten thinks of deceptive signs in systemic terms, as flawed and unreliable

---

[36] Kierkegaard describes irony manifesting itself "through a relation of opposition." Kierkegaard, *The Concept of Irony*, 267–8.

structures of signification, but he fails to countenance the deliberate abuse of language in duplicitous rhetoric and ironic discrepancy.

The third instance of failed rhetorical control also provides a further example of involuntary avowal. It occurs when Innstetten discovers the cache of intimate letters and calls on his friend and colleague Wüllersdorf for support. Innstetten immediately wants to divorce Effi and challenge Crampas to a duel, which prompts the famous conversation about whether it really has to be that way, whether the passage of time does not mitigate the necessity of reciprocal action. They talk about duty, honor, and social norms, and Innstetten refers to some vague social obligation that compels him to go through with the duel and divorce, even though his heart isn't in it (15:278). Although this justification has received a significant amount of attention, it is worth noting that it fails to convince Wüllersdorf, who remains unmoved and indecisive.[37] The more persuasive justification for going forward with the duel is a different one—namely, that Wüllersdorf's knowledge of the affair forces Innstetten's hand. Jeffrey Schneider identifies that sharing of knowledge as "the primary factor forcing Innstetten to direct the paranoid logic of honor against himself. Instead of preventing the duel, it necessitates it."[38] Innstetten says essentially the same thing. He has confided in Wüllersdorf, "Und weil dieser Mitwisser da ist, kann ich nicht mehr zurück" (15:278, And now that somebody else knows, there's no way back for me, 173). By revealing himself candidly and earnestly—by avowing his misery—Innstetten sets in motion the series of events that lead to a death, a banishment, and even more misery.

I want to stress that Innstetten himself interprets this baring of his heart not as an act of courage or principle but rather as a momentary lapse of self-control. He speaks explicitly in terms of control and concealment, saying, "ich hätte mich besser beherrschen und bewachen, alles in mir verbergen, alles im eignen Herzen auskämpfen sollen" (15:279, I should have kept a closer eye on myself, controlled myself, contained it all inside me, battled it out in my own heart, 173). He addresses here both the regime of rhetorical discipline practiced in the novel and its eventual failure. Innstetten does not intend to share his true circumstances with Wüllersdorf or anyone else. But discovering the affair is such a sudden and powerful shock that it overwhelms his self-control. He lets down his guard for a moment and speaks plainly and candidly. In his own estimation, this letting down of his guard establishes his

---

[37] On dueling and the demands of the honor code, see Jeffrey Schneider, "Masculinity, Male Friendship, and the Paranoid Logic of Honor in Theodor Fontane's *Effi Briest*," *German Quarterly* 75, no. 3 (2002): 265–81.

[38] Schneider, "Masculinity," 273.

culpability in the subsequent chain of events. The destructive force in the novel turns out to be the truth coming to light despite a systematic program of repression—not only Effi's involuntary revelation of the affair to Innstetten but also Innstetten's involuntary revelation of the affair to his colleague.

In this regard, the concern in the novel shifts away somewhat from what one finds in earlier works. It moves away from the prospect that irony and unreliable speech could prove to be contagious and uncontrollable, and toward an insight into irony as an instrument of secrecy, reticence, and control. Here it is not irony but rather the force of unintentional avowal that moves like a viral infection across an ever-widening social circle. People use ironic, half-serious, haphazard speech because they aim to suppress meaning, to prevent it from presenting itself via language or gesture. They want to prevent others from establishing a firm connection between their words and their thoughts, beliefs, feelings, and plans. But in *Effi Briest*, unreliable speech does not come across as a grave politico-historical danger, the way it does, say, in *Schach von Wuthenow* or *Unwiederbringlich*. It looks more like a partially effective tool that can delay but not ultimately stop the upwelling of meaning, which functions rather like the dangerous "Schloon" along the beach (15:186–7). Meaning is hidden beneath a surface of fixed reserve, so that most of the time it cannot be perceived, but it's there, in motion, unstable and disruptive, and it has the power to stop everyone in their tracks.

Luise: "You look so unprepared."

Effi Briest dramatizes how the expression of meaning often occurs unintentionally, through an involuntary avowal, through the deviation of meaning from one register to another, or the overlay of unintended significance. This sort of slippage or unintentional communication occurs not only in the story itself, in the interactions among characters, but also at the level discourse, in the way the narrative communicates information to its readers. On the one hand, critics such as Greenberg are undoubtedly correct to interpret *Effi Briest* as a tale that remains partially untold, as a narrative that self-reflexively highlights "its inevitably fragmentary character."[39] On the other hand, though, attending to how reticence and concealment fail reveals a narrative gesture that counters the attempt to control meaning by introducing a surfeit of possible meanings. Language that is supposed to be empty turns out to be full, brimming with potential meaning that will be activated by the novel's subsequent events.

---

[39] Greenberg, "The Resistance of *Effi Briest*," 771.

This argument returns to the novel's opening scenes, in which, over and over again, characters will say one thing, but their words will also signify another meaning, at the same time, without their realizing it. If one commonplace characterization of irony is to say one thing but mean another, then the tragic irony packed into the novel's introduction is that the characters' language speaks truths and alludes to future events, but only in ways that are illegible to the characters who speak or hear them. One sees this, for example, in Effi's defensive question to her mother, "Warum kommt er so früh?" (15:17, Why has he come so early?, 12). She means her question in a limited, local sense. It is not that she is late coming in to get ready; it is, rather, that the baron has arrived earlier than expected, so he should be to blame for her still-disheveled appearance. But like so many passages in the first two chapters, this one operates on two levels, the second level being the allegory of what is to come.[40] There is a tropic movement in her statement that turns it away from a minor concern about tidying up and bends it toward an allegorical plane. For in a broader sense, Innstetten has arrived too early not only in terms of minutes or hours but in terms of Effi's maturity and preparedness. He shows up before she is ready—to leave her parents and friends, to take on adult obligations, to make this abrupt transition. This forward-looking overlay of significance is illegible to Effi, but it is certainly available to the reader, who has been primed by stories of Innstetten courting Louise when he was still too young to make a good marriage match.

Effi's mother, though, provides perhaps the most unintentionally prescient example of speaking on two planes. As Effi, having finally come inside, rushes off to get ready, her mother stops her, saying, "Es ist am Ende das Beste, Du bleibst wie Du bist. Ja, bleibe so. [...] Du siehst so unvorbereitet aus, [...] und darauf kommt es in diesem Augenblicke an" (15:17, Maybe it's as well if you just stay as you are. Yes, just stay as you are. [...] you look so unprepared [...] and that's what matters at a moment like this, 12). In its intended sense, the statement says simply that Effi should just present herself the way she looks right now. She does not appear polished or done up, and the baron will find that attractive. But in the face of the novel's central themes, and with Effi standing on the cusp of a transition of which she is not yet aware, the passage cannot help but acquire additional resonances. Effi looks so unprepared, which, yes, indicates that she has not had a chance to change clothes or fix her hair, but it also points, in another sense, to

---

[40] On the temporal allegory in *Effi Briest*'s opening scenes, see Tucker, "Performing Boredom," 187–9.

how unprepared she is for everything that is about to transpire. She is not ready for a proposal that will catch her off-guard, and as her mother indicates, that lack of preparation is what really matters in this moment.

On a broader scale, Luise's words also express a wish or hypothetical premonition. It would ultimately be best if Effi could just stay the way she is: carefree, playful, excited, surrounded by friends and family, not only as a means of charming their visitor but also more generally, as a way of being in the world. The tension is that the statement's intended meaning—you look alluring the way you are right now—works against the broader meaning by hastening Effi's transition from childhood to adulthood and by increasing the likelihood of a radical rupture in her life. There is, finally, a third potential meaning. One can read the phrase "am Ende" to mean not just "ultimately" but also, in a self-reflexive sense, "in the end," as in "at the end of the story." In fact, Effi will end up, *am Ende*, back where she started, dressed in the same clothes, with the same sundial outside, but it will most certainly *not* be for the best because she will not have remained the way she is now. She will, by that point, have sacrificed the unselfconscious honesty and natural authenticity with which the novel endows her at the outset. The mother's straightforward and practical remark thus gets burdened with layers of unintended meaning, prefiguring events that the characters cannot foresee.

Although a significant amount of attention has been paid to the symbolism and foreshadowing of the novel's opening scenes, such designations do not go far enough to specify the operations of language in the novel.[41] There exists a discrepancy between how the characters' dialogue signifies within the story and how it signifies as an element of narrative discourse to the reader. They often say something other than what their words initially suggest, something more, but they are not aware of the added resonances. Kevin Newmark notes that, in the Romantic tradition, irony "names the possibility that it is precisely the speaking subject who understands least of all the actual meaning of what is being said in its name and through its agency."[42] One could call it a naïve irony—the characters mean something other, something more,

---

[41] Debra Prager, for example, offers an astute analysis of the introduction's imagery and foreshadowing when she details the "carefully constructed architectural and geographic symbolism of the opening scene." Debra Prager, "'Alles so orientalisch': The Elaboration of Desire in Theodor Fontane's *Effi Briest*," *Women in German Yearbook* 29 (2013): 119.

[42] Newmark, *Irony on Occasion*, 44.

than what they say, but it is a meaning from which they themselves are excluded. There is a good deal of reticence and communicative control in evidence in the novel's opening. Effi's mother surely has some ideas about this meeting with the baron, ideas that she withholds from her daughter. And the entire opening revolves around the suggestion of unspoken themes such as abrupt transition, loss of innocence, and female transgression. But the important movement is how this unspoken theme nonetheless gets spoken, in unintended ways, despite the characters' attempts to ignore or even repress it.

The novel's opening is thus constructed not just upon symbolism or foreshadowing but rather on an experience of language in which the characters lose their grip on meaning. It highlights the ways in which their language exceeds their control and comprehension. It is only from the reader's perspective, and especially the reader who already has some inkling of what is to come, that the full import of the characters' words is apparent. The speakers themselves are oblivious to the potential meanings conveyed by their statements. They cannot control the proliferation of meaning, even when those meanings come into conflict with one another. To the extent that the novel's opening engages in foreshadowing, one must recognize a foreshadowing at the level of language and narrative discourse—a performative demonstration of the inability to discipline rhetoric. The proliferation of meaning thus takes on a life of its own and becomes something the characters can no longer control.

Briest: "That takes us *too* far afield."

What to make then of the novel's final line, Briest's well-worn and dismissive expression, "Ach, Luise, laß ... das ist ein *zu* weites Feld" (15:350, Ah Luise, that's enough ... that's *too* vast a subject, 217)? One notices, first, that the story concludes with another of Briest's trite sayings. He is the character in the novel most closely associated with banter, aphorisms, and unserious speech. True to form, he closes the story by reiterating a *Redensart* or empty turn of phrase. But it is not just an empty expression; it is an expression designed to empty the conversation of serious import, to restrict it to a superficial level that ignores uncomfortable questions. In short, it functions as a defense mechanism or instrument of rhetorical control, not unlike the rote expression that Annie employs to ward off future meetings with her mother. The narrative frame of home life in Hohen-Cremmen thus begins and ends with the same issue of control and discipline, with the attempt to contain, even repress, unwanted meanings. Crucially, Briest employs his dismissive expression to parry the very question that comes to light involuntarily in the opening pages—namely, whether Effi was too young to get married. His reflexive move, to curtail conversation and wave away uncomfortable implications, suggests that little has changed over the course of the story. It appears, perhaps bleakly, that people will go on talking in ways that deliberately withhold their true meaning and trying to conceal the gaps over which their conversations are constructed. They will continue to recite banal turns of phrase, employ ambiguity, and cultivate uncertainty as strategies of avoidance and reticence. Briest's final remark feels less like a satisfying summation and more like an expression of resignation and willful ignorance.

Seven All Talk: In Lieu of a Conclusion, *Stechlin*

When we pursue the threads of irony and avowal through Fontane's narrative fiction, it brings to the fore deep-seated concerns with the tension between what is said and what is meant. If I have done my job over the preceding chapters, several points should now be apparent. First, the novels do not present language as having been rendered ineffectual as an inevitable by-product of historical upheaval. They insist instead on an element of agency and volition in the way one uses language, which is important because it reveals the authentic forthrightness of characters such as Melanie van der Straaten and Lene Nimptsch to be acts of rhetorical resistance. They represent the ability to resist assimilating to a fashionable, ironic tone, thereby demonstrating that candor and sincerity remain viable alternatives to society's dominant idiom. Second, although the novels frequently probe problems of language use, they do not luxuriate in the decadence of indifferent chatter, ironic banter, or cynical dissimulation. Instead, they repeatedly draw attention to the deleterious consequences that arise from ambiguous, unreliable speech. Take, for example, Effi's predicament when confronted with Innstetten's ambivalent relationship to the ghost story, or with Crampas's semi-facetious, semi-serious advances. Effi is just one character among many who are flummoxed by the uncertainty of whether to take others' words earnestly or ironically. Fontane's works take a far dimmer view of the use and abuse of irony than commentators have heretofore recognized.

Auerbach complained that Fontane was never able to get beyond the "half seriousness" of idle, sociable talk.[1] But look at how a novel like *Effi Briest* depicts that half-serious tone. It does not merely invoke or cite a semi-earnest, semi-facetious ambivalence; on the contrary, it presents that rhetorical bearing as calculated, cynical, and mean-spirited. It

---

[1] Auerbach, *Mimesis*, 519.

appears as the means to an end of deception and dissimulation. Duplicitous, ironic speech has an insidious and cumulatively harmful effect as it renders language less credible, less reliable, and less effective.

A study that argues, as this one does, that Fontane's works frequently explore the issues emanating from unserious speech cannot conclude without considering *Der Stechlin*. This is true for at least two reasons. First, as Fontane's final finished novel, *Der Stechlin* has sometimes been read as a coda or conclusion to his oeuvre, a reflection on themes that have occupied him throughout his other novels, or as a late-in-life opportunity to take stock of his work.[2] Second, the novel consists mainly of superficial conversations. Its reception history is dominated by the consensus that it is all talk and no action, which is, of course, a viewpoint that Fontane initiated and encouraged. He himself said that next to nothing happens in the novel and that it is "Alles Plauderei, Dialog" (17:495, all talk, dialogue). The philosopher Hans Blumenberg puts it well when he takes *Der Stechlin* "as an epic conversation piece," writing, "The conversations leave out no topic; no conversation is allowed to go below the surface without being interrupted."[3] Blumenberg stands in for a widely held view: that the novel prioritizes talk over plot, that it exists as a grand series of conversations, touching on everything while plumbing the depths of nothing. *Der Stechlin* represents, in other words, the ultimate exacerbation of unserious, haphazard conversation. If Fontane's final novel gives itself over to this kind of insincere chatter, how does that reflect back on the themes of irony and avowal, as they have been examined and developed in the preceding works? Or put differently: how might an examination of irony and avowal in Fontane's fiction relocate this novel vis-à-vis the works that precede it?

On the one hand, *Der Stechlin* appears as a pinnacle of pure talk, as an uninterrupted stream of causerie. And there is a tendency to see in the novel a lot of life wisdom and to read Dubslav as a heartwarming, autobiographical reflection of Fontane the grandfatherly causeur.[4] In some ways, then, the novel resists being subsumed under the argumentative arc of the present book. It could look on this view more like

---

[2] See, for example, Ervin Malakaj, "Senescence and Fontane's *Der Stechlin*," in *Fontane in the Twenty-First Century*, ed. John B. Lyon and Brian Tucker (Rochester, NY: Camden House, 2019), 232–45. He reads the novel as Fontane's coming to grips with issues of aging, influence, and legacy.
[3] Blumenberg, *Gerade noch Klassiker*, 7.
[4] Mecklenburg, *Theodor Fontane*, 166–7, 176–81. See further Fleischer, "*Kommen Sie, Cohn*," 269, who reads Dubslav as a self-portrait that also portrays Fontane's anti-Semitism. He argues that characters such as Baruch and Isidor Hirschfeld reflect Fontane's unease with the growing influence of Jews in German society (274).

an affirmation of spirited, stimulating banter and an elegiac take on a certain urbane tone.

On the other hand, it becomes clear upon closer examination that many of the themes taken up in previous chapters continue to operate in *Der Stechlin*. In addition to the excess of haphazard conversation, there is also a continuing interest in processes of ironization. Dubslav, the narrator reports, has a tendency toward irony that calls the earnestness of everything he says into question. His ironic smirk makes it impossible to tell whether his statements are feigned or sincere (17:8–9). It is a posture that recalls van der Straaten's curious admixture of *Scherz* and *Ernst*, so that Fontane's series of society novels is bookended, front and back, by rhetorical character portraits that foreground an ironic disposition. Melusine, similarly, asserts that she abhors earnest sentiments such as patriotism unless they are cloaked in humor and irony, in which case they are "das beste was man haben kann" (17:309, the best that one can have). Moreover, there are post-truth statements to be found in this novel too. Dubslav at one point contends that "Unanfechtbare Wahrheiten giebt es nicht" (17:8, There are no unassailable truths), and in conversation, he appears indifferent to the truth value of his statements: "Wenn ich das Gegenteil gesagt hätte, wäre es ebenso richtig" (17:29, If I had said the opposite, it would have been just as correct). Eckehard Czucka notes that this sentence eclipses the positing of truth in language and would represent, in an extra-literary discursive context, "the destruction of any possibility of human speech."[5]

Finally, the novel evinces an ongoing suspicion of ambivalence and unreliability in language. Torgelow, the Social Democrat, defeats Dubslav in the election for the Reichstag seat, but once in office, his constituents criticize him for being too "zweideutig," too ambiguous or equivocal. Torgelow appears to be merely a symptom of decadent times when Uncke extrapolates from his example, telling Dubslav, "Alle lügen sie. Was sie meinen, das sagen sie nich und was sie sagen, das meinen sie nich. Is kein Verlaß mehr; alles zweideutig" (17:313, They all lie. They don't say what they mean and they don't mean what they say. No relying on anything anymore; it's all ambiguous). The equivocation lamented here is by now familiar as a form of irony, as a purposeful

---

[5] Eckehard Czucka, "Faktizität und Sprachskepsis. Fontanes *Stechlin* und die Sprachkritik der Jahrhundertwende," in *Theodor Fontane am Ende des Jahrhunderts*, ed. Hanna Delf von Wolzogen and Helmuth Nürnberger (Würzburg: Königshausen & Neumann, 2000), 28. See also Mecklenburg, *Theodor Fontane*, 166, where he points out that the passage resembles Botho's "yes is just as good as no" performance of upper-class conversation and opens that mentality to a similar critique.

discrepancy between the phenomenon of what is said and its underlying meaning or intent. At issue in this conversation is whether Torgelow's dissimulation and unreliability are merely an unfortunate fact of contemporary political life (as the nineteenth century, so the twenty-first, and probably every other era of political existence) or whether they point to a more general dearth of credibility in the world. In short, they are discussing the possibility of a post-truth condition that extends far beyond the exigencies of politics—not necessarily in the radically skeptical sense that truths do not exist, but in the more limited sense that communication has become inured to dissimulation.

According to some in the novel, deceptive ambivalence runs deeper than just a prerequisite for political office; Uncke contends that it has also infected social life and family life. He takes as his second example Baruch Hirschfeld's son Isidor: "der Junge redt […] immer 'von's Prinzip.' Das Prinzip is ihm aber egal. Er will bloß mogeln […]. Und das ist das, was ich das Zweideutige nenne" (17:314, the boy is always talking "about principle." He doesn't care about principle. He just wants to cheat. And that's what I mean by ambiguity). Isidor engages in ironic dissimulation, just like the politicians who disguise their true intent by saying something other than what they mean. He dissembles by talking earnestly about principles to which he is in fact indifferent—his principled rhetoric being merely the disingenuous guise under which he conceals his unprincipled designs. Shortly before his death, Dubslav comes around to Uncke's view of pervasive duplicity, after a visit from the elder Hirschfeld. Although Baruch appears under the pretense of a kindly visit, to check on his old friend's health, it becomes clear that he really wants to press Dubslav into taking on a mortgage and debt. After he leaves, Dubslav remarks to himself, "Sonderbar, Uncke, mit seinem ewigen 'zweideutig' wird am Ende doch recht behalten" (17:376, Strange, Uncke with his perpetual "ambiguous" is actually going to be right in the end). Although *Der Stechlin* famously includes a great deal of talk, there are many indications that one should not be entirely sanguine about its reliability or its consequences.

To make this point taps into a critical vein that sees something flawed and wanting in the novel's abundance of conversation. The characters engage in frequent conversations, but these are just small talk—in German, *Geschwätz* or *Plauderei*—in that they remain superficial and ineffectual. Willi Goetschel notes, for example, that "the conversations are systematically broken off whenever they threaten to escalate from idle talk into actual discussion and dialogue" because this sort of talk functions primarily "as a technique of dissimulating ennui" and "as a parlor game for distraction."[6] Or as Eric Downing writes, "It is a *small talk*

---

[6] Goetschel, "Causerie," 124.

that strives for neither explicit logical connections nor a deeper or true meaningfulness. Rather, it appears on the contrary to be averse to any significance and all connections."[7] The conversations in *Der Stechlin* are more chatter than dialogue. A mere pastime, they eschew significance, context, and the meaningful exchange of ideas.[8]

To connect this back to ideas mentioned at the beginning of this book: the empty banter that abounds in *Der Stechlin* overlaps with Frankfurt's notion of "bullshitting." The characters blithely reject the existence of knowable truths and say whatever it suits them to say at the moment. One is indifferent to truth when one "does not care whether the things he says describe reality correctly. He just picks them out, or makes them up, to suit his purpose."[9] Frankfurt's diagnosis applies well to the indifferent, haphazard talk that one finds throughout the novel, especially when the protagonist Dubslav says that he could have asserted the opposite and it would have been just as true (17:29). He reflects in this instance a society that operates "under the conditions of linguistic arbitrariness."[10] Given the ongoing concern with talk that is untethered from reality and indifferent to its own accuracy, it is hard to read *Der Stechlin* as an unequivocal embrace of that conversational style.

Goetschel contends that one should not mistake the rhetorical ambivalence depicted in the novel for an expression of freedom or detachment. "Instead," he writes, "it should be recognized for what it is: an expression of an inner lack of freedom and a compulsion. Old Stechlin only acts so free with his irony because he is utterly at a loss."[11] The passage supports an important point: in Fontane's conception, irony does not provide an Olympian gaze or a sovereign, above-the-fray sort of detachment. Whatever liberating power it possesses is fleeting and overshadowed by its negative, enthralling tendencies. This is why Dubslav the ambivalent ironist comes across less like a great mind such as Walter Scott and more like the limited Willibald Alexis, who, in Fontane's estimation, remained mired in an ironic tone from which he could not escape (*NA* 21.1:212). Dubslav, with his "natürliche Neigung zum Ausplaudern, zum Plaudern überhaupt" (17:435, natural

---

[7] Eric Downing, "Sprachmagie, Stimmung und Geselligkeit. Überschreitungen des Realismus in Fontanes *Der Stechlin*," in *Herausforderungen des Realismus: Theodor Fontanes Gesellschaftsromane*, ed. Peter Uwe Hohendahl and Ulrike Vedder (Freiburg: Rombach, 2018), 277.
[8] McGillen details how Fontane develops this "art of chatter" or *Plauderkunst* from topical lists compiled from mass media. McGillen, *The Fontane Workshop*, 182.
[9] Frankfurt, *On Bullshit*, 56.
[10] Czucka, "Faktizität und Sprachskepsis," 29.
[11] Goetschel, "Causerie," 120.

inclination toward babbling, toward chatting in general), as well as his tendency toward self-ironization, bathes in the sea of irony and idle talk but has no inclination to come back to shore or to master the ironic moment.

Seeing the novel's ambivalent, ironic tone in this way reveals Dubslav's shortcomings to be of a piece with those of other Fontanean characters. As I have tried to show in the preceding analyses, typically the characters who seem freest with their irony are the ones who are also at a loss: Käthe, when she returns from the curative spa to an ambivalent welcome; Schach, when forced finally to reconcile word and deed; Petöfy, when confronted with the consequences of an insincere vow; van der Straaten, in the moment of his abandonment; Holk, as he plays at the libertine in Copenhagen—the list goes on. These characters seldom say what they mean, but their dissimulation emanates from a position of weakness and compulsion rather than strength. Although the portrait of Dubslav is gentler and more generous than some other Fontanean caricatures of rhetorical excess, *Der Stechlin* still revisits familiar themes and concerns from the earlier society novels. It casts the surfeit of indifferent talk—of mere small talk—as ineffectual, isolating, and unable to enter into dialogue with the wider world. The fundamental ineffectiveness of this manner of speaking comes to the fore in two main ways, through Dubslav's defeat in the Reichstag election and through its contrast with "den großen Zusammenhang der Dinge" (17:320 the grand interrelationship of things), represented by Lake Stechlin and the wired network of telegraphy.

Although *Der Stechlin* has long been recognized as an epic conversation piece sui generis,[12] Fontane also repeatedly highlighted its status as a political novel.[13] Part of its political aspect has to do with how it reveals urbane chatter to be ineffectual. Such chatter is detached from the realities and concerns of the world, even though the telegraph wires and the lake's mysterious, seismographic connection to events around the globe show how interconnected the world (both natural and modern-technological) actually is.[14] This becomes apparent through the special election to replace a deceased Reichstag member. Though the

---

[12] See the contemporaneous reviews cited in Klaus-Peter Möller's editorial appendix to *Der Stechlin*, 17:518.

[13] Fontane, June 8, 1896, *Der Dichter über sein Werk*, 2:471. See further the letter of May 12, 1897, in which Fontane's punctuation (!!) suggests that he too is surprised by the overtly political nature of his latest work. Fontane, *Der Dichter über sein Werk*, 2:474.

[14] On the parallels between Lake Stechlin and the technology of telegraphy, see Christian Thomas, *Theodor Fontane: Autonomie und Telegraphie in den Gesellschaftsromanen* (Berlin: Logos, 2015), 103–4.

All Talk: In Lieu of a Conclusion, *Stechlin*   225

conservatives persuade Dubslav to step forward as their candidate, he hardly mounts a campaign, partly in the hope that Rheinsberg-Wutz still represents a safe district for the party, partly out of indifference to the outcome. A causeur but not an orator, Dubslav cannot speak to people in a way that will motivate them to vote for him. His politics are insincere and superficial, as he is not committed to any particular program other than being the conservative-appointed candidate. While he of course wants nothing to do with "Herumreisen" or "Redenhalten" (17:191, traveling around or giving speeches), the progressives send in a canvasser from Berlin, who goes from town to town, doing the hard work of persuasion. Moreover, the progressive canvasser plies these working-class constituents with the annunciation of political truths in which they can believe—higher wages and an eight-hour workday, "*das sei das Wahre*" (17:194, *that* is what's true). Important here is how political discourse turns on the distinction between true and false (the *true* program of social progress as opposed to the *false* hopes proffered by the church and the nobility) and how it appeals to a truth worth fighting for. Effective political speech is earnest, committed, and very much in the fray.

This stands in sharp contrast to affected forms of upper-class interaction, in which "yes" is indistinguishable from "no" and no statement is more accurate than its contradiction. This manner of speaking, deliberately indifferent to how things actually are, attenuates language's credibility and its communicative function. The predilection for idle talk is too insular to direct itself outward, toward a dialogue with others. It represents, rather, "a retreat into interiority in the face of a threatening world."[15] Barbara Naumann describes the novel's empty talk as an example of dialogue in decay. Referring to Plato, she characterizes the conversations by writing, "In their talkativeness and irony, the dialogues constitute in a sense a citation of Platonic dialogue under non-Platonic conditions—a degenerate form [Verfallsform]."[16] The combination of loquacity and irony ensures that these discussions have a great deal of language but little in the way of commitment, sincerity, or reliability. The novel's conversations, carried out by speakers who revel in their own witty superficiality, are not invested in using dialogic exchange as a means to plumb the depths of an idea and uncover the truth. Dubslav can engage in polished dinner-party banter all night long, but that ability does not mean that he can deliver a compelling campaign speech. The best practitioners of causerie thus turn out to be politically ineffective. It suggests that the nobility cannot effectively countenance and

---

[15]   Goetschel, "Causerie," 124.
[16]   Naumann, "Schwatzhaftigkeit," 22–3.

respond to the pressing concerns of the day. They keep chattering away as they lose relevance and influence.

Goetschel contends that there is one conversation in *Der Stechlin* that stands apart from the others as an exception to the rule of indifferent banter, and this is the encounter between Melusine and Lorenzen during the winter visit to the Stechlin home. This conversation, he writes, "is the only time in the novel that two free persons come face-to-face on equal terms," and "each contributes equally to the discussion" so that for once the novel depicts "the possibility of a genuine dialogue."[17] Goetschel helpfully draws attention to this different kind of conversation in *Der Stechlin*, and I want to make the point that Fontane, even in his late writing, continues to insist on the viability—even necessity—of non-ironic ways of speaking. As in many of his other works, Fontane critiques here the prevalence of an idiom that is ironically detached, indifferent to truth, and thus unreliable. But he continues to offer glimpses of an alternative, a promise of being able to speak more reliably and authentically.

In this case, the conversation between Melusine and Lorenzen stands in contrast to the stream of causerie because it is an earnest, open exchange with a purpose and a point. Note that both characters refer to what is being said as "Bekenntnisse," as being proffered in the mode of avowal, which reinforces the sense that this is a serious discussion rather than just another riff of sociable banter (17:318). This is also the conversation in which Melusine famously asserts the importance of "den großen Zusammenhang der Dinge" (the grand interrelationship of things): "Sich abschließen, heißt sich einmauern, und sich einmauern ist Tod" (17:320, Isolating yourself means walling yourself off, and walling yourself off is death). The fact that her statement occurs in the novel's one exemplary, exceptional dialogue suggests that this grand interrelatedness could be predicated on a bearing of candor and sincerity. Melusine connects with Lorenzen by engaging with him earnestly and openly, and he in turn gives his word to keep supporting Woldemar after the marriage. Whereas the stream of idle causerie reveals itself to be isolating and ineffectual, walled off by its own indifference, Melusine and Lorenzen model here a form of earnest dialogue that can transcend barriers and generate reliable connections—between word and thing, word and deed, and among speaking subjects.

The existence of other, more authentic and reliable communication models once again belies the notion that Fontane presents language as inherently broken or no longer up to the task of conveying information

---

[17] Goethschel, "Causerie," 124.

in a reliable and effective way. Speaking haphazardly, without regard for truth, consistency, or sincerity, appears rather as a predilection that carries ethical and rhetorical implications. The unwillingness of most characters to speak earnestly or in depth on any topic represents a symptom of societal decline. Earlier in the novel, for instance, Lorenzen locates cynical dissimulation at the heart of English cultural degeneration: "sie sagen 'Christus' und meinen Kattun" (they say "Christ" and mean "cotton"). Because they do not say what they mean, because they dissemble via an ironic discrepancy between piety and profit, Lorenzen concludes that their culture is "schrecklich 'runtergekommen" (17:264–5, terribly decayed).

In fact, a large part of the conversation between Lorenzen and Melusine is given over to another grand narrative of historico-cultural development—namely, the rise and decline of Prussian culture. Lorenzen asserts that, although Prussia used to be confident in its superiority, these days "die Begeisterung ist tot" (the excitement is dead), replaced by a "rückläufige Bewegung" (17:323, regressive movement). He pinpoints a conservative tendency to resist the new and to pine for the bygone glory of Prussian highpoints such as the reign of Friedrich Wilhelm I or Frederick the Great. He mentions two waypoints in particular that suggest a rhetorical dimension to the diagnosis of cultural deterioration. He identifies as irretrievable both "das spanische Rohr aus dem Tabakskollegium" (the Spanish cane from the *Tabakskollegium*) and "den Krückstock von Sanssouci" (the walking stick from Sanssouci). "Damit ist es vorbei. Und gut, daß es so ist. Was einmal Fortschritt war, ist längst Rückschritt geworden" (17:323, Those things are done and gone. And good that they are. What once was progress has long since become regression). This is an important passage, as it seems like more than coincidence that the two points Lorenzen mentions, the *Tabakskollegium* of Friedrich Wilhelm I and the intellectual node of Sanssouci under Frederick the Great, also happen to play leading roles in Fontane's genealogy of the Berlin idiom. As he reconstructs it in the "Berlinertum" essay, the *Tabakskollegium* was the birthplace of a distinctive Berlin tone, one that then gets filtered through the literary and intellectual sensibility of Sanssouci to produce the witty, ironic idiom that came to characterize sophisticated Berlin culture by the mid-nineteenth century.

Just as Fontane describes the gradual evolution of a separate Berlin tone over the course of the eighteenth century, so Lorenzen identifies these Prussian rulers with periods in a cultural progression. But the tide has turned in the nineteenth century: what once was progress has given way to regress; evolution has tipped into degeneration. Wit and irony thus no longer constitute the language of enlightened monarchs. They have instead become the indifferent, ineffectual banter of a nobility in decline. These regressive cultural, rhetorical tendencies, coupled with Woldemar's alleged malleability of character, make Lorenzen's ongoing counsel desirable. That he and Melusine are able to have a frank and earnest dialogue suggests at least the potential for future renewal.

Another contrast with the stream of superficial causerie comes through the terse, staccato messages of the telegraph. In the context of *Der Stechlin*, the telegram—concise, to the point, reduced to essential information—delivers a clear counterpoint to the prevailing style of blousy, indifferent conversation. In fact, these stylistic differences, or differences in tone, are precisely why the novel's speakers take issue with telegrams. Dubslav, for instance, complains about the nature of telegraphic composition, saying, "Kürze soll eine Tugend sein, aber sich kurz fassen, heißt meistens auch sich grob fassen. Jede Spur von Verbindlichkeit fällt fort, und das Wort 'Herr' ist beispielsweise gar nicht mehr anzutreffen" (17:28, Brevity is supposedly a virtue, but being brief usually means also being crude. Every trace of courtesy is omitted, and no one ever encounters the word "sir," for example). Dubslav seizes on brevity "as a central defect in language," and it is important to note his specific objections.[18] Concision erases the sense of noblesse oblige courtesy, and perhaps more telling, it erases as superfluous the very titles that reinforce class stratification and social hierarchy. In this democratized communication medium, the word "Herr"—meaning "sir" but also with a connotation of "master"—is nowhere to be found. His complaint tethers communication style to the social and political order that his conservative allies hope to preserve against the demands of progressives and Social Democrats.

Moreover, the telegram's brevity results from the application of cost–benefit analysis and the instrumentalization of language to the conveyance of essential information. Since telegrams charged by the word, the incentive was to minimize cost by conveying as much information as possible in as few words as possible. The cost structure of this new technology thus gave rise to the telegraphic style—a new idiom, a modern and radically efficient manner of communication. Dubslav complains, "Jeder, der wieder eine neue Fünfpfennigersparnis herausdoktert, ist ein Genie" (17:28, Anyone who can finagle a savings of five cents is a genius). The complaints about telegraphy incidentally present what might be the clearest argument in Fontane's writings for an historical—technological—development that breaks language. The novel plays out Dubslav's concern when his son Woldemar sends a clipped telegram from England, and his friends are in disappointed agreement, "daß es

---

[18] Czucka, "Faktizität und Sprachskepsis," 36.

wenig sei" (17:276, that it's not much). A model of concision, it contains no complete sentences, merely a brief list of places and sights; even his own name is abbreviated. According to the dictates of efficiency, it has been stripped of all the pleasantries and courtesies that Woldemar would exhibit in conversation. Only Count Barby defends the virtue of brevity, asserting that it is, on the contrary, "ein sehr gutes Telegramm, weil ein richtiges Telegramm" (17:276, a very good telegram because it's a correct telegram). It is "correct" both in the sense that it corresponds to the conventions of telegraphic communication and that it accurately reflects Woldemar's itinerary in England.

The key point is that the telegram's efficiency, its unadorned directness, is diametrically opposed to the incessant, idle banter of causerie. Whereas the telegraphic style strives to optimize the information-to-language ratio, the novel's many superficial conversations move in the opposite direction. When banter becomes an end in itself, when speaking subjects are indifferent to the accuracy or consistency of what they say, they tend to produce a great deal of language while conveying little in the way of reliable information. Telegraphy supplants the stream of empty language with an electrical *Strom*, a stream or current that carries clipped, hyper-efficient messages.[19]

The telegram's cost structure has another side effect. It is not enough that the message be brief; it must also be clear and unambiguous. It has no space for the ironic ambivalence that Dubslav practices when he appends a rhetorical question mark of uncertainty to everything he says, or when he admits that he could just as easily contradict himself by asserting the contrary of what he had just claimed. Such ambivalence and uncertainty have no place in the telegram because they would only interfere with its communicative function. But to concede this point in the specialized case of telegraphy implies a broader point—namely, that the ambivalence and uncertainty that irony generates interfere with the communicative function of language in general, with its efficiency and reliability.

The appeal of telegraphy, then, is the promise of a medium free from the disruptions of irony, ambivalence, and empty talk. Though its style is terse and impersonal, the telegram also presents as earnest, austere, and credible. It does not dissimulate. From this perspective, the telegram appears as a modern, technological variant of avowal. I do not use "avowal" here in the full Foucauldian sense of that term, as a verbal act through which the subject constitutes itself through the enunciation

---

[19] On the figurative register of "Strom" (current) and the connection between telegraphy and water imagery, see again Thomas, *Theodor Fontane*, 103.

of truth.[20] I mean "avowal" rather in its looser sense as a counterpoint to irony and empty rhetoric, as a medium of communication that is candid, earnest, and effective, one free from irony's destabilizing force. Think, for example, of Foucault's description of *parrhesia* as a mode of truth-telling related to avowal: someone who speaks in this mode "says things as clearly and directly as possible, without any disguise or rhetorical embellishment, so that his words may immediately be given their prescriptive value." It requires a frankness that "leaves nothing to interpretation."[21] This is what telegraphy promises—a vehicle of efficient and reliable truth-telling. In *Der Stechlin*, the telegram punctuates the prevalent style of blousy conversation by being everything those conversations are not: concise rather than meandering, earnest rather than facetious, credible rather than self-contradictory, and predicated on accuracy rather than indifferent to it. Fontane's last completed novel does not offer a conclusion in the sense that it does not resolve the tension between irony and avowal, or more broadly, between reliable and unreliable speech. The tension familiar from other society novels continues to operate here, just in a different guise. *Der Stechlin* carries on the conflict between opposed modes of speaking, and the work as a whole walks a fine line between resignation and optimism. It indicates, on the one hand, that the stream of idle, unreliable talk will continue unabated, but also that this dominant idiom cannot extinguish the possibility of alternative ways of speaking. Beyond the upper-class dinner parties and soirees in Berlin and Brandenburg, there are other networks of communication, invisible messages coursing through subterranean channels or thrumming along telegraph wires suspended in the air. Both promise to convey information more legibly and credibly than any instance of causerie or ironic ambivalence.

Irony has long been regarded as a fashionable, sophisticated literary trope. In the mid-twentieth century, the New Critics even raised irony to a universal component of literary structure.[22] I. A. Richards, one of the foundational proponents of the New Criticism, writes in *Principles of Literary Criticism* that "irony itself is [...] constantly a characteristic of poetry which is [of the highest order]."[23] Within this critical climate, it only makes sense that it would be easier to see in Fontane an affirmative writer of irony rather than a cautious critic of irony. The implicit

---

[20] Foucault, *Wrong-Doing, Truth-Telling*, 17.
[21] Foucault, *Courage of the Truth*, 16.
[22] Cleanth Brooks, "Irony as a Principle of Structure," in *Twentieth Century Criticism: The Major Statements*, ed. William Handy and Max Westbrook (New York: Free Press, 1974), 758–66.
[23] I. A. Richards, *Principles of Literary Criticism* (New York: Routledge, 2001), 248.

syllogism runs: irony is a constitutive element of all serious literature; Fontane's works are serious literature; ergo, Fontane's works are constituted via an ironic tone. Add in a dose of Bakhtinian dialogism, and by the 1970s, Fontane's polyphonic society novels come to seem like German-language embodiments of the most modern, ironic literary sensibility. And when the wave of poststructuralism and deconstruction rolls through the academy, the surfeit of empty talk in Fontane reveals an early insight into the breakdown of language, the unmooring of signification, and the impossibility of ascertaining fixed meanings. This, in a nutshell, is the intellectual provenance of Fontane's reputation as a writer of irony and broken language, a genealogy that links him more to the modernism of Mann, Musil, and Dostoevsky than to other realist writers.

While there is truth to this picture of multivoicedness and detachment in Fontane's works, Bakhtin also wrote about Dostoevsky's representational style in a way that could be helpful in disentangling Fontane's relationship to irony. Specifically, Bakhtin describes the objects of artistic representation: "Dostoevsky was capable of *representing a foreign idea* […], and at the same time maintaining distance as well, not confirming the idea and not merging it with his own expressed ideology."[24] The passage describes a stance of narrative distance, the text's ability to represent an idea without endorsing it. Now consider for a moment how often Fontane's novels turn verbal irony and unreliable language into objects of artistic representation. Bakhtin cautions the reader not to mistake representation for affirmation, and this distinction operates in Fontane's works in even sharper form: one should not mistake a critical portrayal for affirmation. This would look a lot like the intellectual irony that writers such as Martini and Bange have identified in the society novels, except that there is nothing ambivalent or aloof in Fontane's depiction of irony. Fontane's works do not simply maintain a disinterested distance from the phenomenon of pervasive verbal irony; they depict its corrosive effects in a variety of contexts. Even in the gentler light of *Der Stechlin*, ironic ambivalence comes across as ineffectual, a symptom of decline. In the harsher light of other novels, it appears as a malignant force, infiltrating different social strata and discursive spheres and producing a deterioration in language use.

This other image of Fontane—an author concerned with the consequences of ubiquitous irony and unreliable language—has tended to fly under the scholarly radar. But Schlegel contends that an excess of irony can become oppressive, and in our contemporary culture, there is

---

[24] Mikhail Bakhtin, *Problems of Dostoevsky's Poetics*, trans. R. W. Rotsel (Ann Arbor, MI: Ardis, 1973), 68.

a growing sense that irony, ambivalence, and indifference to the truth have become too prevalent, have begun to corrode communication that one expects to be sincere and credible. These days, we could use a bit less irony, a bit less discrepancy between what is said and what is meant. David Foster Wallace was one of the more prescient writers to diagnose this *Zeitgeist* of the late twentieth and early twenty-first centuries. Surveying the 1990s landscape of American television and fiction, he writes that "persistent irony" is "not liberating but enfeebling" because it "serves an exclusively negative function." Even though irony has become a dominant mode of expression, it is "singularly unuseful when it comes to constructing anything to replace the hypocrisies that it debunks."[25] To put the same idea in Kierkegaard's terms: irony is useful only as a mastered moment, as a negative interval in a dialectic, not as a dominant idiom. Unabated irony is tiresome and oppressive, and in the decades since Wallace's essay, the rise of the internet and social media has only exacerbated the involutions of self-referential irony. In our current era, the eclipse of sincerity and the sense of being thrust into a post-truth age have brought to the fore a yearning for earnestness, for reliable connections between language and meaning. And at this particular cultural moment, that other image of Fontane becomes more apparent. In the light of our contemporary concerns, we can read in his works an early meditation on the causes and consequences of a post-truth condition, an indifference to accuracy in language, and ironic ambivalence. There is an elegiac note of resignation in Fontane, to be sure: we might just chatter our way into oblivion while the world burns. But there are hints of resistance and optimism to be found in his novels as well, as they insist on the rhetorical viability of sincerity, reliability, and realism.

One thing Fontane shows clearly is that the calculated deployment of ironic ambivalence—deliberately obscuring the balance of sincerity and insincerity in one's statements—is a key component of the post-truth condition. In that same essay on television and contemporary fiction, Wallace writes that "irony tyrannizes us" because "an ironist is *impossible to pin down*. All irony is a variation on a sort of existential poker-face."[26] Ironic ambivalence produces the impossibility of pinning down whether someone means what he or she says. The society novels alert us early on to a strategy of dissembling whereby one cannot determine whether an expression is meant to be taken earnestly or ironically. Fontane furthermore captures how that ironic ambivalence can be turned into an instrument of dissimulation and rhetorical control—just

---

[25] Wallace, "E Unibus Pluram," 183.
[26] Wallace, "E Unibus Pluram," 183.

look at Schach's feigned acquiescence, Ebba's insincere flirtation, Innstetten's didacticism, or Crampas's slippery maneuvers of seduction. Each of these figures uses ironic ambivalence to exert a kind of tyranny or oppressive power over the other party.

Fontane's novels require an alertness to irony and a sensitivity to predicaments of uncertainty. They are thus timely, in that they speak to issues that continue to occupy us in the present era, one that feels in many ways like it has abandoned any commitment to truth and sincerity. The introduction to this book touched upon the 2016 US presidential campaign and the difficulty of covering a candidate who was indifferent to the accuracy of his statements, one who pitched campaign rhetoric in the indeterminate zone between earnestness and empty "euphemism." The details of that campaign were at issue again in 2019, when Robert Mueller released his investigative report on Russian election interference.[27] One point of scrutiny was Trump's statement during a 2016 press conference, when he said, "Russia, if you're listening, I hope you're able to find the 30,000 emails that are missing."[28] Regarding this odd suggestion, the special counsel's office posed several questions, all of which sought to pin down the statement's underlying meaning. What intent motivated the statement? What was its purpose? What prior knowledge of Russian hacking did it reflect? But Trump's written responses to the special counsel's inquiries confirm that the ironist cannot be pinned down: "I made the statement […] in jest and sarcastically, as was apparent to any objective observer."[29] (The purported sarcasm was not apparent to the Russian intelligence officers who began targeting Clinton campaign email accounts approximately five hours after the request was made.[30]) People have joked about Trump's rhetoric sounding better in the original German, but here the German (or Fontanean) equivalent for his defensive response is clear: he claims that his statement was *scherzhaft*, not *ernsthaft*, and that it would make no sense to scrutinize an ironic statement as if it were a sincere request. It is futile to interrogate an utterance's meaning when the speaker disavows any connection between what he said and what he meant. Wallace identifies in this sort

---

[27] Mueller was appointed as special counsel in spring 2017 to investigate allegations that Russia had interfered in the US presidential election of 2016. His office's report was released in spring 2019.
[28] He refers to messages that Hillary Clinton had allegedly deleted from a private email account. Many interpreted his statement as an appeal to Russian hackers to recover the emails and make them public. Robert S. Mueller, *Report on the Investigation into Russian Interference in the 2016 Presidential Election* (Washington, DC: U.S. Department of Justice, 2019), Appendix C-5.
[29] Mueller, *Report on the Investigation*, Appendix C-18.
[30] Mueller, *Report on the Investigation*, 1:49.

of dismissive gesture "the oppressiveness of institutionalized irony": "the ability to interdict the *question* without attending to its *content*."[31] The deniability of ironic ambivalence acts as an escape hatch; it opens onto the negative freedom of not being bound by the straightforward meaning that others attach to one's words. Note further that this statement and defense occur within an official judicial inquiry, so that, in typical post-truth fashion, one encounters here yet another involution of irony and avowal.

My argument for the timeliness and importance of Fontane's critique of irony rests on instances such as the one cited above—moments when the plausible deniability of irony ("I didn't mean what I clearly said") takes on ethical and political dimensions. Aside from the stakes and the scope of authority, how does Trump's response to the Mueller inquiry differ from Ebba's response to Holk's inquiry? They both claim that obvious, public acts of flirtation were only made in jest. It was all just irony, sarcasm, or euphemism. Whatever one calls it, it is a mode of speaking constituted over the discrepancy between what is said and what is meant. And Fontane's point in a novel like *Unwiederbringlich* is that this penchant for irony has a malignant effect. Copenhagen society, in Fontane's portrayal, is so enthralled by a post-truth, ironic idiom that its official decrees and diplomatic statements (on, e.g., the Schleswig-Holstein question) can no longer be taken at face value. There is always the possibility that what they say is not sincerely meant, or that they mean something other than what they say. In the absence of good-faith sincerity and credibility, international negotiations and diplomatic relations begin to falter. There can be no doubt that the issues Fontane identifies in the nineteenth century pertain just as much, if not more so, to our contemporary society. Indeed, the potential for contagion from individual irony to sweeping, systemic irony is all the greater when the individual in question holds a country's highest public office.

One could draw various conclusions from the congruence between Fontane's concerns and those of the twenty-first-century post-truth age. One possible response is a shrug: the fact that Fontane was fretting already in the 1880s about unreliable language and indifference to truth and that we still are today could indicate that these are perennial anxieties for anyone who attends to language and communication. The perception of a scourge of verbal infidelity traces all the way back to ancient texts, and perhaps it is simply a recurrent lament—namely, that human language is plagued by ambivalence and uncertainty. In other words, perhaps every age perceives itself as a post-truth age, as

---

[31] Wallace, "E Unibus Pluram," 184.

that point in history in which truth was finally eclipsed by dissimulating rhetoric. Petöfy tells Judith that the world will always be mired in Pilate's question, "What is truth?" (7:200). But it could also be that the world will always be mired in the *perception* of a quandary of language, truth, and unreliability. On this view, what fluctuates over time is not the prevalence of irony and unreliability in language but rather a culture's degree of alarm over persistent levels of ambient irony.

Another response would be to make a diachronic comparison and see irony as a particularly modern affliction, one that postmodernism has only exacerbated. Ernst Behler describes postmodernity as "that attitude in which the problems, questions, and issues of modernity accumulate in an unheard-of way" such that postmodernism "becomes a radicalized, intensified version of modernism."[32] That dynamic of intensification pertains to irony too. Fontane worried about irony as a dominant mode of speaking in Prussian society, but that was in an age of industrialization, letter writing, and print media. What would he make of the hall-of-mirrors cultural landscape of today, in the age of digital information, social media, pervasive marketing, and the attention economy? How could he not be bewildered, overwhelmed? The sense of dismay with the cynical irony of mid-nineteenth-century Copenhagen apparent in *Unwiederbringlich* seems downright quaint in a world where mimetic representation has given way to memetic iteration, a world whose motto would not be Pilate's skeptical question but rather "LOL, nothing matters." It is, after all, a world in which the layers of irony and avowal have so interpenetrated one another that it requires tone indicators, such as the sarcasm switch, "/s," and "/srs," to help distinguish between earnest and ironic statements. From this perspective, the rhetorical decadence that Fontane diagnosed in nineteenth-century society has continued in a long, downward slide, plumbing depths of indifference and unreliability that a German realist author would not have thought possible.

And yet I do not believe that Fontane's relevance to the contemporary post-truth predicament should reside primarily in a counsel of despair. To be sure, the novels' weariness (and wariness) of a society saturated by irony and insincerity resonates with present-day concerns about the declining efficacy of public discourse. But Fontane also indicates the potential for points of resistance, for alternatives to the dominant idiom of irony—through the unadorned directness of Lene's authentic speech, for example, through the force of Melanie's avowal, or the terse efficiency of telegraphic communication. The novels show,

---

[32] Behler, *Irony and the Discourse of Modernity*, 5.

often in quiet ways, that ironic indifference is not the only rhetorical bearing, that it remains possible to speak differently, to go against the grain, and to assume a more orderly and reliable relationship to language and truth. The flip-side to the diagnosis of corrosive irony is the countervailing promise that language as such is not inherently broken, that attempts to communicate are not necessarily doomed to fail. Language use remains a matter of agency and intention, and one can still choose to speak earnestly, dependably, credibly.

In short, the novels posit a mode of speaking beyond irony. They suggest that one can still step out of the sea of irony and return to solid ground. Although it might not be the most fashionable stance, I believe that Fontane pushes the reader to see the value and viability of sincerity in a world that seems inclined to dismiss it. His brand of realism calls for drawing a tighter, more reliable connection between words and things, for valuing accuracy and reliability in representation. By bringing to the fore discrepancies between what is said and what is meant, Fontane ultimately challenges individual subjects to bridge that gap and speak otherwise. And if I am correct in identifying in these works an earnest concern with the consequences of unreliable language, then Fontane, so often viewed as writer of gentle ironies, should more accurately be seen as a writer who seeks out the promise of avowal.

Bibliography

Agamben, Giorgio. *The Sacrament of Language: An Archaeology of the Oath.* Translated by Adam Kotsko. Stanford: Stanford University Press, 2011.
Allemann, Beda. "Ironie als literarisches Prinzip." In *Ironie und Dichtung*, edited by Albert Schaefer, 11–37. Munich: C.H. Beck, 1970.
Allen, Julie. "Theodor Fontane: A Probable Pioneer in German Kierkegaard Reception." In *Kierkegaard's Influence on Literature, Criticism, and Art. Tome I: The Germanophone World*, edited by Jon Steward, 61–77. Burlington, VT: Ashgate, 2013.
Althusser, Louis. *Lenin and Philosophy, and Other Essays.* Translated by Ben Brewster. New York: Monthly Review Press, 1972.
Anderson, Paul Irving. "Austro-Hungarian Camouflage: Theodor Fontane's *Graf Petöfy*." *Seminar* 47, no. 3 (2011): 324–8.
Anderson, Paul Irving. *Ehrgeiz und Trauer. Fontanes offiziöse Agitation 1859 und ihre Wiederkehr in Unwiederbringlich.* Stuttgart: Franz Steiner, 2002.
Arendt, Hannah. *The Origins of Totalitarianism.* New York: Meridian Books, 1958.
Arnold-de Simine, Silke. "'Denn das Haus, was wir bewohnen, […] ist ein Spukhaus.' Fontanes *Effi Briest* und Fassbinders Verfilmung in der Tradition des Female Gothic." *Germanic Review* 79, no. 2 (2004): 83–113.
Auerbach, Erich. *Mimesis: The Representation of Reality in Western Literature.* Translated by Willard Trask. Princeton: Princeton University Press, 2013.
Aus der Au, Carmen. *Theodor Fontane als Kunstkritiker.* Berlin: de Gruyter, 2017.
Aust, Hugo. "Fontanes Poetik: Realismus." In *Fontane-Handbuch*, edited by Christian Grawe and Helmuth Nürnberger, 412–27. Stuttgart: Kröner, 2000.
Austin, J. L. *How to Do Things with Words.* Cambridge, MA: Harvard University Press, 1962.
Bade, James. *Fontane's Landscapes.* Würzburg: Königshausen & Neumann, 2009.
Baecker, Dirk. "Ernste Kommunikation." In *Sprachen der Ironie—Sprachen des Ernstes*, edited by Karl Heinz Bohrer, 389–403. Frankfurt am Main: Suhrkamp, 2000.
Bakhtin, Mikhail. *Problems of Dostoevsky's Poetics.* Translated by R. W. Rotsel. Ann Arbor, MI: Ardis, 1973.
Bange, Pierre. *Ironie et Dialogisme dans les Romans de Theodor Fontane.* Grenoble: Presses Universitaires de Grenoble, 1974.
Beckson, Karl, ed. *Oscar Wilde: The Critical Heritage.* New York: Routledge, 2003.
Begemann, Christian. "'Ein Spukhaus ist nie 'was Gewöhnliches … ' Das Gespenst und das soziale Imaginäre in Fontanes *Effi Briest*." In *Herausforderungen des*

Realismus: Theodor Fontanes Gesellschaftsromane, edited by Peter Uwe Hohendahl and Ulrike Vedder, 203–41. Freiburg: Rombach, 2018.

Behler, Ernst. *Irony and the Discourse of Modernity*. Seattle: University of Washington Press, 1990.

Berbig, Roland. *Theodor Fontane Chronik*. 5 vols. Berlin: de Gruyter, 2010.

Berman, Russell. *The Rise of the Modern German Novel: Crisis and Charisma*. Cambridge, MA: Harvard University Press, 1986.

Berman, Russell. "*Effi Briest* and the End of Realism." In *A Companion to German Realism, 1848–1900*, edited by Todd Kontje, 339–64. Rochester, NY: Camden House, 2002.

Bernstein, Richard. *Ironic Life*. Cambridge: Polity Press, 2016.

Blessin, Stefan. "*Unwiederbringlich*—ein historisch-politischer Roman? Bemerkungen zu Fontanes Symbolkunst." *Deutsche Vierteljahrsschrift für Literaturwissenschaft und Geistesgeschichte* 48, no. 4 (1974): 672–703.

Blödorn, Andreas and Friedhelm Marx, ed. *Thomas Mann Handbuch: Leben, Werk, Wirkung*. Stuttgart: J.B. Metzler, 2015.

Blomqvist, Clarissa. "Realism on Stage: Reflections on Language in Theodor Fontane's Theatre Reviews." *Monatshefte* 104, no. 3 (2012): 337–45.

Blumenberg, Hans. *Gerade noch Klassiker. Glossen zu Fontane*. Munich: Carl Hanser, 1998.

Bohrer, Karl Heinz. "Sprachen der Ironie—Sprachen des Ernstes. Das Problem." In *Sprachen der Ironie—Sprachen des Ernstes*, edited by Karl Heinz Bohrer, 11–35. Frankfurt am Main: Surhkamp, 2000.

Booth, Wayne. *A Rhetoric of Irony*. Chicago: University of Chicago Press, 1974.

Bowman, Peter James. "Fontane's *Unwiederbringlich*: A Bakhtinian Reading." *German Quarterly* 77, no. 2 (2004): 170–87.

Bowman, Peter James. "The Lover's Discourse in Theodor Fontane's *Irrungen, Wirrungen*." *Orbis Litterarum* 62, no. 2 (2007): 137–58.

Bowman, Peter James. "*Schach von Wuthenow*: Interpreters and Interpretants." In *Theodor Fontane and the European Context: Literature, Culture and Society in Prussia and Europe*, edited by Patricia Howe and Helen Chambers, 43–62. Amsterdam: Rodopi, 2001.

Brandstettter, Gabriele and Gerhard Neumann. "'Le laid c'est le beau.' Liebesdiskurs und Geschlechterrolle in Fontanes Roman *Schach von Wuthenow*." *Deutsche Vierteljahrsschrift für Literaturwissenschaft und Geistesgeschichte* 72, no. 2 (1998): 243–67.

Breithaupt, Fritz. *Kultur der Ausrede*. Berlin: Suhrkamp, 2012.

Brooks, Cleanth. "Irony as a Principle of Structure." In *Twentieth Century Criticism: The Major Statements*, edited by William Handy and Max Westbrook, 758–66. New York: Free Press, 1974.

Chambers, Helen. "The Inadequacy of the Wife-and-Mother Model: Female Happiness in Theodor Fontane's *Unwiederbringlich*." *Seminar* 47, no. 2 (2011): 285–97.

Cicero. *De Oratore*. Translated by E. W. Sutton and H. Rackham. Cambridge, MA: Harvard University Press, 1948.

Congregation for the Doctrine of the Faith. *Catechism of the Catholic Church*. Vatican City: Libreria Editrice Vaticana, 1994.

Czucka, Eckehard. "Faktizität und Sprachskepsis. Fontanes *Stechlin* und die Sprachkritik der Jahrhundertwende." In *Theodor Fontane am Ende des Jahrhunderts*, edited by Hanna Delf von Wolzogen and Helmuth Nürnberger, 2: 27–39. Würzburg: Königshausen & Neumann, 2000.

Dane, Joseph. *The Critical Mythology of Irony*. Athens, GA: University of Georgia Press, 2011.
D'Ancona, Matthew. *Post-Truth: The New War on Truth and How to Fight Back*. London: Ebury Press, 2017.
D'Aprile, Iwan-Michelangelo. *Fontane. Ein Jahrhundert in Bewegung*. Hamburg: Rowohlt, 2018.
De Man, Paul. "The Concept of Irony." In *Aesthetic Ideology*, edited by Andrzej Warminski, 163–84. Minneapolis: University of Minnesota Press, 1996.
De Man, Paul. "Semiology and Rhetoric." In *Allegories of Reading: Figural Language in Rousseau, Nietzsche, Rilke, and Proust*, 3–19. New Haven: Yale University Press, 1979.
Doebeling, Marion. "Breaking the Mimetic Chain—Pattern of Cultural Unground." In *New Approaches to Theodor Fontane: Cultural Codes in Flux*, edited by Marion Doebeling, ix–xxii. Columbia, SC: Camden House, 2000.
Downes, Daragh. "*Effi Briest*. Roman." In *Fontane-Handbuch*, edited by Christian Grawe and Helmuth Nürnberger, 633–51. Stuttgart: Kröner, 2000.
Downing, Eric. "Sprachmagie, Stimmung und Geselligkeit. Überschreitungen des Realismus in Fontanes *Der Stechlin*." In *Herausforderungen des Realismus: Theodor Fontanes Gesellschaftsromane*, edited by Peter Uwe Hohendahl and Ulrike Vedder, 271–95. Freiburg: Rombach, 2018.
Eberspächer, Martina. *Der Weihnachtsmann: zur Entstehung einer Bildtradition in Aufklärung und Romantik*. Stuttgart: M. Eberspächer, 2002.
Engler-Coldren, Katharina Adeline. "On the 'Right Measure' in *Effi Briest*: Ethics and Aesthetics of the Prosaic." In *Fontane in the Twenty-First Century*, edited by John B. Lyon and Brian Tucker, 121–41. Rochester, NY: Camden House, 2019.
Ferraris, Maurizio. "Was ist der Neue Realismus?" Translated by Malte Osterloh. In *Der Neue Realismus*, edited by Markus Gabriel, 52–75. Frankfurt am Main: Suhrkamp, 2014.
Fleischer, Michael. *"Kommen Sie, Cohn." Fontane und die "Judenfrage."* Berlin: Michael Fleischer, 1998.
Fontane, Theodor. *L'Adultera*. Edited by Helmuth Nürnberger. Munich: Deutscher Taschenbuch Verlag, 1998.
Fontane, Theodor. *Der Dichter über sein Werk*. Edited by Richard Brinkmann. 2 vols. Munich: Deutscher Taschenbuch Verlag, 1973.
Fontane, Theodor. *Effi Briest*. Translated by Hugh Rorrison and Helen Chambers. New York: Penguin, 2000.
Fontane, Theodor. *Große Brandenburger Ausgabe*. Edited by Gotthard Erler, continued by Heinrich Detering and Gabriele Radecke. Berlin: Aufbau-Verlag, 1994–.
Fontane, Theodor. *Irretrievable* [*Unwiederbringlich*]. Translated by Douglas Parmée. New York: New York Review Books, 2011.
Fontane, Theodor. *A Man of Honor* [*Schach von Wuthenow*]. Translated by E. M. Valk. New York: Frederick Ungar Publishing, 1975.
Fontane, Theodor. *On Tangled Paths* [*Irrungen, Wirrungen*]. Translated by Peter James Bowman. New York: Penguin Books, 2010.
Fontane, Theodor. *Sämtliche Werke. Nymphenburger Ausgabe*. Edited by Edgar Gross. 24 vols. Munich: Nymphenburger Verlagshandlung, 1959–75.
Fontane, Theodor. *The Woman Taken in Adultery and The Poggenpuhl Family* [*L'Adultera* and *Die Poggenpuhls*]. Translated by Gabriele Annan. Chicago: University of Chicago Press, 1979.

Foucault, Michel. *The Archaeology of Knowledge and the Discourse on Language.* Translated by A. M. Sheridan Smith. New York: Pantheon, 1972.
Foucault, Michel. *The Courage of the Truth (The Government of Self and Others II).* Edited by Frédéric Gros. Translated by Graham Burchell. New York: Palgrave Macmillan, 2011.
Foucault, Michel. *Wrong-Doing, Truth-Telling: The Function of Avowal in Justice.* Edited by Fabienne Brion and Bernard Harcourt. Translated by Stephen Sawyer. Chicago: University of Chicago Press, 2014.
Frankfurt, Harry. *On Bullshit.* Princeton: Princeton University Press, 2005.
Franzel, Sean. "'Alles ist eitel.' Flüchtigkeit und Dauer in *Schach von Wuthenow.*" In *Herausforderungen des Realismus: Theodor Fontanes Gesellschaftsromane,* edited by Peter Uwe Hohendahl and Ulrike Vedder, 59–84. Freiburg: Rombach, 2018.
Freud, Sigmund. *The Standard Edition of the Complete Psychological Works of Sigmund Freud.* Edited and translated by James Strachey. 24 vols. London: Hogarth Press, 1953.
Garland, Henry. *The Berlin Novels of Theodor Fontane.* Oxford: Clarendon Press, 1980.
Geppert, Hans Vilmar. "Prussian Decadence: *Schach von Wuthenow* in an International Context." In *Theodor Fontane and the European Context: Literature, Culture and Society in Prussia and Europe,* edited by Patricia Howe and Helen Chambers, 105–17. Amsterdam: Rodopi, 2001.
Geulen, Eva. "Realismus ohne Entsagung. Fontanes *L'Adultera.*" In *Herausforderungen des Realismus: Theodor Fontanes Gesellschaftsromane,* edited by Peter Uwe Hohendahl and Ulrike Vedder, 45–57. Freiburg: Rombach, 2018.
Goetschel, Willi. "Causerie: On the Function of Dialogue in *Der Stechlin.*" In *New Approaches to Theodor Fontane: Cultural Codes in Flux,* edited by Marion Doebeling, 116–35. Columbia, SC: Camden House, 2000.
Graevenitz, Gerhart von. *Theodor Fontane: ängstliche Moderne.* Konstanz: Konstanz University Press, 2014.
Grawe, Christian. "*Graf Petöfy.* Roman." In *Fontane-Handbuch,* edited by Christian Grawe and Helmuth Nürnberger, 546–54. Stuttgart: Kröner, 2000.
Grawe, Christian. "*Unwiederbringlich.* Roman." In *Fontane-Handbuch,* edited by Christian Grawe and Helmuth Nürnberger, 604–14. Stuttgart: Kröner, 2000.
Greenberg, Valerie. "The Resistance of *Effi Briest*: An (Un)told Tale." *PMLA* 103, no. 5 (1988): 770–82.
Grevel, Liselotte. "Die 'sanfte Vergewaltigung' im Wort. Der Held im Kräftespiel zwischen Wort und Handlung in Fontanes Erzählung *Schach von Wuthenow.*" In *Theodor Fontane am Ende des Jahrhunderts,* edited by Hanna Delf von Wolzogen and Helmuth Nürnberger, 2:56–67. Würzburg: Königshausen & Neumann, 2000.
Gross, David. "*Kultur* and Its Discontents: The Origins of a 'Critique of Everyday Life' in Germany, 1880–1925." In *Essays on Culture and Society in Modern Germany,* edited by Gary Stark and Bede Karl Lackner, 70–97. College Station: Texas A&M University Press, 1982.
Gruen, Erich. *Rethinking the Other in Antiquity.* Princeton: Princeton University Press, 2010.
Haberland, Detlef. "Theodor Fontanes Roman *Graf Petöfy*—ein 'ungarisches' Drama?" *Zeitschrift für mitteleuropäische Germanistik* 4, no. 2 (2014): 107–25.
Handwörterbuch der Sexualwissenschaft. Enzyklopädie der natur- und kulturwissenschaftlichen Sexualkunde des Menschen. Edited by Max Marcuse. Berlin: de Gruyter, 2001.

Hillerich, Sonja. *Deutsche Auslandskorrespondenten im neunzehnten Jahrhundert. Die Entstehung einer transnationalen journalistischen Berufskultur*. Berlin: de Gruyter, 2018.
Hohendahl, Peter Uwe. "Eindringliche Beobachtung. Zur Konstitution des Sozialen in *Unwiederbringlich*." In *Herausforderungen des Realismus*, edited by Peter Uwe Hohendahl and Ulrike Vedder, 161–86. Freiburg: Rombach, 2018.
Holt, Randall. "History as Trauma: The Absent Ground of Meaning in *Irrungen, Wirrungen*." In *New Approaches to Theodor Fontane: Cultural Codes in Flux*, edited by Marion Doebeling, 99–115. Columbia, SC: Camden House, 2000.
Houghton, Walter. *The Victorian Frame of Mind, 1830–1870*. New Haven: Yale University Press, 1985.
Jens, Walter. *Über Fontane*. Stuttgart: J.B. Metzler, 2000.
Johnson, David. "Ironies of Degeneration: The Dilemmas of Bourgeois Masculinity in Theodor Fontane's *Frau Jenny Treibel* and *Mathilde Möhring*." *Monatshefte* 102, no. 2 (2010): 147–61.
Kakutani, Michiko. *The Death of Truth*. New York: Tim Duggan Books, 2018.
Källström, Sofia. *Das Eigentliche bleibt doch zurück. Zum Problem der semantischen Unbestimmtheit am Beispiel von Theodor Fontanes Effi Briest*. Uppsala: Uppsala University Press, 2002.
Kieffer, Bruce. "Fontane and Nietzsche: The Use and Abuse of History in *Schach von Wuthenow*." *The Germanic Review* 61, no. 1 (1986): 29–35.
Kierkegaard, Søren. *The Concept of Irony*. Translated by Lee M. Capel. Bloomington, IN: Indiana University Press, 1965.
Kobel, Erwin. "Theodor Fontane—Ein Kierkegaard-Leser?" *Jahrbuch der deutschen Schillergesellschaft* 36 (1992): 255–87.
Koschorke, Albrecht. "Facts Shifting to the Left: From Postmodernism to the Postfactual Age." Translated by Michael Thomas Taylor and Sasha Rossman. *PMLA* 134, no. 5 (2019): 1150–6.
Krause, Edith. "Eclectic Affinities: Fontane's Effi and Freud's Dora." *Women's Studies* 32, no. 4 (2003): 431–54.
Lear, Jonathan. *A Case for Irony*. Cambridge, MA: Harvard University Press, 2011.
Liebrand, Claudia. "Geschlechterkonfigurationen in Fontanes *Unwiederbringlich*." In *Theodor Fontane am Ende des Jahrhunderts*, edited by Hanna Delf von Wolzogen and Helmuth Nürnberger, 2: 161–71. Würzburg: Königshausen & Neumann, 2000.
Liebrand, Claudia. *Das Ich und die andern: Fontanes Figuren und ihre Selbstbilder*. Freiburg: Rombach, 1990.
Lohmeier, Dieter. "Vor dem Niedergang. Dänemark in Fontanes Roman *Unwiederbringlich*." *Skandinavistik* 2 (1972): 27–53.
Lyon, John. *Out of Place: German Realism, Displacement, and Modernity*. New York: Bloomsbury, 2013.
Magay, Tamás and László Országh. *Concise Hungarian-English Dictionary*. Oxford: Oxford University Press, 1990.
Malakaj, Ervin. "Senescence and Fontane's *Der Stechlin*." In *Fontane in the Twenty-First Century*, edited by John B. Lyon and Brian Tucker, 232–45. Rochester, NY: Camden House, 2019.
Mann, Thomas. *The Magic Mountain*. Translated by John E. Woods. New York: Knopf, 1995.
Martini, Fritz. "Ironischer Realismus." In *Ironie und Dichtung*, edited by Albert Schaefer, 113–41. Munich: C.H. Beck, 1970.

McGillen, Petra. "*Fontane Goes to J School*. Theodor Fontanes Englandjahre und die Entstehung journalistischer Autorität im *Pre-truth*-Zeitalter." *Colloquia Germanica* 52, no. 1–2 (2019): 11–26.
McGillen, Petra. *The Fontane Workshop: Manufacturing Realism in the Industrial Age of Print*. New York: Bloomsbury, 2019.
McIntyre, Lee. *Post-Truth*. Cambridge, MA: MIT Press, 2018.
Mecklenburg, Norbert. *Theodor Fontane. Romankunst der Vielstimmigkeit*. Frankfurt am Main: Suhrkamp, 1998.
Meyer, Hans. *Der richtige Berliner in Wörtern und Redensarten*. Berlin: Hermann, 1904.
Meyers Großes Konversationslexikon. 6th ed. Leipzig and Vienna: Bibliographisches Institut, 1905–9.
Minden, Michael. "*Effi Briest* and 'Die historische Stunde des Takts.'" *Modern Language Review* 76, no. 4 (1981): 869–79.
Mommsen, Wolfgang. *Imperial Germany 1867–1918: Politics, Culture, and Society in an Authoritarian State*. Translated by Richard Deveson. London: Arnold, 1995.
Mueller, Robert S. *Report on the Investigation into Russian Interference in the 2016 Presidential Election*. Washington, DC: U.S. Department of Justice, 2019.
Mülder-Bach, Inka. "'Verjährung ist […] etwas Prosaisches.' *Effi Briest* und das Gespenst der Geschichte." *Deutsche Vierteljahrsschrift für Literaturwissenschaft und Geistesgeschichte* 83, no. 4 (2009): 619–42.
Naumann, Barbara. "Schwatzhaftigkeit. Formen der Rede in späten Romanen Fontanes." In *Theodor Fontane am Ende des Jahrhunderts*, edited by Hanna Delf von Wolzogen and Helmuth Nürnberger, 2:13–26. Würzburg: Königshausen & Neumann, 2000.
Neumann, Gerhard. "Das Ritual der Mahlzeit und die realistische Literatur. Ein Beitrag zu Fontanes Romankunst." In *Das schwierige neunzehnte Jahrhundert*, edited by Jürgen Barkhoff, Gilbert Carr, and Roger Paulin, 301–17. Tübingen: Max Niemeyer, 2000.
Neumann, Gerhard. "Speisesaal und Gemäldegalerie. Die Geburt des Erzählens aus der bildenden Kunst: Fontanes Roman *L'Adultera*." In *Roman und Ästhetik im 19. Jahrhundert*, edited by Tim Mehigan and Gerhard Sauder, 139–69. St. Ingbert: Röhrig Universitätsverlag, 2001.
Newmark, Kevin. *Irony on Occasion*. New York: Fordham University Press, 2012.
Orwell, George. *In Front of Your Nose, 1945–1950*. Vol. 4 of *The Collected Essays, Journalism, and Letters of George Orwell*, edited by Sonia Orwell and Ian Angos. New York: Harcourt, Brace, Javanovich, 1968.
Osborne, John. "Vision, Supervision, and Resistance: Power Relationships in Theodor Fontane's *L'Adultera*." *Deutsche Vierteljahrsschrift für Literaturwissenschaft und Geistesgeschichte* 70, no. 1 (1996): 67–79.
Passavant, Nicolas von. "Performing the Philistine. Gossip as a Narrative Device and a Strategy for Reflection on Anti-Semitism in Theodor Fontane's *L'Adultera*." In *Fontane in the Twenty-First Century*, edited by John B. Lyon and Brian Tucker, 48–62. Rochester, NY: Camden House, 2019.
Petöfi, Sándor. "National Song." In *Gems from Petöfi and Other Hungarian Poets*, translated by William Loew, 6–7. New York: Paul O. D'Esterhazy, 1881.
Pfeiffer, Peter. "Tod, Entstellung, Häßlichkeit: Fontanes *Schach von Wuthenow*." *Zeitschrift für deutsche Philologie* 113, no. 2 (1994): 264–76.
Prager, Debra. "'Alles so orientalisch': The Elaboration of Desire in Theodor Fontane's *Effi Briest*." *Women in German Yearbook* 29 (2013): 118–41.

Bibliography 243

Quintilian. *The Orator's Education*. Edited and translated by Donald Russell. Cambridge, MA: Harvard University Press, 2001.

Razbojnikova-Frateva, Maja. *Jeder ist seines Unglücks Schmied. Männer und Männlichkeiten in Werken Theodor Fontanes*. Berlin: Frank & Timme, 2012.

Richards, I. A. *Principles of Literary Criticism*. New York: Routledge, 2001.

Ricoeur, Paul. *Freud and Philosophy: An Essay on Interpretation*. Translated by Denis Savage. New Haven: Yale University Press, 1970.

Roebling, Irmgard. "'Effi, komm'—Der Weg zu Fontanes berühmtester Kindsbraut." In *Zwischen Mignon und Lulu. Das Phantasma der Kindsbraut in Biedermeier und Realismus*, edited by Malte Stein, Regina Fasold and Heinrich Detering, 267–313. Berlin: Erich Schmidt Verlag, 2010.

Schiller, Friedrich. *Werke und Briefe*. Edited by Klaus Harro Hilzinger. 12 vols. Frankfurt am Main: Deutscher Klassiker Verlag, 1988–2004.

Schlegel, Friedrich. *Kritische Friedrich-Schlegel-Ausgabe*. Edited by Ernst Behler, Jean Jacques Anstett, and Hans Eichner. Munich: Schöningh, 1958.

Schneider, Jeffrey. "Masculinity, Male Friendship, and the Paranoid Logic of Honor in Theodor Fontane's *Effi Briest*." *German Quarterly* 75, no. 3 (2002): 265–81.

Schößler, Franziska. "Der jüdische Börsianer und das unmögliche Projekt der Assimilation. Zu Fontanes Roman *L'Adultera*." In *Poetische Ordnungen. Zur Erzählprosa des deutschen Realismus*, edited by Ulrich Kittstein and Stefani Kugler, 93–119. Würzburg: Königshausen & Neumann, 2007.

Schwab, Philipp. "Der 'ganze Kierkegaard im Keim' und die Tradition der Ironie. Grundlinien der deutschsprachigen Rezeptionsgeschichte von Kierkegaards *Über den Begriff der Ironie*." *Kierkegaard Studies Yearbook* 14 (2009): 373–492.

Shakespeare, William. "Hamlet, Prince of Denmark." In *The Complete Works of Shakespeare*, edited by David Bevington, 1060–116. New York: HarperCollins, 1992.

Simmel, Georg. *Grundfragen der Soziologie*. Berlin: de Gruyter, 1970.

Strowick, Elisabeth. *Gespenster des Realismus. Zur literarischen Wahrnehmung von Wirklichkeit*. Paderborn: Wilhelm Fink, 2019.

Subiotto, Frances. "The Ghost in *Effi Briest*." *Forum for Modern Language Studies* 21, no. 2 (1985): 137–50.

Szukala, Ralph. "Victoire 1806, Preußen. Zur Spiegelschrift der Bildmotive in Theodor Fontanes *Schach von Wuthenow*." In *In Bildern denken. Studien zur gesellschaftskritischen Funktion von Literatur*, edited by Giovanni Scimonello and Ralph Szukala, 137–53. Bielefeld: Aisthesis, 2008.

Thomas, Christian. *Theodor Fontane: Autonomie und Telegraphie in den Gesellschaftsromanen*. Berlin: Logos, 2015.

Tucker, Brian. "Performing Boredom in *Effi Briest*: On the Effects of Narrative Speed." *German Quarterly* 80, no. 2 (2007): 185–200.

Tucker, Brian. "To Have an Eye: Visual Culture and the Misapprehension of Class in *Irrungen, Wirrungen*. In *Fontane in the Twenty-First Century*, edited by John B. Lyon and Brian Tucker, 63–83. Rochester, NY: Camden House, 2019.

Turk, Horst. "The Order of Appearance and Validation: On Perennial Classicism in Fontane's Society Novel *Schach von Wuthenow*." Translated by Eric Schwab. In *New Approaches to Theodor Fontane: Cultural Codes in Flux*, edited by Marion Doebeling, 1–21. Columbia, SC: Camden House, 2000.

Vedder, Ulrike. "Ringe, Glocken, Tränen. Theatralität und Diskretion in Theodor Fontanes Roman *Graf Petöfy*." In *Herausforderungen des Realismus: Theodor Fontanes Gesellschaftsromane*, edited by Peter Uwe Hohendahl and Ulrike Vedder, 85–105. Freiburg: Rombach, 2018.

Vogt, Ludgera. *Zur Logik der Ehre in der Gegenwartsgesellschaft: Differenzierung, Macht, Integration.* Frankfurt am Main: Suhrkamp, 1997.
Wallace, David Foster. "E Unibus Pluram: Television and U.S. Fiction." *Review of Contemporary Fiction* 13, no. 2 (1993): 151–94.
White, Michael. *Space in Theodor Fontane's Works: Theme and Poetic Function.* London: Modern Humanities Research Association, 2012.
Wilde, Oscar. *The Importance of Being Earnest and Other Plays.* With an introduction by Sylvan Barnet. New York: New American Library, 1985.
Willer, Stefan. "Gesellschaftsspiele. Fontanes *Irrungen, Wirrungen.*" In *Herausforderungen des Realismus: Theodor Fontanes Gesellschaftsromane*, edited by Peter Uwe Hohendahl and Ulrike Vedder, 123–41. Freiburg: Rombach, 2018.
Zuberbühler, Rolf. "'Excelsior!' Idealismus und Materialismus in Kellers und Fontanes Altersromanen *Martin Salander* und *Der Stechlin.*" In *Gottfried Keller und Theodor Fontane: Vom Realismus zur Moderne*, edited by Ursula Amrein and Regina Dieterle, 87–111. Berlin: de Gruyter, 2008.
Zunshine, Lisa. *Why We Read Fiction: Theory of Mind and the Novel.* Columbus, OH: Ohio State University Press, 2006.

Index

adultery novel 8, 89, 113, 115–16, 133–4, 145, 147, 199
Agamben, Giorgio 64, 67, 69, 85–6, 95–6, 105
Alexis, Willibald 24–5, 223
Allemann, Beda 7
ambiguity
    alertness to 198–9
    and irony 115, 176, 203, 222
    and misreading 173–4
    opposed to clarity 136–7
    of tone 131, 149–50, 159–60, 185, 196, 200, 217
Arendt, Hannah 31
Auerbach, Erich 25–6, 219
Aust, Hugo 14
avowal
    in *L'Adultera* 131, 133–40, 142–5
    counterpoint to irony 3–4, 22, 27, 29, 32, 53, 87, 115, 124, 140, 174–6, 230, 235 (*see also* irony)
    definition of 4, 16–18, 35
    in *Effi Briest* 210–13
    in *Irrungen, Wirrungen* 53–6
    in *Schach von Wuthenow* 78–9
    in *Der Stechlin* 226, 229
    in *Unwiederbringlich* 147–8, 160, 163–71, 174–6

Bakhtin, Mikhail 23–4, 158, 231
Bange, Pierre 22–4, 231

banter. *See* small talk
Behler, Ernst 235
Berlin idiom
    caricature 115–17
    emergence 20–1, 46–50, 62, 227
    and wit 73, 94, 117
Berman, Russell 34, 41, 56–7, 206
Bernstein, Richard 11, 26
bildungsroman 185, 188
Blessin, Stefan 178
Blumenberg, Hans 220
Bohrer, Karl Heinz 4
Booth, Wayne 123–4
Bowman, Peter James 39, 72–3, 158
Brandstetter, Gabriele 42
Bregemann, Christian 195

chatter. *See* small talk
Cicero 8
contagion
    narratives of 30
    rhetorical 84–5, 109, 115, 132–3, 141, 156, 182, 234
crisis of language 9, 35, 43, 46, 50, 59, 79
Czucka, Eckehard 221

D'Ancona, Matthew 29, 84
De Man, Paul 123, 125–6, 170
dialogue
    Fontane's portrayal 5, 19, 39, 41, 114, 133

irony in 215
    opposed to empty talk 54, 122, 222, 226, 228
    Platonic 225–6
    surfeit of 220
discipline
    failure of 186, 206–8, 212, 216
    of others 125, 198
    rhetorical 153, 185, 189, 192, 203, 205, 212, 216
discretion 91, 96, 114, 128, 207
dissimulation
    consequences of 219–20
    form of irony 8–9, 22, 88, 185, 204, 224, 232
    opposed to avowal 145
    Orwell on 21
    in *Der Stechlin* 222, 227
Don Quixote 169
Dostoevsky, Fyodor 231
Downes, Daragh 193
Downing, Eric 222–3

Engler-Coldren, Katharina 206
Ernst
    half-seriousness 6, 25–6, 126, 143, 197, 221
    opposed to *Scherz* 3–4, 6, 13, 108, 150, 158, 186–7, 233
    (*see also Scherz*)
    in Socratic irony 3, 118

Ferraris, Maurizio 30
Fontane, Theodor
    L'Adultera (Chapter 4) 16, 18, 93, 147–8, 150, 152, 159, 165–6, 171, 173, 175, 177–8, 189, 210, 219
    Cécile 23
    Effi Briest (Chapter 6) 2, 18, 54–5, 89, 93, 138, 219
    Frau Jenny Treibel 2, 89, 201
    Graf Petöfy (Chapter 3) 13, 16, 32, 57, 235

Irrungen, Wirrungen (Chapter 1) 10, 23, 61, 71–4, 76, 83, 89, 92–3, 107, 115, 117, 123–4, 150, 173, 175, 189, 197, 219
"Die Märker und die Berliner und wie sich das Berlinertum entwickelte" 45–50, 94, 115, 117, 227
Die Poggenpuhls 14, 116
Quitt 204
Schach von Wuthenow (Chapter 2) 13, 16, 93, 109, 115, 118, 137, 153, 173, 179–80, 213
Der Schleswig-Holsteinische Krieg im Jahre 1864 180–3
Der Stechlin (Chapter 7) 9, 18, 24, 28, 114, 202
Stine 129
"Unsere lyrische und epische Poesie seit 1848" 14, 59, 86–8, 136
Unterm Birnbaum 204
Unwiederbringlich (Chapter 5) 2–3, 16, 18, 32, 93, 196–7, 213, 234
Wanderungen durch die Mark Brandenburg 15, 21, 30
Foucault, Michel 16–17, 37, 53–4, 95, 138–9, 144, 230
Frankfurt, Harry 10–11, 15, 50, 223
Franzel, Sean 82, 85
Franzen, Jonathan 89, 109
Frederick the Great 31, 46, 94, 227
Frederick Wilhelm I 46, 227
Frederick Wilhelm III 61, 68–9, 79–80, 85
Freud, Sigmund 201, 207, 209–10
Frith, William 1–5, 32, 55, 169

Geulen, Eva 114, 141–2
Goethe, Johann Wolfgang von 129, 200
Goetschel, Willi 222–3, 226

Gottsched, Johann Christoph 87
Grawe, Christian 194
Greenberg, Valerie 213
Grevel, Liselotte 79
Gross, David 19

Haberland, Detlef 102–3
Hamlet 96
Hannibal 66–7, 83
Heine, Heinrich 200
Hohendahl, Peter Uwe 157, 178, 183
Holt, Randall 19, 35
honor
    false conception 70, 72, 78, 81–3
    guarantor 67–70, 79, 85–6, 110
    Prussian notion 63–5, 212
    symbolic capital 68
humor
    in *L'Adultera* 124, 128, 130, 135–6, 143
    and detachment 24–5
    in *Effi Briest* 201
    and quick wit 94
    in *Der Stechlin* 221
Hungarian Revolution (1848–9) 100–4, 111

indeterminacy
    as effect of irony 9, 108, 159, 170, 176, 193, 197, 200–2, 207
    in politics 182
    semantic 206, 209
infidelity
    marital 55, 90, 93, 95, 103, 108, 113, 118, 122, 125, 127, 141, 199–200, 210
    scourge of 8, 64, 102, 110–11, 234
    to one's word 8, 13, 60, 62, 67, 76, 90–1, 101, 105, 109
irony
    in *L'Adultera* 116, 119–20, 122–3, 129–30, 134–7, 142–5

counterpoint to avowal 3–4, 29, 32, 53, 87, 115, 139–40, 174–6, 230, 235 (*see also* avowal)
critique of 4–5, 12–15, 21–2, 82, 121, 182–3, 219, 232–4, 236
definition of 6–10, 35
in *Effi Briest* 186–7, 191–3, 197–200, 202–4, 207–10, 213–15
in *Graf Petöfy* 91, 107–9
in *Irrungen, Wirrungen* 55
and narrative 22–7, 123–4, 134, 230–1
and post-truth 29, 32, 235
in *Schach von Wuthenow* 70, 79–80
Socratic 3, 11, 118
in *Der Stechlin* 221, 223–5, 227, 229–30
in *Unwiederbringlich* 148, 151, 153–60, 163–7, 170–6, 179

Jesus Christ 31–2, 227
journalism 1, 57–9, 120

Kierkegaard, Søren
    allusions to 155–6
    on the concept of irony 6–7, 9, 159, 173, 183, 196
    on irony as mastered moment 11–13, 27, 232
    on irony of existence 119–20
Koschorke, Albrecht 29–30

Lear, Jonathan 119
Liebrand, Claudia 156
Lohmeier, Dieter 183
Lyon, John 45

Mann, Thomas 5, 13, 22, 129, 231
Martini, Fritz 22–4, 231
McIntyre, Lee 30, 154
Mecklenburg, Norbert 72, 116, 129, 132–3, 200

Meyer, Hans 48
modernization 19, 34, 41–3, 46–7, 59
Ming Dynasty 82–5, 180

Napoleon 16, 48, 71, 83, 85, 179
Naumann, Barbara 225
Neumann, Gerhard 42, 126–7, 137, 140, 200
Newmark, Kevin 9, 215
nihilism 11–13, 23, 27, 29, 162

oath
    Agamben on 67, 69, 86, 96
    in *Graf Petöfy* 90–1, 100–5, 111 (see also vow)
    guarantee 41
    in *Schach von Wuthenow* 61, 69–70, 75
    in *Unwiederbringlich* 170
Orwell, George 20–1, 31, 62

parrhesia 17–18, 37, 230
Petöfi, Sándor 102–5
Pfeiffer, Peter 85, 87
phrase, empty turns of
    in *L'Adultera* 114, 116
    critique of 21, 57–8, 72
    in *Effi Briest* 199, 205, 216–17
    in *Irrungen, Wirrungen* 33, 114
    Redensart 40, 80, 208, 216
    in *Unwiederbringlich* 162
Pietsch, Ludgwig 120–1
Pilate, Pontius 31–2, 97, 154, 235
postmodernism 29–31, 235
post-truth
    in *L'Adultera* 123, 140
    contemporary era of 27–32, 154, 232, 234–5
    Copenhagen and 154, 162–3, 174
    in *Effi Briest* 189
    in *Graf Petöfy* 90, 97
    in *Schach von Wuthenow* 82, 88

skepticism 159, 211, 221–2

Quintilian 8, 170

Razbojnikova-Frateva, Maja 107
realism
    Auerbach on 25–6
    Fontane's program of 14–15, 59, 86–8, 136–7
    irony and 23, 85
    in a post-truth world 174, 232, 236
relativism 154, 159
repression 186, 192, 208, 213, 216
reticence
    in *Effi Briest* 190, 192, 203, 206–7, 209, 213, 216–17
    in *Irrungen, Wirrungen* 56
    in *Schach von Wuthenow* 78
    in *Unwiederbringlich* 167
Richards, I. A. 230

Sanssouci 47, 49–50, 52, 62, 73, 94, 128, 157, 227
Schadow, Johann Gottfried 21, 30
Scherz
    half-joking 6, 126, 129, 143, 197, 201, 221
    opposed to *Ernst* 3–4, 6, 13, 108, 150, 158, 186–7, 233 (see also *Ernst*)
    in Socratic irony 3, 118
Schiller, Friedrich 147, 150
Schlegel, Friedrich 3, 12–13, 25, 118, 121, 231
Schneider, Jeffrey 212
Schößler, Franziska 116
Schwab, Philipp 155
Scott, Walter 24–5, 223
Second Schleswig War (1864) 16, 153, 176, 178–81
small talk 34–5, 37, 41–2, 74–5, 115, 132, 222, 224

Socrates 8, 11, 13, 119
speech acts 14, 95, 134, 137–8, 140, 167
suspicion 188, 192, 198, 211, 221
Storm, Theodor 131–3
Subiotto, Frances 194, 201

telegraph 224, 228–30, 235
Trump, Donald 28, 233–4
trust
    breach of 67–8, 74, 77, 79–80, 104
    erosion of 84–5, 110
    in the face of irony 14, 62, 211

uncertainty
    of avowal's efficacy 176
    consequence of irony 4, 7, 9, 24, 36, 55, 82, 124–5, 150, 154, 157–8, 170, 187, 192–3, 195, 198–9, 202–3, 217, 229, 233

of language 64, 76–7, 170, 234
and modernization 19, 34

Vedder, Ulrike 95, 107
Vogt, Ludgera 68
Von Wildenbruch, Ernst 57–8
vow
    in *Graf Petöfy* 90–103, 106–11
    (*see also* oath)
    in *Schach von Wuthenow* 75–7, 81
    in *Unwiederbringlich* 170

Wallace, David Foster 3, 232–4
White, Michael 153
Wilde, Oscar 147, 175–6

Zito, Salena 28
Zunshine, Lisa 171–2

www.ingramcontent.com/pod-product-compliance
Lightning Source LLC
Chambersburg PA
CBHW062134300426
44115CB00012BA/1915